9

WHAT IS ANALYTIC

MW00534417

Analytic philosophy is roughly a hundred years old, and it is now the dominant force within Western philosophy. Interest in its historical development is increasing, but there has hitherto been no sustained attempt to elucidate what it *currently* amounts to, and how it differs from so-called 'continental' philosophy. In this rich and wide-ranging book, Hans-Johann Glock argues that analytic philosophy is a loose movement held together both by ties of influence and by various 'family resemblances'. He considers the pros and cons of various definitions of analytic philosophy, and tackles the methodological, historiographical and philosophical issues raised by such definitions. Finally, he explores the wider intellectual and cultural implications of the notorious divide between analytic and continental philosophy. His book will be an invaluable guide for anyone seeking to understand analytic philosophy and how it is practised.

HANS-JOHANN GLOCK is Professor of Philosophy at the University of Zurich and Visiting Professor at the University of Reading. His publications include *A Wittgenstein Dictionary* (1996), *Quine and Davidson on Language, Thought and Reality* (2003) and (ed. with John Hyman) *Wittgenstein and Analytic Philosophy* (2008).

WHAT IS ANALYTIC PHILOSOPHY?

HANS-JOHANN GLOCK

Universität Zürich

CAMBRIDGE UNIVERSITY PRESS

CAMBRIDGE UNIVERSITY PRESS
Cambridge, New York, Melbourne, Madrid, Cape Town, Singapore, São Paulo, Delhi

Cambridge University Press
The Edinburgh Building, Cambridge CB2 8RU, UK

Published in the United States of America by Cambridge University Press, New York

www.cambridge.org
Information on this title: www.cambridge.org/9780521694261

First published 2008

Printed in the United Kingdom at the University Press, Cambridge

A catalogue record for this publication is available from the British Library

ISBN 978 0 521 87267 6 hardback
ISBN 978 0 521 69426 1 paperback

For Sonja and Helen
With a fond look back
und einem hoffnungsvollen Blick nach vorn!

[TRUTH]

... alle Begriffe, in denen sich ein ganzer Prozess semiotisch zusammenfasst, entziehen sich der Definition; definierbar ist nur das, was keine Geschichte hat.

(... all concepts which semiotically condense a whole process elude definition; only that which has no history can be defined.)

Friedrich Nietzsche (*Genealogie der Moral* II: 13)

We moved with Carnap as henchmen through the metaphysicians' camp. We beamed with partisan pride when he countered a diatribe of Arthur Lovejoy's in his characteristically reasonable way, explaining that if Lovejoy means *A* then *p*, and if he means *B* then *q*. I had yet to learn how unsatisfying this way of Carnap's could sometimes be.

W. V. Quine (1976: 42).

[clister
of the
?]

[LP] [wow!!
C5
C6]

Contents

There are useful introductions to the problems and techniques of analytic philosophy, notably Hospers (1973) and Charlton (1991). There are also distinguished historical accounts, for instance Skorupski (1993), Hacker (1996), Stroll (2000), Baldwin (2001) and Soames (2003). The current state of analytic philosophy in different subject areas is surveyed by a plethora of companions and guidebooks. Finally, there are spirited pleas for analytic philosophy, such as Tugendhat (1976), Cohen (1986) and Engel (1997).

This book does not belong to any of these genres, though it makes contributions to all of them. It is an attempt to answer the question of what analytic philosophy is in a direct and comprehensive manner. It considers past, present and future; and it tries to distinguish and rule out alternative answers in a sustained manner. To the best of my knowledge, it is the first book devoted to this task. As the title indicates, Dummett's influential *Origins of Analytical Philosophy* concentrates on the historical roots, and it does not engage with rival conceptions of analytic philosophy. Conversely, Cohen's *The Dialogue of Reason* largely ignores historical issues; and its second half is devoted not to analysing analytic philosophy, but to practising it on a specific topic. Finally, D'Agostini's *Analitici e Continentali* surveys both analytic and continental philosophy, which is more than I aspire to. Nevertheless, I shall cast repeated and, I hope, accurate glances at non-analytic ways of philosophizing. For one of my ambitions is to determine what, if anything, the analytic/continental contrast amounts to, not *just* in the past, but also at present and for the future. Nor can I afford to abstain from doing (analytic) philosophy. For it turns out that the historical and taxonomic questions with which the book is concerned raise a host of important and interesting philosophical questions of a conceptual and methodological kind. I shall need to dwell on the nature of linguistic meaning, the purposes of definition and classification, the role of historical knowledge in the resolution of philosophical problems, the threat of incommensurability between theories, the merits of historical relativism,

ix

principles of interpretation, the nature of clarity, different types of philo-sophical argument, essentially contested concepts, the idea of family resemblance, the proper way of demarcating intellectual traditions, and the proper role of philosophy in public debate, among other topics.

The intended audience includes not just analytic philosophers, whether students or professionals, but also non-analytic philosophers, and indeed anyone interested in one of the most exciting, important and controversial intellectual phenomena of the twentieth century. Some acquaintance with the history of philosophy is an advantage, without being a prerequisite. I have used logical formulae where appropriate, but they can be skipped without essential loss. I have also tried to explain any technical vocabulary I employ, and further information on this score is readily available in the now plentiful works of reference.

Although this is not an exclusively historical effort, a sense of time and progression is of the essence. I have therefore used the original publication dates in my references to classics, even in cases in which I cite from later editions or translations. For such works, the Bibliography displays the original date in brackets at the beginning, and then proceeds to specify the edition referred to. I have not, however, tried to impose this system consistently on recent works about analytic philosophy, or on posthumous writings with publication dates far removed from the original composition. At the same time, I feel squeamish about anachronisms like 'Aristotle 2001'. Instead, such giants of yore are quoted using a title and an established system of reference.

The debts I have incurred in writing this book are both diverse and profound. I am grateful for permission to use material from the following articles of mine: 'Philosophy, Thought and Language', in J. Preston (ed.), *Thought and Language: Proceedings of the Royal Institute of Philosophy Conference* (Cambridge University Press, 1997), 151–69; 'Insignificant Others: the Mutual Prejudices of Anglophone and Germanophone Philosophers', in C. Brown and T. Seidel (eds.), *Cultural Negotiations* (Tübingen: Francke Verlag, 1998), 83–98; 'Vorsprung durch Logik: The German Analytic Tradition', in A. O'Hear (ed.), *German Philosophy since Kant* (Cambridge University Press, 1999), 137–66; 'Philosophy', in J. Sandford (ed.), *Encyclopedia of Contemporary German Culture* (London: Routledge, 1999), 477–80; 'Imposters, Bunglers and Relativists', in S. Peters, M. Biddiss and I. Roe (eds.), *The Humanities at the Millennium* (Tübingen: Francke Verlag, 2000), 267–87; 'Strawson and Analytic Kantianism', in H. J. Glock (ed.), *Strawson and Kant* (Oxford: Clarendon Press, 2003), 15–42; 'Was Wittgenstein an Analytic Philosopher?', *Metaphilosophy* 35

(2004), 419–44; 'Wittgenstein and History', in Alois Pichler and Simo Säätelä (eds.), *Wittgenstein: The Philosopher and His Works* (Wittgenstein Archives at the University of Bergen, 2005), 177–204.

I wish to thank Rhodes University (South Africa) for awarding me a Hugh Le May Fellowship in 2002, and the Department of Philosophy, especially Marius Vermaak, for making our sojourn so delightful. I am indebted to the Arts and Humanities Research Council for a sabbatical as part of their Research Leave Scheme. Once more I am grateful to the Alexander von Humboldt Foundation for a grant that allowed me to spend a term at the University of Bielefeld in 2004, and to my hosts Ansgar Beckermann, Johannes Roggenhofer and Eike von Savigny. I wish to thank the University of Reading for its support of my research over many years. It has been both a privilege and a pleasure to work in the Department of Philosophy, and I am forever grateful to John Cottingham for luring me there all those years ago. I also wish to thank my new colleagues at the University of Zurich for the warm and constructive welcome. Julia Langkau and Christoph Laszlo, in particular, have supported this project logistically.

Covering such a huge and diverse area is beyond any single individual. For this reason I had to rely not just on a vast amount of literature, but also on countless conversations and on advice provided by colleagues, students and friends. Even an incomplete list would have to include David Bakhurst, Mike Beaney, Ansgar Beckermann, Jerry Cohen, John Cottingham, Jonathan Dancy, Michael Dummett, Simon Glendinning, Oswald Hanfling, Martina Herrman, Brad Hooker, Geert Keil, Andreas Kemmerling, Anthony Kenny, Vasso Kindi, Wolfgang Künne, Julia Langkau, Diego Marconi, Ray Monk, Kevin Mulligan, Herman Philipse, Carlo Penco, Aaron Preston, John Preston, Alan Richardson, Jay Rosenberg, Katia Saporiti, Eike von Savigny, Joachim Schulte, Peter Schulthess, Hans Sluga, Philip Stratton-Lake, Roger Teichmann, Alan Thomas, Paolo Tripodi, and Daniel Whiting. They have been very generous and helpful in providing answers, and I can only hope that I have asked at least some of the right questions. As on previous occasions, I have also benefited from participating in the St John's College discussion group, which has now, alas, come to an end.

Parts of this book have been aired at Berlin, Bielefeld, Dortmund, Edinburgh, Erfurt, Genoa, Oxford, Reading and Zurich. I am grateful to these various audiences for their questions and objections. I also wish to thank two anonymous readers for the Press for their recommendations and corrections. Peter Hacker, John Hyman, and Christian Nimtz have commented on several chapters. Special thanks go to Javier Kalhat, who read and copy-edited the whole manuscript. Their criticisms and suggestions have been invaluable, and they have saved me, not to mention my readers, from numerous blunders, infelicities, excesses and rhetorical flourishes. I owe a more general and longstanding debt to Peter Hacker for introducing me to both analytic philosophy and its history. He will not agree with some of the answers offered in this book, but he stimulated me to ask the questions.

As ever, my greatest debt is to my family. They have inspired and supported me through good times and bad, and still found the strength to laugh about this project, academic careers and, last but not least, the philosopher in their midst.

CHAPTER I

Introduction

Analytic philosophy is roughly 100 years old, and it is now the dominant force within Western philosophy (Searle 1996: 1–2). It has prevailed for several decades in the English-speaking world; it is in the ascendancy in Germanophone countries; and it has made significant inroads even in places once regarded as hostile, such as France. At the same time there are continuous rumours about the 'demise' of analytic philosophy, about it being 'defunct' or at least in 'crisis', and complaints about its 'widely perceived ills' (Leiter 2004a: 1, 12; Biletzki and Matar 1998: xi; Preston 2004: 445–7, 463–4). A sense of crisis is palpable not just among commentators but also among some leading protagonists. Von Wright noted that in the course of graduating from a revolutionary movement into the philosophical establishment, analytic philosophy has also become so diverse as to lose its distinctive profile (1993: 25). This view is echoed by countless observers who believe that the customary distinction between analytic and continental philosophy has become obsolete (e.g. Glendinning 2002; May 2002; Bieri 2005).

Loss of identity is one general worry, loss of vigour another. Putnam has repeatedly called for 'a revitalization, a renewal' of analytic philosophy (e.g. 1992: ix). And Hintikka has maintained that 'the survival of analytic philosophy' depends on a fresh start based on exploiting the constructive possibilities in Wittgenstein's later work (1998). Searle is one of analytic philosophy's most stalwart and uncompromising advocates. Yet even he concedes that in changing from 'a revolutionary minority point of view' into 'the conventional, establishment point of view' analytic philosophy 'has lost some of its vitality' (1996: 23). Small wonder that those more sceptical about analytic philosophy have for some time now been anticipating its replacement by a 'post-analytic philosophy' (Rajchman and West 1985; Baggini and Stangroom 2002: 6; Mulhall 2002).

Such a combination of triumph and crisis is by no means unprecedented. But it provides a fitting opportunity to address the nature of analytic philosophy from a fresh perspective. In the 1970s, Michael Dummett opened a debate about the historical origins of analytic philosophy with his claim that it is 'post-Fregean philosophy' and that it is based on the conviction that the philosophy of language is the foundation of philosophy in general. Over the last fifteen years the pace of the debate has quickened. In addition to Dummett's *Origins of Analytical Philosophy* there have been several historical surveys of analytic philosophy (Skorupski 1993; Hacker 1996; Stroll 2000; Baldwin 2001; Soames 2003), detailed treatises on more specific aspects (e.g. Hylton 1990; Stadler 1997; Hanna 2001), and at least six collections of essays on the history of analytic philosophy (Bell and Cooper 1990; Monk and Palmer 1996; Glock 1997c; Tait 1997; Biletzki and Matar 1998; Reck 2002). If Hegel is right and the owl of Minerva takes flight only at dusk, analytic philosophy must be moribund. Now, death by historical self-consciousness may not be a bad way to go. Still, even if the analytic enterprise is to be wound up, the process ought to be less one-sided.

So far the debate about the nature of analytic philosophy has focused on two questions: who should count as the true progenitor of analytic philosophy? And at what point did the analytic/continental divide emerge?[1] There has been no sustained attempt in English to combine such *historical* questions with an elucidation of what analytic philosophy *currently* amounts to, and how it differs from so-called 'continental' philosophy. The first part of Jonathan Cohen's *The Dialogue of Reason: an Analysis of Analytical Philosophy* delivers on its sub-title. But it stands alone in its focus on the present, and it explicitly sets aside the historical dimension (1986: 6–7). Moreover, it has little to say about continental philosophy. Yet contemporary Western philosophy is notoriously divided into two traditions, analytic philosophy on the one hand, and continental philosophy on the other. In spite of more than forty years of attempted dialogue and synthesis, this rift is still very real, both philosophically and sociologically. Therefore an account of analytic philosophy should also contrast it with the main alternatives, and not just at the point of its emergence.

The relative neglect of the current status of analytic philosophy is surprising, and not just because of analytic philosophy's general reputation for being ahistorical. From Dummett onwards, the historical questions have been intimately linked to the question of what analytic philosophy is, and to passionate fights for the soul and the future of analytic philosophy.

---

[1] Dummett 1993: esp. chs. 2–4. Hacker (1996: chs. 1–2; 1997) and Monk (1997) join battle with Dummett on the first question, Friedmann (2000) implicitly contradicts him on the second.

Most participants in the debate have tended to identify analytic philosophy with the kind of philosophy they deem proper, and I hope to show that this tendency has led to various distortions.

My ambition is to approach the issue in a fashion that may appear to be at once more analytic and more continental. More analytic in that it scrutinizes the status and purpose of demarcations between philosophical traditions, in that it assesses the pros and cons of various definitions of analytic philosophy in a dispassionate way, and in that it discusses some of the conceptual and methodological problems surrounding the debate. Although I shall not disguise the fact that I am an analytic philosopher, I want to tackle the issue without assuming that analytic philosophy must at any rate equal good philosophy. To put it differently, my main project in this book is to contribute to *descriptive* rather than *prescriptive* metaphilosophy. In this respect my project differs from the explicitly apologetic projects of Cohen (1986: 1–2), Føllesdal (1997) and Charlton (1991). This is not to say that I refrain from defending analytic philosophy against some objections. But I also press criticisms that strike me as well founded and conclude by suggesting ways in which contemporary analytic philosophy might be improved.

In any event, my views on how analytic philosophy should be pursued will be based on a prior attempt to understand what it actually amounts to. My approach to that issue may appear more 'continental' in that it pays attention to the historical background and to the wider cultural and political implications of analytic philosophy and its evolving conflict with other styles of philosophizing. I am not, however, exclusively or even primarily interested in the roots of analytic philosophy, but in what it *presently amounts to*, including the current state of the analytic/continental divide.

My perspective is also continental in a literal sense. As a German who has spent most of his working life in Britain, I can ill afford to be linguistically challenged, and I am aware of contemporary analytic philosophers outside of the Anglophone world. As is common in diasporas, these philosophers show a great degree of self-awareness, and over the last twenty years they have founded various associations and journals devoted to the promotion of analytic philosophy. The 'mission statements' of these ventures are an important source of information about the current self-image of analytic philosophy, and so are some writings for, against and about analytic philosophy that are available only in exotic languages like French, German and Italian. Due to the large scale of this investigation, I shall occasionally be forced to pronounce on historical, exegetical and substantive issues without sustained argument. Some controversial claims will be defended in footnotes, but others will be backed simply by references to relevant literature. I hope, however, that it will become clear how my views on the general questions to which the book is devoted depend on my views on these more specific issues.

I WHY THE QUESTION MATTERS

As the title makes clear, my main focus is on 'What *is* analytic philosophy?' rather than 'Where does analytic philosophy come from?' Nevertheless, the second question will loom large, not just for its own sake but also because of its implications for the first. But do these two questions matter? In one sense, it is patently obvious that they do. Most professional philosophers hold strong views about them. Many of them confine the airing of these views to polite or impolite conversation. But there have also been statements in print on what analytic philosophy is, not least by those who officially declare the topic to be 'unrewarding' (e.g. Williams 2006: 155). These statements provide a second rationale for engaging with the issue. While most of them are instructive and interesting, many of them are false. And I know of no better reason for a philosopher to put pen to paper than the need to combat false views, irrespective of whether these are held by philosophers, scientists, historians or laypeople.

But should one try to replace these incorrect answers by correct ones, or should the questions of what analytic philosophy is and where it comes from simply be dismissed as unanswerable and confusing? Of course, the ultimate proof of that pudding is in the eating. But it is instructive to ponder whether one should give answering these questions a try.

Marx famously remarked 'En tout cas, moi, je ne suis pas marxiste.' Many people since have felt that labels for philosophical positions, schools and traditions are just empty words, superfluous at best, distracting and confusing at worst. Indeed, this sentiment has been particularly vivid among some eminent analytic philosophers, albeit for different reasons. Some early pioneers were suspicious of schools because they felt that all differences of opinion between philosophers could be resolved through the advent of analytic methods. In this spirit, Ayer wrote that 'there is nothing in the nature of philosophy to warrant the existence of philosophical parties or "schools"' (1936: 176, see also 42). Such hopes have faded. But even contemporary analytic philosophers associate schools and -isms with dogmatism and procrastination.

Thus Dummett deplores the analytic/continental divide as follows:

Philosophy, having no agreed methodology and hardly any incontrovertible triumphs, is peculiarly subject to schisms and sectarianism; but they do the subject only harm. (1993: xi)

The most sustained analytic attack on dividing philosophers into schools or positions is earlier and hails from Ryle.

There is no place for 'isms' in philosophy. The alleged party issues are never the important philosophic questions, and to be affiliated to a recognizable party is to be the slave of a non-philosophic prejudice in favour of a (usually non-philosophic) article of belief. To be a 'so-and-so ist' is to be philosophically frail. And while I am ready to confess or to be accused of such a frailty, I ought no more to boast of it than to boast of astigmatism or *mal de mer*. (1937: 153–4)

There is a salutary message here, and not just for those who vilify Ryle as a narrow-minded and pig-headed 'logical behaviourist'. In the first instance, Ryle's professed 'repugnance' is directed at those who not only apply philosophical labels to themselves and their adversaries, but who employ them as weapons of philosophical argument. Such a procedure is annoying and widespread in equal measure, especially when it employs 'dismissal-phrases' (Passmore 1961: 2) such as 'crass materialism', 'naïve realism', 'wild idealism' or 'scholasticism'. Even where a clear sense attaches to a philo-sophical 'ism' and a particular thinker or theory definitely fits the bill, the argumentative weight must be carried by the reflections in favour of or against the position at issue.

Regrettably, we shall see that after World War II Ryle himself engaged in some of the most divisive 'them and us' and by implication school-building rhetoric in the history of the analytic/continental divide (ch. 3.1). More importantly, there is also a less unsavoury use of philosophical labels. We can classify thinkers, works, positions, or arguments without polemical or dialectical intent, namely for the sake of clarifying what their import is and what is at stake in any controversies to which they may give rise. Ryle concedes that

for certain ends, such as those of biography or the history of cultures (though not those of philosophy itself), it is often useful and correct to classify philosophers according to certain general casts of mind or temperaments. (1937: 157)

He has in mind dichotomies such as those between the 'tender-minded' and the 'tough-minded' (James 1907: 10–19, 118–20), between 'inflationists' and 'deflationists' (Berlin 1950), or between 'prophetic' and 'engineering' philosophers.

However, it does not go without saying that such classifications have no place in philosophy itself. For one thing, it is debatable (and will be debated in chapter 4) whether there are hard and fast divisions between philosophy, the history of philosophy and the wider history of ideas. For another, even if there are clear and stable barriers between these disciplines, why should labelling not play a legitimate role in all of them? It would be wrong to reject that suggestion by appeal to the point I conceded just now, namely that philosophical labels carry no argumentative weight. Ryle for one would presumably concede that arguing is not the only activity in which philosophers legitimately engage. They also describe, classify, clarify, interpret, gloss, paraphrase, formalize, illustrate, summarize, preach, etc. Whether all these other activities must ultimately stand in the service of argument is a moot point. What is incontrovertible is that philosophy does not reduce to argument, even if the latter is conceived in a very catholic sense.

In fact, Ryle's rejection of 'isms' is based on two distinct lines of thought. According to the first, there cannot be different philosophical schools A and B which oppose one another on very fundamental issues of principle or method. For in that case supporters of A would have to present proponents of B neither as engaging in a *different kind* of philosophy, nor even as engaging in *bad* philosophy, but rather as *not doing philosophy at all* (and vice-versa).

So the gulf would be one between philosophers and non-philosophers and not between one set of philosophers and another (Astronomers do not boast a party of anti-Astrologists) . . . The members of the opposing school, championing as they do a philosophy which has the wrong general trend, are the victims of a mistake in principle, no matter what acumen they may exercise in questions of detail. Accordingly every school of thought which is conscious of itself as such must and does maintain that the opposing school or schools of thought are in some way philosophically unprincipled. For they are blind to those principles which make its philosophy *a* philosophy and *the* philosophy. (1937: 158, 161)

Alas, this argument rests on an assumption that is not just questionable but wrong. Ryle takes for granted that philosophy is on a par with the special sciences in that a sufficiently fundamental disagreement, notably one on principles, tasks and methods, simply disqualifies one of the disputants from being a practitioner of the subject. Unlike the special sciences, however, philosophy lacks any generally accepted methodological framework. The very nature of philosophy is itself a contested philosophical issue, and views about this issue are philosophically controversial. Although the investigation of the proper aims and methods of philosophy is nowadays known as 'metaphilosophy', it is not a distinct higher-order discipline but an integral part of philosophy itself (Tugendhat 1976: 17–18; Cohen 1986: 1).

The natural sciences have to establish their own fields and methods no less than philosophy. However, at least since the scientific revolution of the seventeenth century, they have done so in ways which have been increasingly less controversial, with the result that disputes about the nature of the subject no longer play a significant role. Even in times of scientific revolutions, scientific debates do not usually concern questions such as what astronomy is. And an introduction to that subject will not be a survey of warring schools on this issue – as it might well be in philosophy.

There are two interrelated reasons for this tendency towards consensus. Someone who has different views about the *subject matter* of a particular science is simply not engaged in that particular field. And although there is methodological debate during scientific revolutions, someone with *radically* deviant *methods*, who for example totally disregards observation and experiment in favour of aesthetic considerations, simply ceases to be a scientist. In contrast, disparate intellectual activities, tackling different problems by incompatible methods and with different aims are still called philosophy. There are, for example, philosophers who would maintain that philosophy should strive neither for knowledge nor cogency of argument but for beauty and spiritual inspiration. Whether anyone who consistently avoids arguments of any kind still qualifies as a philosopher is another moot point. But there are philosophers, including analytic philosophers, who would deny Ryle's claim that the principles of 'any reputable "ism" are established, and only established, by philosophical argument' (1937: 162; see ch. 6.5 above).

This takes us to Ryle's second argument against the existence of genuinely distinct and genuinely philosophical schools and traditions.

The real root of my objection is, I think, the view that I take of the nature of philosophical inquiry. I am not going to expound it in full, but a part of the view is that it is a species of discovery. And it seems absurd for discoverers to split into Whigs and Tories. Could there be a pro-Tibet and an anti-Tibet party in the sphere of geography? Are there Captain Cook-ites and Nansenists? (1937: 156)

Well, yes, as it happens. There are supporters of Alfred Cook and supporters of Richard Peary regarding the question of who first reached the North Pole – Dr Cook-ites and Pearinists, if you please. And there were those who accepted and those who rejected the idea that there is a great land mass around the North Pole, that El Dorado exists or that there is a large continent in the Pacific Ocean. There is room for fundamentally opposing views *within any* area of inquiry, however factual or scientific it may be. In the special sciences, such disputes are eventually settled. Those who still believe that the earth is flat or that π is rational will be disbarred from serious astronomy or mathematics, respectively. But even in the sciences this demarcation is not always clear cut. I for one am hesitant to decide whether, for instance, Lysenkoism or intelligent design theories are simply unscientific, or whether instead they are bad, ideologically motivated, science. I am not hesitant in affirming that no such katharsis has taken place in philosophy. There is literally no position on vaguely philosophical issues that has not been adopted by someone who is generally regarded as a philosopher.

Ryle's arguments for the futility of philosophical labels fail, therefore. This leaves a more general worry. Surely, what matters is not how a particular philosopher or work should be labelled. Who cares whether someone is an enthusiastic Hegelian, a moderate Bradleian, a last-ditch logical positivist, an unswerving pragmatist, a paid-up externalist, a callow consequentialist, or a ruthless eliminativist? What counts, surely, is the *content* of the work, what the philosopher actually wrote and whether the arguments are convincing and the conclusions true!

There is a clear danger in placing excessive weight on philosophical taxonomy and doxography. At the same time, classifications are indispensable to human thought. In order to make sense of things, whether they be material phenomena or intellectual productions, we need to distinguish them by their relevant features. And we do so by applying labels according to certain principles. Historical, exegetical and metaphilosophical investigations are no exception to this rule. Contrasts like Eastern vs Western philosophy, ancient vs medieval vs modern philosophy, empiricism vs rationalism, analytic vs continental philosophy, or labels like 'Thomism', 'Neo-Kantianism' or 'postmodernism' may be simplistic, potentially misleading and downright ugly. Yet some contrasts and some labels are essential if we are to detect important similarities and differences between various thinkers and positions, and if we are to tell a coherent story about the development of our subject. One can hardly engage in an assessment of the historical development and the merits of analytic philosophy without some conception of what it amounts to. What we need, therefore, is not a puritanical avoidance of classifications, but classifications that are scrupulous and illuminating.

Of course, some labels may have acquired so many different uses and connotations that their use casts more darkness than light. Lamenting the radically disparate explanations of the term 'deflationism', Wolfgang Künne counsels:

In view of this terminological chaos, I propose to put the term 'deflationism' on what Otto Neurath once called, tongue in cheek, the *Index Verborum Prohibitorum*. (2003: 20)

Whether or not this is the way forward in the case of 'deflationism', however, it is not an attractive option with respect to 'analytic philosophy'. The term is used much more widely than 'deflationism'. Furthermore, that use has itself become an important part of the history of twentieth-century philosophy. Thirdly, whereas 'deflationism' is often employed with a *specific* meaning introduced *a novo*, 'analytic philosophy' is for the most part used consciously as a label with an established meaning, albeit one that may be vague. Fourthly, this vagueness notwithstanding, there is a general agreement on how to apply the term to an open class of cases. Finally, while there are several potentially clearer alternatives to the label 'deflationism', no such alternatives exist in the case of 'analytic philosophy'. For these reasons clarification rather than elimination should be the order of the day.

2 HOW THE QUESTION SHOULD BE APPROACHED

There remains a strong *prima facie* case for the idea that analytic philosophy constitutes a distinct philosophical phenomenon, whether it be a school, movement, tradition or style. Peter Bieri has recently proposed the following gruelling experiment. For a whole month, read the *Journal of Philosophy* in the morning, and then Seneca, Montaigne, Nietzsche, Cesare Pavese and Fernando Pessoa in the afternoon. Slightly altering Bieri's set-up, and making it even more sadistic, devote the afternoon sessions to Plotinus, Vico, Hamann, Schelling and Hegel, or to Heidegger, Derrida, Irigaray, Deleuze and Kristeva. I think that Bieri's thought-experiment is illuminating. Yet it points in the very opposite direction of the conclusion he favours. According to Bieri, the distinction between analytic and continental philosophy is 'simply a nuisance' that cannot be tolerated (2005: 15). By contrast, I think that three things emerge from the proposed juxtapositions: first, there is at least some overlap concerning the problems addressed; secondly, at least some of these problems are philosophical by commonly accepted standards; thirdly, what goes on in the pages of the *Journal of Philosophy* is a distinctive intellectual activity, one that differs from the activities (themselves diverse) that the other figures engage in.

Small wonder then that the labels 'analytic' and 'continental philosophy' continue to be widely used. This holds even when it is suggested that the distinction is not a hard and fast one. In reviews, for instance, it is commonplace to read not just that a book or author is typical of either the analytic or continental movement, but also that X is unusually sensitive or open minded 'for an analytic philosopher' or that Y is uncharacteristically clear or cogent 'for a continental thinker'. The analytic/continental distinction colours philosophical perception even among those who do not regard it as absolute. More generally, there is no gainsaying the fact that the idea of a distinct analytic philosophy continues to shape the institutional practice of philosophy, whether it be through distinct journals, societies, job advertisements or institutes (see Preston 2007: ch. 1). For instance, it is common and perfectly helpful to explain to students that a particular department or course is analytic in orientation.

At a time when the analytic/continental contrast was emerging, R. M. Hare maintained that there are 'two different ways' in which philosophy is now studied, ways which 'one might be forgiven for thinking … are really two quite different subjects' (1960: 107). And even though Dummett seeks to bridge the analytic/continental divide, this ambition is predicated on the observation that 'an absurd gulf has formerly opened up between "Anglo-American" and "Continental" philosophy'; indeed, 'we have reached a point at which it's as if we're working in different subjects' (1993: xi, 193).

This *status quo* may be neither desirable nor stable. It *may* turn out that either analytic or continental philosophy are pursuing the path of the righteous, in which case followers of the other side should simply follow suit. Alternatively, it *may* transpire that there is a premium on philosophy constituting a unified endeavour, as Western philosophy did until at least the beginning of the twentieth century (see Quinton 1995b: 161). If philosophy works best as a cohesive discipline or at least a single area of discourse, barring factions and communicative barriers, then heads should be banged together, irrespective of whether one side has a monopoly on philosophical wisdom.

But even if the analytic/continental division is regrettable on philosophical or other grounds, it remains real. It must be a starting point for any attempt to get clear about the phenomenon of analytic philosophy, if only for the purpose of overcoming or deconstructing it. The question then is not whether it is legitimate and fruitful to inquire into what analytic philosophy is, but how this should be done.

Some characterizations of analytic philosophy are clearly intended as definitions of some kind, in the sense that *ipso facto* those included do and those excluded do not qualify as analytic philosophers (e.g. Cohen 1986: ch. 2; Dummett 1993: ch. 2; Hacker 1996: 195; Føllesdal 1997). Others are formulated baldly and without qualification – 'Analytic philosophy is …', 'Analytic philosophers do …', 'An analytic philosopher would never ...' Yet they may be intended as non-analytic generalizations which do not *necessarily* apply to all and only analytic philosophers. In other words, they specify characteristic features of analytic philosophy that need not be essential or constitutive features. Finally, there are characterizations which are explicitly qualified in scope, and take forms like 'For the most part, analytic philosophy is ...', 'Most analytic philosophers do ...', etc.

But such generalizations, whether restricted or unrestricted, rely on a certain understanding of what analytic philosophy is. Otherwise they lack a demarcated sample on which they could be based. We need to know by virtue of what someone qualifies as an analytic philosopher, and hence what determines the scope of the terms 'analytic philosophy' or 'analytic philosophers'. For this reason, mere generalizations are no substitute for an explanation of what, if anything, constitutes analytic philosophy or being an analytic philosopher. It is such an account that we should seek in the first instance. In fact, most unrestricted characterizations purport to provide such an account. And even with respect to restricted characterizations it is profitable to ask whether they could be used to define analytic philosophy.

Some philosophers, swayed by Quine's attack on the distinction between analytic and synthetic statements, have general qualms about the distinction between constitutive, defining or essential features of a phenomenon X on the one hand, and accidental features on the other. Elsewhere I have argued that these qualms are unjustified (Glock 2003a: ch. 3). In any event, it would be inapposite to rule out definitions of analytic philosophy *ab initio* on these grounds. If analytic philosophy cannot be defined, whether for general or specific reasons, this is something that should emerge in the course of our exploration. This leaves open entirely the question of *what type* of definition or explanation is appropriate. One important distinction here is that between *nominal* definitions, which specify the linguistic meaning of words, and *real* definitions, which specify the essence of the things denoted by them. Some philosophers, including Wittgenstein and Quine, reject the idea of real essences. But even if this blanket repudiation of essentialism is unwarranted, there are grounds for doubting that analytic philosophy is the proper subject of a real definition.

There can be no question of the label 'analytic philosophy' having a single *correct* or *intrinsic* meaning, independently of how we explain and use it. As Wittgenstein sapiently reminds us:

a word hasn't got a meaning given to it, as it were, by a power independent of us, so that there could be a kind of scientific investigation into what the word *really* means. A word has the meaning someone has given to it. (1958: 28)

Similarly, Davidson writes: 'It's not as though words have some wonderful thing called a meaning to which those words have somehow become attached' (1999: 41). As it stands this is no more than the superficial if incontrovertible observation that meaning is <u>conventional</u> in the sense that it is *arbitrary* that we use a particular sound- or inscription pattern to mean something specific. Instead of 'analytic philosophy' we might have used any number of other signs. A trivial variation – 'analytical philosophy' – is employed by Dummett, among others. More significantly, in German a different label with distinct connotations used to predominate, namely *sprachanalytische Philosophie*.

This trivial point leaves open the possibility that analytic philosophy is a robust distinctive phenomenon, one which has an essence to be captured by a real definition. In that case, any scheme of classification that is faithful to reality would have to include some label or other for analytic philosophy. But it is not easy to see how such a claim might be sustained. If <u>the most popular current account of real essences and definitions</u> is to be trusted, analytic philosophy is a very inauspicious candidate. According to Kripke's (1980) and Putnam's (1975: ch. 12) influential '<u>realist semantics</u>', the reference of natural kind terms like 'water' or 'tiger' is not determined by the <u>criteria</u> for their application – the phenomenal features by which laypeople distinguish things as belonging to those kinds (such as the way something looks or tastes). Rather, it is given by a <u>paradigmatic exemplar</u> and an appropriate '<u>sameness relation</u>' that all members of the kind must bear to this exemplar. 'Water', for instance, refers to all stuff which is relevantly similar to a <u>paradigmatic</u> sample, i.e. any substance which has the same microstructure as that paradigm. Accordingly, natural kinds do not just possess a 'nominal' but also a 'real essence', in Locke's terminology (*Essay* III.3), which in our case is to consist of H_2O.

<u>Whether this account fits natural kind terms for which there are concrete paradigms that can be investigated by science is subject to debate</u> (Hanfling 2000: ch. 12; Jackson 1998: ch. 2). In any event, labels for philosophical schools are *not* natural kind terms. An essentialist account of taxonomic terms in philosophy is totally at odds with their actual role. <u>Nobody could seriously suggest that 'analytic philosopher' applies to all and only those creatures with the same microstructure or genetic code as Rudolf Carnap or Elizabeth Anscombe</u>, let's say, <u>paradigmatic analytic philosophers</u> though they are. Although the labels and distinctions of natural science may be capable of 'carving nature at its joints', in Plato's striking phrase (*Phaedrus*, 265d–266a), this cannot reasonably be expected of historical labels and distinctions.

Even if a definition of analytic philosophy is *nominal* rather than real, however, it is *not* a free for all. Nominal definitions divide into stipulative definitions on the one hand, and reportive or lexical ones on the other. Stipulative definitions simply lay down *ab novo* what an expression is to mean in a particular context, in complete disregard of any established use it may have. Such definitions cannot be correct or incorrect. But they can be more or less fruitful, in that it may be more or less helpful to single out a particular phenomenon through a separate label. Yet with respect to established terms unrestricted stipulation is rarely advisable. For one thing, it invites confusion for no apparent gain. For another, existing terms, as actually employed, stand in relations to other terms that would have to be redefined as well. Even if it deliberately diverges from its established use, an explanation of 'analytic philosophy' can come into conflict with the employments of the constituent terms. Thus one would at least expect that 'analytic' indicates an analogy with chemical or mathematical analysis and a contrast to synthesis. And it would certainly be unacceptable if analytic philosophy were defined as anything other than a kind of philosophy.

Unsurprisingly, most definitions or explanations of analytic philosophy lay claim to some kind of reportive accuracy. For this reason they can be judged by the degree to which they are true to established usage and institutional practice. In assessing these definitions/explanations one should therefore take note of the ordinary use of 'analytic philosophy', its cognates and antonyms. Alas, some contemporaries may find any appeal to ordinary use outdated and downright offensive. But they should be reminded of a few points.

Aristotle, the first to embark on a systematic search for a conception of philosophy, started out from the way people used the term *sophia* (*Metaphysics* I.2; see Tugendhat 1976: ch. 2). Similarly, appeal to the ordinary use of 'analytic philosophy' has been a standard feature of contemporary debates about the nature of analytic philosophy, especially when it comes to criticizing alternative conceptions.

What is more, Aristotle and contemporary metaphilosophers are *right* to set store by the ordinary use of their respective *definienda*. In pursuing any question of the form 'What is X?' we shall inevitably rely on a *preliminary notion* of X, an idea of what constitutes the topic of our investigation. In our case we presuppose a preliminary understanding of analytic philosophy. This is not a fully articulated conception, which would have to emerge from the subsequent debate about what analytic philosophy is, but simply an initial idea of what that debate is about. Such a pretheoretical understanding is embodied in the established use of the term 'analytic philosophy'. Put differently, the way we use and understand a term is not only an innocuous starting point for elucidating its meaning, it is the *only* clue we have at the outset of our investigation.

That much would be underwritten not just by so-called ordinary language philosophers, but also by some of their opponents, notably Quine (1953: 106–7). In the spirit of Quine one might insist, however, that we need to graduate from ordinary use towards a more specialized one based on more exacting scrutiny of the phenomena. But this is not an objection to my procedure. The term 'ordinary use' is ambiguous. It may refer either to the *standard* use of a term as opposed to its irregular use in whatever area it is employed, or to its *everyday* as opposed to its specialist or technical use (Ryle 1953: 301–4). Unlike 'philosophy', 'analytic philosophy' is a technical term used mainly by professional academics, students and intellectuals. And surely there can be nothing wrong with matching suggested definitions against the established or standard use of the experts in the relevant field, if only to establish whether this use actually exemplifies a coherent pattern.

Even if one accepts my general (semantic-cum-metaphilosophical) claims, one may entertain doubts about this particular case. Nobody has done more to defend the appeal to ordinary use against contemporary animadversions than Peter Hacker. Yet he denies that the term 'analytic philosophy' *has* an established use (1998: 14). Hacker is right to point out that 'analytic philosophy' is a term of art and a fairly recent one at that. It does not follow, however, that it has no established use. An established use need not be an everyday one. In fact, what Grice and Strawson (1956) pointed out about the terms 'analytic' and 'synthetic' holds equally of the term 'analytic philosophy'. Although we may lack a clear and compelling explanation, we by-and-large agree in our application of these terms.

Alas, even the most established and clearly circumscribed philosophical taxonomies are liable to misuse. Brian Magee, for example, refers to Fichte, Schelling and Hegel as Neo-Kantians (1983: App. 1). With Neo-Kantians like that, who needs German Idealists? 'Analytic philosophy' is no worse off than more venerable labels. Though there are occasional misapplications, they are generally recognized. Consider the following, presumably rhetorical, question from a circular of Continuum International Publishing Group (21 October 2003):

Are you interested in the continental philosophy of Gilles Deleuze or Theodor Adorno, or philosophy of the analytic tradition such as Friedrich Nietzsche or Mary Warnock?

No prizes for spotting the mistake.

By this token, it would obviously count against a definition of analytic philosophy if it implied that Heidegger and Lacan are analytic philosophers while Carnap and Austin are not. It would also count against a definition if it implied that Russell and Quine are analytic philosophers, while Frege and Hempel are not. Furthermore, we agree not just on what the clear cases are, but also on what count as borderline cases for various reasons, e.g. Bolzano, Whitehead, the later Wittgenstein, Popper, Feyerabend, neuro-philosophers. Finally, the agreement is not to a list, but can be extended to an *open class* of new cases. For instance, perusal of CVs will put most professionals in a position to identify clear-cut analytic and continental philosophers from a list of job applicants.

While there is no case for sheer stipulation, there may be good reasons for modifying generally accepted explanations of 'analytic philosophy'. In assessing such suggestions, we need to trace their consequences. Revisionary definitions can be more or less illuminating for the purposes of historiography and taxonomy. Thus it would count against a definition if it implied either that no philosophers qualify as analytic or that all philosophers do. For in that case the label does no work and has turned into an idle wheel. Distinct characterizations of analytic philosophy have other less immediate consequences, not just for the self-understanding of analytic philosophy, the way in which it conceives of its history, aims, methods and results, but also for the contrast with other philosophical movements such as traditional or continental philosophy.

As I indicated before, in assessing these consequences, we need to rely on a preliminary idea of what philosophers generally count as analytic, and on what grounds. For this reason, I shall be guided by the question whether suggested definitions include all generally acknowledged instances of analytic philosophers and exclude all generally acknowledged instances of non-analytic philosophers. In other words, I shall measure conceptions of analytic philosophy in the first instance against the *commonly acknowledged extension* of the term. In fact, even if a genuine definition of analytic philosophy were a red herring, it would be profitable to ascertain whether and to what extent the countless general claims about it actually hold. By testing these claims for their suitability as definitions, we also test them for their accuracy as generalizations.

While recognized paradigms of analytic philosophy are especially important, however, I shall also consider how proposed definitions deal with cases that, for various reasons, might be considered borderline or controversial. These problematic cases can provide an important litmus test for suggested definitions, especially if it is possible to identify the features that make them problematic. For the same reason, I mention movements like Popper's critical rationalism that have distanced themselves from analytic philosophy, but which nevertheless seem to belong to the analytic tradition.

In this context I should stress that *self*-descriptions are *not* authoritative. Philosophers have investigated and promoted self-knowledge, but they have not uniformly excelled at it. Treating avowals as a touch stone would mean, for instance, including Derrida among the analytic philosophers and excluding Fodor (see ch. 8.1). No fruitful explanation could be tailored to suit such an extension of 'analytic philosophy'.

3   THE STRUCTURE AND CONTENT OF THE BOOK

Although my ultimate focus is on the present, I shall not confine myself to conceptions of 'analytic philosophy' that are *currently extant*. Like any intellectual tradition, analytic philosophy is an intrinsically historical phenomenon, even if this fact alone may not furnish an adequate conception of it. And the same goes for the label 'analytic philosophy', its cognates and antonyms. Without some understanding of relevant developments in the history of philosophy, one cannot appreciate the point of the notion of analytic philosophy and the various reasons for conceiving it in different ways. Such an understanding will also facilitate my discussion of conceptual and methodological issues which arise in the pursuit of an explanation of analytic philosophy.

For these reasons I start out in chapter 2 with a 'Historical survey' of analytic philosophy, a sketch of the emergence and development of the movement to which the label 'analytic philosophy' is generally applied. Unlike previous scholars, I shall examine both the Anglophone and the Germanophone roots, while *also* keeping in mind relevant developments beyond analytic philosophy.

On the basis of this historical survey, the following chapters discuss various ways in which analytic philosophy has been defined or conceived at some stage or other of its career. I have organized them not according to *specific* explanations of analytic philosophy, of which there are way too many, but according to *types* of explanations. Each chapter is in effect devoted to a parameter along which analytic philosophy, or any other philosophical movement for that matter, could be defined. The first five of these parameters turn out to be unsuitable.

Chapter 3, 'Geography and language', deals with geo-linguistic definitions. The image of analytic philosophy as an Anglophone phenomenon is still surprisingly common and embodied in the analytic/continental contrast. But the very label 'continental philosophy' is a misnomer, especially in view of the Central European roots of analytic philosophy. Nevertheless, I shall argue, the contrast between analytic and continental philosophy ties in with, and is reinforced by, stereotypical differences between Anglophone philosophy and academic culture on the one hand, its continental counterparts on the other. In the course of the nineteenth century a conflict between British empiricism and continental rationalism was gradually replaced by geographically and intellectually more complex divisions. I also explore how political developments such as the rise of Nazism and philosophical developments such as the rehabilitation of metaphysics from the 1960s onwards turned the now unduly neglected contrast between analytic and *traditional* philosophy into the analytic vs *continental* divide as we now know it. Still, the Anglocentric conception of analytic philosophy is untenable, and so is its more sophisticated cousin, the Anglo-Austrian conception. At present, analytic philosophy flourishes in many parts of the continent, while continental philosophy is highly popular in North America. Analytic philosophy is neither a geographical nor a linguistic category. Finally, the label 'continental philosophy' fails to distinguish between the twentieth century avant-garde movements inspired by Nietzsche and Heidegger and the traditional or traditionalist philosophy that actually dominates academic philosophy on the continent of Europe.

Chapter 4, 'History and historiography', debates the question of whether analytic philosophy differs from continental and especially from traditionalist philosophy in its lack of historical awareness. In recent years, even some practitioners have accused analytic philosophy of being unduly ahistorical. I aim to show, however, that analytic philosophy in general is not characterized by a dismissive attitude towards the past. Indeed, there has been a recent turn towards history. Furthermore, I shall defend analytic philosophy against historicist animadversions that so far have gone unchallenged. Against the objection that analytic philosophers ignore the past, I argue that for the most part they only resist the unfounded claim that an understanding of history is essential rather than merely advantageous to philosophy. Against the objection that analytic histories of philosophy are anachronistic, I argue that approaching the past in an analytic spirit actually makes for better historiography.

In chapter 5, 'Doctrines and topics', I turn to the idea that analytic philosophy stands out by virtue of a particular range of problems and/or answers to these problems. Definitions by reference to specific doctrines tend to be too narrow. The rejection of metaphysics was never universal

[Suggest such
various definition are
hollow — trying to define all
"Democrats"]

among analytic philosophers and has vanished almost completely.
Dummett defines analytic philosophy as based on the view that an analysis
of thought can and must be given by an analysis of language. But a
linguistic conception of thought and its analysis is neither necessary nor
sufficient for being an analytic philosopher. Dummett's definition ignores
the difference between the rise of logical and conceptual analysis on the one
hand, and the linguistic turn on the other. Similarly, analytic philosophy is
characterized neither by an insistence that philosophy is distinct from
science, nor by the naturalistic assimilation of philosophy to science.
Finally, analytic philosophers do not even agree on topics on which to
disagree. While a preoccupation with theoretical topics was not incidental
to the rise of analytic philosophy, it certainly no longer confines the genre.

The shortcomings of doctrinal approaches encourage methodological or
stylistic definitions. Chapter 6, 'Method and style', argues that even such
definitions are inadequate. It is *prima facie* attractive to tie analytic philosophy to the method of analysis. Unfortunately, this approach faces a
dilemma. If analysis is understood literally, namely as the decomposition
of complex phenomena into simpler constituents, it rules out the later
Wittgenstein and Oxford linguistic philosophy, among others. But if it is
understood widely enough to accommodate such cases, it will also capture
figures ranging from Plato to continental philosophers like Husserl.
Similar difficulties arise for the idea that analytic philosophy is 'science'
as opposed to 'arts centered', in that it is uniformly interested in science
and infused by a scientific spirit. That such a definition would exclude an
exotic case like Wittgenstein might be tolerable. But that it would also
exclude Moore, Ryle and Strawson counts as a decisive objection.

If analytic philosophy has no distinctive method, perhaps it at least
features a particular style. In this vein Bernard Williams has suggested that
analytic philosophy differs from the continental variety in that it avoids
obscurity by using either 'moderately plain speech' or, where necessary,
technical idioms. But the notion of clarity itself stands in urgent need of
clarification. In so far as it is a straightforward matter of prose and
presentation, it is neither universal among analytic philosophers nor confined to them. If a stylistic feature separates continental and analytic
philosophy at present, it is rather different types of obscurantism – aesthe-
ticism on the one hand, scholasticism on the other. This leaves a final
suggestion, namely that analytic philosophy at least aspires to clarity of
thought and argumentative rigour. Rationalist conceptions define analytic
philosophy as a general attitude towards philosophical problems, one
which emphasizes the need for argument and justification. But this

[IN SHORT, THERE
SEEMS TO BE NO
OBVIOUS WAY
TO DEMARC.
AP + CP...!!]

would make the bulk of philosophy analytic. Ever since Socrates, the attempt to tackle fundamental questions by way of reasoned argument has been a distinguishing feature of philosophy as such, e.g. vis-à-vis religion or political rhetoric, not the hallmark of a particular philosophical movement.

The next chapter, 'Ethics and politics', starts out by demonstrating that the analytic tradition is <u>not</u> characterized by the exclusion of moral philosophy and political theory. <u>Next I scotch two conflicting rumours, namely that analytic philosophy is inherently apolitical or conservative, and that it encourages a progressive or liberal attitude and renders its practitioners resistant to political extremism.</u> I also look at what the Singer affair shows about analytic and continental attitudes towards freedom of speech and philosophy's capacity to prescribe specific courses of action. Finally, I consider whether analytic philosophy has an edge over its rivals by dint of refusing to turn philosophical reflection into the handmaiden of preconceived moral and political ideals.

In chapter 8, 'Contested concepts, family resemblances and tradition', I turn to explanations of analytic philosophy that do not take the form of definitions in terms of necessary and sufficient conditions. One such explanation arises out of the rationalist conception, which turns analytic philosophy into an 'essentially contested concept'. In response, I grant that there is an honorific use of 'analytic philosophy'. But, I shall argue, it is less entrenched than the descriptive one and inferior for purposes of philosophical taxonomy and debate. In the remainder, I defend *my own* conception of analytic philosophy, partly by combining two approaches. The first is the idea that analytic philosophy should be explained in terms of *family resemblances*. What holds analytic philosophers together is not a single set of necessary and sufficient conditions, but a thread of overlapping similarities (doctrinal, methodological and stylistic). Thus current analytic philosophers may be tied to Frege and Russell in their logical methods, or to logical positivism and Quine in their respect for science, or to Wittgenstein and linguistic philosophy in their concern with the *a priori*, meaning and concepts, etc. I shall rebut criticisms of the very idea of family resemblance. At the same time, a family-resemblance conception of analytic philosophy once more overshoots the acknowledged extension of the term.

This shortcoming is avoided by combining a family resemblance with a *genetic* or *historical* conception. According to the latter, analytic philosophy is first and foremost a historical sequence of individuals and schools that influenced, and engaged in debate with, each other, without sharing any

single doctrine, problem, method or style. This historical conception conforms to common practice. But it requires supplementation, not least
because it remains unclear how membership of this tradition is determined. To count as an analytic philosopher it is not enough to stand in
relations even of *mutual* influence to members of this list; otherwise one
would have to include, e.g., Husserl and Habermas. Furthermore, a purely
historical conception ignores the fact that philosophers can be more or less
analytic on grounds other than historical ties. These worries can be laid to
rest if we acknowledge that analytic philosophy is a tradition held together
not just by relations of influence, but also by overlapping similarities. In
the final section I delineate the contours of the analytic tradition, and
pronounce on the question of who founded it and when it split off from
traditional and continental philosophy.

Having answered the title question, the final chapter 'Present and future'
turns to the current state of analytic philosophy and of the analytic/
continental divide. I hope to show that the divide plays an important
role in three areas of wider contemporary relevance: the 'culture' and
'science wars'; European fears of Anglo-American 'cultural imperialism';
and the mounting insularity of Anglo-American culture vis-à-vis continental Europe. I also consider some actual or alleged weaknesses of the current
analytic scene. In the final section, I consider the future of analytic
philosophy and its contrast with continental thought. I conclude that the
barriers between the two still exist at present, and that overcoming them is
not an overriding end in itself. Analytic philosophy needs to raise its game
in several respects, yet the ultimate aim should not be a unified philosophical scene, but simply better philosophy.

CHAPTER 2

Historical survey

This chapter charts the career of analytic philosophy. After considering the role of analysis in philosophy before the nineteenth century, it looks at the gradual emergence of logical and conceptual analysis in Bolzano, Frege, Moore and Russell. It then considers two subsequent sea-changes. First the linguistic turn of analytic philosophy at the hands of Wittgenstein, logical positivism and conceptual analysis; then the reversal of that turn, notably through the rehabilitation of metaphysics, the rise of naturalism, the triumph of mentalist approaches to mind and language, and the revival of first-order moral and political theory.

I PREHISTORY

The word 'analysis' stems from the Greek *analusis*, which means 'loosening up' or 'dissolving'. Two notions of analysis have been central to philosophy almost from its inception (see Beaney 2003). The first derives from Socrates' quest for definitions of terms like 'virtue' and 'knowledge', and it features in Plato, who speaks of it as 'division'. Such *decompositional* or 'progressive' analysis applies primarily to what we nowadays call *concepts*. It is the dissection or resolution of a given concept into component concepts, components that in turn can be used to define the complex concept. Thus the concept of a human being – the *analysandum* – is analysed into those of an animal and of rationality, thereby delivering the definition of a human being as a rational animal – the *analysans*. While the *class* of human beings is contained in the class of animals as a proper subset, the *concept* of a human being contains the concept of an animal, in that the latter is part of the explanation of the former.

The second notion derives from Greek geometry and predominates in Aristotle. It may be called *regressive* analysis and applies primarily to *propositions*. Analytic philosophy is sometimes misconceived as a deductive enterprise which derives theorems from axioms and definitions by way of formal proof. Up to Kant, however, this characteristically mathematical procedure of deducing consequences from first principles or axioms was known as the *synthetic method*. The *analytic method*, by contrast, starts with a proposition which has yet to be proven and works back to first principles from which it can be derived as a theorem. What unites decompositional and regressive analysis is the idea of starting with something given (respectively, a concept to be analysed or a proposition to be proven) and identifying something more basic (the components of the analysandum or the axioms from which to deduce the theorem) from which it can be derived (defined or proven).

Whereas Spinoza sought to reason '*more geometrico*', for Descartes synthesis is merely the method of *exposition* or *proof*. The *discovery* of new insights is analytic and consists in identifying the 'simple natures' which constitute reality and the axioms ('primary notions') which specify the links between them (*Meditations* Responses II). Leibniz went even further. According to him in all true propositions the predicate is contained in the concept of the subject; and they can therefore all be proven by *analysing* the latter. Every truth can be reduced to an 'identical truth' by making use of the definitions that result from such analyses. Thus arithmetic equations can be reduced to identical truths by exploiting the fact that each natural number can be defined as its *predecessor plus one*. For instance,

$$7 =_{def} 6 + 1; \quad 5 =_{def} 4 + 1 \text{ and } 12 =_{def} 11 + 1.$$

On this basis

(1) $7 + 5 = 12$

can be transformed into

(1') $(6 + 1) + (4 + 1) = 11 + 1$

and so on, until we reach

(1*) $(1+1+1+1+1+1+1) + (1+1+1+1+1)$
$= 1+1+1+1+1+1+1+1+1+1+1+1.$

Leibniz sought a *characteristica universalis*, a scientific notation which would provide an algorithm both for the analytic method of discovery (the definition of the relevant concepts through decompositional analysis) and the synthetic method of proof (of deriving the theorem with the aid of such definitions).

Whereas Leibniz propagated *logical* and Descartes *ontological* analysis, *psychological-cum-epistemological* analysis was the favoured tool of the

EMPIR. ANAL.

British empiricists, notably in Locke's project of breaking up 'complex' into 'simple' ideas (*Essay* II.2, 22) or in James Mill's *Analysis of the Phenomena of the Human Mind* (1829). The aim was to discover not so much the ultimate constituents of reality in general, but of the human mind, and to show that they are furnished by sensory experience.

In Kant the resolution of mental *episodes* gives way to that of mental faculties like sensibility, understanding and reason. The Transcendental Analytic is a 'logic of truth'; it provides a 'negative touchstone' in that it examines cognitive principles which no empirical judgement can contradict without losing its reference to objects and thereby its status as a bearer of a truth-value – what is nowadays called its *truth-aptness*. By contrast, the Transcendental Dialectic is a 'logic of illusion'; it exposes fallacies to which reason is prone when it makes claims about objects that lie beyond all possible experience (*Critique of Pure Reason* B 85–7).

Kant also uses 'analytic' in a way relating to decompositional analysis (B 1–3, 10–15). In an *analytic* judgement, the predicate is already *contained* in the concept of the subject at least implicitly, as in

(2) All bodies are extended.

By contrast, the predicate of a *synthetic* judgement like

(3) All bodies are heavy

adds something to the subject-concept rather than merely spelling out what is already implicit in it. The analytic/synthetic distinction is connected to that between *a posteriori* knowledge, which is based on experience – whether observation or experiment – and *a priori* knowledge. Unlike the *innate* ideas postulated by the rationalists and repudiated by the empiricists, *a priori* judgements are independent of experience not as regards their *origin*, but as regards their *validity*. Although we have to learn even an *a priori* judgement like (1), we can demonstrate its truth through calculation, without appeal to experience.

Metaphysics aspires to be *both a priori*, unlike the empirical sciences, including Locke's 'physiology of the human understanding', *and* synthetic, unlike formal logic, since it makes substantive claims about reality (A ix, B 18). Leibniz notwithstanding, Kant is confident that the judgements of arithmetic and geometry provide clear instances of synthetic *a priori* knowledge. Even (1) is synthetic: in thinking the sum $7 + 5$ we do not yet think the result $= 12$, since otherwise we would not need to calculate. At the same time Kant realizes that the idea of synthetic knowledge *a priori* is *prima facie* paradoxical. Given that experience is our *only way of getting in touch* with reality, how can a judgement be both synthetic, i.e. tell us something about reality, and yet be *a priori*, i.e. be known independently of experience?

Kant solves this riddle through his 'Copernican Revolution': 'we can know *a priori* of things only what we ourselves have put into them' (B XVIII). There is a difference between our experiences and their objects, and the *content* of experience is *a posteriori*. But the *form* or *structure* of experience is *a priori*, since it is determined not by the contingent input of the objects but by the cognitive apparatus of the subject. We experience objects as located in space and time, and as centres of qualitative changes which are subject to causal laws. According to Kant these are not contingent facts about either reality or human nature, but 'transcendental' preconditions for the possibility of experience, features to which any *object of experience* must conform. Metaphysical judgements like 'Every event has a cause' hold true of the objects of experience (i.e. are synthetic) independently of experience (i.e. are *a priori*), because they express preconditions of *experiencing* objects, preconditions which at the same time determine what is *to be* an object of experience.

Kant's dichotomies and his claim that there is synthetic *a priori* knowledge set the agenda for a debate about the nature of logic, mathematics and metaphysics that continues to be central to analytic philosophy. At an even grander scale, he altered the self-image and institutional organization of philosophy. Before Kant, philosophy was regarded as the 'Queen of the Sciences'. It provided the framework for the special sciences, which is why physics used to be called 'natural philosophy'. In the course of the seventeenth and eighteenth centuries, however, an undeniable contrast emerged: whereas metaphysics remained a 'battlefield' of futile controversy (B XV), the natural sciences progressed by combining empirical research with mathematical tools. This posed a fundamental challenge: can philosophy preserve a distinct role as a separate academic discipline? Or does it face the stark choice between becoming part of the natural sciences or turning into a branch of *belles lettres* unrestrained by standards of truth and rationality?

According to Kant, philosophy is a cognitive discipline, yet distinct from the empirical sciences because, like logic and mathematics, it aspires to *a priori* knowledge. But he rejected the received explanation of this special status. According to Platonists, metaphysics examines abstract entities beyond space and time, according to Aristotelians, it examines 'being *qua* being', the most general features of reality to which we ascend by abstracting from the specific features of particular objects. Kant brought about a fundamental reorientation by insisting that transcendental metaphysics is 'occupied not so much with objects as with the mode of our knowledge *of objects*' (B 25). Science and common sense describe or explain material reality on the basis of experience. Philosophy, by contrast, is *a priori* not because it describes objects of a peculiar kind, whether they be Platonic forms or Aristotelian essences, but because it reflects on the non-empirical preconditions of our empirical knowledge of ordinary material objects.

Kant rehabilitates only a 'transcendental' metaphysics of experience, not the 'transcendent' metaphysics of the rationalists which seeks knowledge of objects beyond all possible experience, like God and the soul. He sweeps away the pretensions of traditional metaphysics without relinquishing the project of philosophy as a *sui generis* discipline distinct from the special sciences. Alas, this otherwise attractive combination comes at a price, namely a form of idealism. Kant neither denies the existence of mind-independent objects, nor does he claim that the mind creates nature, caricatures by some analytic commentators notwithstanding. He does maintain, however, that the mind imposes its *structural laws* on reality. From a philosophical perspective, space, time and causation are 'ideal' rather than 'real'. They apply only to 'appearances', things as they can be experienced by us; they do not hold of 'things as they are in themselves', of which we can have no knowledge whatever.

This 'transcendental idealism' creates numerous tensions. For instance, while causation is supposed to apply only to appearances, the latter result from things in themselves causally affecting the subject's cognitive apparatus. The German idealists tried to overcome these tensions by taking idealism to extremes. The subject furnishes not just the form of cognition, but also its *content*. Reality is a manifestation of a spiritual principle which transcends individual minds, such as Hegel's 'spirit'. Since reality is itself entirely mental, it can be fully grasped by the mind. Philosophy once more turns into a super-science which encompasses all other disciplines. *All genuine knowledge is a priori*, since reason can derive even apparently contingent facts through the method of 'dialectic', which was rehabilitated in the face of Kant's strictures.

These grandiose pretensions proved incompatible with the rapid advances of first the natural and then the cultural sciences in the nineteenth century. The result was the 'collapse of idealism' soon after Hegel's death in 1831. Two main reactions emerged. One was *naturalism*. The naturalists were physiologists by training, who treated the demise of German idealism as a sign of the bankruptcy of all metaphysical speculation and *a priori* reasoning. They held that all knowledge is *a posteriori*, because the allegedly *a priori* disciplines can either be reduced to empirical disciplines like psychology or physiology – this was their preferred line on logic and mathematics, partly inspired by John Stuart Mill's radical empiricism – or be rejected as illusory – their favourite treatment of philosophy.

The other reaction was Neo-Kantianism, a movement that dominated German academic philosophy between 1865 and World War I. If philosophy wanted to preserve its status as a respectable *sui generis* discipline, it had to abandon the hopeless competition with the special sciences. Under the battle-cry 'Back to Kant!', the Neo-Kantians reverted to the idea that philosophy is a *second-order* discipline. It neither investigates a putative reality beyond that accessible to science, nor does it compete with science in explaining empirical reality. Instead, it clarifies the logical, conceptual and methodological preconditions of empirical knowledge, as well as the preconditions of non-philosophical modes of thought more generally.

2 FIRST GLIMMERINGS: MATHEMATICS AND LOGIC

While the flourishing of the special sciences during the nineteenth century put pressure on the idea of philosophy as an autonomous discipline, it also created a need for philosophy. Both the emergence of new disciplines like psychology and the rapid transformation of established subjects raised conceptual and methodological issues and lured scientists themselves onto philosophical territory.

Nowhere is this more evident than in the foundations of mathematics, which became a thriving field, especially in Germany (Gillies 1999). On the one hand, mathematics became increasingly abstract and independent of its empirical applications. Algebra was no longer quantitative and Weierstrass purged analysis of geometrical intuitions and the paradoxical notion of infinitesimals. Both were 'arithmetized' in that their basic concepts were defined in terms of the natural numbers and the arithmetic operations on them. On the other hand, the introduction of non-Euclidean geometries and non-standard algebras cast doubt on the certainty of mathematics, threatening its received status as the paradigm of human knowledge. A 'foundational crisis' ensued. Mathematicians became convinced that what mattered was not so much the intuitive truth of theorems, but their watertight derivation from axioms and definitions. They also developed an interest in the nature of natural numbers, which led to breakthroughs in number theory, such as Dedekind's definitions of infinity and continuity and Cantor's invention of transfinite set-theory. Finally, the interaction between logic and mathematics promised means both for increasing the formal rigour of mathematical proofs and for securing the foundations of that branch of mathematics to which all others seemed reducible – arithmetic.

Several ancestors of analytic philosophy took a leading role in these developments. Bernard Bolzano anticipated by decades both the arithmetization of the calculus and results in number and set theory, e.g. that an infinite set can contain a proper subset which is equally infinite (1851). The most important innovation of Bolzano's formal logic was his method of 'variation' (1837: II §§147–62), which considers what happens to the truth-value of a complex proposition when we alter one of its components – whether it be a concept or another proposition. Variation allowed him to provide precise definitions of a whole raft of logical concepts. His notion of deducibility anticipated Tarski's (1936) notion of logical consequence, and his notion of 'logically analytic' propositions anticipated Quine's notion of logical truth (1960: 65n). In a logical truth only logical particles 'occur essentially'; that is, we can vary all the other components at will, without engendering a change in truth-value. Thus in

(4) Brutus killed Caesar or Brutus did not kill Caesar

we can make any (consistent) substitution for all components other than 'or' and 'not', and the result will still be true.

Bolzano's philosophy of mathematics (1810) harks back to Leibniz. *Pace* Kant, arithmetic is analytic, and it is no more grounded in the *a priori* intuition of time than geometry is grounded in that of space. Logical rigour is to be achieved by 'purely analytical' methods, which do not require recourse to subjective intuitions and pictorial ideas. The same anti-subjectivism and anti-psychologism guides Bolzano's semantic Platonism, which anticipates that of Frege and Moore. He distinguished between mental judgements, linguistic sentences and propositions (*Sätze an sich*). A proposition like Pythagoras' theorem can be expressed by sentences in different languages. It is not true or false in a language or a context, but true or false *simpliciter*, independently of whether anyone ever calls or judges it true. Unlike utterances or judgements, propositions are 'non-actual', that is, they stand outside the causal order of the spatio-temporal world. A proposition is the content of a judgement, and also the sense of the utterance that expresses it. Similarly, we must distinguish the components of propositions – concepts or 'representations-as-such' – from the linguistic components of sentences and the mental components of judgements.

For all his far-sighted innovations, Bolzano's formal logic was old fashioned in one crucial respect. He stuck to Aristotelian syllogistic logic by insisting that all propositions divide into subject and predicate. But the application of mathematical ideas to logic (which had hitherto been the preserve of philosophers) also led to formal systems of an entirely novel kind. By capitalizing on an analogy between the disjunction/conjunction of concepts and the addition/multiplication of numbers, George Boole mathematized syllogistic logic in terms of algebraic operations on sets and presented logic as a branch of mathematics, the algebra of human thinking (1854: chs. 1, 22).

The watershed in the development of formal logic, however, was Gottlob Frege's *Begriffsschrift* of 1879. Frege's system was based on function theory instead of algebra. Like Boole, he mathematized logic. Yet far from seeking to display logic as a branch of mathematics, he pioneered *logicism*, the project of providing mathematics with secure foundations by deriving it from logic. Logicism seeks to define the *concepts* of mathematics in purely logical terms (including that of a set), and to derive its *propositions* from self-evident logical principles.

To pursue this programme, Frege had to overcome the limitations of syllogistic logic. *Begriffsschrift* provides the first complete axiomatization of first-order logic (propositional- and predicate-calculus) and exhibits mathematical induction as an application of a purely logical principle. The basic idea is to analyse propositions not into subject and predicate, like school grammar and Aristotelian logic, but into *function* and *argument*. The expression '$x^2 + 1$' represents a function of the variable x, because the value of $x^2 + 1$ depends solely on the argument we substitute for x – it has the value 2 for the argument 1, 5 for the argument 2, etc. Frege extended this mathematical notion so that functions do not just take numbers as arguments, but objects of *any* kind. Thus the expression 'the capital of x' denotes a function which has the value Berlin for the argument Germany. By a similar token, a sentence like

(5) Caesar conquered Gaul

can be seen as the value of a two-place function (or 'concept') *x conquered y* for the arguments Caesar and Gaul. Frege analyses (5) not into the subject 'Caesar' and the predicate 'conquered Gaul' but into a two-place function-expression '*x* conquered *y*' and two argument-expressions 'Caesar' and 'Gaul'. In Frege's mature system, concepts are functions that map objects onto a 'truth-value'. Thus the value of the two-place concept *x conquered y* is either 'the True' (e.g. for the arguments Caesar and Gaul) or the False (e.g. for Napoleon and Russia), depending on whether the resulting proposition is true or false.

Frege further extended the idea of a truth-function to propositional connectives and expressions of generality. Negation, for example, is a truth-function which maps a truth-value onto the converse truth-value: '*p*' has the value True if and only if (from now on 'iff') '~*p*' has the value False. Similarly

(6) All electrons are negative

is analysed not into a subject 'all electrons' and a predicate 'are negative', but into a one-place function-name 'if *x* is an electron, then *x* is negative' and a universal quantifier ('For all *x* . . .') that binds the variable *x*. 'All electrons are negative' claims of every thing in the universe that *if* it is an electron, it is also negative. Existential propositions ('Some electrons are negative') are expressed through the universal quantifier plus negation ('Not for all *x*, if *x* is an electron, then *x* is not negative'). This quantifier-variable notation is capable of formalizing propositions involving multiple generality, which are essential to mathematics. It captures, e.g., the difference between the true proposition 'For every natural number, there is a greater one' – '$\forall x \exists y (y > x)$' – and the false proposition 'There is a natural number which is greater than all others' – '$\exists y \forall x (y > x)$'. It is also capable of revealing the flaws in the ontological argument. Unlike omnipotence, existence is *not* a 'component' of the concept *God*, a feature which might be part of its definition. Rather, it is a 'property' of that concept, namely the property of having at least one object falling under it. 'God exists' ascribes a property to a concept rather than to an object (its form is '$\exists x Gx$' rather than 'Eg').

Frege was concerned only with the logical 'content' of signs, not, with their 'colouring', the mental associations they evoke. In 'On Sense and Meaning' (1892) he distinguished two aspects of that content: their meaning (*Bedeutung*), which is the object they refer to, and their sense (*Sinn*), the 'mode of presentation' of that referent. While the ideas (*Vorstellungen*) individuals associate with a sign are subjective (psychological), its sense is objective. It is grasped by any individual who understands the sign, yet it exists independently of being grasped. The meaning of a sentence is its truth-value; its sense is the 'thought' it expresses. Like truth-values and concepts, thoughts are mind-independent abstract entities. They are true or false independently of someone grasping or believing them, and they can be shared and communicated between different individuals. Frege uses these truisms not just to combat psychologism, but also to erect a three-world ontology (later revived by Popper). Thoughts are 'non-actual', that is, non-spatial, a-temporal and imperceptible, yet 'objective'. They inhabit a 'third realm', a 'domain' beyond space and time which contrasts with the 'first realm' of private ideas (individual minds), and the 'second realm' of material objects, which are both objective and actual.

According to Frege, although arithmetical propositions are *a priori*, they are analytic in the sense of being provable from logical axioms and definitions alone. In *Grundlagen der Arithmetik* (1884) he brilliantly criticized both Kant's idea that arithmetic is based on *a priori* intuition and Mill's empiricist view that it is based on inductive generalizations. He also tackled the main challenge facing logicism, by providing a definition of the notion of a cardinal number in terms of the logical notion of a set. Frege's logicism culminated in his *Grundgesetze der Arithmetik* (1893 and 1903). Alas, it came to grief because it made unrestricted use of sets which have other sets as their members, and therefore engendered the notorious paradox of the set of all sets which are not members of themselves.

3   THE REBELLION AGAINST IDEALISM

When Bertrand Russell devised this paradox in 1903, he was in the process of developing a logical system closely resembling Frege's. He endeavoured to protect logicism from paradox by means of a theory of types, a 'definite set of rules for deciding whether a given series of words was or was not significant' (1903: xi). This theory prohibits as 'meaningless' formulae that say of a set x what can only be said of x's members, notably that x is (or is not) a member of x itself. The eventual outcome was Russell's and Whitehead's *Principia Mathematica* (1910–13), which provided a definitive statement of logicism and the starting point for a rapid growth of formal logic. Ironically, one of the ensuing results dealt a serious blow to the logicist project. According to Gödel's 'incompleteness theorems' (1931) no logical system strong enough to derive arithmetic can establish its own consistency. Therefore there is no system of self-evident and demonstrably consistent axioms capable of generating all mathematical truths, which militates against the epistemological aspiration behind logicism, namely to secure the foundations of mathematics against any conceivable threat of doubt or inconsistency. As a result, the contemporary philosophical importance of logicism lies more in its spin-offs for the methods of logical analysis than in attaining its original goal.

Like Frege, Russell thought of his formal system as an *ideal language*, one which avoids the apparent logical defects of natural languages – ambiguity, indeterminacy, referential failure, and category-confusion. But his interests were wider. He applied the new logical techniques not just to the foundations of mathematics but also to traditional problems of epistemology and metaphysics. Indeed, he hoped that they would set philosophy as a whole on the secure path of a science. The reason for this wider scope lies in Russell's intellectual roots. Though initially trained as a mathematician, he also held a degree in philosophy and became steeped in a philosophical system, namely the 'British Idealism' epitomized by Bradley and McTaggart.

British Idealism was a belated assimilation of German Idealism which held sway in Britain between the 1870s and the 1920s. For the British Idealists the view that there are mind-independent individual things leads to contradictions that can be exposed by Hegelian dialectic. Common sense and science are at best 'partially' or 'relatively true' and their findings must be qualified by philosophy. According to Bradley, individual things are mere appearance, and the underlying reality is a single indivisible whole, the all-encompassing Hegelian 'Absolute'. In so far as one can distinguish any aspects of this whole, the relations between them are necessary or 'internal', that is, constitutive of the relata, rather than contingent or 'external' (Passmore 1966: chs. 3–4).

Russell and his Cambridge contemporary G. E. Moore had initially sympathized with British Idealism. Their 'revolt' against it marked a decisive moment in the emergence of analytic philosophy.

It was towards the end of 1898 that Moore and I rebelled against both Kant and Hegel. Moore led the way, but I followed closely in his footsteps . . . I felt a great liberation, as if I had escaped from a hot house into a wind swept headland . . . In the first exuberance of liberation, I became a naive realist and rejoiced in the thought that grass really is green. (1959: 42, 62)

For Moore, the monistic denial of external relations between independent objects evinces confusions concerning identity and difference, and runs counter to the common-sense insight that some facts are contingent. He also accused idealism of 'too psychological a standpoint' (1898: 199). For one thing, Kant's Copernican revolution wrongly makes *a priori* truths dependent on the nature of the human mind, which is a contingent matter. For another, whether a proposition is true is not a matter of degree and must not be confused with whether it is thought or known to be true. Finally, the objects of knowledge or thought are not psychological phenomena in the minds of individuals. They are *propositions*, complexes of concepts that exist independently of being known or thought about. While Moore and Russell repudiated the idealists' coherence theory of truth (according to which a proposition is true iff it is part of a coherent system of propositions), they did not immediately opt for a correspondence theory. A true proposition does not correspond to a fact, it *is* a fact and therefore itself part of reality. Similarly, the concepts that feature in propositions exist independently of our minds and their activities (Moore 1899: 4–5).

The British Idealists had *prima facie* compelling arguments for their paradoxical answers to philosophical questions. In response, Moore insisted that the *questions themselves* must be *questioned*. The 'difficulties and disagreements' that have dogged philosophy are due mainly

to the attempt to answer questions without first discovering precisely *what* question it is which you desire to answer ... [philosophers] are constantly endeavouring to prove that 'Yes' or 'No' will answer questions, to which *neither* answer is correct ... (1903: vi)

According to Moore, philosophy needs common sense and painstaking analysis rather than dazzling dialectics: 'a thing becomes intelligible first when it is analysed into its constituent concepts' (1899: 182). He regarded analysis as a decomposition of complex concepts – including propositions – into simpler concepts by way of definition.

Russell was even more expansive in his praise for analysis. He maintained apodictically that 'all sound philosophy begins with *logical analysis*', and that this realization represents 'the same kind of advance as was introduced into physics by Galileo' (1900: 8; 1914: 14, see also 68–9). With hindsight he wrote:

Ever since I abandoned the philosophy of Kant and Hegel, I have sought solutions of philosophical problems by means of analysis; and I remain firmly persuaded, in spite of some modern tendencies to the contrary, that only by analysing is progress possible. (1959: 11)

Whereas Moore was mainly concerned with combating the *idealist* denial of mind-independent objects, Russell's main bugbear was the *monistic* denial of a plurality of entities. For Russell there are two types of philosophers, those like Bradley who take the world to be a bowl of jelly – an indivisible whole – and those like himself who think of it as a bucket of shot, consisting of discrete, physical or logical atoms (Monk 1996a: 114).

Russell initially described analysis in decompositional terms, namely as the identification of the simple parts of mind-independent, non-linguistic complexes (1903: xv, 466). For the same reason, he adopted a luxuriant ontology similar to those of Moore and Meinong, accepting as real all the things that our meaningful terms seem to stand for, including not just abstract objects but also fictional entities like the Homeric gods and impossible entities like the round square.[1]

---

[1] According to a revisionist reading, Russell's ontology never included non-existing entities (Griffin 1996; Stevens 2005: ch. 2). There are passages which deny that, e.g., chimera are things denoted by

But Russell's conception of analysis was also inspired by the aforementioned discovery that mathematical notions like infinity and continuity could be defined in a way that does not lead to the contradictions diagnosed by Hegelianism. Like Frege and unlike Moore, Russell was a pioneer of *logical* rather than *conceptual* analysis. The new logic provided ways of *paraphrasing* philosophically puzzling propositions in a formal language. More specifically, analysis provides a means of showing that our generally accepted propositions do not commit us to the existence of dubious entities. This enabled Russell's self-proclaimed 'robust sense of reality' (1919: 170) to reassert itself.

For Frege, a sentence of the form 'The *F* is *G*' has a sense but lacks a meaning if nothing which is *F* exists. By this token,

(7) The present King of France is bald

expresses a thought but lacks a truth-value, i.e. it is neither true nor false. Russell rejected Frege's sense/meaning distinction. His famous theory of descriptions analysed such sentences into a quantified conjunction, viz.

(7′) There is one and only one thing which is a present King of France, and every thing which is a present King of France is bald.

In formal notation, (7) is expressed as

(7*) $\exists x((x$ is a present King of France & $\forall y (y$ is a present King of France $\rightarrow y = x))$ & x is bald)

Expressions like definite descriptions ('the so-and-so') are 'incomplete symbols'. They have no meaning – do not stand for anything – on their own; yet they can be paraphrased in the context of the meaningful sentences in which they occur.

The theory of descriptions was described by Frank Ramsey as a 'paradigm of philosophy' (1931: 263), since it seemed capable of resolving age-old puzzles about existence and identity. Analysis was no longer just decomposition of the entities apparently denoted by the *terms* of a

concepts. But Russell also opined that 'in some sense nothing is something' and wrote: 'Whatever may be an object of thought, or may occur in any true or false proposition, or may be counted as *one*, I call a *term* ... every term has being, *i.e. is* in some sense. A man, a moment, a number, a class, a relation, a chimera, or anything else that can be mentioned, is sure to be a term; and to deny that such and such a thing is a term must always be false' (1903: 73, 43). Griffin tries to defuse this list by insisting that Russell is inadvertently talking about terms when he means to be talking about *denoting concepts*. But this is not an option, since the list is part and parcel of a key passage in which Russell *explains* his notion of a *term*. Note also that the orthodox interpretation is in line with Russell's own later account of his development.

sentence; it turned into the transformation of a *whole* sentence into one from which incomplete symbols have been eliminated. Such analysis aims to uncover the true *logical form* of propositions and facts, a form which can differ substantially from the often misleading *grammatical form* of the sentence in the vernacular which expresses that fact. Russell put logical analysis into the service of a *reductionist* project. In the spirit of Occam's razor and of earlier empiricists, the unnecessary reification of objects of discourse is avoided by 'analysing away' the troublesome expressions (1956a: 233; see Hylton 1990: ch. 6; Hacker 1996: 9–12). More generally, he pursued a *metaphysical aim* by *logical means*: true sentences properly analysed are supposed to be *isomorphic* to the facts they express, and therefore logical analysis can reveal the ultimate components and structures of reality.

4 THE LINGUISTIC TURN

Frege and Russell had revolutionized formal logic and demonstrated its philosophical potency. At the same time, they had left the *nature* of logic obscure. That, at any rate, was the view of Ludwig Wittgenstein, an Austrian who came to Cambridge in 1911, initially as Russell's student but soon as his equal and remorseless critic. At the time, there were four accounts of the nature of logic. According to Mill, logical propositions are extremely well corroborated inductive generalizations. According to psychologism, logical truths or 'laws of thought' describe how human beings (by and large) think, their basic mental operations, and are determined by the nature of the human mind. Against both positions Platonists like Frege protested that logical truths are objective and necessary, and that these features can only be explained by assuming that their subject matter – logical objects and thoughts – are abstract entities inhabiting a 'third realm' beyond space and time. Finally, Russell held that the propositions of logic are supremely general truths about the most pervasive traits of reality, traits to which we have access by abstraction from non-logical propositions. For instance, 'Plato loves Socrates' yields the logical form '$x\Phi y$' and thereby a proposition like 'Something is somehow related to something'.

Wittgenstein's *Tractatus* (1922) eschews all four alternatives. The propositions of logic like '$(p \lor \sim p)$' are neither inductive generalizations, nor descriptions of how people think, of a Platonist *hinterworld* or of the most pervasive features of reality. Rather, they are vacuous 'tautologies'. They *say nothing*, since they combine empirical propositions in such a way that all factual information cancels out. 'It is raining' says something about the weather – true or false – and so does 'It is not raining.' But 'Either it is raining or it is not raining' does not. The necessity of tautologies simply reflects the fact that they do not make any claims the truth-value of which depends on how things actually are. Just as logical propositions are not statements about a special reality, the logical constants (propositional connectives and quantifiers) are not names of peculiar logical entities, as Frege and Russell supposed. Rather, they express the truth-functional operations through which complex propositions are created out of simpler ones.

According to Wittgenstein, all logical relations between propositions are due to the complexity of molecular propositions, the fact that they are built up from 'atomic' or 'elementary propositions' solely through truth-functional operations. By the same token, all meaningful propositions can be analysed into logically independent elementary propositions. The ultimate constituents of such propositions are unanalysable 'names' (the simplest components of language). These names have as their meaning, i.e. stand for, indestructible 'objects' (the simplest components of reality). A similar type of *logical atomism* was developed by Russell. Furthermore, Wittgenstein shared Russell's conviction (1900: 8; 1914: ch. 2; 1918: 108) that philosophy is identical with the logical analysis of propositions into their ultimate constituents, and that this would also display the building-blocks of reality.

Whereas Russell was driven by the empiricist idea that these constituents of reality should be objects of sensory 'acquaintance', Wittgenstein pursued a Kantian project. His prime concern was not to establish the precise nature of objects, but rather to show that they *must exist* if we are to be able to represent reality. Echoing Kant's ambition to draw the bounds between legitimate discourse and illegitimate speculation, the aim of the *Tractatus* is to 'draw a limit to thought'. At the same time, Wittgenstein gave a linguistic twist to the Kantian tale. Language is not just a secondary manifestation of something non-linguistic. For thoughts are neither mental processes nor abstract entities, but themselves propositions, sentences which have been projected onto reality. Thoughts can be completely expressed in language, and philosophy can establish the limits of thought by establishing the limits of the linguistic expression of thought. Indeed, these limits cannot be drawn by thoughts about both sides of the limit, since, by definition, such thoughts would be about something that cannot be thought. The limits of thought can only be drawn 'in language' (1922: Pref.), namely by showing that certain combinations of signs are bereft of sense, as in the case of 'A-sharp is red'.

For Wittgenstein, the logical calculus developed by Frege and Russell is not an ideal *language*, one that avoids the alleged defects of natural

languages, but an ideal *notation* which displays the logical structure that all
natural languages must have in common under their misleading surface.
Wittgenstein tries to capture the preconditions of linguistic representation
through his so-called picture theory. The essence of propositions – 'the
general propositional form' – is to state how things are. The logical
structure of language is identical with the metaphysical structure of reality,
because it comprises those structural features which language and reality
must share if the former is to be capable of depicting the latter. Elementary
propositions are pictures or models which depict a 'state of affairs', a
possible combination of objects. To do this, their constituent names
must go proxy for these objects, and they must have the same 'logical
form' as the depicted state of affairs. An elementary proposition is true iff
that state obtains, i.e. iff the named objects are actually combined as it says
they are.

Empirical propositions have sense by virtue of depicting a possible state
of affairs and logical propositions are 'senseless', since they say nothing. By
contrast, the pronouncements of metaphysics are 'nonsensical'. They try to
say what could not be otherwise, e.g. that the class of lions is not a lion. But
any attempt to refer to something nonsensical, if only to exclude it, is itself
nonsensical. For we cannot refer to something illogical like the class of lions
being a lion by means of a meaningful expression. What such metaphysical
'pseudo-propositions' try to *say* is *shown* by empirical propositions properly analysed. In fact, the pronouncements of the *Tractatus* itself are in the
end condemned as nonsensical. By outlining the essence of representation
they lead one to the correct logical point of view. But once this is achieved,
one must throw away the ladder which one has climbed up. Philosophy
cannot be a 'doctrine', since there are no meaningful philosophical propositions. It is an 'activity', a 'critique of language' by means of logical
analysis. Positively, it elucidates the meaningful propositions of science;
negatively, it reveals that metaphysical statements are nonsensical (1922:
4.0031, 4.112, 6.53–6.54).

With engaging modesty, Wittgenstein felt that the *Tractatus* had solved
the fundamental problems of philosophy and abandoned the subject after
its publication. Meanwhile, the book had come to the attention of the
logical positivists of the Vienna Circle. The logical positivists aimed to
develop a 'consistent empiricism'. They agreed with British empiricism
and Ernst Mach that all of human knowledge is based on experience, but
tried to defend this position in a more cogent way, with the help of modern
logic, a point they stressed by using the label 'logical empiricism'. Inspired
by Frege, Russell and Wittgenstein they employed logical rather than

ANTI-PSYCHOL.

psychological analysis to identify the elements of experience, reality and language (Carnap *et al.* 1929: 8). Moreover, they invoked the *Tractatus* to account for the propositions of logic and mathematics, without reducing them to inductive generalizations (Mill), lapsing into Platonism (Frege), or admitting synthetic *a priori* truths (Kant). Logic and mathematics, they conceded, are necessary and *a priori*; yet they do not amount to knowledge about the world. For all *a priori* truths are analytic, that is, true solely in virtue of the meanings of their constituent words. *Logical* truths are tautologies which are true in virtue of the meaning of the logical constants alone, and *analytical* truths can be reduced to tautologies by substituting synonyms for synonyms. Thus

(8) All bachelors are unmarried

is transformed into

(8') All unmarried men are unmarried

a tautology of the form ' $\forall x ((Fx \ \& \ Gx) \rightarrow Gx)$ '. Necessary propositions, far from mirroring the essence of reality or the structure of pure reason, are true by virtue of the conventions governing our use of words (Carnap *et al.* 1929: 8–10, 13; Blumberg and Feigl 1931; Ayer 1936: 21–4, ch. 4).

Nowadays the logical positivists are best known for verificationism, the view that the meaning of a proposition is its method of verification (the 'principle of verification'), and that only those propositions are 'cognitively meaningful' which are capable of being verified or falsified (the verificationist 'criterion of meaningfulness'). On the basis of this criterion, they condemned metaphysics as meaningless, because it is neither *a posteriori* – like empirical science – nor analytic – like logic and mathematics. Metaphysical pronouncements are vacuous: they neither make statements of fact that can ultimately be verified by sensory experience, nor do they explicate the meaning of words or propositions.

Legitimate philosophy boils down to what Rudolf Carnap called 'the logic of science' (1937: 279). Its task is the logico-linguistic analysis of those propositions which alone are strictly speaking meaningful, namely those of science. Rounding off this linguistic turn, Carnap reformulated philosophical problems and propositions from the traditional 'material mode' – concerning the nature or essence of objects – into the formal mode – concerning linguistic expressions, their syntax and semantics.

The logical positivists took over the analytic methods of logical atomism while repudiating the (diverse) metaphysical rationales given for them by Russell and Wittgenstein. From the latter they inherited the linguistic turn,

MATH. PHIL.: how ve LPS
BEYOND M.¼
F., G!
+ t.
Kant.

{ WHAT A DEPRESSING INSIGHT — another sign of the — ... — HUMILITY!]

VERIF.

ANTI-MP

ONLY SCI.
STATEMENTS ARE MEANINGFUL,
∴ ONLY SCI. IS WORTHY OF PHIL. STUDY

from the former the ambition to vindicate empiricism by means of reductive analysis. They were committed to the 'unity of science', the idea that all scientific disciplines, including the social sciences, can be unified in a single system with physics as its foundation. The theoretical terms of science are defined through a more primitive observational vocabulary and this makes it possible to break down all significant propositions into propositions about what is 'given' in experience.

These so-called 'protocol-sentences' or 'observation-sentences' occasioned the first major split within the positivist movement. According to the 'phenomenalists', led by Schlick, these sentences are about subjective sense-experiences; according to the physicalists, led by Neurath and later joined by Carnap, they are about physical objects rather than mental episodes. The physicalist option does justice to the fact that the objects of science must be intersubjectively accessible. The price to be paid is that even the propositions which constitute the empirical foundations of science are fallible, a view which was also supported by Karl Popper, an associate of the Vienna Circle.

Another controversy arose over the status of philosophy vis-à-vis science. All logical positivists believed that philosophy should emulate the rigour and the cooperative spirit of the formal and empirical sciences. But whereas Schlick and Carnap held fast to a qualitative distinction between the empirical investigation of reality and the philosophical analysis of the propositions and methods of science, Neurath adopted a naturalistic stance according to which philosophy itself dissolves into a unified physicalist science.

Carnap had originally been impressed by Wittgenstein's strictures against any attempt to talk about the relation between language and reality, and he had therefore restricted the analysis of language to logical *syntax*, the intra-linguistic rules for the combination of signs. But in 1935 Alfred Tarski published a seminal paper that defined the central semantic notion of truth in a way that avoids semantic paradoxes (like that of the liar). This persuaded Carnap to drop the restriction to syntax, and his subsequent attempts to explicate semantic notions – notably through the idea of possible worlds (1956) – had a profound influence on analytic philosophy of language.

Verificationism also came under pressure. The principle of verification was attacked by conceptual analysts, who pointed out that linguistic meaning attaches not just to declarative sentences capable of being true or false and hence of being verified or falsified, but also, for example, to interrogative, imperative and performative sentences. In response, logical positivists restricted the principle to what they called 'cognitive' as opposed to e.g. emotive meaning (Carnap 1963, 45; see Stroll 2000, 84–6).

This concession deprives the principle of verification of its semantic role, unless it can be shown that even non-declarative statements have a truth-apt and hence verifiable component. It does not threaten the verificationist critique of metaphysics, since metaphysics aspires to descriptions of reality with cognitive content. But traditional philosophers objected that the criterion of meaningfulness is self-refuting, since it is neither empirical nor analytic, and hence meaningless by its own light (Ewing 1937). And logical positivists like Hempel (1950) realized that the criterion is either *too strict*, in that it rules out sentences which are part of science ('All quasars are radioactive' cannot be conclusively verified and 'Some quasars are not radioactive' cannot be conclusively falsified), or *too liberal*, in that it allows metaphysical sentences like 'Only the Absolute is perfect.'

5 LOGICAL CONSTRUCTIONISM VS CONCEPTUAL ANALYSIS

Meanwhile in Cambridge there emerged a new generation of logical analysts, Ramsey pre-eminent among them. The Cambridge analysts shared neither the anti-metaphysical fervour of the logical positivists nor their verificationism. They did, however, share with them Wittgenstein's 'thesis of extensionality' (simple propositions occur in a complex one only in such a way that the truth-value of the latter depends solely on those of the former). They also shared with them Russell's empiricist aspiration of analysing propositions and concepts into constructions referring exclusively to the contents of experience. Alas, their attempts to reduce all meaningful propositions to truth-functional constructions out of elementary propositions about sense-data were no more successful than Carnap's heroic effort in *Der Logische Aufbau der Welt* (1928).

Analysis worked well enough when it came to showing that – grammatical appearances notwithstanding – we are not committed to the existence of the present king of France, the round square or the average Briton. Such 'logical' or 'same-level analysis' aims to present the actual logical form of a proposition and thereby its implications. It contrasts with 'new-level' or 'metaphysical analysis', a reductionist procedure supposed to eliminate things of one kind in favour of things of an ontologically more basic kind (Stebbing 1932; Wisdom 1934). The flip-side of new-level analysis was *logical construction*, the demonstration of how propositions and terms that seemed to denote the eliminated entities can be constructed out of propositions and terms that refer only to entities of the less problematic kind.

New-level analysis had more or less succeeded in mathematics, where numbers had been reduced to sets. But it failed in other areas. Even the *prima facie* undemanding analysis of propositions about nation-states into propositions about individuals and their actions proved tricky. When it came to the phenomenalist reduction of propositions about material objects to propositions about sense-data, the difficulties proved insuperable. Other stumbling-blocks included attributions of belief: the truth-value of 'Sarah believes that Blair is honest' is not determined simply by that of 'Blair is honest', contrary to the thesis of extensionality (see ch. 6.1 and Urmson 1956: 60–74, 146–62).

As regards the analysis of *concepts*, an additional hurdle was the so-called 'paradox of analysis' (Langford 1942), which is in fact a dilemma. Suppose that 'brother' is analysed as 'male sibling'. Either the analysandum has the same meaning as the analysans, in which case the analysis is *trivial* and nothing is learned by it; or the two are not synonymous, in which case the analysis is *incorrect*.

It is tempting to blame the failure of reductive analysis on the vagaries of ordinary language: the proposed analysis fails to say precisely the same thing as the analysandum simply because the analysandum does not say anything precise to begin with. This is the attitude of a strand within analytic philosophy that is known as 'ideal language philosophy' and comprises Frege, Russell, Tarski, the logical positivists and Quine. It holds that owing to their logical shortcomings, natural languages need to be replaced by an ideal language – an interpreted logical calculus – at least for the purposes of science and 'scientific philosophy'.

According to Carnap, the attempt to reveal the underlying logical form of sentences in the vernacular is futile; analysis should instead take the form of *logical construction*, not just in the sense that eliminated phrases are reconstructed out of acceptable ones, but in the sense of devising *entirely new artificial languages*. 'The logical analysis of a particular expression consists in the setting-up of a linguistic system and the placing of that expression in this system' (1936a: 143). Carnap's procedure of 'rational reconstruction' or 'logical explication' bypasses the paradox of analysis (1928: §100; 1956: 7–9). The objective is not to provide a synonym of the analysandum, but to *replace* it with an alternative expression or construction, one which serves the cognitive purposes of the original equally well while avoiding drawbacks such as obscurity and undesirable ontological commitments. For instance, talk about numbers can be replaced by talk about sets of sets. Encouraged by the emergence of Brouwer's intuitionist logic, Carnap espoused a 'principle of tolerance' in logic (1937: §17). We are at liberty to construct novel calculi, constrained only by the demand for consistency and considerations like ease of explanation and avoidance of puzzlement. This pragmatist attitude put him at odds not just with the *Tractatus*, for which there is a single 'logical syntax' common to *all* meaningful languages, but also with those like Russell who held that an ideal language should uniquely mirror the metaphysical structure of reality.

An alternative to both reductive analysis and logical constructionism emerged from 1929 onwards, when Wittgenstein returned to Cambridge and subjected his own earlier work to a withering critique. The eventual result was *Philosophical Investigations* (1953).

Wittgenstein came to realize that nothing could possibly fit the bill of logically independent elementary propositions. This had the further consequence that there are logical relations between propositions which do not result from the truth-functional combination of such elementary propositions. Ordinary language is not 'a calculus according to definite rules' (§81). Its rules are more diverse, diffuse and subject to change than those of artificial calculi. The atomistic idea of indecomposable objects and unanalysable names is a chimera. The distinction between simple and complex is not absolute, but relative to one's analytic tools and purposes. The collapse of logical atomism also undermines the picture theory. The explanation of how propositions represent possible facts cannot be that they are arrangements of logical atoms which share a logical form with an arrangement of metaphysical atoms. Moreover, the possibility of linguistic representation does not presuppose a one-to-one correlation between words and things. The underlying referential conception of meaning is doubly wrong. Not all words refer to objects. Indeed, even in the case of referring expressions, their meaning is *not* the object they stand for. The meaning of a word is not an entity of any kind, but its use according to linguistic rules (§43).

Both the picture theory and verificationism restrict meaningful propositions to statements of fact. Wittgenstein now denies that the sole function of language is to describe reality. In addition to statements of fact there are not just questions and commands but 'countless' other kinds of language games, e.g. telling jokes, thanking, cursing, greeting, praying. Furthermore, the constitutive rules of a whole language – Wittgenstein refers to them as the 'grammar' of that language – do not mirror the structure of reality but are 'autonomous'. They are not responsible either to empirical reality or to a Platonic realm of 'meanings'. Signs *by themselves* don't have meanings; we *give* them meaning by explaining and using them in a certain way. Language is not the self-sufficient abstract system as it is presented in the *Tractatus*. Rather, it is a human practice which in turn is embedded in a social 'form of life' (§23).

Wittgenstein still held that philosophical problems are rooted in misunderstandings of language. But he rejected both logical analysis and logical construction as means of achieving clarity. There are no logically independent elementary propositions or indefinable names for analysis to terminate with. Indeed, not all legitimate concepts can be sharply defined by reference to necessary and sufficient conditions for their application. Such *analytic definition* is only one form of explanation among others. Many philosophically contested concepts are united by 'family resemblances', overlapping similarities rather than by a common characteristic mark. In particular, propositions do not share a common essence, a single propositional form. Finally, the idea that analysis can make unexpected discoveries about what ordinary expressions really mean is misguided. The rules of language cannot be 'hidden'. Rather, competent speakers must be capable of recognizing them, since they are the normative standards which guide their utterances. To fight the 'bewitchment of our understanding through the means of our language' we require neither the construction of artificial languages nor the uncovering of logical forms beneath the surface of ordinary language. Instead, we need a description of our public linguistic practices, which constitute a motley of 'language games' (§§65–88, 108, 23).

Wittgenstein's new ideas, combined with Moore's common-sense philosophy, had a profound impact on a movement which emerged around the turn of the 1930s and dominated British philosophy until the 1960s. Its opponents called it 'ordinary language' or 'Oxford philosophy', since its most eminent proponents – Ryle, Austin and Strawson – were based there.[2] They themselves preferred labels such as 'conceptual analysis' or 'linguistic philosophy'. For they regarded philosophical problems as conceptual and concepts as embodied in language. To possess a concept is to know the meaning of certain expressions; by the same token, concepts are neither mental occurrences nor entities beyond space and time, but abstractions from our use of words.

Linguistic philosophers tried to resolve philosophical problems not through substituting artificial terms and constructions for the idioms of natural languages, but through clarifying the latter. More specifically, they described the ordinary uses of philosophically troublesome terms and contrasted them with their uses in philosophical theorizing. If

---

[2] The first to use the contrast 'ideal' vs 'ordinary language' philosophy was Gustav Bergmann, himself an ideal language philosopher (Rorty 1967: 6–9, 15–24).

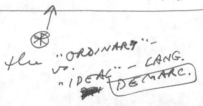

philosophical problems originate in our actual conceptual framework, as ideal language philosophers granted, the introduction of a novel scheme will merely sweep these problems under the carpet, *unless* its relation to the old one is properly understood. Once we have elucidated ordinary language, conceptual analysts like Strawson continued to reason, we no longer require an artificial one. For the problems arise not out of ordinary language as such, but out of its distortion and misunderstanding in philosophical theories (1963; see Rorty 1967: 15–19). [*i.e. the phils.*]

What survives the rejection of logical and reductive analysis is conceptual analysis and linguistic paraphrase. Philosophical problems are resolved by explaining expressions and by establishing the status and inferential powers of the statements in which they occur. The structure of 'I have a pain' is the same as that of 'I have a pin'; yet Wittgenstein maintained that these propositions are entirely disanalogous moves in the language game (1953: §§572–3). Similarly, Ryle advocated that philosophy should chart the 'logical geography' of our concepts. In *The Concept of Mind* he argued that the Cartesian dualism of mind and body results from 'category-mistakes': it treats mental concepts which signify behavioural dispositions as if they referred to processes that are just like physical ones, only more ethereal. Ryle rejected Wittgenstein's therapeutic image according to which 'the philosopher treats a question like a disease' (1953: §255). Yet he accepted that philosophy is a meta-discipline which does not 'talk sense with concepts' but tries to 'talk sense about concepts' (1949: 9–10). The paradox of analysis disappears, since the task is <u>not</u> to provide novel information about a realm extrinsic to us. According to Wittgenstein, philosophy reminds us of rules that we have mastered in practice but which mislead us in the course of philosophical reflections. According to Ryle, it takes us from the *knowledge how* to use words to an explicit *knowledge that* they are used according to certain rules. Either way, analysis is not a trivial pursuit, because the explanation of philosophically interesting concepts is complex and rich, especially when it places these concepts in their diverse contexts (everyday, scientific, philosophical).

J. L. Austin exemplified linguistic philosophy, especially to its enemies, since he was a master of observing minutiae of linguistic use – '*what we should say when*, and so why and what we should mean by it'. For example, he carefully contrasted apparently equivalent terms such as 'appear', 'look' and 'seem' by looking at the different situations that license their application. But his interest in language was not motivated solely by the desire of rectifying confusions, and he toyed with the idea that linguistic analysis might turn into a branch of linguistics (1970: 181, 231–2). By a similar token, whereas some linguistic philosophers regarded the quest for systematic theories as a misguided intrusion of scientific methods into philosophy, Austin founded a systematic approach to language, namely speech act theory. At the same time, even Austin was suspicious of the craving for uniformity that logical positivism shared with traditional philosophy. In line with Wittgenstein and Ryle he condemned as a 'descriptive fallacy' the dogma that language has just a single function, namely to describe or report facts. Moreover, he insisted that while 'ordinary language is *not* the last word . . . it *is* the *first* word' (1970: 103, 185; Wittgenstein 1953: §120). All neologisms, those of science included, need to be explained, and this can ultimately be done only in ordinary terms that are already understood. Therefore it is a precondition of sound philosophy that it should pay attention to the way in which central notions are employed in their normal surroundings, whether this be everyday language or the specialized language of a scientific discipline.

6 THE COLLAPSE OF LOGICAL POSITIVISM

The rise of Nazism forced most logical positivists to emigrate, mainly to the USA. By the forties, their views had achieved the status of orthodoxy. Labels like 'logical', 'philosophical' and 'conceptual analysis' had been rife since Russell and Moore, and they were soon joined by 'linguistic philosophy' and 'the analysis of language'. But pertinent uses of 'analytic(al) philosophy' came relatively late. One of the first occurs in Ernest Nagel (1936; also Bergmann 1945: 194). But the name caught on only after the war, perhaps through Arthur Pap (1949; see von Wright 1993: 41n; Hacker 1996: 275–6n). Later it was extended from logical positivism to conceptual analysis (Beck 1962; Ayer 1959: 3; Butler 1962; Montefiori and Williams 1966). Even before then, both Urmson's *Philosophical Analysis* (1956) and the Preface of Feigl's and Sellars' *Readings in Philosophical Analysis* (1949) had suggested that the Cambridge movement of Moore, Russell and Wittgenstein and the logical empiricism of Vienna and Berlin, along with their more recent continuations, should be considered as part of a single analytic approach to philosophy.

Thus, between the 1930s and 1950s analytic philosophy established itself as a self-conscious philosophical movement or tendency, albeit one splitting into two distinct branches – logical constructionism and conceptual analysis. At the same time, however, some assumptions uniting these two branches came to be questioned. The main protagonist of this development was the Harvard logician W. V. Quine. Quine was heavily indebted to the logical positivists. He shared their predilection for artificial languages, the conviction that natural science constitutes the paradigm of human knowledge, their vision of a unified science, their suspicion of abstract entities, and the empiricist credo that sensory experience provides not just the evidence on which our beliefs rest but also endows our language with its meaning. 'Whatever evidence there *is* for science *is* sensory evidence', and 'all inculcation of meaning of words must rest ultimately on sensory evidence' (1969: 75). But just as the logical positivists had tried to improve on Hume and Mach, Quine tried to improve on them, replacing their logical empiricism by a more pragmatist variety.

Quine first came to fame in 1951 through 'Two Dogmas of Empiricism'. The article vigorously attacked the two pillars of the logical positivists' conception of philosophy, namely the distinction between analytic and synthetic propositions and the project of reductive analysis. The linguistic turn promised a distinctive role for philosophy, without dubious appeals to a Platonic realm of abstract entities, Aristotelian essences or Kantian pure reason. While science results in empirical propositions that describe reality – and are hence synthetic – philosophy results in analytic propositions which unfold the meaning of the terms employed by science and/or common sense.

A similar line was taken by Wittgenstein and linguistic philosophers. In spite of their considerable disagreements, these philosophers accepted that there is a qualitative difference between science, which is concerned with factual issues and hence *a posteriori,* and philosophy, which is concerned with conceptual issues, and hence *a priori.* Quine overturned this picture by denying that there is a qualitative difference between apparently *a priori* disciplines like mathematics, logic and philosophy on the one hand, and empirical science on the other. Unlike Mill, Quine did not simply assimilate necessary propositions to empirical generalizations. Instead, he questioned the distinctions that had traditionally been used to set philosophy and science apart, in particular the analytic/synthetic distinction. He thereby challenged the idea that there is a distinct type of proposition which articulates conceptual connections rather than empirical facts, and reinvigorated radical empiricism, according to which even apparently *a priori* disciplines are ultimately based on experience.

Quine's attack on the analytic/synthetic distinction involved two lines of reasoning – one concerning epistemology and scientific method, the other concerning semantics and ontology. The impetus of the first line is that the analytic/synthetic distinction presupposes a second dogma of empiricism, namely 'reductionism', the view that every meaningful statement is translatable into a statement about the immediate experiences that confirm it. Reductionism would allow one to define analytic statements as those which are confirmed come what experience may. However, Quine argues, it is at odds with the *holistic* nature of scientific belief-formation: our beliefs form a 'web' in which each belief is linked to all others, and ultimately to experience. This means that it is impossible to specify confirming evidence for individual statements. It also means that any belief can be abandoned for the sake of preserving other parts of the web, and hence that there are no *a priori* statements, i.e. statements immune to empirical revision.

Quine's semantic argument is that analyticity is part of a circle of intensional notions – notions concerning what expressions mean or say – that cannot be reduced to purely extensional notions – notions concerning what expressions stand for or apply to like reference. But, he insisted, all these notions are obscure, because there are no criteria of identity for 'intensions': while we know what it is for two expressions to have the same extension, we do not know what it is for them to have the same intension. In *Word and Object* Quine supported this bold contention by focusing on 'radical translation', the translation of a completely foreign language from scratch (1960: ch. 2). Because such translation cannot assume any prior understanding, it helps to appreciate that translation is 'indeterminate': there is no fact of the matter as to whether two expressions are synonymous, and hence there are no criteria of identity for intensions. As a result, scientific philosophy should eliminate them from its ontology.

The result of Quine's assimilation of the analytic and the synthetic, the *a priori* and the empirical, is a thoroughgoing naturalism. Philosophy is a branch of, or continuous with, natural science (metaphilosophical naturalism). There is no genuine knowledge outside natural science (epistemological naturalism), and the latter provides the sole standard for what is real (ontological naturalism). The naturalistic conception of knowledge in turn requires a new, 'naturalized epistemology'. Like traditional epistemology, this novel discipline investigates the relationship between our beliefs and the empirical evidence for them. Yet it does so not by providing an *a priori* 'rational reconstruction' (à la Carnap) of the *reasons* we have for accepting scientific theories, but through a *scientific* investigation – behaviourist psychology or neurophysiology – of what *causes* us to adopt them. In the wake of Quine, this naturalistic conception of philosophy has achieved the status of orthodoxy, especially in the USA.

Reductionism and verificationism proved to be an Achilles heel of logical positivism not just in the philosophy of language, but also in the philosophy of science. Their failure undermined *logical* empiricism, but other versions soon came to the fore. Like Quine's *holism*, Popper's *fallibilism* (1934) rejects the idea of infallible protocol-sentences. Popper also criticized the verificationist criterion of meaningfulness on several grounds. First, separating meaningful science from nonsensical metaphysics is *neither* feasible *nor* desirable, since metaphysical speculation provides an invaluable stimulus to scientific research. Secondly, what is needed is a demarcation not between sense and nonsense, but between empirical science and other disciplines. Finally, the criterion for that demarcation cannot be verifiability. Science depends on universal laws, and these can never be conclusively verified, since they cover an infinite number of cases. Instead, it is *falsifiability*. A theory is scientific if it allows for the derivation of predictions that can be falsified by empirical data. Science proceeds not by fine-tuning inductive generalizations, but by bold conjectures, the logical deduction of predictions from these conjectures, and their ruthless refutation in the light of novel data.

For the logical positivists, scientific theory-formation was an ahistorical activity, namely of constructing theoretical frameworks to fit the available empirical evidence. Popper introduced a historical element, because a scientific theory is judged largely by the extent to which it can explain the observations that refuted its predecessors. He nevertheless retained the image of scientific progress as a linear rational process, in which theories are conclusively falsified and replaced by new ones which increasingly approximate the truth. This image was questioned by Thomas Kuhn (1962) and Paul Feyerabend (1975). They maintained that the history of science does not consist of rational shifts from inferior to superior theories, but of 'paradigm-shifts' which are partly dictated by non-cognitive factors (social, aesthetic, etc.). There is no universal scientific rationality which would allow us to maintain that more recent theories are objectively better than their predecessors. They also questioned the Kantian distinction between the 'context of discovery' and the 'context of justification', which had allowed the logical positivists to keep the rational reconstruction of scientific theories apart from an explanation of their origins, whether it be physiological or sociological.

Although few swallowed their relativistic conclusions, Kuhn and Feyerabend turned philosophy of science from ahistorical methodological questions to the history and, to a lesser extent, the sociology of science. Since the 1970s, the preoccupation with methodology also came under pressure from metaphysics. Disregarding the positivistic proscriptions, philosophers of science increasingly maintained that unobservable theoretical entities and the laws of nature are mind-independent features of reality rather than merely linguistic expedients for the explanation and prediction of experience.

7   THE REHABILITATION OF METAPHYSICS

In this respect, post-positivist philosophy of science was part of a more general trend. The ground for this rehabilitation of metaphysics had been cleared by the aforementioned withdrawal of the verificationist criterion of meaningfulness. Into this soil analytic philosophers planted three distinct metaphysical seeds.

The first was Quine's naturalistic approach to ontology. For Carnap, the only genuine questions of existence are scientific questions like 'Are there neutrinos?' or 'Are there prime numbers greater than 10^{10}?'; they concern particular groups of entities and can be solved within a specific 'linguistic framework'. By contrast, philosophical questions like 'Are there material objects?' or 'Do numbers exist?' concerning whole categories of entities are either meaningless or 'practical' in nature. They boil down to the pragmatic question of whether for scientific purposes it is convenient to adopt a linguistic framework like that of the natural numbers.

By contrast, Quine's naturalism resulted in a 'blurring of the boundary between speculative metaphysics and natural science' (1951: 20). Philosophy is concerned with the 'limning of the most general traits of reality'. It investigates the fundamental 'furniture of our universe', and differs from science only quantitatively, in the generality and breadth of its questions. Quine is 'no champion of traditional metaphysics'. He denies that *a priori* philosophical reflection can establish what kinds of things there are, in the style of rationalism. Nevertheless, he finds a place for ontology (1960: 161, 254; 1966: 203–4). Like traditional ontology, Quine's naturalistic variety seeks to establish what kinds of things there are. But it does not pursue this aspiration directly or in isolation. Instead, it helps science in drawing up an inventory of the world. It translates our scientific theories into an ideal formal language ('canonical notation') and thereby clarifies and, where possible, reduces their 'ontological commitments', the types of entities the existence of which these theories presuppose. A canonical notation displays our ontological commitments and allows us to paraphrase them in order to keep them to a minimum. While

(9) Red is a colour

contains a name for a property, and thereby seems to commit us to the existence of an intensional entity, the paraphrase

(9') $\forall x \, (x \text{ is red} \rightarrow x \text{ is a colour})$

avoids any such commitment. Decisions on whether to admit entities that cannot be paraphrased away are guided by a pragmatic trade-off between the systematic efficacy (explanatory power) attained by admitting them and the ontological economy achieved by excluding them.

Like Carnap, Quine does not analyse our existing notions but explicates them, i.e. replaces them by analogues deemed to be scientifically more respectable. But whereas the logical positivists aspired to an ideal language that avoids metaphysical problems, Quine's ideal language aims to reveal *the metaphysics of science*. This has become a guiding principle of contemporary naturalists. By exploring what things our best current scientific theories *take* to exist, they also purport to provide the best account of what things *actually* exist.

A contrasting rehabilitation of metaphysics was provided by Strawson. His early writings criticized orthodoxies of logical analysis by reference to ordinary use. But in *Individuals* Strawson's concern shifted to what he called *descriptive metaphysics*. This Kantian enterprise differs from previous conceptual analysis in its greater scope and generality, since it seeks to 'lay bare the most general features of our conceptual structure'. These are not discernible in the motley of ordinary use, but in fundamental functions of discourse, notably those of *reference* – singling out an individual item – and *predication* – saying something about it. Descriptive metaphysics 'is content to describe the actual structure of our thought about the world', by contrast to *revisionary metaphysics*, which aspires 'to produce a better structure' based either on *a priori* insights, as in traditional metaphysics, or on the perceived demands of science, as in naturalism. It also differs from both in that it elucidates not the most abstract features of the *world*, but the preconditions of our *thought* about the world, of our 'conceptual scheme' (1959: 9).

This idea is also central to Strawson's epistemology, which revived the idea of *transcendental arguments*. Such arguments aim to show that sceptical doubts are incoherent or self-refuting, because they question preconditions of any meaningful discourse, the sceptic's own doubts included. The sceptic saws off the branch on which he is sitting, because his doubts employ concepts which make sense only on the tacit assumption of conceptual connections he explicitly rejects.

Critics have protested that transcendental arguments establish at best that we must employ concepts like those of a mind-independent object, not that they are *actually* satisfied by anything in reality (Stroud 1968).

Nevertheless, the idea of establishing the preconditions of experience, thought or discourse continues to inspire philosophers who wish to avoid both the Scylla of scepticism and the Charybdis of naturalized epistemology, which simply bypasses the normative issue of whether our beliefs are justified. The same goes for descriptive metaphysics, the attempt to make explicit the fundamental notions and implications of our conceptual scheme (e.g. Jackson 1998: 31–3).

The final source of contemporary analytic metaphysics has two inter-related roots. The first is the thriving of modal logic, in particular the idea that the logic of terms like 'necessarily' and 'possibly' can be explicated in terms of Leibniz's notion of a possible world. The second is the rise of theories of 'direct reference', according to which many expressions, notably proper names and natural kind terms, refer to their denotata directly, without the mediation of Fregean senses, i.e. of 'modes of presentation', which are most straightforwardly conceived as properties that the denotata uniquely possess. Quine had followed the logical positivists in treating the necessary, the analytic and the *a priori* as equivalent. This is at odds not just with Kant, but also with contemporary essentialism. For Kripke (1980: 34–9), the *a priori* is an epistemological category, necessity a metaphysical one, and analyticity a logical one. In the wake of Kripke, the following definitions have found favour: a truth is *a priori* iff it can be known independently of experience; it is *necessary* iff it is true in all possible worlds; it is *analytic* iff it is true by virtue of meaning. According to Kripke's and Putnam's 'realist semantics', these categories differ not just in their intension, but also in their extension. Theoretical identifications like

(10) Water is H_2O

are *both a posteriori*, because they are discovered by science, *and* necessary. For natural kind terms (like proper names) are 'rigid designators'. In all possible worlds in which they pick out anything at all, they pick out the same thing, namely a substance with a particular microstructure (H_2O in our case), and that microstructure constitutes the *essence* of the natural kind. With characteristic foresight, Quine had anticipated the essentialist implications of modal logic, yet he ridiculed the idea that philosophers are capable of getting essences into the hair-crosses of their intellectual periscopes. Ironically, instead of undermining modal logic, his warnings led to a revival of essentialism. What is more, this revival can appeal to Quine's own naturalism. Quine holds that philosophy must forsake necessity and essences because it is continuous with science. But if some necessary truths – truths about the essence of things – are *a posteriori*, philosophy can be continuous with science precisely because it scrutinizes such essences.

This presupposes, however, that sense can be made of modal notions like that of possible worlds. In line with his general attack on intensions, Quine complained that there are no criteria for trans-world identity. The essential features of an individual are those which it possesses in all possible worlds in which it exists. But what determines who is who in different possible worlds? Another issue is the ontological status of possible worlds. According to Lewis' hyper-realism, possible worlds are just as real as the actual one. Each world is a self-contained space-time with no connection to any other world. According to Kripke's realism, by contrast, a possible world is a way this world might have been, it is something real yet abstract. And according to fictionalism, a possible world is a fiction, a totality of consistent representations. To say that it is possible that *p* is to say that there is a consistent description of a world according to which *p*. Reality attaches not to the unactualized possibilities themselves, but rather to our representations of them (see Glock 2003a: 95–101; Baldwin 2001: ch. 6).

"PROPHE-TIC OF MULTI-VERSE"?

Irrespective of these disputes, essentialism has spawned a new genre, one in which metaphysical questions are answered by appeal to modal intuitions, intuitions about whether there is a possible world satisfying certain conditions. For instance, the question whether the mind is identical with the body is tackled by contemplating whether there is a possible world with 'zombies', creatures physically identical to us yet bereft of any kind of mental life (Chalmers 1996).

Their metaphysical ambitions notwithstanding, all three projects remain faithful to the linguistic turn, in so far as they proceed through reflections on language. Quine's contribution to the investigation of reality lies in devising a canonical notation for the ontologically parsimonious formulation of scientific theories. For Strawson, the metaphysically fundamental categories are those that play a central role in our conceptual scheme as embodied in language. And although essentialism is after necessities which concern reality rather than our conceptual scheme, it identifies these through the workings of language, notably the rigid fashion in which proper names and natural kind terms designate. This is why Kripke and Putnam (1975) constantly appeal to 'what we would say' about certain counterfactual situations, e.g. a 'Twin Earth' on which a substance which shares all the surface properties of water turns out to have a chemical composition other than H_2O.

8 FROM LANGUAGE TO MIND

For logical positivism, Wittgenstein and linguistic philosophy, language mattered because it provided a means for resolving philosophical problems. For logical atomism as well as for Quine and essentialism it matters, because it provides a guide to the ontological constitution of reality. But the linguistic turn also encouraged an interest in language as a topic in its own right. From the 1960s onwards, it became common to contrast linguistic philosophy unfavourably with the *philosophy of language* (Searle 1969: 3–4; Dummett 1978: 441–3). Two differences were diagnosed. First, whereas philosophy of language is a *discipline* just like the philosophy of law, linguistic philosophy is a *method*, namely for the resolution of problems from all areas of philosophy. Secondly, linguistic philosophy proceeds by the piecemeal investigation of particular expressions, constructions and locutions, whereas philosophy of language requires a *systematic* account of language. Even among those eager to utilize linguistic analyses for the resolution of philosophical problems, many felt that without such an account these analyses would lack a proper foundation.

Philosophy of language is interested in the workings of actual languages rather than in the construction of artificial ones. But this does not determine the role which formal logic has to play. Strawson (1971: 171–2) highlighted the 'Homeric struggle' between formal semanticists, who treat language primarily as an abstract system of complex formal rules, and those who regard it primarily as a kind of human activity. Yet many figures straddle this divide. This holds for Quine and his pupil Donald Davidson (1984b). Both combine formal semantics with a pragmatist emphasis on language as a form of social human behaviour. Whereas Quine is ultimately interested in artificial languages, however, Davidson has been the most eminent champion of a *theory of meaning for natural languages*. Before him, a theory of meaning was supposed to provide an analysis – in a suitably loose sense – of the concept of meaning (as in referential, behaviourist, verificationist and use theories of meaning). By contrast to such *analytic* theories, Davidson envisages a *constructive* theory which does not explain directly what meaning is. Instead, for each sentence of a specific natural language like Swahili the theory generates a theorem that specifies the meaning of that sentence. Such a theory is empirical; and actually to construct it is a task for empirical linguistics. The philosopher's brief is to establish the requirements that such theories must fulfil. This is done by *Tractatus*-like reflections on the essential preconditions of language. Thus it is argued that speakers can produce and understand a potentially infinite number of sentences, and that this 'semantic productivity' requires a 'compositional' theory, one which displays the meaning of each sentence as rigidly determined by that of its components (drawn from a finite lexicon) and the mode of their composition.

According to Davidson, a Tarskian truth-theory satisfies these requirements, because with a finite number of axioms it permits for each sentence of *L* the derivation of a 'T-sentence'. For instance, a theory for German delivers

(11) 'Schnee ist weiss' is true iff snow is white.

Whereas Tarski tried to define *truth*, Davidson employs T-sentences to state the *meaning* of sentences by specifying the *conditions under which they are true.* Unlike Tarski, Davidson is optimistic that such theories can be devised not just for formal but also for natural languages. He argues that they allow of empirical confirmation under conditions of 'radical interpretation' (a variant of radical translation), namely if one ascertains the conditions under which alien speakers assent to sentences of their own language.

For Davidson it is a precondition of radical interpretation, and hence of linguistic understanding in general, that the interpretees hold beliefs which are by and large correct. According to his 'principle of charity', speakers of interpretable natural languages cannot be fundamentally mistaken. Therefore a theory of meaning can answer questions about reality by ascertaining the logical form of natural languages. In particular, it can demonstrate the existence of events by showing that certain inferential patterns of ordinary discourse ontologically commit us to events (1980: ch. 7). Dummett's 'anti-realism' (1978) also regards theories of meaning as a guide to metaphysical insights. Against Davidson's truth-conditional semantics, however, he maintains that the meaning of sentences is determined not by the conditions under which sentences are true, which are independent of our ability to decide whether they obtain, but by the conditions 'which warrant their assertion'.[3]

In another respect, Davidson and Dummett are on the same side. Like many icons of mid-century analytic philosophy (Wittgenstein, linguistic philosophy, Quine, Sellars) they adopt a *third-person perspective* on language, holding that the meaning of words and sentences is determined by observable behaviour. All of the aforementioned also tend to assign priority to language over thought. Both claims conflict with a powerful recent

---

[3] They further disagree on how to meet the challenge of accounting for non-declarative sentences in terms of either truth- or assertion conditions (see Glock 2003a: 159–65).

trend. The slogan that meaning is use came under scrutiny by Grice's theory of conversational implicatures. Grice (1989) maintained that many of the patterns of linguistic use highlighted by conceptual analysts are semantically irrelevant, since they are due not to the meaning of specific expressions, but to pragmatic principles governing discourse in general. Furthermore, a common theme in linguistic philosophy is that language is a form of intentional behaviour. This suggested to Austin that the philosophy of language is a branch of the philosophy of action. Taking this proposal one step further, Grice and Searle turned it into a sub-domain of the philosophy of mind, by trying to reduce semantic notions to psychological ones like intention.

Gricean theories still hold that expressions derive their meaning from the use to which speakers put them. Approaches influenced by Chomsky's 'revolution in linguistics' (1965) shed any vestige of the common-sense idea that meaning and language are rooted in communication. Thus Fodor (1975) argued that both the meaning of public languages and the intentionality of thought can be explained by a 'language of thought'. *External* sentences are meaningful because they are correlated with *internal* symbols, sentence-like representations in the brain which constitute our thoughts. Fodor's 'language of thought hypothesis' is highly representative of contemporary approaches. It extols the priority of private minds over public languages, while retaining the machinery and vocabulary (meaning, content) of logico-linguistic analysis, because it regards thinking as a process of logical computations on internal sentences.

This reversal of the linguistic turn has turned the philosophy of mind into the most thriving part of analytic philosophy. Nevertheless the subject received its initial impetus after the war from Wittgenstein and Ryle.[4] Through the mainstream of modern philosophy from Descartes to phenomenalism runs the idea that private experiences provide the foundations not just of empirical knowledge but also of language. It seems that the meaning of words can be fixed only if the individual speaker associates them with experiences that only he can have and know about. Wittgenstein's famous private language argument challenged this assumption (1953: §§243–314). A ceremony of naming can only lay down standards for distinguishing between correct and incorrect uses of a word, and hence provide the latter with meaning, if it can be explained to and understood by others. This attack on Cartesianism was reinforced by Ryle's assault on the myth of the

---

[4] Though Broad 1925 was a prescient anticipation of the subsequent debate on the place of the mind in a physical world.

'ghost in the machine', the idea that perception and action are cases of an immaterial soul interacting with the physical world.

Both Wittgenstein and Ryle distinguished sharply between establishing the causal preconditions of mental phenomena, such as the firing of neurons, and the analysis of mental concepts, which specifies features that are *constitutive* of mental phenomena. Quinean naturalism led to a very different outlook, according to which the philosophy of mind is a branch of psychology, biology or neuroscience. The widely accepted task is to *naturalize* mental phenomena, i.e. to show that they are fully explicable in the terms of physical science.

Wittgenstein's and Ryle's attacks on Cartesian dualism found favour. But their denial that mental terms refer to inner states which cause our outward behaviour was repudiated, especially by 'Australian materialists' like Place, Smart and Armstrong (see Baldwin 2001: 47–52, 201–3). And if these inner states are not irreducibly mental, they must be physical. The result was the mind-brain identity theory: the mind is identical with the brain and mental properties are identical with neurophysiological properties. The identity theory was not presented as a *semantic* or *analytic* reduction showing that mental terms mean the same as terms referring to neurophysiological phenomena. Instead, it was put forward as a *scientific* or *synthetic* reduction based on *a posteriori* discoveries. The identity of the mind with the brain is supposed to be on a par with that of the identity of water with H$_2$O. In effect, however, the identity theory combined the conceptual claim that mental terms refer to inner states that cause behaviour with the scientific claim that this causal role is played by certain neural states.

This combination soon came a cropper. As Putnam (1975: chs. 18–21) and Fodor (1974) pointed out, mental phenomena are *multiply realizable* through psychochemical phenomena, not just in principle (a human being, a Martian and a computer could all entertain the same thought) but in fact, and not just across species. When different test persons solve one and the same problem, slightly different parts of the brain are activated. This led to a novel form of materialism. According to *functionalism*, mental states are functional states of a machine. What is constitutive of a mental phenomenon is not the particular physical process but the *causal role* or *function* that it performs, a role which could be realized or implemented in diverse physical states. Pain, for instance, can only be identified with the function of correlating a stimulatory input (e.g. injury) with a behavioural output (e.g. crying), not with the firing of specific neurons.

The mind-brain identity theory maintained that types of mental states are identical with *types* of neurophysiological states. Davidson's 'anomalous monism' (1980) abandons this 'type-type' identity. But it retains the idea that each 'token', each instance of a mental state or event occurring in an individual, is identical with a particular neurophysiological event or state. Like functionalism, it also holds on to the idea that mental properties *supervene* on physical properties. While there can be a physical difference between individuals without any mental difference, there cannot be a mental difference without a physical difference.

Though hugely popular, functionalism faced objections on two fronts. At one end it was castigated for failing to do justice to the indelibly subjective nature of the mind. Thus Thomas Nagel (1974) and Jackson (1986) argued that materialism in general and functionalism in particular cannot account for 'qualia', the private feel of mental phenomena. At the other end, it was alleged that functionalism cannot explain intentionality, and in particular the content of our thoughts. Searle's Chinese room argument uses a thought experiment in the style of conceptual analysis to show that the mere 'syntactic' ability to produce an appropriate output of symbols in response to an input does not amount to genuine understanding or thought about the world, since it is present even in a system that merely simulates these achievements. Furthermore, externalists denied that the content of an individual *A*'s thoughts is exclusively determined by her intrinsic (mental or physiological) properties. Instead, what *A* thinks depends at least partly on facts 'external' to, and often unknown to, *A*, facts about *A*'s physical (Putnam 1975: chs. 8 and 12) or social (Burge 1979) environment. Two physically identical individuals might have different thoughts. When a physical duplicate of mine on a 'Twin-Earth' thinks about the transparent, odourless and potable liquid surrounding him, the content of his thoughts differs from mine: he cannot be thinking about water, since he is surrounded by XYZ rather than H_2O.

A radical, some would say desperate, reaction to the travails of existing variants of materialism is *eliminative materialism* (Churchland 1981). It treats our ordinary psychological beliefs and concepts as part of a theory – 'folk psychology' – which is simply wrong and does not refer to real phenomena. Therefore folk psychology should be replaced by a more scientific, purely neurophysiological theory. Like Quine's nihilism about meaning, this is a form of *eliminative* naturalism. Statements which involve concepts that cannot be accommodated within natural science – notably about thought and meaning – are not *analysed*, not even in the weaker sense of scientific reduction. Instead, they are simply *replaced* by naturalistically acceptable statements and notions.

9 MATTERS OF VALUE

For Moore, the question of how 'good' is to be defined was the most fundamental problem of ethics. But his famous 'open question' argument drove him to the conclusion that 'good' is indefinable, since goodness is a simple quality which has no parts. Consider any definition of the form:

(12) Good is X.

(Candidates for 'X' include 'that which causes pleasure'). For any substitution for 'X' – other than 'good' itself – it is always an intelligible and in that sense 'open' question as to whether (12) is true. Therefore, even if things which are X are in fact good, 'X' cannot *mean* the same as 'good' and hence cannot be used to define it. In particular, any attempt to define 'good' in terms of natural properties is bound to fail, the contrary view being dubbed by Moore the 'naturalistic fallacy' (1903: 10–16). Good is a non-natural simple property, to which we have access by a kind of rational *intuition.* Nevertheless, this property supervenes on natural properties: any two things with exactly the same natural properties would also have to be equally good.

Later analytic philosophers tended to accept Moore's conclusion that moral properties cannot be analytically defined in terms of natural ones, while rejecting his intuitionism. This led many to the conclusion that moral judgements are not descriptive or factual and hence not strictly speaking truth-apt at all. According to the logical positivists, cognitively significant propositions are either analytic or *a posteriori*. But moral statements fit neither category. They concluded that moral statements are not cognitively significant, and that their real function is not to make factual claims, but rather to express our emotions, in particular of approval or disapproval (Ayer 1936: ch. 6). According to Stevenson (1944), emotivism also explains why moral statements are intrinsically action-guiding, whereas descriptions of fact seem to be motivationally neutral: it would be odd to say 'Φ-ing is the right thing to do, but I am in no way in favour of Φ-ing.'

Emotivism runs the risk of reducing moral statements to interjections like 'boo' and 'hurrah', and to ignore the role that reason plays in moral argument. This shortcoming was addressed by Hare, the most influential moral philosopher among the Oxford conceptual analysts. According to Hare's 'universal prescriptivism', moral statements are closer to imperatives than to avowals of emotions: their purpose is to guide action. But unlike imperatives they are universalizable: if one morally condemns a lie, one is committed to condemning all lies in circumstances of a similar kind. The question of whether the person making a moral statement can consistently desire this kind of universalization provides scope for reasoned argument, even though there are no moral facts.

Because of this last point, and in spite of its Kantian provenance, universal prescriptivism came to be lumped with emotivism under the heading of 'non-cognitivism'. Hare's work set the scene for the subsequent debate. In line with the linguistic turn, he initially restricted moral philosophy to 'meta-ethics' – a second-order discipline which does not issue any moral claims but instead analyses moral concepts, examines the status of moral judgements, and delineates the structure of moral argument. 'Ethics, as I conceive it, is the logical study of the language of morals' (1952: v). H. L. A. Hart (1962) provided a comparable stimulus to legal and political theory. He tried to avoid futile metaphysical disputes about the nature of obligations and rights through the analysis of legal concepts. But under the influence of Wittgensteinian ideas he rejected the search for analytic definitions in favour of a more contextual elucidation of the role such concepts play in legal discourse.

Non-cognitivism was challenged in the first instance by conceptual analysts who cast doubt on its picture of moral discourse. Geach (1972: ch. 8.2) argued that it cannot do justice to the occurrence of moral statements in inferences, because the latter requires propositions that are truth-apt. Later cognitivists set store by the fact that we ordinarily call moral judgements true or false and that moral discourse displays the full grammar and logic of assertions. Foot and Warnock maintained that the sharp distinction between descriptive and prescriptive uses of language is untenable. Among the most pervasive moral concepts are 'thick concepts' such as rudeness, concepts which include both descriptive and prescriptive elements. And Searle (1969: ch. 8) argued that by appeal to institutional facts it is after all possible to derive prescriptive from descriptive statements, an 'ought' from an 'is'.

Putnam (1981) pointed in a similar direction when he insisted that the philosophy of science no longer supports the fact/value distinction, since scientific inquiry itself rests on norms. And McDowell (1998) and Wiggins (1991) urged a rethink of the non-cognitivist dichotomy of the subjective (expression, prescription) and the objective (description), by exploring the analogy between values and secondary qualities like colours. More generally, similarities between moral and perceptual judgements were explored by a revival of intuitionism, especially in Britain under the label 'particularism' (Dancy 2004).

At the same time, both non-cognitivism and intuitionism had to face a novel, methodological challenge. Can meta-ethical issues about the logic of moral discourse really be kept separate from substantive moral questions? For one thing, Hare himself moved from an allegedly neutral meta-ethics to a position which tries to draw substantive ethical conclusions (in his case of a utilitarian bent) from the nature of our moral concepts. For another, there were Quinean animadversions against distinguishing the analysis of concepts from the discovery of matters of fact (Harman 1977). Thirdly, the 1960s and 1970s brought to the fore issues like war, nuclear deterrence, abortion, civil disobedience, and the destruction of the natural environment. Through the student rebellion, these concerns impinged directly on university syllabi and research. Many philosophers realized that these involve substantive moral questions that cannot be left to either religious dogma or political ideologies like Marxism. 'Applied ethics' became the name of the attempt to deal with such specific moral issues in a cogent rational manner. Finally, the rebirth of normative ethics was completed by the realization that grand normative theory beyond conceptual analysis remained possible. Rawls' *A Theory of Justice* (1972) was a compelling trend-setter. It marked the rise of political theory, hitherto neglected, within the analytic tradition. Rawls attempted to justify a principle of distributive justice by considering the kind of rules which agents ignorant of their future place within society should rationally opt for. Rawls also inspired a revival of the Kantian idea that there is such a thing as objective practical reasons for action, over and beyond the means-ends rationality explored by decision theory, and independent of any contentious ontology of moral facts.

These developments did not spell the end for meta-ethics, but instead led to an intertwining of meta-ethical and ethical discussions. Furthermore, the focus shifted from specific moral notions to investigations into the nature of moral justification and the metaphysical status of values. Naturalism also reasserted itself at this level (see Railton 1998). One variant maintains that moral concepts can be accommodated within naturalism once we give up the misguided ambition of analysing them. Moral predicates meet naturalistic demands because the properties they attribute – e.g. contributing to human flourishing – play a role in the best explanatory theories of empirical science (Boyd, Sturgeon), or because they are idealizations of psychological properties (Lewis, Harman). But there is also a contrasting, eliminative version of naturalism. According to Mackie's 'error theory' (1977), moral concepts and judgements are indeed descriptive or factual. The trouble, according to Mackie, is that nothing corresponds to moral concepts in reality, which is purely physical. From this he draws the disconcerting conclusion that our moral judgements are all and sundry mistaken.

An equally iconoclastic attack on the very terms of moral debate was launched by neo-Nietzscheans like MacIntyre (1984) and Williams (1985). They suggested that philosophy is impotent to fill the moral gap left by the decline of religion. The demand for objective, rational and impersonal validation unites all major positions in normative ethics. But, the neo-Nietzscheans urged, it is of dubious origins, unfeasible, and lacks sufficient credibility to sustain the project of a philosophical ethics. Although the neo-Nietzscheans are less infatuated with science than the naturalists, in one respect they point in a similar direction. Even as regards matters of value, the story goes, philosophy is not an autonomous discipline; rather, it needs to be supplemented by other modes of discourse, whether they be natural science, the social and historical sciences, or even art and religion.

CHAPTER 3

Geography and language

This chapter discusses geo-linguistic conceptions of analytic philosophy. Section 1 presents the Anglocentric version of such a conception, which arose in conjunction with the analytic/continental contrast. Section 2 rejects the Anglocentric conception by reference to the Germanophone roots of analytic philosophy. Section 3 discusses a possible comeback, namely that the Germanophone pioneers of analytic philosophy were aberrations in a philosophical culture that was generally hostile to the analytic spirit. Section 4 turns to a modification of the Anglocentric conception. According to the 'Neurath-Haller thesis' analytic philosophy, though not simply Anglo-Saxon, is at any rate Anglo-Austrian in origin and character. While both suggestions contain kernels of truth, they distort the complex roots of analytic philosophy, especially the impact of German thinkers and of Kantian ideas. The final section argues that *any* geo-linguistic conception falls foul of both historical facts and the status quo. The dichotomy between analytic and continental philosophy is not just a cross-classification, it also fails to exhaust the options, since it ignores pragmatism and traditionalist philosophy. The real philosophical divisions cut across all geographical and linguistic borders.

1 FOG OVER CHANNEL – CONTINENT CUT OFF!

In so far as analytic philosophy is contrasted with continental philosophy, it is natural and indeed common to conceive of it in geographic terms. Strictly speaking, these terms are *geo-linguistic*. On the one side, we find analytic philosophy which is referred to as (in decreasingly parochial terms) 'British', 'American', 'Anglo-Saxon', 'Anglo-American' or 'Anglophone'. It is the kind of philosophizing that predominates in the English-speaking world – notably North America, the British Isles and Australasia. On the other side we find the kind of philosophizing that prevails in continental Europe, and in some other parts of the globe such as Latin America (e.g. Charlton 1991: 2–3).

The origins of this *Anglocentric* conception of analytic philosophy are closely connected to those of the label 'continental philosophy'. This tag emerged in at least three different contexts. The first, to which we shall return below, was J. S. Mill's discussion of the German influences on Coleridge. Mill speaks of 'Continental philosophers' and 'the Continental philosophy' (1840: 191), as well as of 'the Germano-Coleridgean doctrine' and 'the French philosophy'.

The label re-emerged after World War II. Some British representatives of analytic philosophy recognized that their style of philosophizing was distinctively *different* from simultaneous trends in continental Europe. The British context explains the choice of terminology. In so far as Americans of the period recognized a geographic divide within Western philosophy, it featured *European* philosophy as one of its poles (Blumberg and Feigl 1931; Nagel 1936). By contrast, the British still regarded themselves as European. At the same time fascism and the war had alienated them from *continental* Europe not just politically and culturally, but also philosophically.

British philosophers introduced the term 'Continental philosophy', in the first instance to denote phenomenology and its existentialist offspring. In the twenties Ryle had given an 'unwanted course of lectures, entitled "Logical Objectivism: Bolzano, Brentano, Husserl and Meinong." These characters were soon known in Oxford as "Ryle's three Austrian railway-stations and one Chinese game of chance"' (Ryle 1970: 8). He had studied Husserl's *Logische Untersuchungen*, had met the man himself, and had even published a respectful though critical review of Heidegger's *Sein und Zeit* (Ryle 1928). By the time of the Anglo-French colloquium at Royaumont in 1958, however, Ryle's attitude had hardened dramatically. He was keen not just to distance his conceptual analysis from phenomenology – the title of his paper was 'Phenomenology versus *The Concept of Mind*' – but also to attack continental philosophers with the aid of cultural stereotypes.

(1) Apart from one or two brief flirtations, British thinkers have showed no inclination to assimilate philosophical to scientific enquiries; and *a fortiori* no inclination to puff philosophy up into the Science of sciences. Conceptual enquiries differ from scientific enquiries not in hierarchical rank but in type . . . I guess that our thinkers have been immunised against the idea of philosophy as the Mistress Science by the fact that their daily lives in Cambridge and Oxford Colleges have kept them in personal contact with real scientists. Claims to *Fuehrership* vanish when postprandial joking begins. Husserl wrote as if he had never met a scientist – or a joke.

(2) Even inside philosophy, no privileged position has with us been accorded to the philosophy of mind . . . We have not worried our heads over the question Which philosopher ought to be *Fuehrer*? If we did ask ourselves

this question, we should mostly be inclined to say that it is logical theory that does or should control other conceptual enquiries, though even this control would be advisory rather than dictatorial. At least the main lines of our philosophical thinking during this century can be fully understood only by someone who has studied *the massive developments of our logical theory*. This fact is partly responsible for the *wide gulf* that has existed for three-quarters of a century between *Anglo-Saxon* and *Continental philosophy*. For, on the Continent during this century, logical studies have, unfortunately, been left unfathered by most philosophy departments and cared for, if at all, only in a few departments of mathematics. (1962: 181–2; my emphasis)

Donner und Blitzen! Was Husserl a philosophical goose-stepper rather than a Jew persecuted by the Nazis? And were major advances in logic achieved at Oxford of all places, rather than at Jena, Göttingen, Vienna and Warsaw?

The blow on reading this passage is cushioned when it transpires that, mention of mathematics notwithstanding, by 'the massive developments of our logical theory' Ryle means not the advances in formal logic but the progression in *philosophical* logic from Russell's theory of descriptions to Wittgenstein's later account of meaning. But only slightly. Ryle refers to these developments as 'The *Cambridge* Transformation of the Theory of Concepts'. As Monk points out, this bypasses 'the slightly awkward fact that Wittgenstein was more Germanic than Anglo-Saxon. Wittgenstein, for all that he wrote in German and felt like an alien in England, was, it seems, a Cambridge man through and through, and not really a "Continental" at all' (1996b: 3). At the Royaumont conference, Ryle seemed interested less in establishing whether there was a wide gulf between analytic and 'Continental' philosophy than in ensuring that there would be. In the discussion following Ryle's paper, Merleau-Ponty suggested 'Notre programme, n'est-il pas le même?'; Ryle curtly responded 'J'espère que non' (Beck 1962: 7; see also Glendinning 1998a: 8–10; Rée 1993).

Finally, the term 'continental philosophy' became institutionally established in North America during the late 1960s. Like logical positivism, phenomenology, existentialism and critical theory were introduced to America by expatriate Europeans around the time of World War II, people like Horkheimer, Adorno, Alfred Schutz and Herbert Spiegelberg. During the 1950s and 1960s continental authors from Germany and France were assimilated by American philosophers, theologians, literary, social and political theorists (see Brogan and Risser 2000). Interest in this field was further stimulated by regular visits of famous continentals such as Gadamer, Habermas, Derrida and Ricoeur. During the sixties, the same developments in politics and educational policy that fanned the re-emergence of normative ethics and the birth of applied ethics within analytic philosophy also led to a clamouring for courses devoted to these thinkers, since they were (wrongly) assumed to be uniformly on the political left and (rightly) assumed to be outside the Anglophone philosophical mainstream. The titles of these courses often included 'continental philosophy' and variants of it. From a term of abuse it had turned into the appropriated name for an intellectual movement and an academic field. Soon Anglophone philosophers of all locations and persuasions began to use it. The contrast between analytic and continental philosophy as we know it was born!

A majority of recent commentators have repudiated the simple-minded geo-linguistic model of analytic philosophy which this contrast implies (notably Dummett, Sluga, Hacker, Friedmann and proponents of the 'Neurath-Haller thesis'). Nevertheless, for a long time it was received 'wisdom'. At a party of the Oxford sub-faculty in 1986, my confession to be German elicited the immediate and sincere response 'You must be an existentialist, then!', notwithstanding the fact that I wasn't sporting a turtle-neck and that the only uncontroversial existentialist *philosopher* (as opposed to theologian) from Germany – Karl Jaspers – had died in 1969. Even at present the geo-linguistic conception exerts a profound influence among a wider philosophical public. Indeed, in subtle and subliminal ways it affects even contemporary historians of analytic philosophy. In the Oxford University Press 'A History of Western Philosophy Series' the two volumes devoted to analytic philosophy bear the respective titles *English-Language Philosophy 1750–1945* (Skorupski 1993) and *Contemporary Philosophy: Philosophy in English since 1945* (Baldwin 2001). Similarly, Soames introduces his overview of 'the analytic tradition in philosophy' as follows: 'With a few notable exceptions, the leading work in this tradition was done by philosophers in Great Britain and the United States; even that which wasn't written in English was, for the most part, quickly translated and had its greatest impact in the world of English-speaking philosophers' (2003: xi). Contemporary continental philosophers also give succour to the Anglocentric model by identifying analytic philosophy with Anglo-American philosophy (e.g. Schroeder 2005: xvi, 346).

The analytic/continental dichotomy and the Anglocentric picture of analytic philosophy contain a kernel of truth. There is no gainsaying the fact that a substantial majority of contemporary analytic philosophers hail from English-speaking areas, and that these include the most famous specimen. In part, this is due to brute institutional facts, especially the numerical strength of American philosophers and philosophical publications (Rescher 1993) compared to philosophers and publications elsewhere, whatever the tongue or philosophical persuasion. In part, it reflects the fact that in philosophy the centre of gravity has moved during the course of the twentieth century, from Germanophone to Anglophone countries, initially to Britain and then, over the last forty years, to North America.

Nevertheless, the analytic/continental dichotomy contrasts a non-geographic and a geographic category and therefore involves 'a strange cross-classification – rather as though one divided cars into front-wheel drive and Japanese' (Williams 1996a: 25). For related reasons, the Anglocentric picture is untenable. In its parochial and insular outlook it is reminiscent of the headline attributed to *The London Times*: 'Fog over Channel, Continent Cut Off'. As Engel puts it: 'That the climate of a country or its breakfast should be continental may just about pass muster, but its philosophy?' (1997: 9).

2 *VORSPRUNG DURCH LOGIK*: GERMANOPHONE ROOTS OF ANALYTIC PHILOSOPHY

It is true that the roots of what is known as continental philosophy lie on the Continent of Europe. More specifically, as regards its origins, continental philosophy is predominantly Germanophone philosophy (notable exceptions being Kierkegaard and Bergson, Croce and Ortega y Gasset). The dialectical, existentialist, phenomenological and hermeneutical traditions were inaugurated almost exclusively by German speakers – respectively, Hegel and Marx, Schopenhauer and Nietzsche, Brentano and Husserl, Dilthey and Heidegger. The same goes for psychoanalysis, which has exerted a tremendous collateral influence on continental philosophy; indeed, in cases like that of Lacan it is tempting to speak of collateral damage. Although Anglophone analytic philosophers have saved most of their bile for twentieth-century French philosophy, the latter consists largely of takeoffs from Germanophone thinkers: Sartre and Merleau-Ponty from Husserl, Althusser from Marx, Foucault from Nietzsche, Lacan from Freud, and Derrida from Heidegger.[1] It might seem therefore that the analytic vs continental conflict could be added to the list of Anglo-German contrasts: tea vs coffee, ale vs lager, bangers vs sausage, back four vs sweeper, shame vs guilt.

---

[1] You ought to mistrust such a claim coming from a German who has spent eighteen years in Britain. But it has been substantiated by a French study – Ferry and Renaut 1985. See also Critchley 2001: 16.

Needless to say, this will not do either, since analytic philosophy is also to a large extent the invention of German speakers. Of course its emergence owes much to Russell, Moore and American Pragmatism. Yet it owes even more to Frege, Wittgenstein and logical positivism. No one would think of analytic philosophy as a specifically Anglophone phenomenon, if the Nazis had not driven many of its pioneers out of central Europe.

As we have seen in the previous chapter, the 'revolution in rigour' (Gillies 1999: 179) in mathematics and logic played a crucial role in the emergence of analytic philosophy. That revolution was a highly international affair. In addition to aforementioned contributors, the founder of American pragmatism C. S. Peirce reinvented the quantifier-variable notation independently of Frege and made important contributions to the logic of relations. Admittedly, Russell's work constitutes the major immediate input of that nineteenth-century revolution for the development of analytic philosophy in the early twentieth century. But Russell was a polyglot and cosmopolitan, and he benefited immeasurably from 'continental' influences. The logical notation which rendered *Principia Mathematica* so much more surveyable than Frege's *Grundgesetze* derived from the Italian Peano. And about a trip in 1895 Russell later wrote:

I viewed America in those days with the conceited superiority of the insular Briton. Nevertheless, contact with academic Americans, especially mathematicians, made me realise the superiority of Germany to England in almost all academic matters. Against my will, in the course of my travels, the belief that everything worth knowing was known at Cambridge gradually wore off. (1967–9: 135)

Weierstrass, Dedekind and Cantor demonstrated to Russell that the problems in the foundations of mathematics, which he had regarded as proof of absolute idealism, could actually be solved by formal methods. For this reason they played a crucial part in his conversion from idealist monism to pluralistic realism (Monk 1996a: 113–15) and in inspiring his logicist programme.

Furthermore, Russell owed the analytic tools with which to pursue this programme in large measure to Frege. Before his study of Frege in 1903, Russell did not have a workable account of quantification (Stevens 2005: ch. 2). In the Preface of *Principia Mathematica* Russell and Whitehead wrote: 'In all questions of logical analysis, our chief debt is to Frege' (1910–13: viii). Russell also credits Frege with having provided 'the first complete example' of 'the logical-analytic method in philosophy' (1914: 10). Wittgenstein for his part proclaimed in the Preface of the *Tractatus* his indebtedness to the 'great works of Frege'.

In many respects World War I marked a watershed in the philosophical relations between Anglophone and Germanophone countries (Kuklick 1984), and in the decline of German as an academic language. Yet the leading position of Germanophone thinkers and publications in formal logic continued into the thirties. When Quine came to Harvard in 1930 to do graduate work in formal logic, he was disappointed to note that in spite of the presence of Whitehead and Sheffer, the real action was on the European continent. That is why his European tour to Vienna, Prague and Warsaw in 1933 had such a lasting impact on him (1986: 7–13). Even the work of logicians from outside Germany and Austria (notably Skolem and Tarski), reached a wider audience only through its publication in German. In 1996 Quine told me in conversation that when he held in hand the German translation of his doctoral work he felt 'Now it's official!'

The decisive role of Wittgenstein and the logical positivists for the further development of analytic philosophy is even more evident. In 1959 Russell noted, albeit with a note of displeasure: 'During the period since 1914 three philosophies have successively dominated the British philosophical world: first that of the *Tractatus*, second that of the Logical Positivists, and third that of Wittgenstein's *Philosophical Investigations*' (1959: 160). Hacker underwrites Russell's historical assessment and concludes: 'Wittgenstein bestrides fifty years of twentieth-century analytic philosophy somewhat as Picasso bestrides fifty years of twentieth-century painting' (1996: 1).

One factor in Wittgenstein's importance is the influence of his later work on the transition from Cambridge analysis to Oxford linguistic philosophy. Even more important, however, is the influence of his early work on the predominantly Germanophone logical positivists (see Hacker 1996: ch. 3). At its weekly meetings, the Vienna Circle twice read and discussed the *Tractatus* line by line (1924 and 1926). Their interpretation was highly selective (ignoring in particular the saying/showing distinction and the reflections on the mystical). Nonetheless, some members of the Vienna Circle (Schlick, Carnap, Waismann) recognized it as a 'decisive turning point' in the history of philosophy (Schlick 1931/2), because of its promise to terminate the fruitless debates of metaphysics with the aid of logical analysis. Schlick described the *Tractatus* as 'the most significant work of our time' and its insights as 'absolutely crucial to the destiny of philosophy'. Carnap regarded Wittgenstein as 'the philosopher who, apart from Russell and Frege, had the greatest influence on my thinking' (1963: 24). And Hahn commended the *Tractatus* 'for having clarified the role of logic' (1980: xii). Neurath was least enamoured of Wittgenstein and poignantly criticized the *Tractatus* idea of ineffable metaphysical truths (1931: 535; see Geier 1992: 26). For all that, the Manifesto of the Vienna Circle, which he co-authored with Carnap and Hahn, honoured Wittgenstein as one of the inspirations of a scientific world-view along with Russell and Einstein, albeit much to Wittgenstein's chagrin (see Glock 2001: 207–13).

Logical positivism in turn became what is by common consent – though not necessarily common acclaim – the most influential philosophical school of the last one hundred years, especially through its impact on American philosophy (Feigl 1981: 57–94; Hacker 1996: ch. 7.1; Friedman 1998; Haller 1993: 1). The dispersion of logical positivism and of related movements and thinkers from central Europe was inevitable, given the rise of fascism. Under the Nazis the philosophers and scientists concerned faced the prospect of being silenced at best, and of being murdered at worst.[2] Many were politically on the left, although they ranged from moderate liberals like Schlick through democratic Socialists like Carnap to unorthodox Marxists like Neurath. Some of them, like Tarski, Popper and Waismann, were Jews.

The exodus of analytic philosophy was a gradual affair. It was anticipated by visits of leading figures such as Schlick to America and by Feigl's move there in 1931. It started in earnest in 1933 with Hitler's rise to power in Germany, which forced Reichenbach and Hempel into exile. It gathered pace during the 1930s, partly because of the rising fascist threat, which drove out Neurath and Carnap, and partly because of Schlick's murder by a deranged student in 1936. It was completed by the Nazi invasion of Poland in 1939, which destroyed the Polish school of logic. Tarski barely escaped, because he happened to be visiting the USA to attend one of the Unity of Science conferences that the indefatigable Neurath organized to keep logical positivism alive in exile.

The net result was the transplantation of logical positivism to the Anglophone world. Neurath and Waismann found asylum in Britain, and Popper eventually settled there after a spell in New Zealand. But the main influx was into the USA (see Hardcastle and Richardson 2003). This process was aided by the existence of an indigenous form of logically minded empiricism derived from American pragmatism, which included

---

[2] Of the members of the Vienna Circle, only Kraft and von Juhos survived the war in Vienna, and the Nazis murdered Grelling of the Berlin group as well as several members of the Warszaw–Lodz group (Hacker 1996: 316n3).

Charles Morris, Ernest Nagel and the young Quine. The receptive audience also included scientists with instrumentalist or operationalist convictions such as Bridgman and behaviourist psychologists such as Skinner. Logical positivism soon set up centres at UCLA through Reichenbach and later through Carnap, the University of Minnesota, through Feigl and his young associate Sellars, the University of Iowa, where Bergmann founded a school of Platonist positivists, Chicago, through Morris and Carnap, Princeton, through Tarski and Hempel, and Harvard, the permanent abode of Quine and host to a whole string of illustrious visitors from Europe.

The impact of these émigrés was colossal, first in formal logic, philosophy of language and the philosophy of science, later in all areas of theoretical philosophy, notably the burgeoning philosophy of mind. In conversation, Quine has dated the arrival of analytic philosophy in America to an incident which he also relates in print, in which Carnap countered a diatribe by Lovejoy in a characteristically meticulous and rational manner (Quine 1966: 42; Beckermann 2001: VIII). And it is probably no more than mild hyperbole when Davidson (1980: 261) states that he got through graduate school at Harvard in the late 1940s by reading Feigl's and Sellars' anthology of predominantly positivist writings. Even those contemporary analytic philosophers in the USA who reject virtually all doctrines associated with logical positivism, in particular their hostility to metaphysics and their verificationism, pay homage to the fact that they introduced rigorous methods and precise logical tools into the subject (Plantinga 1995: 139; Burge 2003: 201n). Borradori writes: 'In America, the definition of analytic philosophy has always been posed in opposition to European thought' (1994: 7). *Nein!* Those Americans who coined the label 'analytic philosophy' explicitly used it to refer to a *European* movement (Blumberg and Feigl 1931; Nagel 1936).

3 BRITISH EMPIRICISM VS GERMAN ROMANTICISM

At this juncture, it is tempting to adopt a radically opposing view of the origins of analytic philosophy, though still one conceived in geo-linguistic terms. Dummett writes:

Important as Russell and Moore both were, neither was the, or even *a*, source of analytical philosophy; and pragmatism was merely an interesting tributary that flowed into the mainstream of the analytical tradition. The sources of analytical philosophy were the writings of philosophers who wrote, principally or exclusively, in the German language; and this would have remained obvious to everyone had it not been for the plague of Nazism which drove so many German-speaking philosophers across the Atlantic. (1993: ix)

Leaving aside the question of who founded analytic philosophy for the time being (see ch. 8.4), there is much to applaud in this passage. But we should not simply turn the Anglocentric conception on its head and assign exclusive priority to Germanophone thinkers. As a distinctive philosophical movement, analytic philosophy is unthinkable without Russell and Moore. Furthermore, defenders of the Anglocentric conception have a *prima facie* plausible rejoinder. Frege, Wittgenstein and the Vienna Circle stand radically apart from the mainstream of Germanophone philosophy (Wedberg 1984: ch. 1; Coffa 1991: 1–4). In so far as they belong to a tradition at all, the story goes, it is that of Anglophone analytic philosophy, which received either these thinkers or at least their ideas with open arms. The German and Austrian origins of Frege, Wittgenstein and the Vienna Circle are, it appears, merely an unfortunate coincidence, just like the origins of Händel, Freud, Einstein, the House of Windsor or the Christmas tree.

This idea also finds indirect support in some continental philosophers. According to Critchley, the analytic vs continental philosophy division reflects a deeper cultural conflict between two habits of thought, which he refers to as 'empirical-scientific' and 'hermeneutic-romantic' (2001: 41–8; 1998 15n4). Referring to Mill's aforementioned introduction of the term 'Continental philosophy', he associates the analytic/continental divide with Mill's opposition between Bentham and Coleridge, and hence between the questions 'Is it true?' and 'What is the meaning of it?' (1840: 177). Critchley emphasizes that the mention of Coleridge implies that we are not dealing with a strictly geographical divide, and in the sequel he disregards the geo-linguistic aspect and compares the analytic/continental divide to C. P. Snow's 'internal' contrast between *The Two Cultures* (1959), science on the one hand, the arts and humanities on the other.

But Coleridge had no significant impact on British philosophy. This concession leaves open the possibility, therefore, of drawing a contrast between analytic and continental *philosophy* along geo-linguistic lines, namely by reference to the contrast between British science and empiricism on the one hand, German romanticism and rationalism on the other. Indeed, the contrast between analytic and continental philosophy ties in with, and is reinforced by, some stereotypical differences between Germanophone and Anglophone thought. Acrimonious conflict between Anglophone and Germanophone philosophy is nothing new. In 1873, long before the rise of analytic philosophy, John Stuart Mill complained about the baleful influence of German philosophy. 'The German or a priori view of human knowledge . . . is likely for some time (though it may be hoped in a diminishing degree) to predominate among those who occupy themselves with such [logical] enquiries, both here and on the continent' (1873: 171). Understandably, Mill found this fact all the more galling given his own excellent treatment of the issue in *A System of Logic*.

At roughly the same time, Marx and Nietzsche lampooned the ahistorical and superficial nature of Anglo-Saxon empiricism, utilitarianism and pragmatism. Throughout *Das Kapital*, Marx complains about Mill's shallow syncretism. Jeremy Bentham gets off less lightly. He is described as a 'purely English phenomenon', an 'insipid, pedantic, leather tongued oracle of the ordinary bourgeois understanding' and 'a genius in bourgeois stupidity'. Why? Because Bentham assumes that the human condition is that of the 'English philistine'. And about the utilitarian principle that one should promote the greatest happiness of the greatest number, Marx complains: 'at no time and in no land has a homespun commonplace ever swaggered so complacently' (1867: ch. 22.5). While Marx condemned utilitarianism as the ideology of English capitalism, his epigones have condemned pragmatism as the ideology of American imperialism (e.g. Klaus and Buhr 1976: 963).

Nietzsche, never knowingly outdone in philosophical rudeness, looks down on the 'indefatigable, inevitable English utilitarians', 'with derision, though not without pity', because they lack 'creative powers and artistic conscience'. Like Marx, he deplores what he regards as self-deceived universal pretences of a parochial outlook. The utilitarians promote 'English morality', not realizing that the alleged 'happiness of the greatest number' is in reality 'the happiness of England' (1886: §§225, 228). 'One has to be English to be capable of believing that human beings always seek their own advantage' (1906: §930). Well, it certainly helps! On the other hand, it may help to be German if one is to hold, with Nietzsche, that the 'blond Arian beasts' should promote neither the happiness of the greatest number, nor even their own happiness, but strive heroically and selflessly to wreak as much death and destruction as possible.

Nietzsche is even more definite than Marx in blaming the deficiencies of empiricism on the English national psyche (like many continentals, he was oblivious to the difference between England and Britain). The English 'are no philosophical race', he informs us, they lack '*real* power of spirituality, real *depth* of spiritual insight, in short, philosophy'. Their 'profound mediocracy' is not only to blame for utilitarianism, it has 'once before brought about a collective depression of the European spirit', namely in the form of British empiricism. Against the empiricist slogan, 'there are only facts', Nietzsche insists that sense must be projected into facts, there are 'no facts-in-themselves', only interpretations (1886: §§252, 253, 481, 556).

So pronounced was Nietzsche's abhorrence of Anglo-Saxon empiricism that it even led him to invoke the anti-empiricist spirit of Kant, Schelling and Hegel. This is ironical, since these philosophers are otherwise among his favourite bogeys. Yet Nietzsche's ambivalence is no coincidence. Although Kant and Hegel resisted the claims of empiricism, their stress on the role of reason placed them firmly in the enlightenment tradition which Nietzsche sought to debunk. Other German thinkers, including Schelling and the romantics, are closer to Nietzsche in that they rejected the enlightenment as such. However, in sharp contrast to Nietzsche, they deplored the Western roots of the enlightenment, which they opposed in the name of Germanism. Moreover, their prime targets were the French, on account of the French revolution and Napoleon, not the British, who had the proto-romantic Shakespeare and the reactionary Burke to their credit (for a brief rendering of this sorry tale, see Beck 1967).

Such complications notwithstanding, a contrast emerges between British common sense and German profundity. In moral philosophy there is a conflict between a pragmatist pursuit of utility and an idealistic pursuit of 'higher' goals, whether religious salvation, world-revolution, or the *Übermensch*. In theoretical philosophy there is a conflict between an *empiricist* stress on facts and science and a *rationalist* stress on the need for theory and interpretation, the alternative being an *irrationalist* rejection of *both* reason *and* experience. Russell alluded to this conflict when he remarked à propos Köhler's apes: 'It seemed that animals always behave in a manner showing the rightness of the philosophy entertained by the man who observes them ... Animals observed by Americans rush about frantically until they hit upon the solution by chance. Animals observed by Germans sit still and scratch their heads until they evolve the solution out of their inner consciousness' (1959: 96).

At the same time, this contrast did not coincide completely with national boundaries. There were 'traitors' on both sides. Thus in 1831, the year of Hegel's death, Friedrich Eduard Beneke deplored the German propensity for constructing grandiose philosophical systems in disregard of the results of natural science. Moreover, he blamed these shortcomings on Germany's cultural isolation:

Only we Germans are excluded from this association, as if divided from all other nations by insurmountable barriers. While we declare these [nations] to be bereft of all true philosophical spirit (strangely enough, given their past achievements, and especially those of English philosophy), they regard us as daydreamers, as caught up to such an extent in amorphous mirages and conceit, that we are hardly ever capable of casting a dim glance at the real world down here. Which is why anyone who wants to live peacefully among humans, and who wants to form a clear conception and understanding of their nature and their relations, must be on guard against our spiritual productions. (Beneke 1831: 114; see Bubner 1996)

However, the end of the nineteenth century witnessed something akin to a philosophical role-reversal between Britain and Germany. Beneke's exhortations were a founding document of German Neo-Kantianism, a movement that triumphed over German Idealism, romanticism and physiological naturalism by developing a philosophical outlook closely associated with both the natural and the social sciences.[3]

At the same time, Britain was in the grips of Absolute Idealism, a belated assimilation of Hegelian idealism tempered by British moderation. The Absolute idealists were craving for a philosophical outlook that would be spiritually more nourishing than empiricism, utilitarianism and Darwinism, but which could nevertheless be reconciled with modernity. Hegelianism was just the ticket, since it reconciled everything with anything in a 'higher synthesis', the 'Absolute' (previously known as God). But in spite of the fact that common sense and the Absolute were briefly trading places, they could never deny their respective roots. German Neo-Kantians were conscious of the debt they owed to British philosophy and science. Conversely, British Idealists proclaimed to the bitter end that due to their endeavours British philosophy was 'rejoining the main stream of European thought' (Muirhead 1924: 323; see Hacker 1996: 5).

It may seem, therefore, that analytic philosophy fits better into the Anglophone than into the Germanophone philosophical world, and that the Anglocentric conception of it can be defended, provided that it is taken in a qualified and more contextual spirit.

4 THE ANGLO-AUSTRIAN AXIS

Even such a modified Anglocentric picture will not find favour with a group of scholars who hold that empiricist and science-oriented thought in the spirit of analytic philosophy had a long tradition *within* the Germanophone world. The received contrast, they would say, fails to

---

[3] According to Cooper (1994: 8), at the turn of the nineteenth century France upsets the geographical stereotypes as much as Germany, since it was dominated by positivism à la Comte. But Bergson's eminence at the time militates against this claim.

notice that Germanophone philosophy divides into *two utterly distinct branches*. On the one hand there is a *German* tradition deriving from Kant, and stretching through the German idealists to Heidegger. On the other hand there is an *Austrian* tradition which starts with Bolzano, continues with the Brentano school and includes the Polish school of metaphysics and logic founded by Twardowski and Kotarbinski (Smith 1994; Simons 1999; Uebel 1999). Even Dummett, a stalwart supporter of the idea that analytic philosophy originates in Frege, claims that analytic philosophy 'would better be called "Anglo-Austrian" than "Anglo-American"' (1993: 1–2).

On this version of a geo-linguistic conception, the contrast is not between Anglophone and Germanophone, or between analytic and continental philosophy *per se*. Rather, there is an 'Anglo-Austrian Analytic Axis' (Simons 1986) which includes Britain on the one hand and the former Habsburg empire (especially Austria, Czechoslovakia and parts of Poland) on the other. According to these commentators, the contrast is between a level-headed and realist Austrian tradition close to, and partly inspired by, British empiricism and an obscurantist and idealist German tradition going back to Kant.[4]

The idea of an Anglo-Austrian analytic axis of light is the radicalized version of the so-called 'Neurath-Haller thesis' (Smith 1994: 14–20). According to Neurath, Austrian philosophy differs markedly from the rest of Germanophone philosophy, in that it 'spared itself the Kantian interlude' (1936: 676) and goes back to Bolzano instead. It was characterized, Neurath opines, by a rejection of all forms of idealism, an emphasis on psychological and linguistic analysis, respect for empirical science, a mistrust of speculation, and stylistically by the avoidance of obscure profundities in favour of clarity of exposition. Neurath's idea was taken up and elaborated by Haller (1991). Haller drew attention in particular to the 'proto-Vienna circle', a group of pre World War I philosophers and scientists including Neurath and Hahn, which was heavily influenced by the Austrian physicist Ernst Mach.

---

[4] One could even reverse the priority in the Anglo-Austrian axis. Bell (1999) argues that the archetypal British contribution to the rise of analytic philosophy, the revolt from idealism, was in fact a re-enactment of a Central European upheaval. According to Bell, Moore rather than Russell was the driving force behind the rebellion, and Moore's realistic conception of propositions was indirectly influenced by Brentano and Meinong, with Stout serving as a conduit. Bell's conjecture cannot be refuted. Still, the alleged influence did not register with Moore, who was honest in acknowledging his intellectual debts. Furthermore, Russell's revolt did not simply build on Moore. It had a different trajectory and different roots, the latter being *German mathematics* rather than *Austrian psychology*.

Proponents of the Neurath-Haller thesis have done a great service in bringing to light a fascinating chapter of intellectual history, and one which is of great relevance to the rise of analytic philosophy. Furthermore, many of their claims are correct and important. Leading Habsburg philosophers like Bolzano and Brentano attacked Kant vehemently, even on issues on which they essentially agreed with him, like the definition of truth or the analytic/synthetic distinction. And they were even more contemptuous of the German Idealists that dominated German philosophy between 1800 and 1831. Furthermore, the style of writers like Bolzano, Brentano or Kotarbinski contrasts favourably with that of the German Neo-Kantians, even when the philosophical pursuits of the latter were in close proximity to British empiricism and contemporary science (Smith 1994: 4).

Nevertheless, the Neurath-Haller thesis is lop-sided and the stronger thesis of an Anglo-Austrian analytic axis is incorrect. What is wrong is not the claim that there were distinctive philosophical currents in the Habsburg empire, that these had an important impact on analytic philosophy, or that there were notable differences in philosophical atmosphere between the Habsburg empire and Germany. It is rather three suggestions: first, that there is a single, unified and unique current of 'scientific', proto-analytic philosophy which dominated Austrian philosophy; secondly, that the proto-analytic/analytic movement was entirely alien to Germany; and thirdly, that this movement was universally characterized by realism and hostility to Kant.

The idea that there was a *single* Austrian tradition going back to Bolzano is a propagandistic invention of Neurath's. As Haller himself acknowledges, there are at least *two* strands in Austrian philosophy, a predominantly *realist* one going from Bolzano through the school of Brentano, especially Meinong, to Husserl and Polish philosophy, and a predominantly *empiricist* one going from Mach and Boltzmann to the Vienna Circle. This split should not come as a surprise, moreover. From Locke to Quine, empiricism and realism have always been uneasy bedfellows, since it is tempting to suppose that what is immediately given in experience is some kind of mental intermediary that stands between the observer and material reality. Neither Mach's sensualism nor the phenomenalism of the early logical positivists is realist by any stretch of the imagination. Secondly, there could not be a greater contrast than that between the patently metaphysical ideas of Bolzano and Meinong on the one hand, and the anti-metaphysical zeal of Carnap and Neurath on the other, or between Brentano's long list of synthetic *a priori* truths and the blanket repudiation of the synthetic *a priori* by Wittgenstein and the logical positivists. Thirdly, there is an important split between the anti-psychologism of Bolzano, Wittgenstein and most logical positivists on the one hand, and the invocation of mental 'intuitions' in Brentano's act psychology, an invocation which is duly continued in Husserl's phenomenology.

Even within any of these various camps and movements, there is no Austrian continuity at the exclusion of German philosophers. It is true that for various political reasons, Kant and German Idealism did not play the role in Austria that they did in Germany.[5] However, both Leibniz and Herbart exerted a strong influence on Austrian philosophy from Bolzano onwards. Brentano, for his part, was a pupil of Trendelenburg, an important German philosopher who mediated between Aristotelian and Kantian modes of thought. By contrast, he hardly ever mentions Bolzano. Unlike his pupil Husserl, to be sure. But the latter is unsuitable both as a realist and as a progenitor of analytic philosophy. There was a tenuous link between Bolzano and later developments in Vienna, namely Alois Höfler. But he does not fit the bill of a raving anti-Kantian, since he warned contemporaries against precisely the kind of contempt for Kant that one senses in some proponents of the Neurath-Haller thesis (see Uebel 1999: 259–66).

More generally, the analytic axis thesis ignores the intimate cultural, political and academic connections between Germany and the Habsburg empire. There was no cultural or academic chasm between the German states and Imperial Germany (after 1871) on the one hand, and the German speaking parts and constituencies of the Habsburg empire and its successor states on the other. Even the political division is a relatively recent artefact of Bismarck's *kleindeutsche Lösung* of 1866. And there was completely free movement among academics, including those associated with Austrian

---

[5] Smith would have us believe that 'Kant, Fichte and Hegel are like Goethe and Schiller popular icons (*Volksheiligtümer*), and it is the duty of every German to keep their memory sacred' (2000: 16). In fact, the reputation of Kant and the German Idealists has waxed and waned, and they rarely occupied a central place even in the world of German letters. German Idealism never recovered its reputation after 1831. Thereafter, Hegel and Schelling were best known, respectively, for giving *Geschichtsphilosophie* and *Naturphilosophie* a bad name. Their critics Schopenhauer and Nietzsche were much more popular. The Nazis had very little use for Kant's rationalism, ethical univeralism and cosmopolitanism, yet adored Nietzsche. Conversely, since World War II Fichte's ultra-nationalism and anti-semitism have rightly been perceived as sources of embarrassment, by the select few who have heard of him. For good reasons, Kant has enjoyed the highest and steadiest reputation among German philosophers; yet in a recent nationwide poll on the greatest Germans not even he made it into the top ten, unlike Bismarck, Goethe and Bach. Smith supports his claim by reference to the personal impression Sidney Hook gained in 1930! The only hard evidence Hook provides is that in Germany some streets are named after philosophers. Enough to show that the Germans have on occasion taken more public pride in their philosophers than the Anglo-Americans have in their's (let's face it, they could hardly have taken less); not nearly enough to show that German philosophers are public icons that play a central role in the national psyche.

philosophy by various commentators (this is confirmed, e.g., by the short biographies in Haller 1993: 253–61). Husserl and von Mises moved from the Habsburg empire into Germany. Yet more damaging to the Anglo-Austrian conception is the fact that the traffic was even heavier in the opposite direction. Brentano and Stumpf were both originally German (and the latter returned there after a spell in Vienna). And the same goes for two of the three most eminent members of the Vienna Circle, namely Schlick and Carnap.

Indeed, Carnap is widely acknowledged as the most important logical positivist. Furthermore, logical positivism consisted not just of Schlick's *Wiener Kreis*. There was also the Berlin *Gesellschaft für Empirische Philosophie*, later renamed *Gesellschaft für Wissenschaftliche Philosophie* (see Danneberg *et al.* 1994). It was led by Reichenbach, and also boasted the young Hempel, thereby accounting for another two of the most distinguished logical positivists. It is also the origin of the positivist journal *Erkenntnis*. Finally, even if one leaves aside the impact of mathematicians like Weierstrass, Dedekind and Cantor on Russell, by far the most important early Germanophone pioneer of analytic philosophy was Frege.

These facts have not deterred some advocates of Austrian philosophical supremacy. Thus Smith opines:

The native German philosophers who have made serious contributions to exact philosophy or to the philosophy of science in the modern sense are, in contrast, remarkably few, and of these – one thinks in particular of Hans Reichenbach, Carl Hempel, and Kurt Grelling – it can often be asserted that the true flowering of their thought and influence occurred precisely through formal or informal collaboration with their teachers or contemporaries in Austria. (1994: 9)

In a footnote Smith suggests that even Frege is not a straightforward exception, since 'even here we can point to Wittgenstein's role in disseminating Fregean ideas'. By the same logic, the true flowering of Plato's and Aristotle's thought and influence depended on an Arabic context, because of the essential role that the Arabs played in transmitting their ideas to posterity.

There is no evidence for the claim that German philosophers were capable of analytic work only when prompted by Austrians. On the other hand, there is plenty of evidence for a contrasting view, even if one prescinds from the towering figure of Frege. Brentano wrote his best and most influential work, *Psychologie vom Empirischen Standpunkte* (1874), in Würzburg, *before* setting up shop in Vienna. Schlick authored *Allgemeine Erkenntnistheorie* (1918) in Germany, thereby setting in motion the *real* Vienna Circle, which, for good reasons, was also called the 'Schlick Circle'.

And if Herbert Feigl is to be trusted, Vienna had a bad influence on Schlick, because of 'the enormous effect of Wittgenstein'. 'To my chagrin Schlick ascribed to Wittgenstein philosophical ideas that he had already expounded much more lucidly in his 1918 book on epistemology. I was also disappointed with Schlick's compromise with positivism (phenomenalistic version) – and the abandonment of his critical realism as "metaphysically suspect"' (1981: 8). In a complete reversal of the Neurath-Haller thesis, Feigl pits realism made in Germany against Austrian phenomenalism. Carnap's *Aufbau*, now widely regarded as his most important work, was completed in Vienna but based on his German *Habilitation*. Finally, Reichenbach and Hempel received their education in Germany and achieved their ultimate flourishing in America, far removed from any Austrian muses.

Defenders of the Anglo-Austrian conception might dig in their heels by maintaining that the relevant contributions to analytic philosophy came from German scientists and mathematicians rather than from German philosophers. The former are often contrasted favourably with the latter, regarding both content and style (e.g. Gillies 1999). But as a defence of the Anglo-Austrian conception this will not do. *Au pied de la lettre*, it accounts for all the German influences on Russell, since even Frege was professor of mathematics. But it blithely ignores the indisputable fact that during the late nineteenth and early twentieth centuries many crucial philosophical contributions were made by thinkers who were not working in philosophy departments, figures such as Helmholtz. The philosophical implications of even Frege's formal work is beyond dispute. Moreover, if Frege can be disqualified on account of being a mathematician, then so can Bolzano, who held a chair in theology and did much of his work in mathematics, and Brentano, who was an ordained priest and worked as a psychologist. Furthermore, the Vienna Circle consisted of philosopher-scientists many of whom were not philosophers by training or affiliation. In any event, it is the incessant refrain of many proponents of the Neurath-Haller thesis that scientific philosophers bridge the gap between philosophy and the sciences.

Turning to the final bone of contention, proponents of the Anglo-Austrian conception are not alone in regarding analytic philosophy as a sustained revolt against Kant. The idea carries some weight. After flirtations with Kant and Hegel, Moore and Russell rebelled against idealism and initiated the complementary programmes of conceptual and logical analysis. Subsequently, the credo of the most influential school of analytic philosophers, the logical positivists, was the rejection of Kant's idea that there are synthetic judgements *a priori*. Next, proponents of Oxford conceptual analysis frowned upon the system-building that characterized both Kant and Neo-Kantianism, and they replaced it by piecemeal investigations into the use of philosophically relevant expressions. Finally, in the wake of Quine analytic philosophy has increasingly been dominated by naturalism, and hence by the anti-Kantian idea that philosophy is continuous with empirical science.

Nevertheless, the received contrast between Kant on the one hand, analytic philosophy or even the Austrian tradition on the other, is untenable. For one thing, there is a distinctive anti-naturalist tradition within analytic philosophy, which insists that philosophy – especially logic, epistemology and semantics – differs from natural science not just quantitatively but qualitatively (see ch. 5.3). Among its godfathers are not just proclaimed adversaries of Kant, like Bolzano and Moore, but also Frege and Wittgenstein. Both of these thinkers developed Kant's anti-naturalism, albeit in strikingly different ways. Frege defended the Neo-Kantian idea of the *a priori* and autonomous status of philosophy (in particular of logic and epistemology) against the encroachments of science, in sharp contrast to Brentano's naturalism (Glock 1999b). There are also clear Kantian themes in Wittgenstein, whose work owes much more to Schopenhauer and Frege than it does to the indigenous Austrian tradition of Bolzano and Brentano (Glock 1997a, 1999a).

For another, Kant's account of metaphysics and *a priori* knowledge set the agenda even for those who rejected the synthetic *a priori*. The linguistic turn of logical positivism was ostensibly directed against Kant's suggestion that philosophical propositions are synthetic *a priori*. Nevertheless, Reichenbach, Schlick and Carnap all had strong roots not just in Poincaré's conventionalism – itself influenced by Kant – but also in German Neo-Kantianism. Carnap was a pupil of the Neo-Kantian Bruno Bauch, and Schlick's conventionalism emerged out of the Neo-Kantian debates on relativistic physics (Friedman 1998).[6] In spite of their rejection of the synthetic *a priori* and their occasionally virulent anti-Kantian rhetoric, many logical positivists accepted the Kantian idea that philosophy is a *second-order discipline*. Unlike science or common sense, philosophy is *a priori* not because it describes objects of a peculiar kind, such as the abstract entities or essences postulated by

---

[6] On the issue of Neo-Kantianism, Smith's defence of the Anglo-Austrian conception is unconvincing. He rightly characterizes 'Natorp and the lesser Neo-Kantians' as 'truly belonging to the mainstream German tradition' (2000: 9n). On the other hand, after grudgingly conceding that the Anglo-Austrian interest in science was shared by German Neo-Kantians like Bauch, Natorp and Cassirer, he continues that these 'exceptions . . . are overwhelmingly thinkers outside the mainstream of German philosophy' (2000: 4). Yet Cassirer was the epitome of an establishment figure (see Friedman 2000). And as regards Natorp, Smith needs to have it both ways.

Platonism and Aristotelianism, respectively, but because it articulates the conceptual scheme that science and common sense employ in their empirical descriptions and explanations of reality.

This Kantian undercurrent is no coincidence. The *Tractatus*, arguably the most important text in the rise of analytic philosophy, sets philosophy the Kantian task of drawing 'the limit of thought', of demarcating legitimate and illegitimate forms of discourse, rather than that of adding to our scientific knowledge of the world. Schlick and Carnap accepted the division of labour suggested by Wittgenstein, presumably because they were steeped in Neo-Kantian ideas through their philosophical apprenticeship in Germany. Indeed, there is only a single step from the claim of the Marburg school that philosophy is the metatheory of science to Carnap's slogan that philosophy is the 'logic of science' (1937: 279), that step being the linguistic turn of the *Tractatus*, according to which the logical limits of thought are to be drawn in language.

The upshot is that analytic philosophy does not contrast with German or French philosophy. At most it contrasts with the irrationalist current that includes romanticism and *Lebensphilosophie*. But even that current has influenced analytic philosophy – not just Wittgenstein, but also Carnap. More importantly, as Critchley points out, the romantic and existentialist spirit cuts across all national boundaries. And so does its antipode, the spirit of the enlightenment. National stereotyping in philosophy is a baleful Hegelian legacy, and it cannot sustain a proper conception of analytic philosophy.

5 CONTEMPORARY FAILINGS OF GEO-LINGUISTIC CONCEPTIONS

That the Anglocentric picture falls foul of the Germanophone origins of analytic philosophy has been widely recognized in recent years. It is less appreciated that geo-linguistic conceptions of analytic philosophy *in general* are untenable, and not just for historical reasons. The analytic/continental dichotomy suffers from at least four *non-historical* weaknesses. It is indifferent to geographic variations within continental Europe, the present ascendancy there of analytic philosophy, the importance of non-analytic ways of philosophizing in Anglophone countries, and the fact that continental philosophy is neither the only nor in many respects the major alternative to analytic philosophy.

The generic term 'continental' conceals important geographical differences. In Scandinavia, analytic philosophy has been the dominant force almost since its inception, mainly through the pioneering efforts of two

Finns, Kaila, an early convert to logical positivism, and von Wright, Wittgenstein's most distinguished pupil (see Olson and Paul 1972; Haaparanta and Niiniluouto 2003).

In Germany and Austria, the story was, alas, different. The Nazi take-over had relatively little impact on the content of mainstream academic philosophy, which concentrated on purely historical work. Its main philosophical consequence was that certain movements were driven abroad – including not just logical positivism, but also Marxism and psychoanalysis. The only avant-garde movements that survived largely intact were phenomenology and existentialism, even though individuals like Husserl and Jaspers had been silenced. As a result of emigration, post-war Germanophone philosophy was for some years rather provincial. In West Germany however, it rediscovered and reappropriated not just Hegel and Marx, but also analytic philosophy.[7]

Some philosophers without prior allegiances embraced analytic philosophy wholeheartedly, and became mainstream analytical philosophers. This holds true especially of the 'Munich School' of Wolfgang Stegmüller, and of related developments in Austria, which were facilitated by historical and personal links with the pre-war Vienna Circle. Other German philosophers approached analytic philosophy from their own indigenous perspective (many of them taught for some time at Heidelberg, Gadamer's university). This holds of Habermas and Karl-Otto Apel. They have used Wittgenstein and speech act theory to defend the hermeneutic distinction between the causal explanations provided by the natural sciences and the understanding of human action and speech sought by the social sciences against positivist objections. But it also holds of the more genuinely analytic efforts by Tugendhat and Künne to reformulate and clarify traditional philosophical problems in an analytic idiom.

Analytic philosophy is now thriving in Germany, Austria and Switzerland. Although some practitioners still like to think of themselves as a persecuted minority, it is without the shadow of a doubt a growth industry and the most powerful single movement. This holds true in terms of numbers – the *Gesellschaft für Analytische Philosophie* (GAP) which represents Germanophone analytic philosophers counts 800 members and rising in 2005, and its tri-annual meetings are among the largest conferences

---

[7] In East Germany, as in Eastern Europe more generally, the shape of academic philosophy was dictated by the ideological exigencies of the communist regimes. Analytic philosophy was condemned as a product of bourgeois capitalism and Anglo-American imperialism. Serious discussion of it was largely confined to formal and historical work, which could get by with paying lip-service to 'the classics of Marxism-Leninism' in the preface.

on analytic philosophy in Europe. But it also holds in terms of furnishing the point of orientation. Analytic positions on any given issue are the ones that others cannot afford to ignore. Every phenomenologist, hermeneutician and critical theorist has a line on analytic theories in her field, even if that line may sometimes strike analytic colleagues as uninformed, prejudiced or slightly out of date. By contrast, few analytic philosophers of the younger generation feel any need to have a line on non-analytic doctrines.

The development of analytic philosophy in France has been a slower and more painful process. This had less to do with the impact of fascism, however, than with the indigenous academic climate. There was the legacy of Bergson, the untimely death of figures such as Nicod, Jourdain and Herbrandt, the emphasis on historical studies, and finally the orientation of the more creative thinkers such as Kojève and Sartre towards non-analytic Germanophone figures, whether they be Hegel, Husserl or Freud. But even in France analytic philosophy is at present the fastest growing movement, thanks to the patient and ultimately successful efforts of pioneers like Jacques Bouveresse (1983). It is no coincidence, moreover, that some of the most vigorous proponents of analytic philosophy and opponents of the continental alternative, such as Bouveresse and Pascal Engel (1997), are French. The situation in Italy, Spain and many Eastern European countries is similar.[8] Accordingly, another major failing of geo-linguistic conceptions is that at present analytic philosophy flourishes in most if not all parts of the continent.

But geo-linguistic conceptions also come a cropper at the other philo-sophical end. After World War II, the ascendancy of analytic philosophy entirely eclipsed other movements in most centres of Anglophone philos-ophy. But it did not prevent phenomenology, existentialism, hermeneutics and post-structuralism from taking roots in some ecological niches, such as Catholic universities in the USA or in Ireland or The New School for Social Research in New York. Furthermore, from the 1960s onwards continental modes of thought became immensely popular in North America. Indeed, it is arguable that within this Anglophone setting they had a wider impact on subjects outside of philosophy than they ever did in continental Europe.

In his history of post-war analytic philosophy Baldwin associates an 'analytic' concern for arguments in philosophy with the English tongue.

---

[8] An umbrella organization, the European Society for Analytic Philosophy or ESAP, was founded in 1991. Its website http://www.dif.unige.it/esap features links to Central European, Croatian, French, German, Italian, Portuguese and Spanish societies of analytic philosophy. ESAP also regularly organizes major conferences.

He duly acknowledges that 'among many writers about philosophy, especially those whose main background and sympathies are in the humanities' (2001: 273–4), there is great sympathy for the later Rorty, who rejects philosophical argument in both theory and practice. But it seems that Baldwin wishes to contrast these 'writers about philosophy' with genuine philosophers. And it is common to play down the role of continental thought within Anglophone *philosophy* by insisting that its main impact has been on *other* disciplines. But this would be precipitate. *Bona fide* philosophers with an allegedly 'continental' scepticism about the power of rational argument include not just Rorty and his followers, but also Cavell and his admirers. They further include Anglophone Nietzscheans and postmodernists, several acolytes of Kuhn and Feyerabend, and some Wittgensteinians, notably proponents of the so-called 'New Wittgenstein'. In any event, continental thought in the English-speaking world is no stranger to philosophy departments proper. Most of the contributors to a recent reader with the revealing title *American Continental Philosophy* are philosophers by training and/or institutional association.[9] And continental philosophers have successfully overcome their erstwhile marginalisation within the American Philosophical Association (see Preston 2007: 12–14).

A final and most serious failing of geo-linguistic conceptions concerns the taxonomy of current positions with which it is connected. For one thing, there is at least one important movement which does not fit neatly into either the analytic or the continental category, namely American pragmatism. Pragmatism was founded by C. S. Peirce, popularized by William James, and further developed by John Dewey, G. H. Mead and C. I. Lewis. The demise of German idealism in the middle of the nineteenth century sparked off various intellectual trends that tried to overcome religious and metaphysical mystery-mongering by stressing the importance of human practice. Pragmatism is the Anglo-Saxon version of this move from the Absolute to action. Although it had followers elsewhere, e.g. E. C. S. Schiller in Oxford, it is the only philosophical movement which is indigenous to the United States. It differs from its continental cousins – Marxism, existentialism, hermeneutics – in its empiricist and utilitarian tendencies, and in its association with natural science in general, and with Darwinism in particular.

---

[9] Brogan and Risser 2000. In their Introduction the editors also demonstrate that when it comes to irony, American continental philosophers are second to none: 'This non-sedimented, open spirit, which shuns a narrowly nationalistic perspective, makes America uniquely receptive to the multiple directions of continental philosophy that emerge from many different countries' (8).

With respect to the analytic/continental divide, pragmatism occupies an ambivalent role. On the one hand, pragmatism, especially in the hands of Peirce, has strong affinities with analytic philosophy and thereby prepared the ground for the latter's favourable reception from the 1930s onwards. As mentioned above, Peirce made important contributions to the development of formal logic. Furthermore, in line with the linguistic turn he tried to ground his logic in an account of meaning and reference. In a passage reminiscent of the *Tractatus*, he described logic as 'only another name for *semiotic*, the quasi-necessary or formal doctrine of signs' (Hookway 1998). Finally, his pragmatism is best known for a semantic maxim: the content of a concept or belief is determined by the experiential consequences we would expect our actions to have if the concept applied or the belief were true. By this token, the meaning of a word like 'acid' consists of the 'conceivable experimental phenomena' implied by affirming or denying that it applies in a given case (1934: 273). This position directly anticipates the operationalism and verificationism of the logical positivists. Furthermore, these and other pragmatist ideas, notably a holistic and instrumentalist conception of knowledge and the emphasis on human action, also influenced later analytic philosophers, notably Quine, Davidson, Putnam, Haack and Brandom.[10]

On the other hand, pragmatism has been regularly contrasted with analytic philosophy. What is more, as developed by James and Dewey, it has clear affinities to continental philosophy. It is no coincidence that many contemporary proponents of pragmatism in America, most notably Richard Rorty (1982), are hostile to analytic philosophy and sympathetic to continental modes of thought. Following James, many pragmatists conceive of truth in terms of usefulness. According to James, a belief is true if it is expedient for us to believe it (1907: 99–100). This not only makes truth partly dependent on human beings, it forges a link between truth and human welfare, and hence between cognitive and moral issues. This connection is reinforced by the conviction, particularly pronounced in Dewey, that scientific inquiry can function as an ideal in ethics and politics. In our context, this idea has a two-fold significance. For one thing, it indicates that American pragmatists are fond of 'debunking of dualisms' (Rorty 1986: 333, 339), including Kantian dichotomies like those between theoretical and practical reason, and between philosophy and other disciplines.

---

[10] Glock 2003a: 18–23 argues that Quine and Davidson can be described as 'logical pragmatists', because their relation to American pragmatism is analogous to that of the logical empiricists to classical empiricism. They develop *some* pragmatist ideas in a clearer and more cogent way, with the help of techniques and doctrines from analytic philosophy.

This not only chimes with continental philosophy, it is a direct result of Hegelian influences on the early American pragmatists. For another thing, the link means that pragmatist philosophizing is often inspired by moral and political aspirations that are more prominent in continental than in analytic philosophy. Indeed, according to Rorty and West (1989), pragmatism reaches its climax in a form of social prophecy which is uniquely American.

Pragmatism thus presents a double challenge to the analytic/continental divide. First, it is a borderline case. Secondly, it may even constitute a distinct philosophical movement or tendency at the same grand strategic level as analytic and continental philosophy (e.g. Margolis 2003 and Rockmore 2004). In my view, pragmatism is an ambivalent phenomenon in this respect. On the one hand, like some specific movements – e.g. Thomism or phenomenology – it can be characterized by reference to certain basic convictions (e.g. concerning the importance of human action). On the other hand, it does not even come close to possessing a common method or style, or to constituting a single web of discussion.

There is, however, a movement or tendency at the same somewhat diffuse level of generality as analytic and 'continental' philosophy, and one whose recognition is long overdue. In many contexts the main *alternative* to analytic philosophy does not qualify as continental philosophy by the currently established standards. At present, that tag is predominantly used to refer to a family of avant-garde movements from the nineteenth and twentieth centuries. Originally, however, in its positivistic and linguistic phase, analytic philosophy was contrasted neither with continental nor with European philosophy, but with 'traditional philosophy' or 'established school philosophy', both favourite bogeys of the positivist crusade against metaphysics. 'Looking back we now see clearly the *essence of the new scientific world-view*: its contrast to traditional (*herkömmlichen*) philosophy', which is any philosophy that propounds philosophical propositions rather than confining itself to the logical analysis of scientific propositions (Carnap, Hahn and Neurath 1929: 18; see also Carnap 1928: xvii).

More generally, it was *traditional* philosophy that provided the point of departure as well as the acknowledged antipode to analytic philosophy (see Tugendhat 1976). Taking seriously the talk of a *Revolution in Philosophy* (Ayer *et al.* 1956) and of a 'turning point' (Schlick 1930/1), it was felt on all sides of the linguistic and philosophical divides that analytic philosophy at least aspired to a radical break with the *philosophia perennis*, the grand and hitherto universally respected tradition of Western philosophy ranging from the Pre-Socratics to Kant. This contrast between analytic and traditional philosophy was superseded by the contrast between analytic and *continental* philosophy as we now know it only because of a combination of two entirely distinct developments, one political, the other philosophical. On the one hand, the exodus of analytic philosophers from continental Europe enforced by the scourge of Nazism rendered possible the idea of contrasting analytic philosophy with philosophy on the continent. On the other hand, the rehabilitation of metaphysics and the reversal of the linguistic turn within analytic philosophy from the 1960s onwards removed the most fundamental doctrinal conflicts with traditional philosophy.

Most non-analytic philosophers of the twentieth century do not belong to continental philosophy. This obviously holds for the Anglophone opponents of analytic philosophy, ranging from the contributors to Lewis 1963 through Mundle (1970) to Kekes (1980). More significantly, it also holds of academic philosophers on the continent. A majority of them are devoted to the study – the interpretation and exposition – of the aforementioned *philosophia perennis*. In *quantitative* terms, academic philosophy on the continent remains dominated by historical and exegetical work (see also Bouveresse 2000: 131). Plato rather than phenomenological reduction, Descartes rather than *différance*, Spinoza rather than *Seinsgeschichte* and Leibniz rather than logocentrism are still the order of the day. A typical German dissertation bears a title like 'The Concept of History from Augustine to Dilthey'. This explains the *prima facie* curious fact that the label 'continental philosophy' remains least popular on the continent in question.

Even if we confine ourselves to *Western* philosophy, leaving aside not just Islamic, Chinese and Indian philosophy but also the burgeoning fields of world and ethno-philosophies, analytic philosophy contrasts not just with continental philosophy, but also with two other closely connected phenomena: *traditional* philosophy up to and including Kant on the one hand, and *traditionalist* philosophy, which pursues the scholarly study of traditional philosophy.

In conclusion, the current state of affairs confounds the analytic/continental divide and thereby geo-linguistic conceptions of analytic philosophy no less than the latter's historical roots. At the highest level of generality we have to distinguish between at least three different extant philosophical tendencies:
- analytic philosophy
- continental philosophy, so-called
- traditional-cum-traditionalist philosophy.

At the highest level! Obviously traditional philosophy is not a homo-geneous phenomenon, even on the question of whether philosophy can furnish metaphysical insights into the nature of reality. But analytic philosophy owes its birth to a break with the past, a past which it tended to view as uniform and predominantly misguided.

Both past and present, the lines between these tendencies cut across all geographical and linguistic boundaries. Therefore geo-linguistic conceptions of analytic philosophy are misguided. By the same token, the very label 'continental philosophy' is a misnomer. Some who recognize this fact have tried to rectify matters by using the labels 'Post-Kantian Philosophy', 'Post-Kantian Continental Philosophy' or 'Modern European Philosophy' instead. But these are equally misleading. As regards the first, emblematic analytic philosophers like Strawson, Sellars, Rawls and Bennett (to name just the incontestable cases) have drawn on Kant, while many continental philosophers have condemned him furiously, in the case of Nietzsche apparently even without much knowledge of the texts. Adding 'continental' does not solve the problem, since the analytic philosophers with important Kantian affinities include Frege, Wittgenstein, Schlick, Reichenbach and Carnap. 'Modern European Philosophy' makes matters worse. As a prefix to 'philosophy', 'modern' already has an established use, namely to signify the period after Descartes. 'Contemporary European Philosophy' will not do either. We should not allow demagogues to conceal the fact that geographically and culturally speaking Britain is part of Europe, as is the analytic philosophy which has flourished there. A last ditch attempt would be 'Contemporary Continental Philosophy'. But this not only ignores the fact that traditionalist plus analytic philosophers form a decisive majority of professional philosophers on the Continent. It also excludes figures and movements which constitute a central part of continental philosophy as an established field of academic study, as is transparent from syllabi, textbooks and works of reference. Admittedly, that field includes contemporary avant-garde movements such as critical theory (Habermas), feminism (Irigaray, Kristeva), postmodernism (Lyotard, Baudrillard) and post-structuralism (Foucault, Derrida, Deleuze). But it also includes movements and figures from the nineteenth and early twentieth centuries – German Idealism, the philosophy of life (Schopenhauer, Kierkegaard, Bergson), phenomenology (Husserl, Sartre, Merleau-Ponty), Western Marxism (Lukacs, Horkheimer, Adorno), and Heidegger (Critchley 2001: 13).

There is no obviously superior alternative to 'continental philosophy'. Furthermore, the label has become entrenched even among those apprised of its misleading connotations, whether they be on the continental or analytic side (respectively, Glendinning 1998a; Glendinning 2006: chs. 4–5 and Mulligan 1991). Summing up the attitude of those in the know, Cooper writes: 'The continent, for our purposes, is not a place, but a tendency' (1994: 2). In view of this situation, I shall reluctantly retain the misnomer and drop the scare quotes and qualifications for the remainder of this book. I shall diverge even from the more enlightened practice, however, by insisting on the difference between continental philosophy on the one hand, traditional and traditionalist philosophy on the other. In the next chapter I shall examine a proposal connected to the latter phenomenon, namely that what sets analytic philosophy apart is its attitude towards history.

CHAPTER 4

History and historiography

If not by reference to space (geography and language), perhaps analytic philosophy can be conceived by reference to time. A disregard for historical issues is often mentioned as one of the distinctive features of analytic philosophy (Agostini 1997: 73–4; Engel 1997: 184–96). Furthermore, this alleged fact is almost universally used as a stick with which to beat analytic philosophy. Without good cause, I feel. Not *just* because analytic philosophers take a greater interest in the past than is commonly assumed, but *also* because their neglect of *some* historical issues is not the mortal sin their critics make it out to be.

The accusation that analytic philosophy lacks historical awareness unites its two main rivals within contemporary Western philosophy, continental and traditionalist philosophy. More surprisingly, perhaps, the criticism is also shared by some who by common consent are analytic philosophers themselves. From a continental-cum-pragmatist perspective, Rorty accuses analytic philosophy of being 'an attempt to escape from history' (1979: 8–9), and Wilshire takes exception to its 'radically ahistorical and modern-progressivist point of view' (2002: 4). From a traditionalist perspective, Ayers has lambasted analytic philosophers for their historiographical failings (1978), and from a traditionalist-cum-continental perspective Rée complains about their 'condescension' towards the past (1978: 28). The analytic critics, finally, include historians of the analytic movement like Sluga (1980: 2), Baker (1988: ix) and Hylton (1990: vii), who deplore its lack of historical self-consciousness. They also include Bernard Williams, who has urged analytic philosophy to adopt a more historical and genetic perspective in general (2002a).

For present purposes I shall use the label 'historicism' for any position that promotes historical thinking in philosophy and warns against ignoring or distorting the past. There is an ongoing debate about the virtues of 'doing philosophy historically' (Hare 1988; Piercey 2003). But it suffers from a failure to distinguish different *types* of historicism.

According to *intrinsic* historicism, proper philosophy is *ipso facto* histor-ical. Thus Krüger assures us that the reason for studying history is not just the 'pragmatic' one of 'studying historical material in order to produce trans-historical philosophical insight', since the only philosophical insight to be had is itself historical in nature (1984: 79 and n). In the same vein, Critchley repudiates the 'validity of the distinction between philosophy and the history of philosophy operative in much of the analytic tradition' (2001: 62). According to *instrumental* historicism, studying the past is *necessary*, yet only as a *means* to achieving ends which themselves are not historical in nature. This view is exemplified by Taylor, who holds that one 'cannot do' systematic philosophy without also doing history of philoso-phy (1984: 17). And according to *weak* historicism, a study of the past is *useful* to such a pursuit, without being indispensable (Hare 1988: 12; Kenny 2005: 24).

It is also important to distinguish two historicist criticisms of analytic philosophy. The first is that analytic philosophers tend to *ignore* the past – the charge of *historiophobia*. The second is that in so far as they consider the past, they *distort* it by reading features of the present into it – the charge of *anachronism*. My aim is to show that analytic philosophy and history are not such a mismatch after all, even though they have been through some rough patches. Neither historiophobia nor anachronism are characteristic features of analytic philosophy. Indeed, there is virtually no approach to history that has not been adopted by at least some analytic philosophers. Furthermore, in so far as analytic philosophers tend to share such an approach, it is one that stands them in good stead. Sections 1–2 deal with the charge of historiophobia. It fails, because analytic philosophers by-and-large accept weak historicism, and they have reason to avoid the stronger positions. Intrinsic historicism is misguided, and the case for instrumental historicism remains unproven. Sections 3–4 deal with the charge of anach-ronism. Some forms of analytic history succumb to this ill, but the problem-oriented historiography favoured by most analytic historians is superior to the relativism of their historicist critics. Approaching the past with a view to substantive issues makes not just for better philosophy but also for better history.

I   HISTORIOPHOBIA VS INTRINSIC HISTORICISM

Analytic philosophers invite the charge of historiophobia in that they have often prided themselves on the ahistorical nature of their enterprise. But they have done so for diverse reasons.

To the analytic enemies of metaphysics the history of philosophy appeared primarily as a history of nonsense or mistakes. According to the *Tractatus*, 'the whole of philosophy' is full of the 'most fundamental confusions' and 'errors' based on failure to grasp the logic of our language. As a result, 'most of the propositions and questions to be found in philosophical works are not false but nonsensical' (3.323–3.325, 4.003). The early Wittgenstein directed the charge of nonsense even-handedly at all philosophy, including not just many pioneers of analytic philosophy, but even the metaphysical pronouncements of his own *Tractatus* (6.54). By contrast, his disciples in the Vienna Circle confined the accusation to what they variously called metaphysics, 'traditional' or 'school philosophy'. 'The representatives of the scientific world-view ... confidently approach the task of removing the metaphysical and theological debris of millennia' (Carnap, Hahn and Neurath 1929: 9–10, 19). They focused especially on post-Kantian German philosophy – German Idealism, vitalism and Heidegger (Carnap 1963: 875). But scholastic metaphysics, the 'hidden metaphysics' of Kant and twentieth-century apriorism were equally in the target area, and so was even the realist attempt to assert the existence of the external world or of other minds. While they were at it, the logical positivists also included ethics and aesthetics. These disciplines consisted of 'pseudo-propositions' bereft of cognitive meaning, of misguided attempts to answer vacuous 'pseudo-questions' or 'pseudo-problems'.

In the domain of *metaphysics*, including all philosophy of value and normative theory, logical analysis yields the negative result *that the alleged statements in this area are entirely meaningless* ... Our thesis, now, is that logical analysis reveals the alleged statements of metaphysics to be pseudo-statements. (Carnap 1932: 60–1; see also 1934b: §2)

Such sweeping accusations of nonsense are no longer *en vogue*. But a naturalistic view with similar implications has taken their place. Analytic philosophy, the new story goes, is a scientific discipline; it uses specific techniques to tackle discrete problems with definite results, and hence no more needs to seek refuge in discussing the past than does natural science. Thus Quine dismisses exegetical worries about attributing the essence/accident distinction to Aristotle by adding 'subject to contradictions by scholars, such being the penalty for attributions to Aristotle' (1960: 199). And he is widely credited with the quip: 'There are two kinds of people interested in philosophy, those interested in philosophy and those interested in the history of philosophy' (MacIntyre 1984: 39–40). Finally, Williams reports: 'in one prestigious American department a senior figure had a notice on his door that read JUST SAY NO TO THE HISTORY OF PHILOSOPHY' (1996b: 18).

The culprit turns out to be Gilbert Harman (Sorell and Rogers 2005: 43). It could equally have been Fodor, who boasts about his 'ignorance of the history of philosophy' and his ability to write a 'book about Hume without actually knowing anything about him' (2003: 1). On this issue, there is even convergence between contemporary naturalists and Wittgenstein. Wittgenstein confessed:

As little philosophy as I have read, I have certainly not read too little, *rather too much*. I see that whenever I read a philosophical book: it doesn't improve my thoughts at all, it makes them worse. (MS 135: 27.7.47; quoted Monk 1990: 495)

According to Ryle, moreover, Wittgenstein 'not only properly distinguished philosophical from exegetic problems but also, less properly, gave the impression, first, that he himself was proud not to have studied other philosophers – which he had done, though not much – and second, that he thought that people who did study them were academic and therefore unauthentic philosophers, which was often but not always true'. Ryle, by contrast, balked at the superior attitude towards previous philosophy which he detected in Wittgenstein and the Vienna Circle. Not only had figures of the past 'sometimes said significant things', they should be treated 'more like colleagues than like pupils' (1970: 10–11).

As this quotation demonstrates, however, historiophobia is not a universal affliction among analytic philosophers. Even for those who abstain from historical discussions, the reason is often not principled doubts about their potential philosophical value, but rather reluctance to enter an increasingly specialized field for fear of being contradicted by scholars (Wilson 1991: 461–2). More importantly, many analytic philosophers have laid claim to the philosophical mantle of thinkers from the past. Leibniz provided Russell with the inspirational idea that 'all sound philosophy begins with *logical analysis*' (1900: 8). Ayer described logical positivism as 'the logical outcome of the empiricism of Berkeley and David Hume' (1936: 41). And Reichenbach (1951) purported to lay bare the historical roots of both the analytic movement and the speculative philosophy it aspired to replace. Even historiophobic analyticians occasionally succumb to 'precurorism'. Thus Quine dabbled in historical questions by discussing Russell's ontological development or the origins of the linguistic turn and contextualism (1981: chs. 7–8). Indeed, since the 1960s there has been an upsurge in analytic work on the history of philosophy, prompting von Wright to speak of a 'retrospective turn' (1993: 47; see also Wilson 1991: 454; Critchley 2001: 61).

Analytic interest in the past has always included ancient Greek philosophy, to which analytic philosophers have felt a strong affinity, though their approach has been condemned as anachronistic (Annas 2004). But it has by no means been confined to it, and now extends to all periods.

Accordingly, historiophobia is not a necessary condition for being an analytic philosopher. But is it a sufficient one? By (my) definitions, historiophobia is incompatible with *traditionalist* philosophy. But it is not unknown among traditional and continental philosophers. In the Preface to the *Prolegomena* Kant wrote:

There are scholars to whom the history of philosophy is itself their philosophy; the present Prolegomena are not written for them. They will have to wait until those who endeavour to draw from the fountain of reason have finished their business, and thereupon it will be their turn to apprise the world of what happened.

For Kant's admirer Schopenhauer historical studies represented the very opposite of true philosophy, since they are by nature unsystematic and incapable of penetrating the veil of mere appearances:

history has always been a favourite study among those who want to learn something without undergoing the effort required by the real branches of knowledge, which tax and engross the intellect. (1851: II, §233)

Schopenhauer in turn influenced Nietzsche. As we shall see, Nietzsche's idea of genealogy has inspired historicist thinkers in- and outside of analytic philosophy. Ironically, his *Vom Nutzen und Nachteil der Historie für das Leben* is in fact an eloquent *attack* on nineteenth-century historicism. Knowledge of the past is to be avoided, Nietzsche informs us, when it hinders rather than expedites 'life', the pursuit of the interests of the present.

It emerges that historiophobia is not a distinguishing feature of analytic philosophy. But its attitude towards the past might yet prove to be distinctive. While Ryle's passage repudiates historiophobia, it also indicates a conflict with historicism. He insists that the *exegetical* question of what a philosopher believed can and must be distinguished from the *substantive* question of whether those beliefs are correct (Russell 1900: xi–xii). More generally, analytic philosophy is guided by the conviction that there is a difference between *philosophy* and the *history of philosophy* (Engel 1997: 193–4), contrary to the intrinsic historicism to which much of continental philosophy seems to subscribe.

Nevertheless, not even the rejection of intrinsic historicism is a universal feature of analytic philosophy. There is a form of intrinsic historicism which inverts naturalistic historiophobia and which has been propounded by philosophers with analytic training.

Naturalistic historiophobia relies on two premises. The *first* is the claim that proper philosophy is part of, or continuous with, the natural sciences, and should therefore emulate the latter's aims and methods. The *second* premise is that natural science is a thoroughly ahistorical enterprise. 'A science that hesitates to forget its founders is lost' (Whitehead: 1929: 107). Scientific investigations rarely proceed by arguing with the great dead, and students of the natural sciences are not introduced to their subjects through their history.

Nevertheless, some intrinsic historicists have welcomed the first premise, while repudiating the second. In this, they are inspired by two ideas from post-positivist philosophy of science. The first is Kuhn's historicist per-spective on science. 'History, if viewed as a repository for more than anecdote or chronology, could produce a decisive transformation in the image of science of which we are now possessed' (1962: 1). The second is the thesis – associated with Quine and Kuhn – of the underdetermination of theory by evidence: any given set of empirical data can be accommodated by mutually incompatible scientific theories.

Drawing on these ideas, Krüger insists that a novel scientific theory T_n cannot be judged solely by comparing it to the empirical data; it must also be pitted against the previously accepted theory T_{n-1}. Scientific theories can only be understood as alternatives to their *historical predecessors*, because the empirical evidence is equally compatible with different theories (1984: 93). MacIntyre is even more forthright:

the history of natural science is in a way sovereign over the natural sciences . . . the superior theory in natural science is that which affords grounds for a certain kind of historical explanation.

By the same token, the history of philosophy 'is sovereign over the rest of the discipline'. The ultimate test of a philosophical theory 'occurs not at all at the level of argument', but rests on its capacity to provide a historical explanation of its rivals (1984: 44, 47).

Scientific theories emerge through evolution and, on occasion, revolu-tion rather than out of the blue. But even if the underdetermination of theory by evidence is granted, it only entails that in assessing the cognitive virtues of T_n we cannot solely rely on empirical data, not that we must compare and contrast it with a historical rival T_{n-1}. Indeed, some scientific theories do not have predecessors, either because they mark the dawn of a discipline or because they concern newly discovered phenomena such as quasars or autism. Finally, even where a scientific theory pits itself against a rival, this process is not *historiographical*. Proponents of T_n have ample motivation to explain both the failures and the successes of a preceding orthodoxy T_{n-1}. Yet their target is not to provide a *historical* explanation of T_{n-1} itself, an account of its origins and development, of the motivations of its proponents and its cultural and political context. It is rather to provide a *scientific* explanation of the *natural phenomena* that are pertinent to the tenability of T_{n-1}.

Neither scientists nor philosophers can afford to disregard the theories of their *immediate* predecessors, since these are the rivals against which they have to prove their mettle. *In so far* as the naturalistic historiophobes counsel such complete abstinence they are clearly mistaken. It is unclear, however, how far that actually is. Furthermore, as regards *more remote* predecessors the argument does not even deliver the weak claim that it is advantageous to take an interest in them, not to mention the stronger claim that it is unavoidable.

It is unsurprising, therefore, that most intrinsic historicists contest the *first* premise of the naturalistic argument, the identity of philosophy and natural science. Their preferred route has been to align philosophy with the humanities and social sciences. For Gadamer (1960), philosophy is hermeneutics, an investigation of the method of interpretation, because the fundamental structures and limits of human existence are determined by the interpretation of meaningful actions and their products. Philosophy turns into a dialogue with texts and with the history of their effects. One of the historical blind spots of analytic philosophers is supposed to be that they are oblivious to the need of situating ourselves in the Gadamerian 'conversation which we are' (Rorty *et al.* 1984: 11).

This hermeneutic variant of intrinsic historicism is rare among analytic philosophers. Few of them would accept Rorty's claim that a key task of philosophy is 'the colligation of hitherto unrelated texts' in a historical narrative (1991: 94). But there are notable exceptions. In his revealingly entitled *Tales of the Mighty Dead* (2002) Brandom colligates energetically by forging Spinoza, Leibniz, Hegel, Frege, Heidegger and Sellars into an 'inferentialist' tradition, a tradition opposed to the idea that the representation of reality is the central function of thought and language. Furthermore, Brandom accepts Gadamer's claim that philosophy is essentially a matter of 'talking with tradition'.

Is the majority of analytic philosophers correct in resisting such claims? There is no gainsaying the fact that the cultural sciences are inherently historical, since they seek to describe and explain the development of evolving human practices. *If* philosophy is simply one of the *Geisteswissenschaften*, it is inherently historical. Natural and cultural sciences do not exhaust the options, however. By tradition philosophy, like logic and mathematics, has been regarded as *a priori*, independent of sensory experience. Its problems cannot be solved, its propositions cannot be supported or refuted, by observation or experiment, irrespective of whether these concern the natural world or human culture. Though often derided at present in the name of naturalism, this rationalist picture squares well with the actual practice of philosophers, naturalists included. Philosophy as a distinctive intellectual pursuit is constituted at least in part by *problems* of a peculiar kind. These problems include questions such as 'Can human beings acquire genuine knowledge?', 'What is the relationship between mind and body?' and 'Are there objective moral principles?' They are not just supremely abstract and fundamental, but also *a priori*, at least in the sense that the characteristically philosophical disputes about them concern not the scientific findings themselves, but at most the relevance these findings have for such problems.

This lesson applies to the cultural sciences with a vengeance. If neuroscience by itself does not solve the mind-body problem, and if biology by itself cannot tell us whether one can derive normative from factual statements (an 'ought' from an 'is'), the historical sciences will be completely out of their depths. There is no reason why the empirical findings of these disciplines should possess greater potency for solving philosophical problems than those of the natural sciences. More specifically, problems of this kind cannot be solved or dissolved by recording their history. The observation that Descartes espoused a substance dualism in reaction to such-and-such historical circumstances neither answers the mind-body problem nor does it show the problem to be misguided. If philosophy were simply a historical science, it would no longer speak to the philosophical problems. This also explains a *profound irony* about intrinsic historicism. The great philosophers whom it urges us to study did precisely *not* identify philosophy with historiography; they tackled non-historical problems and aspired to insights of a *non-historical* kind.

The hermeneutic version of intrinsic historicism is tenable only if the aspiration to tackle philosophical problems by way of either solution or dissolution must be abandoned. This defeatist conclusion is not just the explicit view of some continental philosophers, it is also an inevitable consequence of the historicist relativism propounded by some historians of analytic philosophy to which we turn in section 3. Right now we should simply note that historiophobia is neither prevalent in nor exclusive to analytic philosophy, and that intrinsic historicism is not the preserve of non-analytic philosophers.

2 INSTRUMENTAL VS WEAK HISTORICISM

The rationalist conception of philosophy underlies Kant's rejection of intrinsic historicism. In one respect, however, rationalism points in the opposite direction. If philosophy is *a priori*, then, unlike the science of the past, the philosophy of the past cannot simply be *superseded* by novel empirical findings. Therefore it may have something to teach us, just as weak historicism has it. Kant allows for this possibility. He only resists the view that history of philosophy is philosophy enough. This view was still powerful in the doxographic climate of the eighteenth century, and it re-emerges in intrinsic historicists of the present.

Willy-nilly, Kant even provided an impetus for instrumental historicism. For Kant philosophy is *a priori* not because it describes abstract entities or essences, but because it is not concerned with objects of any kind. Instead, it is a *second-order discipline* which reflects on the preconditions of experiencing ordinary objects, that is, on the conceptual structures that science and common sense presuppose in their descriptions and explanations of reality. Kant treats this conceptual scheme as an immutable mental structure – 'pure reason'. From Hegel onwards, however, it was held that our scheme can change, at least in parts. For Hegel 'philosophy [is] its time apprehended in thought' (*Philosophy of Rights*: Preface). It articulates and synthesizes the different branches of the culture of an epoch into a superior form of wisdom. Less ambitiously, according to Collingwood (1940), metaphysics spells out the 'absolute presuppositions' of an epoch, fundamental intellectual commitments that can only be brought to light with the benefit of hindsight through historical reflection.

A different mutation of the Kantian picture emerged in the analytic tradition. Wittgenstein accepted that philosophical problems defy empirical solution because they are rooted in our conceptual scheme rather than reality. Unlike Kant, however, Wittgenstein regarded this scheme as embodied in language. In his later philosophy he recognized, moreover, that language is a practice and hence subject to change. Although Wittgenstein personally was immune to the charms of historical scholarship, this opens the door to a historical understanding of concepts, and hence of the philosophical problems in which they feature. Philosophy is not *ipso facto* history, yet historical knowledge may be indispensable to tackling the conceptual problems with which it deals.

Contemporary instrumental historicists follow this trajectory. The underlying idea is that philosophy aims at a special kind of *self-understanding*, an understanding not so much of the non-human world as of our thoughts and practices. In the words of Williams:

The starting point of philosophy is that we do not understand ourselves well enough … Philosophy's methods of helping us to understand ourselves involve reflecting on the concepts we use, the modes in which we think about these various things [nature, ethics, politics]; and it sometimes proposes better ways of doing this. (2002b: 7)

Similarly, for Taylor, philosophy 'involves a great deal of articulation of what is initially inarticulated', namely the fundamental assumptions behind the way we think and act (1984: 18).

Instead of Collingwood's 'absolute presuppositions' let us use the more neutral 'framework' for the system of concepts, modes of thought and assumptions that underlie a given culture. As both Williams and Taylor acknowledge, the immediate philosophical task is to articulate *our current* framework, since the 'concepts which give rise to the questions are ours' (Williams 2002b: 7). Why then should philosophy require an understanding of the *past*? There are two ways of responding to this challenge. One is to argue that philosophy must look at the history of the philosophical *characterizations* of our framework; the other that it must take into account the development of that framework *itself.*

Taylor adopts the first strategy. According to him, successful articulations of our world-view presuppose recovering previous articulations. His example is that the most successful challengers to the Cartesian conception of the mind – Hegel, Heidegger and Merleau-Ponty – had recourse to history. Taylor recognizes the objection that 'it didn't have to be so'; the critics just happened to be German and French professors with 'a notorious professional deformation which makes them compulsively engage in expositions and re-interpretations of the canonical texts' (1984: 19). Worse still, it wasn't even so. Wittgenstein's attack on the Cartesian picture is at least as compelling; yet it is entirely ahistorical, revolving around a dialogue between the author and a fictitious interlocutor.

Taylor's second argument excludes this possibility *ab initio*. It maintains that the only way of appreciating that a prevailing philosophical position 'is one of a range of alternatives' is learning about its origins and the prior orthodoxies that the current one had to contend with. '[Y]ou need to understand the past in order to liberate yourself', because this is the only way of realizing that there are alternatives to the *status quo* (1984: 20–2; similarly Baker 1988: xvii).

This line of reasoning is vulnerable on three counts. First, even if one can challenge a given philosophical articulation A_2 only by being acquainted with an alternative A_1, that alternative need not lie in the past. *Synchronic* diversity can take the place of *diachronic* diversity. Secondly, even if some articulations are without extant competitors, we would only have to know a past articulation. It would not follow that we have to know the *history* leading from A_1 to A_2. Mere doxography (the recording and contrasting of opinions held by philosophers) would do just as well. Finally, the argument assumes that one can only overcome a philosophical position A_n if one is familiar with a prior alternative A_{n-1}. That assumption is not just unfounded, it also engenders a vicious regress. For it entails that our immediate predecessors could only have moved from A_{n-1} to A_n because they were already familiar with A_{n-2}, and so on. Perhaps Augustine anticipated Descartes' *cogito* and Hegel anticipated Wittgenstein's private language argument. Strawson reports fatuously announcing to George Paul in 1949 'that I had a new theory of truth; to which he sensibly and characteristically replied: "Come on now, which of the old ones is it?"' (1998: 8). Nevertheless, this is one regress of which we know that it stops somewhere. Even in philosophy, someone at some time must have had a genuinely original idea.

Let us therefore turn to the second option. The proposal is that articulating our framework presupposes knowledge of *its* history. According to Williams, more baneful than the neglect of the history of philosophy has been the neglect of 'the history of the concepts which philosophy is trying to understand' (2002b: 7). This position underwrites a broader form of historicism, since it makes philosophy dependent not just on the history of *philosophy* but on the entire *history of ideas* and perhaps even on *history in general*, depending on the forces that shape our concepts. But how can it be sustained, given that the philosophical problems we currently confront have their roots in our present framework?

One suggestion is to transpose the need for *alternatives* from the philosophical articulation to the articulated framework. Knowing about the history of our current framework liberates us from regarding the latter as unavoidable. Thus Skinner writes that 'the indispensable value of studying the history of ideas' is to learn 'the distinction between what is necessary and what is the product merely of our own arrangements' (1969: 52–3).

If we are to understand our framework in a philosophically fruitful way it is indeed crucial to establish what aspects of it, if any, are indispensable rather than optional products of contingent circumstances. Otherwise we cannot assess, for instance, Strawson's claim that 'there is a massive core of human thinking which has no history – or none recorded in histories of thought' because it is not subject to change (1959: 10). Nevertheless, the historicist argument runs into trouble. As regards philosophical articulations, at least there was no doubt as to the existence of diversity. As regards the framework itself, it is not even beyond dispute that there *are* genuine alternatives. From Kant to Davidson philosophers of a rationalist persuasion have argued that *au fond* we all share the same framework. Confronted with different epochs, they insist that the alleged differences are merely superficial. If they are right, the argument that philosophers need to be familiar with alternative frameworks from the past is a non-starter.

There are good reasons for resisting the rationalist attack on the possibility of alternative frameworks (Dancy 1983; Hacker 1996). In that case, however, the historicist argument fails on other grounds. If the apparent diversity of human cultures cannot be dismissed as deceptive, then it is *synchronic* as well as diachronic. Our framework differs from that of the ancient Greeks; yet it also differs, for instance, from that of extant hunter-gatherers. Once more, synchronic diversity can take the place of diachronic diversity. Historiography is only one source for recognizing diversity, the other being *cultural anthropology*. What is more, Wittgenstein and Quine have self-consciously raised the possibility of alternative frameworks by using *fictional* rather than actual anthropology, envisaging tribes that use elastic rulers or talk about undetached rabbit-parts rather than rabbits. This may even have the advantage that we can tailor the envisaged forms of speech and action to the philosophical problems under discussion.

Williams relies on a different argument for the need to look at the history of the framework. According to him, in the case of scientific concepts like that of an atom the question whether the same or a different concept is employed in different epochs and cultures does not matter much to 'what may puzzle us about that concept now (for much the same reason that the history of science is not part of science)'. Unfortunately, Williams does not divulge these reasons. Instead, he argues that the question *does* matter for some philosophically contested concepts, those that are intimately tied to human interaction and communication, like freedom, justice, truth and sincerity. In these cases it is imperative, he insists, to appreciate that their historical variants represent 'different interpretations' of a 'common core'. We may be able to understand that core through a functionalist reflection on the role these concepts fulfil in satisfying the demands of human life, as in fictions of a 'State of Nature' which purport to explain the emergence of ethical values, language or the State. Such a functional explanation is not *per se genetic*. It is one thing to know the function of an organ, another to know its evolutionary emergence. Similarly, one can reflect on the function of our concept of knowledge, without speculating about its origins. 'But', Williams continues, 'the State of Nature story already implies that there must be a further, real and historically dense story to be told'. Therefore we need a Nietzschean 'genealogy', a 'method that combines a representation of universal requirements through the fiction of a State of Nature with an account of real historical development' (2002b: 7). A genealogy is a 'narrative that tries to explain a cultural phenomenon by describing a way in which it came about, or could have come about, or might be imagined to have come about', given different circumstances (2002a: 20).

Within analytic philosophy, Kant's distinction between *quaestio facti* and *quaestio iuris* and the ensuing Neo-Kantian distinction between genesis and validity has fuelled a pervasive, if largely implicit, suspicion of the so-called 'genetic fallacy', the mistake of deducing claims about the *validity* of a theory or the *content* of a concept from information about its historical origins, including information about the causes of its emergence. Thus Frege granted that 'the historical perspective' has a certain justification, while insisting that one cannot divine the nature of numbers from psychological investigations into the way in which our thinking about numbers evolved (1884: Introduction).

Williams defends genealogy against the charge of a genetic fallacy. According to him it 'overlooks the possibility that the value in question may understand itself and present itself and claim authority for itself in terms which the genealogical story can undermine'. Thus liberal conceptions of morality, 'claimed to be the expression of a spirit that was higher, purer and more closely associated with reason, as well as transcending negative passions such as resentment', and hence a genealogy is capable of displaying them as 'self-deceived in this respect' (2002b: 7–9; see 2002a: 20–40, 224–6).

If Williams is right, one reason why history is essential to philosophy is that the genesis of certain concepts or beliefs is crucial to their content and validity. But he has not managed to dissipate the charge of a genetic fallacy. All he shows is this: *if* a practice, belief or mode of thought *defines* or *justifies itself* in terms of a particular origin, then that origin becomes relevant to its justification. The reason is *not* that there is after all no distinction between genesis on the one hand, content or validity on the other. Participants in the Catholic practice of ordination actually defend it by reference to the idea of apostolic succession, and hence to a particular origin. In other cases the genesis of a practice provides a reason for or against it even if it is not actually adduced, e.g. when a legal norm has not been adopted through proper procedures. Yet the investigation of either the actual or the best possible reasons is not *per se* genetic, it merely takes on a genetic aspect in specific cases.

Concepts like that of a sunburn or of lava are genetic in that they apply only to things with a certain origin. Even in these cases, however, it is not the history of the *concept itself* which is part of its content, but the history of its *instances*. To elucidate that content, philosophy only needs to note that historical dimension; unlike empirical disciplines which apply such concepts it does not have to examine the actual origin of potential candidates.

Most importantly, it is the *status quo alone* which determines whether a given concept is genetic or whether the actual or optimal justification of a belief or practice mentions its origins. Even if Williams is right in maintaining that liberal morality originally laid claim to superior breeding, this entails *neither* that its current proponents justify it in this manner *nor* that this is the best possible justification. If neither of these options holds, genealogy will be immaterial to the philosophical merits of liberal morality. And whether they hold depends exclusively on the present.[1]

Williams may be right to claim that some of our *specific* discursive practices are or should be based on genetic justifications or that some philosophically relevant concepts are genetic – indeed, the concept of analytic philosophy may itself be such a case (see ch. 8.3). Yet he has not provided a *general* reason why any philosophical reflection on a concept or belief should *require* either a historical or a fictional account of its emergence.

The absence of a general case for instrumental historicism should not come as a surprise. It is notoriously difficult to demonstrate for *any* specific method that it is *essential* to philosophy as such; some practitioners even believe that they can attain philosophical insights without rational argument (but see 6.5). Still, there remains a general case for weak historicism. The points raised by instrumental historicists may not be essential to

---

[1] Williams' own purportedly genealogical vindication of truthfulness does not presuppose any history, actual or invented. He considers a fictional State of Nature. But the net yield of the exercise is that a practice of acquiring true beliefs and sharing them with others is advantageous to social creatures, since it allows them to pool information that is not directly available to any one individual. Williams argues that this practice would be unstable unless its participants regarded accuracy and sincerity as good in their own rights. To this end he enriches the functional story by considering further aspects of the context of the practice, as well as potential threats to it. But the vindication relies purely on what would be beneficial for creatures with human capacities, limitations and requirements within various scenarios. It does not depend on how the creatures or the scenarios emerged. The philosophical case of *Truth and Truthfulness* is anthropological-cum-epistemological rather than historical.

philosophy, but they are certainly advantageous. The reason lies in the aforementioned difference between philosophy and empirical disciplines. Like other cognitive endeavours, philosophical understanding is a communal achievement. But given the partly *a priori* and conceptual nature of philosophy, and the combination of continuity and change in the relevant concepts, the community of ideas relevant to our contemporary philosophical problems is not exhausted by contemporaries. The problems, methods and theories of the past have not simply been superseded by empirical progress. As a result the endeavours of past thinkers remain a valuable source of inspiration, both positively and negatively.

Benefits attach not just to knowledge of past philosophical reflections, but also to knowledge of the evolution of our framework. For one thing, alternatives to our current framework that belong to our own history are more likely to be pertinent to issues we are concerned with, and are phrased in a language or idiom that we can understand without undertaking a special study. For another, certain previously dominant features of our own framework may have receded, and yet play an important role in our current philosophical puzzles. While in principle it is possible to retrieve these features from the current employment and function of these concepts, it may be easier to bring them into view by looking at earlier stages. Thus Anscombe (1958) and MacIntyre (1981) have suggested that some of our deontological concepts originally derived from the idea of a divine command. *If* they are right, it will help to explain why these concepts seem to lay claim to an authority which may appear puzzling from a secular perspective. Finally, if we are to profit from the philosophical reflections of the past, we must recognize conceptual differences and shifts concerning key terms.

3 ANACHRONISM VS ANTIQUARIANISM

There are strong arguments in favour of weak historicism, then, and this position is occupied by a majority of analytic philosophers. This leaves the second historicist protest: analytic philosophy is anachronistic, because it treats the figures of the past simply as if they were contemporaries whose ideas have an immediate connection to current preoccupations. According to Ayers, analytic philosophy pursues a 'programme of flattening the past into the present' (1978: 55). Hacking speaks of the 'pen-friend approach to the history of philosophy' (1984: 103), while Baker and Hacker accuse mainstream interpreters of treating Frege 'as an absent colleague, a contemporary fellow of Trinity on extended leave of absence' (1984: 4).

Some analytic philosophers have responded to the charge of *anachronism* with that of *antiquarianism*. Historicists, they would say, regard the history of philosophy as a museum which is to be treated with veneration rather than critical scrutiny. As a result their narratives are irrelevant to substantive philosophical problems, whatever their historical accuracy. In this vein Broad contrasts his own 'philosophical' approach to history with a 'historical and philological' one (1930: 2). The spirit of a history of ideas which brackets questions of philosophical truth and cogency was epitomized by Ross. After a lecture, the famous scholar was asked by a student whether Aristotle was right. He replied: 'My dear child, you must not ask me such questions. I merely try to find out what Aristotle thought. To find out whether what he thought is true or not is not my business but that of the philosophers' (quoted Künne 1990: 212). As this statement indicates, however, such a history of ideas leaves open the *philosophical* issues raised by the past. It should not come us a surprise, therefore, that analytic historians have gone beyond it. But they have moved in different directions.

One historiographical perspective with distinctive analytic echoes is what Passmore calls 'polemical' (1966: 226). Its ultimate aim is to expound the commentator's own views, and it thereby turns past thinkers into mouthpieces of contemporary views. In this vein, Broad suggests that scholarship is philosophically irrelevant. The only interest of our predecessors, he contends, is that 'the clash of their opinions may strike a light which will help us to avoid the mistakes into which they have fallen' (1930: 1–2).

The polemical approach invites an immediate objection. One cannot assess 'whether the old boy got anything right' unless one has established what his views were (Rorty *et al.* 1984: 10; also Baker 1988: xii; Rée 1978: 30). This point is well taken, however, by most analytic historians. The only way of avoiding it is to bracket questions of interpretation. In line with many authors after him, Broad declares that he is interested only in the answers to the substantive questions 'suggested' by previous authors. More recently, Kripke's discussion of Wittgenstein's rule-following considerations purports to provide an account of 'Wittgenstein's argument as it struck Kripke', rather than a faithful exegesis (1982: 5). In so far as it uses a past figure merely as a Rorschach spot for stimulating questions and ideas of an entirely non-historical kind, such an approach amounts to historiophobia by the backdoor.

A third analytic stance is doxography. It does not abstain from attributing views to figures of the past. At the same time, it rests content with comparing and contrasting positions, without fretting over chronological relations, lines of intellectual influence or the wider context. Dummett recounts a 'history of thought' – of propositions and arguments standing in abstract relations of support or conflict – rather than a 'history of thinkers' (1993: ch. 1). Such an account is committed to exegetical accuracy, yet in so far as it tells a developmental narrative at all, it is a fictional reconstruction from a contemporary or atemporal perspective. Thus Dummett, for all his assiduousness as a systematic thinker, had no scruples to speculate that Frege may have contributed to the demise of German Idealism, when the latter in fact preceded Frege's birth in 1848.[2]

To varying degrees, therefore, polemical, Rorschach and doxographical approaches invite the charge of anachronism. Fortunately, they do not exhaust the options for analytic historians. A majority of them favours what Passmore labels 'problematic histories' or the 'history of problems' approach. This approach is based on the aforementioned idea that philosophy has its roots in problems of a special kind, and that its history is an evolution of these problems and their solutions. Problematic historians ask questions like: Why were people exercised by certain problems, why did they utilize certain methods for tackling them, and why did they find certain solutions attractive?

Problematic history is by no means the prerogative of analytic philosophers. It was anticipated by Hegel and made explicit by Windelband (1892). But it has been especially congenial to analytic historians. On the one hand, problematic histories deal with the actual development of philosophy. On the other hand, they do so in a philosophical spirit. They seek to understand how these developments contributed to our present philosophical situation.

Problematic history has not been spared historicist fire. Krüger complains that it 'replaces genuine temporal development by a spurious present'. Its 'assumption of the persistence of problems is at odds with the claim that philosophy advances', to which it is also committed, and leaves it at a loss to explain the emergence of new problems. Furthermore, philosophical problems are not 'autonomous' but change along with the wider cultural and social *context* (1984: 81–5).

But problematic histories need not assume that philosophy inevitably progresses. Furthermore, progress does not rule out the persistence of problems. For it can consist in gaining a *better understanding of the problems* and of the options for dealing with them. Such an understanding is precisely one of the things that analytic philosophers have aspired to.

---

[2] 1973: 683. When the error was pointed out by Sluga, Dummett corrected it (1981: 71–2, 497).

Moore put philosophical difficulties down to 'the attempt to answer questions without first discovering precisely *what* question it is which you desire to answer' (1903: vi). And in a spirited plea for analytic philosophy, Beckermann notes that philosophical progress 'often amounts to the clarification rather than the solution of problems' (2004: 10; see also Kenny 2005).

Problematic history also allows for the gradual transformation of problems. After all, one of its concerns is precisely how the problems of the past evolved. Finally, it can acknowledge the embeddedness of philosophy. Analytic historians like Passmore, von Wright and Kenny are fully aware of the embeddedness of philosophy. Understanding a text properly often requires acquaintance with its cultural context.

One real bone of contention is whether it inevitably requires knowledge of external social factors, as historicists (Rée 1978: 30; Hylton 1990: 3) and sociologists of knowledge (Kusch 1995) suggest. What contextual features have what kind of relevance to interpretation is a moot question. In so far as it has a general answer, it depends on hermeneutic issues that historicists have tended to shirk (see section 4). It should be obvious that those aspects of the context which the author assumes to be familiar to readers or which concern tacit assumptions of her reasoning are more important than the economic conditions of the text's production. More generally, if we seek a philosophical understanding of the content of a text rather than a genetic (historical, sociological, psychological) explanation of its creation, there is a strong case for insisting that only those contextual features matter which the author herself could adduce in its explanation and defence (Skinner 1969: 28; Frede 1987: ix–xxvii; Engel 1997: 188–92).

The ultimate crux is whether embeddedness militates against an ambition which *is* central to analytic historians: to understand the past in order to derive substantive philosophical lessons (see Sorell and Rogers 2005: 3–4). While this ambition is compatible with acknowledging the impact of the context, it presupposes that there is also continuity across time. The problems, methods and solutions of a remote philosophical theory must be intelligible from a contemporary perspective, so that it is possible to assess the theory for its *trans-historical merits*. Context is important in understanding what claims a philosophical text propounds, but the validity of these claims is not relative to historical context.

By contrast, at least since Collingwood (1939: 69), historicists inside and outside the analytic camp have insisted that the views of the past can only be understood properly from within their own temporal context, not from the perspective of our current preoccupations and convictions. As a result,

Baker contends, 'attempts to pass judgement on the worth of philosophical positions *sub specie aeternitatis* are misconceived' (1988: xii). Rée inveighs against the idea of 'eternally available' philosophical problems or positions (1978: 12, 28). MacIntyre maintains that the 'sense of continuity' driving analytic historians is 'illusory'. There is insufficient 'agreement in concepts and standards to provide grounds for deciding between the rival and incompatible claims' of different 'modes of philosophical thought' (1984: 33–4). And Rorty summarizes this historicist relativism by claiming that different philosophical positions are incommensurable: they cannot be assessed objectively from a neutral standpoint (1979: ch. VII).

Incommensurability comes in two versions, semantic and epistemic. *Semantic* incommensurability has it that there is no objective standard because of semantic variance between the vocabularies of different theories. But *meaning variance* does not entail *translation failure*. There is no one-to-one correspondence between Russian and English colour terms, for instance, but this does not militate against compound translations such as 'light blue'. Even in more fraught cases, such as those familiar from scientific revolutions, nothing prevents followers of a theory T_2 from *modifying* their conceptual apparatus in order to gloss T_1, notably by introducing new terms or constructions based on their own vocabulary. It is a moot question whether such procedures always yield a perfect match between synonymous constructions. But even this kind of translation failure does not entail mutual *unintelligibility*, since proponents of T_2 can acquire the conceptual apparatus of T_1 without endorsing it. Aristotelians and Kantians who hold to the centrality of enduring particulars are capable of mastering the 'perdurantist' idiom of space-time worms, even if they regard it as derived and confusing. 'Aetna erupted' is not synonymous to 'Part of the life-long filament of space-time taken up by Aetna is an eruption'. Nevertheless, one cannot understand both sentences without realizing that they necessarily have the same truth-value. By this token, there is no semantic obstacle to comparing statements from different theories for their truth-value.

According to historicist relativism, the statements of a past philosopher cannot be transplanted from their original context into our contemporary idiom; for outside that context these statements no longer have the same content. Bennett, by contrast, is confident that 'we understand Kant only in proportion as we can say, clearly and in contemporary terms, what his problems were, which of them are still problems and what contribution Kant made to their solution' (1966: back cover). Ayers replies that we can only interpret a past thinker 'in his own terms' (1978: 54). Taken literally, this confines interpreters to the vocabulary of the author. The obvious difficulty is that this vocabulary is often unfamiliar to us. In such cases, Ayers' prescription obliges us to explain an obscure phrase, sentence or text in other, equally unfamiliar terms. But in order to understand a text properly we must be able to explain it in terms that are *intelligible to us*. It may be objected that we might render it intelligible by immersing ourselves in the old vocabulary, without being able to explicate it in our own. Alas, this leaves us with the mystifying suggestion that an individual could operate two distinct vocabularies *with* understanding, yet *without* any capacity to explain the terms of one in terms of the other to any degree. Even if the idea of such semantic schizophrenia is coherent, it should be the last resort in accounting for the relation between different theories.

In any event, semantic incommensurability is not a viable option for historicists. If the figures of the past were so alien that we could never comprehend them in contemporary terms, studying them would be futile. It should not come as a surprise, therefore, that even historicists ultimately grant semantic commensurability, at least when their own readings of the past are at stake (e.g. MacIntyre 1984: 42–3). Apparently the threat of incommensurability hangs like a thick fog over the history of our subject when it is approached by the rude searchlights of analytic philosophers, yet miraculously lifts when historicists cast an elegant glance on it.

Historicism must instead hinge on *epistemic* incommensurability. Thus for Rorty there is no vantage point from which one could adjudicate between philosophical positions from different periods, since there is no '*independent* test of accuracy of representation', no way of stepping outside of our belief system and conceptual apparatus as a whole and comparing it with reality (1991: 6).

As Baldwin points out, it is far from obvious that objective philosophical assessment requires such an incoherent feat (2001: 272–3). One alternative is to judge theories by their internal consistency and the extent to which they meet their own targets. At the same time epistemic incommensurability is susceptible to several objections. For one thing, its relativistic conclusion may be self-refuting, because it is implicitly committed to claiming a kind of correctness which it explicitly rejects (Engel 1997: 194). Consistent relativists would have to regard their own animadversions against analytic historiography as no more than the expression of a different *Zeitgeist*.

Moreover, from the fact that specific philosophical ideas must be understood before the background of a more or less extensive context, it does not follow that they can only be understood by *accepting* that context. We may acknowledge, for example, that a particular statement is intelligible, plausible or compelling given other assumptions accepted by the author. Yet this does not prevent us from questioning the statement, provided we have reasons to reject those assumptions. Conversely, we can criticize a claim which we may regard as correct on the grounds that it is incompatible with assumptions the author herself takes for granted. Either way, the need to reckon with context in no way removes the possibility of rational assessment.

Finally, as a stick with which to beat analytic historians incommensurability is question-begging. It assumes what the latter deny, namely that there is insufficient continuity for rational debate. Historicist relativists incline towards circular reasoning. On the one hand relativism is supposed to be a lesson from history; on the other hand that lesson will only be revealed to those who approach history in the right relativistic spirit. Hacking has drawn attention to the immediate way in which Descartes speaks to contemporary undergraduates (1984: 107–8). There is no reason to regard them as deluded. Descartes' claim that nothing in my experience indicates whether I am awake or dreaming must be understood historically, as a heuristic device aimed at laying foundations for a new positive science. But this in no way precludes its use as a sceptical argument. Nor does it prevent a rational confrontation between Descartes' claim and the counter claims of later epistemologists.

4 HERMENEUTIC EQUITY

There is no compelling argument against the analytic project of assessing ancient philosophical theories for their truth and cogency. In fact, the boot may be on the other foot. Far from being the only way of revealing the past, to abstain from judgement may even mean to conceal it. To understand his subject, the historian needs to have a genuine sense of what it is to be troubled by a philosophical problem, and to take a stance on it. The detached attitude prescribed and occasionally affected by historicists is at odds with the engaged attitude of most past philosophers. To refrain from praising or blaming their predecessors would not have occurred to them.

There is a further argument against philosophical abstinence. In the hermeneutic tradition we encounter a 'principle of equity' according to which a good interpretation of a text presumes that its author is rational, unless the opposite has been demonstrated. And in the analytic discussion of radical translation we find a 'principle of charity' according to which we should not translate utterances of an entirely alien language as being obviously false.

To the combatants in the historicism battle, such hermeneutic principles are a double-edged sword. On the one hand, they intertwine exegetical and substantive issues, by suggesting that we cannot as much as *understand* a text without taking a stance towards its claims. On the other hand, they threaten to open the substantive case only to shut it at once, since they seem to imply that the stance we must adopt is an *affirmative* one. Instead of favouring a hard-hitting analytic approach, this would give succour to the reverential attitude of traditionalist philosophy.

But how sharp is the sword anyway? Note first that the hermeneutic term 'equity' is superior to the analytic 'charity', since it avoids the suggestion that the interpreter needs to show some kind of – moral or cognitive – forbearance. Next, we must keep apart at least three dimensions of equity:

1 assuming that the expressed views are by-and-large true;
2 assuming that these views are by-and-large coherent;
3 assuming that the utterance/text is suited to the speaker's/author's purposes.

Some formulations of equity make it appear as if proper interpretation precludes the possibility of ascribing irrational views. In fact, however, equity demands only a *fallible presumption* of rationality, which can be defeated in any individual case. Its proponents insist on a 'supporting consensus' (Gadamer 1967: 104–5), a background of shared assumptions which enables disagreement in detail while ruling out 'massive error' (Davidson 1984b: 168–9).

Quine prohibits only the ascription of beliefs that are evident empirical falsehoods or explicit logical contradictions. Davidson, by contrast, occasionally applies charity 'across the board', to all types of beliefs, and entreats us to 'maximize agreement' with the interpretees. This procedure is forced upon us, he reckons, because in radical interpretation we neither know what the natives think nor what their utterances mean. Assuming that they believe what we do is the only way of solving this equation with two unknowns (1984b: xvii, 101, 136–7).

This kind of equity would indeed open the case of the substantive merits of a philosophical text only to shut it. But it is misguided. In normal 'domestic' communication – philosophical exchanges included – we rightly take for granted an agreement in the understanding of most expressions, an agreement which opens up the possibility of disagreeing in our beliefs. Even in radical interpretation the maximization of agreement is not inevitable; on the contrary, it would often lead to misinterpretation (Glock 2003a: 194–9). It is wrong to ascribe to people opinions we take to be correct even in cases in which there is no explanation of how they could have acquired them. Interpretations should ascribe beliefs that it is epistemically *plausible* for people to have, whether or not they coincide with ours.

A second argument for maximizing agreement concerns reference. It would be misguided to entertain the possibility that the beliefs of a subject about a topic X are *all and sundry* wrong; for in that case we have no longer any grounds for assuming that these views are indeed views about X. 'Too much attributed error risks depriving the subject of his subject matter' (Davidson 1984a: 18). This observation does not, however, support Davidson's stronger thesis that *most* of a subject's beliefs about X must be true, and that the errors we normally lumber our predecessors with are too massive:

... how clear are we that the ancients ... believed that the earth was flat? *This* earth? Well, this earth of ours is part of the solar system, a system partly identified by the fact that it is a gaggle of large, cool, solid bodies circling around a very large, hot star. If someone believes *none* of this about the earth, is it certain that it is the earth that he is thinking about? (1984b: 168)

'Yes!' is the correct, if unsolicited, answer to Davidson's rhetorical question. To be speaking about the earth one does not need to be right on the recherché scientific topics he mentions. All that is needed is an identification like: 'The vast body on which we are currently standing' or 'The body which comprises the continents and the oceans'. If someone points to the ground and says sincerely: 'We are currently standing on an enormous flat disk. If you continue moving in the same direction you'll eventually fall off the edge,' he clearly believes the earth to be flat, just as we believe it to be spherical.

Two of these general lessons apply directly to philosophical interpretation. First, we cannot simply maximize agreement, since it would be blatantly anachronistic to credit ancient texts with (actual or presumed) insights which became available only later. Secondly, the need to comprehend the background does not entail an obligation to adumbrate it. To understand Kant's *Critique of Pure Reason* fully requires a host of contextual knowledge, from details like the legal background of his term 'deduction' to the strategic tension between his surprisingly a prioristic conception of natural science on the one hand, and his surprisingly empiricist animadversions against metaphysics on the other. But an interpreter can avail herself of any part of this background without condoning it, and without averting her eyes from the aforementioned tension.

In other respects philosophical texts present a unique challenge. Philosophical disputes are of a very fundamental kind, yet without revolving around the basic observational errors that even moderate equity rules out. Often the disagreement – whether consciously or not – is not about the factual truths of empirical claims but about the understanding of particular concepts or terms. While we can take many terms for granted here, this does not hold for those which are philosophically contested in a particular passage. Accordingly, factual truth is largely irrelevant and conceptual truth cannot be taken for granted.

What about the second aspect of equity? There is a respectable case for holding that one cannot believe an *explicit* contradiction of the form 'p & $\sim p$'. If someone utters sentences of this form sincerely and without qualifying them (e.g. concerning time or respect) this is a criterion for his not having understood at least one of the terms involved, and therefore incompatible with his thereby expressing the alleged belief. If so, it is unclear how one *could* entertain a belief of this kind without undermining one's status as a rational agent and hence as a genuine subject of beliefs. Nevertheless, one can hold beliefs which *turn out* to be contradictory, i.e. which defy being spelled out in a coherent fashion.

When it comes to interpreting texts, even the ascription of explicit contradictions is not off limits. For a text is not an immediate expression of a single belief. It may rather manifest beliefs which the author held at different stages of composition. Because of inattention an author may also fail to recognize that a belief expressed on page X is incompatible with one expressed on page Y, or he may simply have committed a slip in writing down the text.

Such mishaps afflict even giants. Kant, for instance, calls the principle 'every alteration has its cause' a non-pure synthetic judgement *a priori* on B 3 of *The Critique of Pure Reason*, while according to B 5 it is a *pure* synthetic judgement *a priori*. Rather than impose elaborate revisions on the interpretation of the text, it is more equitable to diagnose an inconsistency. Indeed, in this case knowledge of the troubled genesis of the text should decrease our readiness to read deeper significance into some apparent inconsistencies. Commentators who believe that one must never ascribe inconsistent views to an author have, I suspect, never bothered to reread their own writings.

Similar considerations apply to the third aspect of equity. On occasion it is more equitable to regard a text as an obscure expression of the author's intended message, simply because the alternative would lumber it with views which are either mistaken or at odds with other parts of the corpus.

This goes to show that different aspects of equity can come into conflict, and that equity can never reign supreme, but must be tailored to text and author. At the end of the day we must weigh different considerations, based on our overall knowledge of the individual case.

We saw that in order to achieve more than a nominal understanding we need to relate the text to our terms, interests and beliefs. Now it emerges that we need not project most of our beliefs onto the interpretees. In conjunction these two points favour the critical engagement espoused by analytic historians. Perhaps the most striking formulation of this conjunction hails from Gadamer, however. On the one hand we must relate the text to our own concerns and convictions, on the other hand the text poses a challenge, in so far as its claims about the matter at issue are at variance with what we take to be the truth (1960: 286–90). The ideal result is a dialogue, a 'fusion of horizons'. The interpreter is open to the text precisely because she treats it as a philosophical challenge. She allows the text to question both her own understanding of it *and* her prejudgements about the matter at issue. The dialogue may either necessitate a revision of the interpretation, or of those prejudgements, or it may confirm the original attribution of error. In none of these cases can the interpreter simply ignore issues of truth and cogency.[3]

Resisting charity across the board makes room not just for counting the interpretees wrong. It may transpire that on some issues they not only hold *different* views, but that they are right and we are wrong! In approaching a foreign text or culture, we must keep in mind the possibility that we might have something to learn. That is one lesson of the hermeneutic tradition which its analytic admirers have yet to assimilate. But it is a lesson which chimes with the dominant attitudes and practices of analytic historians: we should learn from a text by taking it seriously as raising issues and evincing claims of substantive interest.

The historicist bracketing of such issues ultimately fails because philosophical texts make cognitive claims of a non-historical kind. Comprehension of these claims is aided by knowledge of the issues discussed. The idea that the history of a subject profits from remaining neutral as to the validity of the examined claims or even from ignorance about the subject matter of those claims is no more plausible with respect to philosophy than it is with respect to science. The alleged impudence of treating

---

[3] Mulligan (1991: 116) quite properly grumbles about a passage in which Gadamer forswears critical analysis of ancient texts. My point is that some of Gadamer's own hermeneutic principles point in the opposite direction.

philosophical texts *sub specie aeternitatis* in fact amounts to no more than this: analytic philosophers speak in their own voice, instead of constantly disavowing their own beliefs. Mindful of the difference between belief and truth they are also aware of the possibility that their beliefs will turn out to be false. And if they are historically conscious, and a rising number of them are, they will also be aware that reading a text from the past puts both the author and the interpreter to precisely this test.

In conclusion, neither historiophobia nor anachronism is a distinguishing feature of analytic philosophy. And in so far as many (though by no means all) analytic philosophers resist the excesses of historicism (intrinsic and instrumental historicism, historical relativism, undiscriminating charity), they are on the side of the angels.

CHAPTER 5

Doctrines and topics

Many readers will feel that up to this stage I have been beating about the bush. In so far as analytic philosophy constitutes a genuine philosophical movement, tradition or current, shouldn't its proponents be united by certain philosophical interests or views? It is high time to spare a thought for the rather obvious suggestion that analytic philosophy is characterized by certain topics and/or doctrines. We might call such topical or doctrinal conceptions of analytic philosophy 'material', to distinguish them from formal (methodological and stylistic) conceptions to be considered in the next chapter.

Philosophers have a notorious penchant for disagreement, and closer inspection tends to reveal diversity even within paradigmatic schools or movements. In the case of analytic philosophy, this general phenomenon is particularly pronounced. Most commentators would concur with Soames' denial that analytic philosophy is a 'highly cohesive school or approach to philosophy, with a set of tightly knit doctrines that define it' (2003: xii). Even with respect to specific currents, contemporary scholars go out of their way to stress that they involved greater variety than commonly assumed. Both Hacker (1996: 228–9) and Warnock (1998) point out that the label 'Oxford ordinary language philosophy' was only used by opponents, and that post-war Oxford philosophy did not constitute a uniform school. Similarly, historians of logical positivism maintain that it was not the monolithic philosophical faction of popular repute (Haller 1993; Uebel 1991). As we had occasion to observe (ch. 1.2), many analytic philosophers regard philosophical schools and -isms as intellectually unwholesome, since they smack of the kind of dogmatism that they would rather associate with their opponents.

As regards specific trends within analytic philosophy, however, protestations of diversity and heterodoxy must be taken with more than a pinch of salt. After all, the logical positivists self-consciously devised and applied labels to their own position: 'scientific philosophy', 'scientific world-view', 'logical positivism', 'logical empiricism', etc. They had their own societies (*Verein Ernst Mach* in Vienna, *Gesellschaft für Wissenschaftliche Philosophie* in Berlin), journals (*Erkenntnis*), series of publications (*Schriften zur Wissenschaftlichen Weltauffassung*) and conferences (especially on the Unity of Science). The Vienna Circle even had its own 'Manifesto' (Carnap, Neurath and Hahn 1929). The logical positivists also had their internal disputes and factions – notably what are now known as the left and the right wing of the Vienna Circle – as befits any proper philosophical school. Furthermore, their early writings abound with purple passages about common aims, convictions, and enemies, and about the need for collaboration and 'collective work' of the kind familiar from the natural sciences (1929: 6–7). What is more, during their heyday the logical positivists were indeed united in their rejection of metaphysics and of synthetic *a priori* knowledge, and in their commitment to empiricism and the unity of science.

With the possible exception of Austin, conceptual analysts did not aspire to scientific collaboration or to forming a cohesive group under a single philosophical banner. Nevertheless, they shared an *ésprit de corps* especially in their dealings with outsiders like the dreaded logical positivists and the despised continentals (see ch. 3.1). Furthermore, they shared some general views about the nature of philosophy. They were united in taking a linguistic turn, in distinguishing between philosophy and science, and in preferring analysis and paraphrase of the vernacular to the construction of artificial languages.

At present, there are countless schools and -isms within analytic philosophy, even if one leaves aside labels like 'California semantics' and 'right-wing Wittgensteinians' which are used pejoratively by opponents. Some -isms derive from the great pioneers and heroes. To name but a few, there are Wittgensteinians, New Wittgensteinians, Quineans, Sellarsians and Davidsonians. In addition, there are '-isms' of a more or less general kind: naturalism, physicalism, descriptivism and (semantic) anti-realism. There is also a crop of *neo*-isms (neo-Fregeans, neo-Russellians) and *quasi*-isms ('quasi-realism'), and some opponents of Hare's and Mackie's meta-ethical views proudly called themselves 'anti-noncognitivists'. In short, analytic philosophy has thrown up taxonomic labels to rival even the most baroque continental efforts. At least one group, which calls itself 'The Canberra Planners' and is based at the Australian National University, even publishes a *Credo* on the internet: < web.syr.edu/~dpnolan/philosophy/Credo (28.10.2004) > . The *Credo* professes, among other things: 'We believe in the substantial correctness of the doctrines of David Lewis about most things (except the nature of possible worlds).' It ends with 'Amen', as befits such outpourings of piety. Though tongue in cheek, this *Credo* nevertheless bears witness to the fact that some analytic philosophers feel the intellectual or emotional urge to subscribe publicly not just to a common set of *doxa* but also to a figurehead.

In so far as the image or self-image of analytic philosophy is determined by one or other of its various movements or schools, the idea of defining it by reference to topics or doctrines is strikingly plausible. The obvious problem is that analytic philosophy features *different* and often *warring* authors, schools, movements and doctrines. As a result, material definitions of analytic philosophy are too narrow. Nevertheless, it is worth teasing out their strengths and weaknesses, not least because some of them have been propagated by eminent practitioners and scholars.

Analytic philosophers are no strangers to controversy. Atomists line up against holists, theists against atheists and agnostics, materialists and realists against phenomenalists and idealists, utilitarians against deontologists and virtue theorists, conflicting theories of meaning and of the mind are cheaper by the dozen, and so on, and so forth. To be even remotely plausible, therefore, the purportedly defining doctrines must be suitably general and have implications for the method and self-image of philosophy. I shall discuss definitions of analytic philosophy by reference to four doctrines: the rejection of metaphysics (section 1), the linguistic turn (section 2), the division of labour between philosophy and science (section 3), and naturalism (section 4). The final section turns to the question of whether analytic philosophers are united by the exclusion of certain topics or an obsession with other topics.

I   THE CRUSADE AGAINST METAPHYSICS

The earliest doctrinal conception associates analytic philosophy with the repudiation of metaphysics. This view of analytic philosophy was quite common among early opponents, though they often referred to it under other labels, notably logical positivism, analysis and linguistic philosophy (Blanshard 1962; Lewis 1963). It persists to this day, especially on the continent (e.g. Müller and Halder 1979: 18; Hügli and Lübcke 1991: 35). As mentioned in chapter 3.5, the current division between analytic and continental philosophy was preceded by a division between analytic and *traditional* philosophy. Traditional philosophy was predominantly committed to the idea that metaphysics can provide us with distinctively philosophical insights into the nature of reality. To the traditionalist philosophers that keep the flag of traditional philosophy flying today, analytic philosophy still tends to be epitomized by the anti-metaphysical crusade of the logical positivists. Even continental philosophers without a brief for traditional metaphysics (Babich 2003) have scolded analytic philosophy for adopting a deflationary attitude that seeks to dissolve philosophical problems rather than to revel in their profundity.

The members of the Vienna Circle characterized their common outlook as a *Scientific World View*, as in the title of their manifesto (Carnap, Hahn and Neurath 1929). This scientific world-view conceives of science as the epitome of human rationality which would sweep away theology and metaphysics as the vestiges of the Dark Ages. The logical positivists regarded metaphysics as theology in disguise, and hence as an expression of super- stition or misguided artistic impulse. In truly Teutonic fashion, they fancied themselves in the role of 'storm-troopers of the anti-metaphysical and resolutely scientific school of research' (Frank 1935: 4). In their crusade against metaphysics, our Viennese storm troopers wielded three devastating weapons: the new logic of Frege and Russell, the *Tractatus* claim that all necessity is tautological, and the verificationist criterion of meaningfulness, which they derived from their contacts with Wittgenstein. In this vein, Carnap and Ayer complained that the Hegelian notion of the Absolute is a mere pseudo-concept. A sentence like 'Only the Absolute contains the truth as such' has no more literal or cognitive meaning than the sound-sequence 'Ab sur ah', since no experience could establish its truth or falsity. Similarly, Heidegger's pronouncements 'We know the Nothing' or 'The Nothing noths' are on a par with 'Caesar is and'. They violate the rules of logical syntax by treating the term 'nothing' – a logical quantifier which indicates the absence of things of a certain kind – as if it were the name of a particularly mysterious thing (Carnap 1932; Ayer 1936: 59).

But how could some of the most intelligent members of the human race – a self-image readily accepted by analytic and continental philosophers alike – mistake sheer gibberish for profound insights into the essence of reality? The positivists' answer to this question is equally striking, and it owes more than a passing debt to Nietzsche's *Lebensphilosophie* and his critique of metaphysics. Metaphysical statements have no cognitive mean- ing, since they are neither verifiable nor falsifiable. But they constitute a kind of 'conceptual poetry'. They express or arouse certain emotions, or a certain attitude towards life (*Lebensgefühl*). Unfortunately, they do so in a misleading and unsatisfactory way, because they clad these emotions or attitudes in the form of a statement about the essence of the world (Carnap 1963: 4; 1932: 78–80; Ayer 1936: 59–61; Schlick 1926: 158). Metaphysicians are 'misplaced poets', or 'musicians without musical talent'. Monistic metaphysicians are failed Mozarts, because they express a harmonious attitude to life, dualists are failed Beethovens, because they express a heroic attitude in an equally misguided fashion. What kind of metaphysics would a failed Vaughan Williams produce? The mind boggles!

In spite of his designated role as a supplier of arms, Wittgenstein disapproved of the war on metaphysics waged in his name. He criticized the logical positivists on the (justified) grounds that 'there was nothing new about abolishing metaphysics' (Nedo and Ranchetti 1983: 243). In conversations with members of the Vienna Circle Wittgenstein not only defended Schopenhauer, he even feigned to understand what Heidegger means by *Sein* and *Angst* (1979: 68; Carnap 1963: 26–7). Wittgenstein was alienated by the scientistic trajectory of the positivist overcoming of metaphysics. Nevertheless, he was officially hostile to all metaphysical statements both in the early and in the later work. To be sure, the *Tractatus* had maintained that there are metaphysical truths about the essential structure which language and the world must share. At the same time he maintained that these truths cannot be 'said' – meaningfully expressed in philosophical propositions – but are 'shown' by empirical propositions properly analysed. But this idea of an ineffable metaphysics stands in stark contrast to the metaphysical tradition. Furthermore, in his later work Wittgenstein abandoned the idiosyncratic idea of an ineffable metaphysics, *without* reinstating the more venerable project of effable metaphysics (Glock 1996: 330–6; Hacker 2001: chs. 4–5). Metaphysical theories, he continued to insist, are 'houses of cards' erected on linguistic confusions. They need to be torn down by bringing 'words back from their metaphysical to their everyday use', i.e. by reminding us of the way in which words are used outside of metaphysical discourse (1953: §§116–19).

To a lesser degree, the anti-metaphysical definition also covers the abstention from metaphysical claims practised by most Oxford philosophers. But that abstention was overcome, at least in name, by Strawson's descriptive metaphysics. Furthermore, the definition leaves out Moore and Russell, who explicitly espoused lavish metaphysical doctrines throughout their careers. While Russell welcomed the positivists' aspiration to make philosophy scientific through the use of logical analysis, he resisted their attacks on metaphysics (1940: 21, chs. 22 and 25; 1950).

At the same time, both Moore and Russell contributed to the ideas that inform the attack on metaphysics. Many philosophers of the past have disparaged the theories of their predecessors as false, unfounded or pointless. But the early Wittgenstein accused metaphysical theories of suffering from a more basic defect, namely that of being nonsensical. It is not just that they provide wrong answers, but that the questions they address are misguided questions to begin with (what the logical positivists called 'pseudo-questions'). This *critique of (non-)sense* was inspired by Moore's tactic of questioning the question: Moore tried to *dissolve* rather than answer questions which lead to misguided philosophical alternatives. It was also inspired by Russell's theory of types, which introduced a systematic dichotomy between propositions which are true or false and statements which are meaningless, although they may be impeccable as regards vocabulary and syntax (e.g. 1919: 137).

The idea that at least *some* metaphysical theories fail to make sense crops up earlier still. In the course of criticizing Fichte, Schelling and Hegel, Bolzano confesses that he doubts whether he has fathomed the correct meaning of these authors (1837: I §7), thereby anticipating scores of similarly ironical confessions of analytic philosophers. Even Frege's attitude to metaphysics is ambivalent. On the one hand, his philosophy of logic and mathematics commits him to weighty metaphysical claims about abstract objects. On the other hand, while he did not condemn metaphysics, he insisted that it should play second fiddle to logic. Logic can no more be based on a metaphysical foundation than on a psychological one, since it is presupposed in all other cognitive endeavours: 'I regard it as a failsafe sign of error if logic stands in need of metaphysics and psychology, disciplines which themselves require logical principles. After all, where is here the real foundation, on which everything rests? Or is it as in the case of Münchhausen, who pulled himself out of the bog by his own tuft?' (1893: XIX).

Even this minimal claim, however, is rejected by some contemporary analytic philosophers. One recurrent theme in recent publications is that metaphysics is not just legitimate but the most fundamental subject both inside and outside of philosophy. Disregarding Frege's reminder that, by its very definition, it is *logic* which investigates the principles of reasoning presupposed in *all* cognitive disciplines, Lowe maintains that metaphysics is 'the most fundamental form of rational inquiry' (1998: vi).

This change of fortune is particularly striking in the case of ontology. The logical positivists had denounced ontology as either trivial or meaningless. But attitudes changed from the fifties onward, in the wake of Quine's naturalistic conception of ontology. Instead of having a good laugh about Heidegger's 'The Nothing noths', analytic philosophers took up ontology themselves, and with a vengeance. The war cry that philosophy should concern itself with things instead of words, with reality instead of concepts, has gained wide currency (e.g. Wolterstorff 1970: xii;

Armstrong 1980: 37–9). Even today, most analytic philosophers would repudiate the idea that ontology investigates 'Being' or 'Nothing' as based on reification (but see Jubien 1997: 1; Jacquette 2002). Nevertheless, it is generally assumed that ontology deals with two problems which are more fundamental than those of epistemology, semantics and perhaps even logic (e.g. Laurence and MacDonald 1998: 3–4; cf. Glock 2003: ch. 2).

What kinds of things exist?

What is the nature or essence of these kinds?

While Quine's naturalistic conception of ontology rehabilitated the first question against logical positivism, the second question was reinstated against Quine by the Kripke-led revival of essentialism. As a result of both developments, most contemporary practitioners regard the earlier hostility to ontology and metaphysics as an infantile disorder of analytic philosophy. Putnam writes: 'while at one time (during the period of logical positivism) [analytic philosophy] was an anti-metaphysical movement, it has recently become the most pro-metaphysical movement on the world philosophical scene' (1992: 187). Although I do not know what alternatives he has in mind, I share his diagnosis. Many continental philosophers subscribe to the project of deconstructing metaphysics. And history has taught many traditionalist philosophers to respect metaphysical systems more for their ingenuity than for providing apodictic information about the nature of reality. The current analytic mainstream, by contrast, is confident that one last heave will get them to the bottom of things (see ch. 9.2). In short: hostility to metaphysics is absent both at the beginning of analytic philosophy and at present. Therefore it does not provide an acceptable characterization of the analytic movement, even though it fits important representatives between the wars.

2 LANGUAGE, CONTEXTUALISM AND ANTI-PSYCHOLOGISM

In the eyes of traditionalist philosophers, analytic philosophy is not just characterized negatively by the rejection of metaphysics, but positively by the idea that philosophy should turn into the logical or conceptual analysis of language. This reorientation towards language is often referred to as the 'linguistic turn' – following Rorty (1967) – or as the method of 'semantic ascent' – following Quine (1960: §56).

When twentieth-century philosophy is compared with its predecessors, an obsession with language does indeed emerge as one of its most striking features. For the most part, this phenomenon is greeted with hostile incredulity by external observers. Surely, they say, if philosophy is the profound and fundamental discipline which it has purported to be for more than two millennia, it must deal with something more serious than mere words, namely the things they stand for, and ultimately the essence of reality or of the human mind.[1]

This reaction is not confined to laymen and -women, but shared by many philosophers who are far removed from common sense. Indeed, Dummett has claimed that the concern with language is the elusive factor, long sought for in vain by Anglo-European conferences, which separates the phenomenological tradition on the continent founded by Husserl from Anglophone analytical philosophy. Dummett proposed the following 'succinct definition':

analytic philosophy is post-Fregean philosophy . . . we may characterize analytic philosophy as that which follows Frege in accepting that the philosophy of language is the foundation of the rest of the subject . . .

Only with Frege was the proper object of philosophy finally established: namely, first, that the goal of philosophy is the analysis of the structure of *thought*; secondly, that the study of *thought* is to be sharply distinguished from the study of the psychological process of thinking; and, finally, that the only proper method for analysing thought consists in the analysis of *language*. (1978: 441, 458)

Without the emphasis on Frege, the proposal reoccurs in *Origins of Analytical Philosophy*:

What distinguishes analytical philosophy, in its diverse manifestations, from other schools is the belief, first, that a philosophical account of thought can be obtained through a philosophical account of language, and, secondly, that a comprehensive account can only be so obtained . . . Analytical philosophy was born when the 'linguistic turn' was taken. (1993: 4–5, see chs. 2, 12–13)

Dummett contrasts analytic philosophy with the philosophy of thought – developed in Husserl's phenomenology – which retains the idea that philosophy should investigate thought, but claims that this investigation is independent of, and antecedent to, an understanding of language.

Dummett's definition has been tremendously influential, if perhaps more by way of provocation than inspiration (e.g. Williamson 2004). Most contemporary commentators reject the idea that a linguistic turn is the defining feature of analytic philosophy. But the idea continues to find favour, not least among those who, whether rightly or wrongly, would reject the label for themselves (see ch. 8.1). In assessing it, we must keep in

---

[1] Gellner's attack on Oxford philosophy (1959) provides an amusing, if unsophisticated, example.

mind that criticisms of Dummett to the effect that the linguistic turn leads philosophy astray (or even round the bend) are not to the current point. Our question is not whether taking a linguistic turn is necessary and/or sufficient for philosophical success, but whether it is necessary and/or sufficient for being an analytic philosopher.[2] It is imperative, moreover, to distinguish the different claims that make up the linguistic turn and hence analytic philosophy as portrayed by Dummett:

1 The basic task of philosophy is the analysis of the structure of thought.
2 The structure of thought must be distinguished from the structure of thinking.
3 The only proper way of analysing the structure of thought consists in analysing the structure of the linguistic expression of thought.
4 Consequently, the philosophy of language is the foundation of philosophy.
5 Central to the linguistic turn is contextualism, the idea that sentences are semantically prior to their components.

According to Dummett, the linguistic turn was first taken through Frege's famous 'context-principle' (Dummett 1993: 4–5). Similarly Kenny: 'If, therefore, analytic philosophy was born when the "linguistic turn" was taken, its birthday must be dated to the publication of *The Foundations of Arithmetic* in 1884, when Frege decided that the way to investigate the nature of number was to analyse sentences in which numerals occur' (1995: 211). As we shall see, Kenny's qualification concerning the link between analytic philosophy and the linguistic turn is sapient. What about the link between the linguistic turn and the context-principle?

Among Frege's 'fundamental principles' for the conduct of logical inquiry is not just 'always to separate sharply the logical from the psychological, the subjective from the objective', but also 'never to ask for the meaning of a word in isolation, but only in the context of a sentence'. Further on he adopts a strong restrictive context-principle: 'Only in the context of a proposition do words mean something' (1884: Pref. and §62).

In the wake of Frege, contextualist ideas of various types and strengths have been repeated by countless philosophers of language, Wittgenstein, Quine and Davidson pre-eminent among them (Glock 1996: 86–9; 2003a: 141–6). Contextualism and its more radical cousin holism constitute highly

---

[2] This disposes of those passages by Cohen (1986: 8, 12–34) in which he argues against the philosophical fecundity of the linguistic turn. As regards its claim to define analytic philosophy, Cohen objects that analytic philosophers couldn't disagree if they were merely concerned with language. As the philosophy of language makes depressingly clear, however, there is no reason to suppose that philosophers are more likely to reach consensus on language than on any other topic.

important strands within analytic philosophy. Nevertheless, it is problematic to tie either the linguistic turn or analytic philosophy to contextualism.

As Quine (1953: 37–42; 1981: 68–9) and Hacker (1996: 281) noted, the idea that 'the way to investigate X is to look at sentences in which "X" occurs' was first propounded in Bentham's theory of fictions (1817: App. IX), over fifty years before Frege's *Foundations*. More importantly, contextualism is neither necessary nor sufficient for taking a linguistic turn. The idea that the truth-apt whole is in some sense *prior* to its components can easily be transposed from a linguistic onto a mentalist or Platonist plane, from sentences and words to, respectively, judgements and concepts or propositions and concepts. Thus Kant famously (or not so famously, judging by analytic debates on contextualism) insisted that the sole function of concepts is to be used in judgements (*Critique of Pure Reason* B 92–3). Furthermore, it is possible to take a linguistic turn while endorsing an atomistic rather than a contextualist conception of meaning and language. This has been done by pre-analytic empiricists (see Quine 1981: 67–8). It is certain, moreover, that combining atomism and a linguistic turn would not disqualify someone from being an analytic philosopher.

Having dismissed the suggestion that contextualism is definitive of the linguistic turn, let us turn to the question of whether the linguistic turn is definitive of analytic philosophy. Dummett deserves credit not just for having reopened the debate about the nature of analytic philosophy, but also for drawing attention to the important role that the contrast between thought and language has played in its career. Taken with a pinch of salt, moreover, his four claims can be portrayed as central themes in early Wittgenstein, the logical positivists, Quine and Davidson. Even if one takes into account the scope of the canvas on which Dummett paints, however, his brush-strokes are inaccurate.

As regards (1), we can readily grant that thought is an important topic in the philosophy of mind. But why should it be *the* topic of philosophy as a whole? Now, according to (2), what (1) is driving at is not the process of thinking – goings-on in the minds of individuals – but thought in the sense of what is thought. This would mean that the fundamental task of philosophy is to analyse propositions. (2) has the merit of drawing attention to the role played by *anti-psychologism* in the formation of analytic philosophy. In spite of the revolutionary progress in the formal or technical aspects of logic, the nineteenth-century debate about the *nature* of logic proceeded on the traditional assumption that logic studies the *laws of thought*, laws of correct thinking and reasoning, as in the title of Boole's major work – *An Investigation of the Laws of Thought* (1854). What unites all psychologistic accounts of logic is the idea that these laws describe how human beings (by and large) think, their basic mental operations, and that they are determined by the nature of the human mind. By the same token, logic is ultimately a branch of psychology, as Mill insisted (1865: 245–6). Beyond this general consensus, however, psychologism comes in at least three different forms – transcendental, empiricist and naturalistic.

The former two are united in explaining logical laws by reference to *subjective* mental goings-on which are accessible to introspection. According to the empiricist version, the structures and operations of the mind are contingent on human nature, and to be investigated by empirical psychology (Mill, Erdmann). According to the transcendental version, they are immutable and necessary features without which experience would be unintelligible. Naturalistic psychologism agrees with the empiricist version on the empirical nature of logic-*qua*-psychology, but rejects its subjectivism and introspectivism. Thus the German naturalists followed Mill in maintaining that psychology rather than logic or metaphysics is the fundamental science (Czolbe 1855: 8). However, unlike the British empiricists, they conceived of psychology and experience in physiological terms, as concerning movements of the nervous system.

Against psychologism, Frege protested that logical laws do not describe how we actually think, but prescribe how 'one *should* think'. They are strictly necessary and objective laws of 'truth', not contingent laws of 'holdings-to-be-true' (1893: XV–XIX). Whereas psychology is an empirical science dealing with individual minds on the one hand, logic is an *a priori* discipline concerned with objective principles on the other. We must distinguish sharply between *thinking* as a subjective mental act or episode and a *thought* as the objective content of such an episode.

Anti-psychologism unites Frege with Bolzano, Moore, middle Russell, Wittgenstein and Carnap. The latter complains, for instance, that epistemology as hitherto practised is an 'unclear mixture of psychological and logical constituents' (1936b: 36). This does not vindicate (2), however. On the one hand, anti-psychologism is not a uniform feature of analytic philosophy. In fact, both its empiricist and its naturalistic streaks strongly tend towards psychologism. The account of meaning furnished by the later Russell was psychologistic. And while that account may have had little impact (Green 2001: 520–1), the opposite holds of Quine's naturalized epistemology. Yet this subject dissolves both epistemology and semantics into empirical psychology no less than the systems of Fries, Beneke, Mill and Hamilton. In fact, the lecture on which Quine's eponymous 'Epistemology Naturalized' was based originally had the sub-title 'The

Case for Psychologism' (Willard 1989: 287–8). To be sure, Quine avoids
the subjectivism of empiricist forms of psychologism, since the psychological basis of both knowledge and meaning is provided by intersubjectively accessible neural stimulations rather than private ideas or sense-data
(Glock 2003: 185–8). But this simply displays a physiological approach to
psychology itself, reminiscent of the German naturalists. In any event, a
majority of contemporary naturalists sympathize with the cognitive turn in
philosophy of language, philosophy of mind and the behavioural sciences;
and they rely heavily on the notion of a mental representation, conceived as
a phenomenon in the mind of individuals. As Smith points out, the 'earlier
aversion of analytic philosophers to psychology has been abandoned' in
'much contemporary work on logic and meaning in the field of cognitive
science' (1994: 189; also Willard 1989: 286–7).

On the other hand, anti-psychologism is not the preserve of analytic
philosophers. Husserl's *Logische Untersuchungen* is a *locus classicus* of anti-
psychologism. Husserl insists that logical laws, far from being reducible to
psychological regularities, 'belong to a theoretically closed round of abstract
truth, that cannot in any way be fitted into previously delimited theoretical
disciplines' (1900: 80, see also 76). Admittedly, this anti-psychologism may
have been influenced by Frege's criticism of Husserl's youthful *Philosophie
der Arithmetik*. Furthermore, *Logische Untersuchungen* can be portrayed as a
proto-analytic work by an Austrian philosopher who was later led down the
garden path (Mulligan 1990: 228–32). This is cold comfort for Dummett,
however, since claiming it for analytic philosophy is out of the question if
that label is tied to the linguistic turn specified in (3) and (4).

Furthermore, non-analytic opponents of psychologism were not confined to Husserl. It is popular to accuse Kant, Hegel and their various
nineteenth-century successors of confusing logic not just with metaphysics
and epistemology, but also with psychology (Kneale and Kneale 1984, 355;
Carl 1994: chs. 1–2; cf. Dipert 1998). There is some justice in this picture.
Kant's transcendental idealism treats the necessary preconditions of experience as features to which the objects of experience have to conform
because they are imposed on them by our cognitive apparatus in the course
of processing the incoming data. This transcendental psychology was one
of the main sources of nineteenth-century psychologistic logic (another
one being associationist and introspectionist psychology), because it suggests that the mind can underpin apparently necessary propositions in
logic, mathematics and metaphysics.

At the same time, Kant also inaugurated crucial anti-genetic and anti-
psychologistic modes of thought. What makes a belief *a priori* is not how

we acquire it, but rather how it can be verified. Furthermore, he distinguished between the question of how we acquire a certain kind of experience or belief (*quaestio facti*) and the question of what the logical and epistemological status of that experience or belief is (*quaestio iuris*). By the same token, he separated transcendental philosophy from 'empirical psychology', notably Locke's 'physiology of the human understanding' (see A 84–5/B 116–17; A ix; 1783: §21a). As regards logic, he insisted on the purity of *formal* logic – a term he coined, incidentally – separating it from psychology, metaphysics and anthropology.[3] Like Frege, he also insisted on the *topic-neutrality* and *normativity* of logical laws (B VIII; see Trendelenburg 1840: 35).

Kant inspired Lotze, Sigwart, Liebmann and the Southwest school of Neo-Kantianism, who in turn anticipated and influenced core tenets of Frege's anti-geneticism and anti-psychologism (Sluga 1997; Glock 1999b; Anderson 2005; cf. Dummett 1973: 676). They are united in the view that logic and epistemology are autonomous, distinct not just from psychology, but also from other natural sciences such as physiology. Thus Lotze (1874: 316–22) and Windelband (1884: I 24) distinguished explicitly between the genesis of our beliefs and their validity. While being (*Sein*) and genesis (*Genese*) are investigated by empirical science, investigating the validity of knowledge claims is the prerogative of philosophy (logic and epistemology). In the same breadth, these thinkers *separated* logic from natural science by insisting on its normative character, just as Frege did. Finally, they drew an increasingly pronounced distinction between the act of judging – what Frege calls a judgement – and the content of the judgement – what Frege calls a judgeable content or thought.

Anti-psychologism even extends to Hegelianism. The absolute idealists in Britain were no less adamant in rejecting any attempt to ground logic in mental operations than Moore and Russell (Hacker 1996: 5–6). What is more, Hegel himself had already complained about Kant's 'psychological idealism' (1816: II 227; see Aschenberg 1982: 61). And this is not simply disingenuous. Their image among analytic philosophers notwithstanding (e.g. Dummett 1973: 683), neither German nor British Idealism reduced reality to episodes in the minds of individuals. Instead, they insisted that reality is intelligible only because it is the manifestation of a divine spirit or rational principle. Though obviously problematic for other reasons, this

---

[3] In this respect Kant is close to Frege, and contrasts (favourably, in my view) with Bolzano, who saw fit to include under the heading of logic various methodological and pedagogic recipes, thereby making the subject 'dependent on psychology' (1837: I §§7–13).

position is entirely immune to Bolzano's and Frege's criticisms of *subjective* idealism and psychologism.

(1) can no more serve as a defining credo of analytic philosophy than (2). One counter-example is invoked by Williamson (2004: 108), namely philosophers of mind who reckon with non-conceptual representations that may not qualify as thought. But the investigation of non-conceptual mentality is compatible with what Williamson calls the 'representational turn' and what I have called the 'reflective turn' (1997b). It does not contradict the Kantian idea that philosophy is a second-order discipline which reflects on the way we represent reality, whether in language, conceptual thought or non-conceptual perception.

Other analytic philosophers reject that idea in all its manifestations. Throughout his career, Russell insisted that the fundamental task of philosophy is 'to understand the world as well as may be', rather than merely to analyse thought or language. Indeed, this was his heartfelt complaint against the later Wittgenstein and Oxford conceptual analysis. By his own admission, ahead of exposure to the early Wittgenstein, he was not interested in language and meaning, since he regarded them as 'transparent'. Logic is central to philosophy precisely because it is 'concerned with the real world just as truly as zoology, though with its more abstract and general features', because it provides an 'inventory' of 'the different forms that facts may have' (Russell 1959: 161, 108; 1919: 169; 1918: 216). Similarly for Moore, 'The first and most important problem of philosophy is: to give a general description of the *whole* universe' (1953: 1–2). Last but not least, there are numerous recent manifestations of such a view. They include all those who have taken an ontological turn and regard the metaphysical investigation of reality as philosophy's defining vocation, and they range from Quinean naturalists through Kripkean metaphysicians to Searle, who seeks a 'unified theory of reality' (2004).

In one passage, Dummett attributes to analytic philosophy the metaphysical aim of describing 'the most general structural features of reality', but through 'pure reflection, unaided by empirical investigation' and hence 'by extrapolating from the most general structural features of our thought or of our language'. 'It makes no difference whether language is taken to be prior to thought in the order of philosophical explanation, or thought to be prior to language. The former is the order of priority traditional in analytical philosophy indeed, until quite recently, a common mark of analytical philosophy' (1992: 133–4). According to Green, this defuses the threat posed to his definition by the indisputable fact that Moore and Russell were interested in the world rather than thought or language. For 'what Dummett means by an account of thought, is an account of the objects of our thoughts, or an account of the world about which we think', an account of 'the furniture of the universe about which we think and talk' (2001: 519–20).

But this defence trades on an equivocation between the *content* of our thinking and its *object*. The content of one of my long-standing beliefs is that Vesuvius is a volcano, its object is Vesuvius. Only the object, not the content, is part of 'the world about which we think'. Dummett's analysis of thought does not scrutinize the predominantly material objects that most of our thoughts are about, otherwise it would precisely have to be an empirical investigation. Rather, it analyses what contemporary philosophers are fond of calling the 'propositional content', what is thought by the subject and said by the sentence expressing the thought.

Green is correct in noting the parallel between Dummett's passage and analytic philosophers who contend or assume that analysing the contents of our thoughts or sentences can yield knowledge about the ultimate constituents of reality.[4] But she fails to notice that this is inconsistent with Dummett's original definition. According to (1), analysing thought is not a *method* for achieving metaphysical insights into reality, it is the intrinsic *goal* of analytic philosophy. This, in conjunction with (3), is supposed to provide the rationale for (4), the claim that the philosophy of language is the foundation of the subject, which Dummett treats as definitive of analytic philosophy.

Opponents to that claim include all those who regard the philosophy of language as a branch of the philosophy of mind. They also include thinkers ranging from Foot through Rawls to Williams who pursue moral and political theory without relying on a theory of meaning. Finally, and most decisively, they include paradigmatic proponents of a linguistic turn. According to the Vienna Circle *Manifesto*, the 'task of philosophical work' lies in 'clarification' of 'traditional philosophical problems' rather than in 'the propounding of special "philosophical pronouncements"' (1929: 8), pronouncements about language and meaning included. And Wittgenstein explicitly renounced the suggestion that the philosophy of language is the foundation of philosophy. The fundamental task of philosophy is not to investigate *either* thought *or* language, but to *resolve philosophical problems*, questions that seem intractable because they are

---

[4] For Russell, philosophy studies the logical form of propositions. Since there is a fundamental identity of structure between true propositions and facts, an inventory of the logical forms of propositions will reveal the essential structure of reality (1914: 33, 216–17; 1917: 75; 1918: 197, 216–17, 234).

not attributable to factual ignorance. By contrast to Dummett, he also denied that we have to clarify concepts like 'language' and 'meaning' before we can clarify other concepts (see Glock 1996: 247).

What if we concentrate on (3)? The weakened link between analytic philosophy and the linguistic turn would then run somewhat as follows: *in so far as* philosophy is concerned with the analysis of the content of thought, rather than the genesis of thinking, the constitution of reality or the tenability of moral principles, it does so by way of analysing the meaningful expression of thought.

Understood in a suitably loose way, this general approach is indeed taken by Wittgenstein and his followers, a majority of logical positivists and conceptual analysts, Quine, Davidson and, of course, Dummett himself. Ayer, for instance, once underpinned it by the blunt contention: 'The process of thought is not distinct from the expression of it' (1947: 25).

At the same time, this linguistic conception of thought is repudiated by many representatives of the contemporary mainstream in Anglophone philosophy. They reverse the order of explanatory priority between thought and language, reckon with the possibility of pre-linguistic thoughts and 'non-conceptual content', and hence regard the philosophy of language as secondary not just in terms of the ultimate goal but also in terms of the method of philosophy. Dummett himself acknowledges this for the Oxford philosophers Gareth Evans and Christoper Peacocke (1993: 11, 112). John Searle, Thomas Nagel and Colin McGinn also spring to mind, and so do Chisholm and Castañeda from a previous generation.

Dummett is prepared to bite the bullet of accepting that such philosophers no longer count as analytic. His unflinching stance has been defended, moreover, on the grounds that these thinkers simply indicate that, partly as a result of its enmeshment with cognitive science, analytic philosophy is losing its distinctive identity and heading for a rapprochement with phenomenology (Green 2001: 512–13, 526–8). The problem is far more wide-reaching, however.

The idea that thought is independent of and prior to language even in the order of analysis reaches back to the dawn of analytic philosophy. It is therefore imperative to distinguish between the *rise of analytic philosophy* on the one hand, its later *linguistic turn* on the other. As Dummett himself recognizes, 'the extrusion of thoughts from the mind' (1993: ch. 4) leads in the first instance to a Platonistic rather than linguistic conception of thoughts, one in which thoughts appear as abstract entities rather than as abstractions from what people say or could say. To Bolzano and Frege it seemed that the objectivity and necessity of logic can only be secured if its subject matter – propositions or thoughts – is resettled from the mental realm into an abstract third realm beyond space and time. Several scholars have argued that this Platonist conception prevented Frege, Dummett's analytic philosopher *par excellence*, from ever taking a linguistic turn (e.g. Baker and Hacker 1983). Frege regarded his semantic reflections as subservient to the logicist project (Sluga 1997), a project which is ultimately an epistemological one since it seeks to provide mathematics without secure foundations. To be sure, he showed considerable interest in natural languages and occasionally relied on ordinary grammar for constructing his formal system. He also regarded language as the only mirror of thoughts we have. But he put this down to limitations of human cognition rather than to the intrinsic nature of thoughts. Language is a distorting mirror, which is why the concept-script departs from ordinary language in order to mirror the structure of thought more faithfully. Logic should conduct a 'ceaseless struggle against ... those parts of grammar which fail to give untrammeled expression to what is logical'. 'It cannot be the task of logic to investigate language and determine what is contained in a linguistic expression. Someone who wants to learn logic from language is like an adult who wants to learn how to think from a child. When men created language, they were at the stage of childish pictorial thinking. Languages are not made so as to match logic's ruler' (1979: 6–7; 1980: 67–8).

In Russell's writings we encounter diverse statements on this issue. 'The study of grammar, in my opinion, is capable of throwing far more light on philosophical questions than is commonly supposed by philosophers. Although a grammatical distinction cannot be uncritically assumed to correspond to a genuine philosophical difference, yet the one is *prima facie* evidence for the other' (1903: 42). But he also held that the abstract nature of logic defeats natural languages. For 'ordinary language is rooted in a certain feeling about logic, a certain feeling that our primitive ancestors had' (1918: 234).

Moore was preoccupied with analysing or defining concepts; he regarded propositions and concepts as components of the world rather than of thought or language (1953: 1–2; 1899: 4–8). For this reason he sought *real* rather than *nominal* definitions of the analysanda. This is to say that he did not try to report the meaning of expressions (some of his later admirers among linguistic philosophers notwithstanding), but to scrutinize the elements of the concepts and propositions that they stand for. He distinguished sharply between establishing the verbal definition of a word and inspecting in the mind's eye the concept it denotes (1903: 6; 1942: 664; see Hacker 1997b).

It is correct that the logical atomism of middle Russell and early Wittgenstein revolves around the idea that logic has metaphysical implications because the structure of reality is identical with the structure of thought, just as for Kant epistemology has metaphysical implications because the structure of reality is identical with that of experience. But this is not tantamount to accepting the further identification of the structure of *propositions* with the structure of *sentences*, and the analysis of propositions with the analysis of language. By contrast to Frege, early Moore and Russell regarded propositions and concepts as immediate components of reality rather than senses of linguistic expressions, and their analysis had no intrinsic link to an analysis of language (Monk 1997: 47–50).

There remains a possible rejoinder on Dummett's behalf. The most striking dissidents from a linguistic approach to thought are either contemporaries or figures from the inception of analytic philosophy. But, one might argue, both the beginning and the end of a tradition constitute hard cases for any taxonomy, and hard cases make for bad law. Even if this response were legitimate, however, it would not solve another problem. Dummett's linguistic definition not only *excludes* paradigmatic analytic philosophers, whether they be early Platonists or late mentalists, it also *includes* paradigmatic continental philosophers. A work by Heidegger bears the title *On the Way to Language*. For better or worse, Heidegger's followers have reached that destination. The jargon of much current philosophy on the continent – notably of French post-structuralism – is taken not from metaphysics or psychology, but from linguistics and semiotics (Derrida 1967; Foucault 1973: 386; see Rorty 1982: xx). Moreover, the idea that human thought and experience are essentially linguistic is a commonplace among hermeneutic philosophers. Gadamer writes that 'Being that can be understood is language' (1960: 450; see also 1967: 19), and Ricoeur is well known for his aphorism 'the symbol sets us thinking' (quoted in Thiselton 1998).[5]

In fact, the dominant empiricist strand within analytic philosophy, forever obsessed with the raw given presented to individual minds (impressions, sense data, neural stimulations), seems less equipped to do justice to a complex intersubjective phenomenon like language than the hermeneutic tradition. In 1918, when German philosophers like Hamann, Herder, Humboldt, and Schleiermacher had been exploring the social and

---

[5] I leave aside the linguistic turn that critical theory took when Habermas got into the driving seat (e.g. 1979), since he and his friend Apel (1980) were inspired partly by analytic philosophy.

historical nature of linguistic understanding for over a hundred years, an analytic genius like Russell remained so obsessed with the idea that the meanings of words are private sense-data that he was capable of claiming that people 'would not be able to talk to each other unless they attached quite different meanings to their words' (1918: 195). Contrast Gadamer: 'Understanding is itself to be conceived not so much as an act of subjectivity but rather as a move into a place within the occurring tradition' (1960: Preface).

Mulligan (1991: 17–18) sounds a note of caution. Comparisons between the analytic and the continental turns to language are 'empty', he maintains, since they disregard the fact that the latter are embedded in various forms of (transcendental) idealism. In my view Nietzsche and Gadamer are clear exceptions to this claim. But if it were right, it would provide a different grist to my mill. For in that case the distinguishing feature of analytic philosophy is precisely not a preoccupation with language *per se*. But realism is equally unsuitable as a distinguishing feature. It is notoriously unclear what the realism/idealism contrast amounts to in any philosophical tradition. Furthermore, there is literally no form of idealism that has not been condoned by some analytic philosopher or other: from the transcendental solipsism of the *Tractatus* through the phenomenalism of Russell and the early Vienna Circle to Berkeleian idealism (Foster 1982), or from the verificationism of the positivists to Putnam's internal realism and Dummettian anti-realism.[6]

Let me end on a more positive note. We must distinguish the metaphilosophical theory and the philosophical practice of counter-examples to Dummett's definition. The latter owes its plausibility to the fact that philosophers can take a linguistic turn in their actual proceedings, without having endorsed it. Both Moore's analysis of concepts and Russell's reductive analysis in the theory of descriptions in effect operate at a linguistic level, in the former case by checking the definition of a term against commonly accepted views about its applicability, in the second case by paraphrasing sentences with the help of a novel notation. Indeed, even card-carrying mentalists like Fodor remain preoccupied with language and semiotic themes. This is no coincidence. First, the linguistic turn placed the nature of intentionality at the centre of philosophy. It thereby set the

---

[6] Cooper (1994) also demurs at crediting continentals with a linguistic turn. His reason is that they reject the analytic project of a theory of meaning which renders explicit a system of rules which is supposed to guide linguistic competence. But even if one can disregard Habermas' and Apel's acceptance of that project, some analytic philosophers are equally hostile to it. These include Wittgensteinians (Baker and Hacker 1984) as well as followers of Quine and the later Davidson (see Glock 2003a: ch. 8.4).

agenda for current theories of meaning and content. Even the linguistic approach to this agenda remains pertinent. Whether or not it is prior to thought, language provides the paradigmatic and clearest case of intentionality, and shapes the discussion of the latter. Secondly, when it comes to the philosophical elucidation of thought, not even the most ardent subjectivist can abstain from considering sentences. For it is through their linguistic expression alone that thoughts are amenable to intersubjective paraphrase and analysis into components. Thirdly, at least in practice most analytic philosophers concede not only that the analysis of concepts and the paraphrase of propositions constitutes an important *part* of philosophy (if perhaps a propaedeutic one); they also accept the connection between concepts and propositions on the one hand, and the meaning of words and sentences on the other. Finally, analytic philosophy is to a considerable extent informal logic – 'critical thinking' in the lingo of contemporary syllabi – applied to philosophical discourse. Yet when it comes to ascertaining the import of questions, the content of claims and the cogency of arguments, it is crucial to get clear about the precise meaning of the expressions in which those questions, claims and arguments are phrased.

Nevertheless, even though analytic philosophy continues willy-nilly to employ linguistic methods, the linguistic turn is not a *doctrine* to which all and only analytic philosophers subscribe.

3 PHILOSOPHY AND SCIENCE

A third group of doctrinal definitions revolves around the relationship between philosophy and science, in particular the natural sciences. But it is somewhat disconcerting to note that there are in fact two diametrically opposed accounts of how analytic philosophy views this relation.

According to one view, analytic philosophy subscribes to a Kantian-cum-Wittgensteinian distinction between the *a priori*, conceptual analysis of philosophy and the *a posteriori*, factual descriptions and explanations of science. This view is intimated by Hacker in passages which maintain that Quine challenges the analytic movement rather than forming a part of it.[7] It covers Wittgenstein and, in his wake, the conceptual analysis practised in Cambridge and later in Oxford. It also covers the official position of the Vienna Circle, which distinguished between science and philosophy and treated the latter as a second-order discipline that reflects on the 'logic of science'.

---

[7] 1996: xi, 195, ch. 1. Hacker's official account is a historical one: he regards analytic philosophy as a historical movement, though one which excludes Quine. See ch. 8.2–4.

But the idea of philosophy as qualitatively distinct from science fits neither the beginnings of analytic philosophy in Russell nor the current naturalistic mainstream. For Russell, as we have seen, philosophy is no less in the business of investigating reality than science. It deals with the most general and pervasive traits of reality. Russell also regarded philosophy as a proto-science, dealing with questions that are not yet amenable to the methods of empirical science. It struggles with a problem which may appear insoluble, until, as a result of philosophical progress and then scientific breakthrough, it can be taken over by a new empirical discipline which splits off from philosophy. Underlying both views is a hankering for 'scientific method in philosophy', one that ushers in a 'truly scientific philosophy' capable of the kind of piecemeal yet steady progress attained by the natural sciences (Russell 1903: xv, 3–11, 106; 1912: 90; 1914: ch. 2; 1925: 32).

According to Quine, proper or 'scientific philosophy' does not just emulate the methods of the deductive-nomological sciences; it is itself 'continuous with science', and in fact *part* of science. Quine wants to 'rub out or at least blur the distinction between philosophy and various sciences' (1970: 2; 1994: 57, 47, 51). But he provides diverse accounts of the role philosophy is to play within science. In some places he follows Locke's famous image of philosophy as an *underlabourer*: philosophy is a 'hand-maiden to science' with the task of 'tying up loose ends' such as paradoxes and questions of evidence, problems that working scientists tend to ignore. In others he is closer to the more flattering Aristotelian image of philosophy as the *queen* of the sciences. It deals with the 'general, basic concepts of science' such as truth, existence and necessity (1994: 57, 47–8). In more typical passages, he follows Russell and expresses the same view by reference to reality rather than concepts. Philosophy is concerned with 'a limning of the most general traits of reality'. It investigates the fundamental 'furniture of our universe', and differs from science only quantitatively, in the generality and breadth of its questions and categories (1960: 161, 254, 228–9, 275–6).

Hacker is aware, of course, that Quine's conception of analytic philo-sophy as continuous with science reverts in many respects to that of Russell. He maintains, however, that this does not militate against his conception of analytic philosophy on the grounds that this Russellian conception had lain dormant for forty years, and that Quine did not share Russell's account of logical analysis (1996: 319–20n). Both claims are contentious. Neither the American converts to logical positivism (Nagel, Morris) nor the strong anti-Wittgensteinian branch of the Vienna Circle led by Neurath sub-scribed to a demarcation between philosophy and science. Witness the following contrast. In 1930 Schlick wrote:

But what is [philosophy], then? Well, not a science indeed, but still something so great and significant that it may continue to be honoured henceforth, as in former days, as the queen of the sciences; for it is nowhere laid down that the queen of the sciences must herself also be a science. We now see in her ... not a system of knowledge but a system of *acts*; philosophy, in fact, is the activity whereby the *meaning* of statements is established or discovered. Philosophy elucidates propositions, science verifies them. (1979: II 157)

In 1931 Neurath responded:

All members of the Vienna Circle agree that there is no 'philosophy' with its own special statements. Some people, however, still wish to separate the discussions of the conceptual foundations of the sciences from the body of scientific work and allow this to continue as 'philosophizing'. Close reflexions show that even this separation is not feasible, and that the definition of concepts is part and parcel of the work of unified science. (1983: 52)

Furthermore, even if before Quine there had not been any subscribers to Russell's views on the relationship between philosophy and science, Russell's views were never remotely forgotten, even amongst those in thrall to his antipode Wittgenstein. They remained an indispensable point of reference for all analytic philosophers, even during the heyday of the distinction between philosophy and science between the 1930s and the 1960s. Indeed, Austin even shared Russell's image of philosophy as a proto-science:

In the history of human inquiry, philosophy has the place of the initial central sun, seminal and tumultuous: from time to time it throws off some portion of itself to take station as a science, a planet, cool and well regulated, progressing steadily towards a distant final state ... Is it not possible that the next century may see the birth, through the joint labours of philosophers, grammarians, and numerous other students of language, of a true and comprehensive *science of language*? Then we shall have rid ourselves of one more part of philosophy (there will still be plenty left) in the only way we ever can get rid of philosophy, by kicking it upstairs. (1970: 232)

This is precisely the kind of vision that drives current interdisciplinary efforts in cognitive science, in their case a vision inspired by Quinean naturalism.

The case for regarding Quine as emblematic of a particular strand of analytic philosophy is overwhelming. He is regarded as the most eminent analytic philosopher after Wittgenstein by a majority of those who regard themselves as analytic philosophers, including many who do not subscribe to his doctrines. Furthermore, Quine is explicitly preoccupied with logical analysis and paraphrase. Examples of it 'are legion in *Word and Object*', and just as Ramsey treated the theory of descriptions as a paradigm of philo-sophy, Quine does the same for the explication of the ordered pair (Hylton 1998: 50). Finally, Quine's logical analysis is quite close to Russell, not just in its instruments, notably the theory of descriptions, but also in one other respect (and here I disagree with Hylton). He strives to devise an ideal language or canonical notation which will display the real structure of reality, rather than, e.g., the disguised logical form underlying ordinary language.

Some academics, such as certain 'neuro-philosophers', take Quine liter-ally and try to solve philosophical problems directly through empirical investigations, in complete disregard of *a priori* and conceptual issues. There may be a case for insisting that they should no longer count as analytic philosophers, or even as philosophers *tout court*. But there is no gainsaying the fact that important analytic philosophers like Russell, Neurath and Quine have regarded philosophy as part of, or at any rate continuous with, science.

The second doctrinal definition based on the relationship between philosophy and science goes in the opposite direction of the first. It identifies analytic philosophy with naturalism. In the wake of Quine, few analytic philosophers these days would dare to publish a book on the philosophy of mind, without at least professing allegiance to some form of naturalism in the preface. Thus Jackson states: 'Most analytic philoso-phers describe themselves as naturalists' (2003: 32). Kim confines the point to the present: 'If current analytic philosophy can be said to have a philosophical ideology, it is, unquestionably, naturalism' (2003: 84). And Leiter (2004a: 5) diagnoses a 'naturalistic turn' in philosophy that rivals the earlier linguistic turn in importance. Nevertheless, to maintain that ana-lytic philosophy is essentially or even predominantly naturalistic is just as erroneous as to dissociate it from naturalism. Although there has been a notable swing towards naturalism in recent years, it has been resisted by eminent figures such as Strawson, Kripke, McDowell, Dummett and Putnam (see Putnam 1992: ix–x). But in order to appreciate the relation between analytic philosophy and naturalism we first require a more dis-cerning conception of the latter.

In 1954 Ernest Nagel observed: 'the number of distinguishable doctrines for which the word "naturalism" has been a counter in the history of philosophy is notorious' (1954: 3). This remark is even more apposite today (see Keil 2008). There are almost as many definitions of naturalism as there are proponents. Nevertheless, one can distinguish at least three different types of naturalism:

- Metaphilosophical naturalism claims that philosophy is a branch of or continuous with natural science;
- Epistemological naturalism is nothing other than scientism: it insists that there is no genuine knowledge outside natural science;
- Ontological naturalism denies that there is any realm other than the natural world of matter, energy, and spatio-temporal objects or events.

There are important connections between these positions. What counts as natural to ontological naturalism can be formulated through independent metaphysical criteria, e.g. as anything within the 'spatio-temporal-causal realm' (Katz 1990: 239; similarly Armstrong 1983: 82). This type of naturalism is a monistic position on what exists or is real. It is a version of materialism or, assuming that modern post-mechanistic physics allows for phenomena that are not material, a version of physicalism. Alternatively, what counts as natural can be explained epistemically, as comprising anything that features in scientific explanation as explanandum or explanans (Danto 1967: 448). In Sellars' famous words: 'in the dimension of describing and explaining the world, science is the measure of all things, of what is that it is, and of what is not that it is not' (1963: 173).

One reason why naturalists often prefer the second option (apart from the obvious one of insulating their ontological claims from direct philosophical criticism) is that it defuses a potential conflict between ontological and metaphilosophical naturalism. Instead of pronouncing on what exists *ex cathedra*, on the basis of *a priori* contemplation, naturalism follows the lead of science. The question of what exists turns into the question of what science reckons with. This idea goes back to Quine, whose naturalistic ontology rests on the conviction 'that it is within science itself, and not in some prior philosophy, that reality is to be identified and described' (1981: 21).

Metaphilosophical naturalism, for its part, is also known as 'methodological naturalism', since it concerns the topics, procedures and results of proper philosophizing, and entreats philosophers to emulate the methods of the special sciences (e.g. Maddy 1998: 161; Leiter 2001: 82–4). Metaphilosophical naturalists variously characterize philosophy either as *part* of science or as *continuous* with it. The first version is in play when Quine describes naturalized epistemology as a 'chapter of psychology and hence of natural science' (1969: 82; also Papineau 1993: 5). The second features when he writes: 'Naturalistic philosophy is continuous with natural science' (1995: 256–7).

It is natural to suppose that metaphilosophical naturalism is but the application of epistemological naturalism to the subject of philosophy.

This presupposes, however, that philosophy aspires to knowledge. Of course, many will exclaim in exasperation, though not without opposition from some analytic philosophers. As we have seen, the early Wittgenstein and Schlick rejected this cognitivist assumption. Indeed, they are committed to combining epistemological naturalism – the only propositions with sense and hence the only *candidates* for knowledge are those of empirical science – with metaphilosophical anti-naturalism – philosophy is an analytic activity rather than a doctrine and *a fortiori* distinct from science.

The question of what counts as science is a festering thorn in the side of epistemological naturalism. Its representatives hold that 'unqualified cognitive value resides in science and nothing else' or that 'science is the highest path to truth' (Moreland 1998: 37; Quine 1995: 261). But which academic disciplines are extolled and which are humbled by these verdicts? Hawks under the sway of the unity of science restrict science to the hard natural sciences, and in particular to physics, and allow other disciplines only in so far as their laws can be derived from those of physics. Doves, often of a pragmatist bent, welcome any discipline that is cognitively successful, including biology, psychology and even the social and historical sciences. There is a whole spectrum of possible stances here, and many naturalists waver between different locations on that spectrum (cf. Quine 1969: 24 and 2000: 411).

Finally, all versions of naturalism come in both an *eliminativist* and a *reductionist* form. Faced with apparent counter-examples – philosophical methods that do not rely on science, knowledge claims of a non-scientific kind or entities beyond the natural world – a naturalist has two options. She can either dismiss them as spurious or try to show that on closer scrutiny they boil down to a scientific or natural phenomenon. It is exclusively the reductionist option, however, which fuels the ubiquitous projects of *naturalizing* a certain phenomenon such as intentionality, meaning or morality. The aim of such an enterprise is to demonstrate that the phenomenon in question is real only because it is *really something else* (Fodor 1987: 98), namely something which is part of the natural order and can therefore be accommodated within science. By the same token, the discipline dealing with the phenomenon will be transformed into a branch of science that provides a causal explanation of it, e.g. psychology.

An obvious problem for a naturalistic definition of analytic philosophy is that each and every one of these tenets has been rejected by an illustrious and indeed paradigmatic specimen. As we have seen, rightly or wrongly an overwhelming majority of analytic philosophers before the 1980s repudiated the naturalization of morality, and their flag is kept flying by present-day Kantians and neo-intuitionists. The attempt to naturalize logic is nothing other than psychologism. That attempt was mocked by Frege: the causal 'explanation of a mental process that ends in taking something to be true, can never take the place of proving what is taken to be true'. We must distinguish between the causal conditions for holding a belief and the logical conditions for its truth, lest we think that the proof of Pythagoras' theorem might have to mention the phosphate content of our brain (1884: XVIII, 1979: 5; see Glock 1999b). Inspired by Frege, Geach does not mince his words on reductionist naturalism:

> When we hear of some new attempt to explain reasoning or language or choice naturalistically, we ought to react as if we were told someone had squared the circle or proved $\sqrt{2}$ to be rational: only the mildest curiosity is in order – how well has the fallacy been concealed? (1977: 52)

This unbridled hostility carries over directly to epistemic naturalism. The idea that there is no knowledge other than that of natural science was rejected by Frege – who pointed out the autonomy of logic and mathematics from *a posteriori* disciplines – greeted with incredulity by Moore – who insisted on the existence of non-scientific knowledge in ethics and common sense – and incensed the later Wittgenstein, who loathed the scientistic spirit of his age. It has provoked even a mild-mannered philosopher like Strawson to comment: 'From such philistinism as this we can only avert our eyes' (1997: 35; see also Dummett 2007: 10).

One important strand within continental philosophy, hermeneutics, resists epistemic naturalism by insisting that the methods of the human and social sciences are *sui generis*, revolving around understanding rather than the causal explanations of the deductive nomological sciences. And it is true that analytic philosophers, notably Hempel, have combated this methodological pluralism in the name of the unity of science. But the unity of science and its assimilation of the social to the natural sciences is not a hallmark of analytic philosophy (*pace* Mulligan 1991: 116, 119). There is also an analytic version of hermeneutics, and it covers not just Wittgensteinians like von Wright (1971) who contrast reasons and causes, but also Davidson (1980), who identifies them. A distinction between natural and social science is also drawn by Searle (1995).

There may be knowledge outside of science, yet *philosophy* might still be allocated a place within science, just as metaphilosophical naturalism has it. We must distinguish, however, between the idea that philosophy should emulate certain highly general ideals of modern science – such as precision, intersubjective scrutiny of results and collaboration – and the idea that it pursues the same goals and employs the same methods. This second claim is repudiated not just by the usual suspects – Wittgensteinians and conceptual analysts – but also by many who aim to philosophize in the scientific spirit of the first claim.

Frege not just denied that logic is a natural science; he also insisted that it is more fundamental than either metaphysics or psychology (1893: XIX). The Wittgensteinian idea that there should be a *division of labour* between science and philosophy was explicitly preached by Schlick and Waismann. In a more technical and science-oriented manner, this image is also evident in Carnap. Philosophy is not a doctrine consisting of propositions but a method, namely of logical analysis. Negatively, it reveals metaphysical nonsense. Positively, it turns into the 'logic of science', namely the linguistic analysis or explication of scientific propositions, concepts and methods (1937: 279). This demarcation of philosophy and science underlies Carnap's distinction between analytic and synthetic propositions in *The Logical Syntax of Language*, and his distinction between internal and external questions in 'Empiricism, Semantics and Ontology' (1956). He reasserted it late in life. Scientific philosophy is not philosophy that meddles in the scientific investigation of reality. Instead, it is philosophy that reflects on this investigation in the same rational and collaborative spirit as the one which guides the first-order explorations of the scientists themselves (1964: 133–4).

As regards the fundamental question of how philosophy stands to science, the front lines within the Vienna Circle ran neither between the 'right wing' conservatives (Schlick, Waismann) and the 'left wing' progressives (Neurath, Carnap, Hahn), nor between the phenomenalists (Schlick, early Carnap) and the physicalists (Neurath, later Carnap). It ran between the Wittgensteinians (Schlick, Waismann and Carnap) on the one hand, and Neurath on the other, who anticipated Quine's assimilation of philosophy to science.

We cannot salvage the idea of analytic philosophy as committed to metaphilosophical naturalism by restricting ourselves to the present, the way Kim does. Quine's repudiation of the analytic/synthetic distinction has won widespread approval, and numerous authors still appeal to what they take to be axiomatic wisdom. But there are also growing signs of dissent. Followers of Wittgenstein, Grice and Strawson still demur. Even in the USA, which has traditionally inclined towards naturalism, Carnap has undergone a revival. Thus Friedman has argued that a Carnapian distinction between analytic and synthetic propositions is called for rather than precluded by the attempt to make sense of natural science (1997). In addition, various forms of an analytic/synthetic distinction have been rehabilitated by thinkers as diverse as Boghossian, Putnam and McDowell. Indeed, though curiously ignored by acolytes, Quine himself came to recognize that there is a legitimate dichotomy between the analytic and the synthetic, one which approximates the intuitive conception of analyticity: 'a sentence is analytic if *everybody* learns that it is true by learning its words' (1974: 79; see Glock 2003a: 81–6). And the idea of philosophy as conceptual analysis has been defended in a novel fashion by Jackson (1998), notwithstanding his naturalistic sympathies.

Even if all analytic philosophers had jettisoned the analytic/synthetic distinction, this would only bar them from setting philosophy apart on the grounds that it aspires to or results in (non-obvious) analytic or conceptual truths. They could still demarcate philosophy from science along other lines. The most obvious one is the idea of philosophy being *a priori*. Combining epistemological and metaphilosophical naturalism, Devitt insists that 'there is only one way of knowing, the empirical way, that is the basis of science'; hence, 'from a naturalistic perspective, we should deny that there is *any* a priori knowledge' (1996: 2, 49).

For reasons already touched upon, however, this is actually a *minority* view in the career of analytic philosophy. Frege rejected the empiricist thesis that all knowledge is based on induction; while he did not deny Mill 'a spark of good sense', he deplored that it is 'no sooner lit than extinguished, thanks to his preconception that all knowledge is empirical' (1884: 9, §3n, 4n). Both Russell and Moore accepted the possibility of *a priori* knowledge and regarded philosophy as an *a priori* discipline. Dissent from Mill's claim that all knowledge is *a posteriori* was also the driving force behind the conventionalism of the logical positivists. Wittgenstein, conceptual analysis and their contemporary off-shoots all insist on the non-empirical character of logic, mathematics and philosophy.

Even some of their opponents are committed to *a priori* knowledge. Bonjour has recently rushed to the 'defense of pure reason' (1998), though not in a way that Kant would have appreciated. More significantly, Kripke and his numerous followers hold that some propositions – e.g. 'The standard metre is 1 metre long' are contingent yet *a priori*. Furthermore, their defence of *a posteriori* necessary propositions combines scientific discoveries, e.g. that water consists of H_2O molecules, with *a priori* reflections on the semantics of proper names and natural kind terms. More generally, there is widespread acceptance that post-Kripkean metaphysics features non-empirical problems, propositions and lines of reasoning at least among other things (Jackson 2003; Williamson 2004: 127–8).

Finally, Williams sets philosophy apart without appeal to either the analytic or the *a priori*, by insisting that it requires a humanistic and historical understanding absent from the natural sciences (2006).

The widespread impression that contemporary analytic philosophy, at least, is tied to metaphilosophical naturalism owes an unfortunate debt to intellectual salesmanship. Quine and his followers oppose the goal of a 'prior' or 'first philosophy' on the grounds that the natural sciences are 'fallible and corrigible but not answerable to any supra-scientific tribunal'. 'I see philosophy not as an *a priori* propaedeutic or groundwork for science, but as continuous with science' (1981: 72; 1969: 126).

Through this ploy they have managed to tarnish their opponents – linguistic philosophers like Wittgenstein, Carnap or Ryle – with the brush of two ideas that have apparently been consigned to the dustbin of history by the development of science. One is the Aristotelian doctrine according to which philosophy off its own bat provides the axioms from which the special sciences proceed. The other is the Cartesian quest for absolute certainty. But this is a caricature. What linguistic philosophers aspire to is not a super-science, one which provides mere science with unshakeable foundations, but a second-order discipline which deals with problems of a different – conceptual or methodological – kind. In fact, these reflections have predominantly resulted in a rejection both of the Aristotelian conception of philosophy as the queen of the sciences and of Cartesian foundationalism. At the same time, these two positions have also had followers within analytic philosophy. Foundationalists, for instance, range from Ayer through Chisholm to contemporaries like Alston, Audi and Sosa.

A naturalistic conception of analytic philosophy cannot be based on either the epistemological or the metaphilosophical variety. Ontological naturalism may seem a better bet. For many distinguished practitioners seek to steer a middle course between the Scylla of epistemological naturalism and the Charybdis of ontological *super*naturalism. Wittgenstein famously compared language to a game like chess. On the one hand, a chess-piece is a piece of wood that can be described by physics. On the other hand, one cannot explain what a chess-piece or what the game of chess is in purely physical terms. But the difference between a chess-piece and a simple piece of wood is not that the former is associated with an abstract entity or with a process in a separate mental realm. It is rather that the chess-piece has a role in a rule-guided practice (1953: §108).

Following Wittgenstein's analogy, contemporaries like Brandom, Hacker, McDowell and Putnam have developed the idea that human beings are special not because they are connected to a reality beyond the physical world of space, time and matter (a Platonist third realm or Cartesian soul substances, for example), but because they can only be adequately understood from a normative perspective, one that is alien to the natural sciences. There is knowledge outside of natural science, knowledge of language, logic and mathematics, for example. Yet the special status of such knowledge does not derive from a special subject matter – supernatural entities beyond space or time; it must instead be explained by reference to normative practices (speaking, reasoning, calculating). These practices in turn presuppose agents with distinctively human capacities. But while these capacities cannot be adequately characterized in physical terms, they do not transcend the natural world. They are perfectly intelligible features of animals of a unique kind; and their causal prerequisites and evolutionary emergence can be explained by science.

Without appealing to normativity, Davidson (1980: ch. 11) steers a parallel course. His anomalous monism is 'ontological monism coupled with conceptual dualism'. It tries to reconcile the naturalistic (anti-Platonist and anti-Cartesian) claim that there is no realm beyond the physical with a recognition that mental and semantic discourse is neither reducible to nor replaceable by the idiom of natural science. 'There are no such things as minds, but people have mental properties ... These properties are constantly changing, and such changes are mental events' (1994: 231).

Strawson distinguished a soft, catholic or liberal naturalism from a hard, strict or reductive one (1986: 1–2, 38–41). In the same spirit, McDowell distances his own 'naturalism of second nature' from 'bald naturalism' (1996: chs. IV–V), and Hornsby (1997) her 'naïve naturalism' from scientistic versions. This is indicative of a general trend among those opposed to scientism and reductionism, namely to distinguish between good (ontological) and bad (epistemological) types of naturalism. However, analytic philosophy also features important thinkers who resist the allure of both (see Corradini and Lowe 2006). To appreciate this one only needs to remember that ontological naturalism rules out at least three venerable positions – theism, Platonism and mind-body dualism. Neither a transcendent creator God, nor abstract entities beyond space and time, nor Cartesian souls, egos or selves are denizens of the spatio-temporal realm. There is a distinguished tradition of analytic theists, including Plantinga, van Inwagen and Swinburne. There is also the more specific yet equally flourishing enterprise of analytic Thomism.

Platonism was not just a guiding force in the emergence of analytic philosophy in Bolzano, Frege, Moore and Russell. It was also espoused by Church and Popper, among others. And it remains a live option to this day, for instance in neo-Fregeans like Wright (1983). Indeed, it is generally acknowledged that both full-blooded naturalists and proponents of the third way have their work cut out for them in accounting for logic and philosophy by way of either reduction or elimination. Even Quine, meta-philosophical naturalist *par excellence*, grudgingly admits abstract objects – namely classes – into his ontology, since they are indispensable to science and cannot be paraphrased away (1960: §§53–5). Mind-body substance dualism is in many respects the least popular branch of anti-naturalism. But even it has been vigorously defended by authors like Swinburne (1986) and Lowe (2000). Indeed, whether rightly or wrongly, the emerging consensus is that qualia may constitute a lethal stumbling block to physicalism (see Chalmers 1996; Kim 2004) and hence to ontological naturalism.

Even if we define naturalism disjunctively over all three of its main versions, important figures throughout the history of analytic philosophy would be excluded. Some characterizations go further still, transforming naturalism from a broad church into an all-encompassing one, fool-proof against threat from heathens and heretics. Thus Quine qualifies his onto-logical credo that 'the world is as natural science says it is' by adding the proviso 'insofar as natural science is right' (1992: 9). Ironically, this is analytic. To use Quine's own terminology, in this sentence the term 'natural science' does not occur essentially; it can be replaced by the name of any other entity capable of saying how the world is, whether it be 'Bush', 'astrology', or even, shock-horror, 'deconstructivism'.

Another famous naturalist described naturalism as guided by 'respect for the conclusions of natural science'; a second famous naturalist described it as 'less a philosophical system than a recognition of the impressive impli-cations of the physical and biological sciences', and declared 'We are all naturalists now.' Not unreasonably, given this minimalist conception. But as the son of that second naturalist observed: 'As for Naturalism. That, too, had negative overtones at home. It was as wishy-washy and ambiguous as Pragmatism. One could believe *almost* everything about the world and even *some* things about God, and yet be a Naturalist. What was needed was a new, nonreductive materialism'. The first naturalist was Dewey (1944: 2), the second R. W. Sellars (1922: i), and the third his son Wilfrid Sellars (1979: 2). Sellars junior is absolutely right to inveigh against a conception of naturalism which encompasses even theists – however tempted some contemporary theists may be to jump onto the naturalistic bandwagon. Furthermore, even if it were legitimate and fruitful to characterize naturalism in such an indiscriminating fashion, this would not salvage a naturalist definition of analytic philosophy. For Dewey, R. W. Sellars and those the latter referred to as 'we' were *not* analytic philosophers. They are excluded not just by common philosophical usage but also by any criterion that is even remotely plausible. The same goes for Nietzsche with a vengeance, his naturalistic leanings notwithstanding. 'Long live physics!', he enthused in *The Gay Science* (1882: §335).

4 TOPICAL DEFINITIONS

While accepting that analytic philosophers disagree even on fairly fundamental doctrines, some commentators maintain that they are united by the topics on which they disagree. Cohen (1986: 10–11, 57) may be alone in explicitly advancing a topical definition of analytic philosophy to be contrasted with doctrinal and methodological ones. But several authors characterize analytic philosophy in topical terms. It is even more common to find remarks such as these: 'John Searle was raised in the tradition of analytic philosophy, but he transcends that tradition. One reason is that he writes on a variety of topics even though his tradition encourages its supporters to focus narrowly on certain aspects of one or two topics' (Fotion 2000: 1).

One popular prejudice about analytic philosophy is that it tends to concern itself with a very narrow set of topics belonging to theoretical philosophy, in particular to (formal and philosophical) logic, philosophy of science, philosophy of language, metaphysics and philosophy of mind. The role of ethics and politics within analytic philosophy will be discussed in chapter 7. There we shall see that analytic philosophy has entirely overcome its relative neglect of moral and political theory between 1910 and 1960.

The case of aesthetics resembles that of ethics. Judgements of aesthetic value were regarded as bereft of cognitive content by both the logical positivists and the early Wittgenstein (1922: 6.42–6.421), and aesthetics was therefore restricted to the analysis of aesthetic concepts and the examination of the status of aesthetic statements. As in the parallel case of ethics, however, the proscription of first-order investigations was gradually lifted after World War II. And as regards second-order investigations, Wittgenstein's later ideas about family-resemblance initiated a lively debate about the very possibility of analysing or defining terms like 'art' and 'work of art' (see Davies 1998). Goodman's iconoclastic reflections on pictorial representation stimulated aesthetic debate of yet another kind (see Hyman 2006).

But there are other topics which, in the eyes of some, have been neglected by analytic philosophers and pursued instead by their rivals. Thus Passmore opines that 'Franco-German-Italian philosophy' has been 'centrally concerned with the issues which have preoccupied theology', while 'Anglo-American philosophy' devoted 'its attention to epistemology, mind and language' (1985: 11). As Cooper (1994: 3) points out, however, Passmore's own discussion of continental thinkers completely omits religion, and instead focuses on their views concerning – epistemology, mind and language! One might add that analytic philosophy has produced most of the twentieth century's leading philosophers of religion, figures as diverse as Kenny, Mackie, Phillips, Plantinga and Swinburne. Furthermore, philosophy of religion plays a much greater role in Anglo-American countries than on the continent. This is no coincidence, since religious convictions are much more widespread in the USA than in secular societies like France, Germany or Italy, and hence more liable to be a fulcrum of philosophical attention.

At the same time, Cooper himself claims two other distinctive interests for continental philosophy, namely the background condition of inquiry and the fall of the self. But both topoi have also featured in analytic philosophy. Different types of background conditions for knowledge have played a role in Wittgenstein's *On Certainty*, Quine's naturalized epistemology and Searle's theory of social reality. Even sociological background conditions have been popular themes in analytic philosophy since Kuhn and Feyerabend.

The idea that continental philosophy has a special love-hate relation to the self which is absent from analytic philosophy is *prima facie* more plausible, or at any rate more popular. Henrich, a leading German neo-Hegelian, informs us that 'continental philosophy takes the relation between the transcendental constitution of the person and the concept of philosophy as constitutive of philosophy, whereas empiricist philosophy tends to emphasize scientific and critical standards' (2003: 7). And in *Continental Philosophy since 1750: the Rise and Fall of the Self*, Solomon (1988) manages to portray philosophers on the continent – including even Kant and Husserl – as concerned mainly if not solely with inflating or deflating the sense of their own egos in accordance with their emotional needs and political foibles.

Though hardly an admirer of Post-Kantian continental philosophy, I am loathe to accept that it reduces to precisely this rigmarole. In any event, however, a concern with the problem of the self is definitely not the prerogative of the continentals. When it comes to attacking the 'self' as an illusion or fiction imposed by linguistic appearances, the tradition running from Wittgenstein and Russell through Ryle and Strawson to Dennett and Hacker is second to none. But there are also unflinching defenders of a metaphysical self (see G. Strawson 2005).

In general, after the war analytic philosophy became both more wide-spread and more catholic in its coverage. Exotic topics abound at recent APA meetings (Stroll 2000: 269–70). At present there is literally no area that has escaped the attention of analytic philosophers, whether it be the philosophy of the body and of sexuality (Soble 1998), eco-philosophy (Naess 1989), feminist epistemology (Alcoff and Potter 1993), the philosophy of computing (Floridi 2004), or psychoanalysis (Gardner 1993). For any significant area of human thought *x*, there is not just a *philosophy* of *x* but also an *analytic* philosophy of *x*. With respect to traditional and central areas, this analytic philosophy of *x* post-dated the traditional philosophy of *x*. Analytic theory of knowledge and analytic moral philosophy are obvious examples. But with respect to more peripheral or more recent topics, the analytic philosophy of *x* often came first, especially in the area of moral philosophy (see ch. 7.1).

Accordingly, the *exclusion* of certain topics is not a distinctive feature of analytic philosophy. What about the *emphasis* on other topics? For reasons mentioned in chapter 2.2, analytic philosophy arose in the context of discussions about mathematics and logic, and, to a lesser extent, discussions of natural science and psychology. The linguistic turn transformed its concern with these areas and linked it to an interest in language. And the revival of metaphysics and the turn to the mind transformed them once again. But an interest in these areas was never the prerogative of analytic philosophy. Science has been central to traditional philosophy and plays a role even in continental philosophy. And metaphysics has of course been a central part of philosophy throughout its history.

If analytic philosophy is characterized by a topic, it had better be more specific. Some historians have linked the analytic tradition to a very particular topic, one which we owe to Kant. Robert Hanna writes: 'The history of analytic philosophy from Frege to Quine is the history of the rise and fall of the concept of analyticity, whose origins and parameters both lie in Kant's first *Critique*' (2001: 121). The idea that analytic philosophy consists of predominantly hostile footnotes to Kant also emerges from Coffa (1991), in spite of his antipathy to Kant and Neo-Kantianism. It is a salutary reminder of Kant's importance to analytic philosophy.

The topic of analyticity is very important, because it is linked to the status of logical, mathematical and philosophical (metaphysical) propositions which plays such a dominant role in the early development of analytic philosophy. Hannah's pronouncement covers Frege, whose logicism is an answer to Kant's question of whether arithmetic is analytic. It also covers Wittgenstein, whose philosophy revolves in a very Kantian way around the connection between the nature of philosophy and the nature of necessity and a priority (Glock 1997a). Furthermore, it covers the logical positivists, who were just as obsessed with the possibility of synthetic *a priori* knowledge as Kant was, though they reached the opposite conclusion. Even Quine fits the picture. It is no coincidence that his revival of radical empiricism and naturalism proceeds through an attempt to undermine the analytic/synthetic distinction, and the associated distinction of *a priori* and *a posteriori* knowledge. The new Kripkean essentialism tries to undermine the Kantian dichotomies in yet another way. But in doing so it pays homage to the archetypal Kantian conundrum of how we might come by substantive knowledge about reality without the aid of experience.

At the same time, the importance of analyticity and the synthetic *a priori* must not be exaggerated. Though Moore and Russell on occasion employed versions of the analytic/synthetic distinction, their work did not revolve around it. The same goes for Cambridge analysis between the wars, and for much Oxford philosophy, especially for Austin. The characterization also excludes a lot of post-positivist and post-Quinean analytic philosophy in the metaphysical vein, which has moved beyond these topics, if only by treating Quine's attack on the analytic/synthetic distinction as axiomatic. Finally, in the ever expanding field of moral and political theory, the analytic/synthetic distinction has never played a central role.

What is correct is this. There is a more general Kantian problem, namely whether, and if so how, philosophy can be conceived as an autonomous discipline distinct from the empirical sciences. And this problem has loomed large in the work of most analytic philosophers who have engaged in metaphilosophical reflections. But not all analytic philosophers are given to such reflections.

Conversely, a preoccupation with analyticity and the synthetic *a priori* would include much of early continental philosophy. Both the Neo-Kantians and Husserl were profoundly concerned with the possibility of synthetic *a priori* knowledge. As mentioned before, the Neo-Kantian position provided the starting point for leading logical positivists such as Schlick, Reichenbach and Carnap. Furthermore, Husserl's extended list of synthetic judgements *a priori* constituted a major challenge for both Wittgenstein (1979) and the logical positivists, who discussed examples like 'Nothing can be red and green all over at the same time' *ad nauseam*. And the more general Kantian problem about the status of philosophy vis-à-vis science plays an even more pervasive role in continental philosophy (see Critchley 2001).

Cohen's topical definition faces the same obstacles. He defines analytic philosophy as the *Dialogue of Reason*, which is to say that it is 'the reasoned investigation of reasons', 'the reasoned discussion of what can be a reason for what' (1986: 49–50, 57). Cohen struggles valiantly to show that this covers not just analytic philosophy's discussion of scepticism, the paradoxes and the theory of action, but also, e.g., its preoccupation with meaning and the mind-body issue. But he relies on at least two questionable manoeuvres. The first is to move from the observation that a certain topic of analytic philosophy is connected to reason to the conclusion that it is *au fond* reason itself that is the focus of interest. For instance, he observes that the analysis of concepts often specifies conditions for the application of words, and draws the conclusion that concepts are of interest to analytic philosophy only because of the reasons for their application. The second manoeuvre is to observe that analytic philosophy aspires to tackle a topic like the mind-body problem in a *rational manner*, and to conclude from this that its real interest is 'to investigate how we can reason coherently on such issues' (1986: 51). Yet there is an obvious difference between the all too common discussion of how the mind is related to the body and the much rarer metaphilosophical discussion of how that issue is to be tackled.

Cohen is alive to the converse problem that a preoccupation with reason is a rather ostentatious feature of *non*-analytic philosophers such as Hegel. In excluding such cases he ultimately relies on a feature which is already explicit in his definition, namely that analytic philosophy is a *reasoned* investigation of reason. That only goes to show one thing, however. In spite of his explicit rejection of methodological conceptions, Cohen's own definition is not a purely topical one, but instead involves a methodological aspect, a reference to how any given topic is to be approached. And it is to such definitions that we must now turn.

CHAPTER 6

Method and style

In the last chapter we considered the most straightforward way of defining a philosophical movement, material definitions in terms of shared doctrines or interests. We found that this is not a viable option in the case of analytic philosophy. To some commentators, this negative result casts doubt on the very idea that analytic philosophy is a distinctive phenomenon. Thus Aaron Preston insists that analytic philosophy *must* be definable by adherence to a certain doctrine or 'theory', or else relinquish its claim to count among the 'philosophical groups ("schools," "movements," or whatever)' (2004: 445–6; see also Preston 2007; de Gaynesford 2006: 21). Preston concedes that there is an 'ordinary', 'precritical, or unprecisified concept of analytic philosophy', according to which it is first, 'a school of philosophy that now exists', and, secondly, one that originated around the turn of the twentieth century. He thinks, however, that this ordinary concept is just as vacuous as that of a witch. Since there is no common doctrine uniting the people normally classified as analytic philosophers, 'there is no such thing as analytic philosophy is ordinarily conceived to be', and it makes scant sense to continue to talk about analytic philosophy (2004: 453–9).

A different reaction is more plausible: if our concept of analytic philosophy does not capture a single set of doctrines, perhaps it captures *something else*. Preston rejects this option *ab initio*. His argument in effect runs as follows:

P₁ A school requires that there should be 'defining criteria' for membership in it.

P₂ To use 'philosophical' as a 'differentia' for a school, implies that the defining criteria for that school 'have to do with philosophy'.

P₃ Philosophy is a 'theoretical discipline', i.e. in the business of advancing theories.

C The defining criteria of a philosophical school must be acceptance of a certain theory.

As we have seen, P₃ would not be accepted by Wittgenstein and many of his followers. Furthermore, *pace* Preston it makes sense to distinguish between a closely knit philosophical school and looser groupings such as movements or traditions (see ch. 8.3). Even if his argument were sound, therefore, analytic philosophy might still be a respectable taxon. In any event, however, the argument is fallacious. From P_3 it follows only that when it comes to distinguishing philosophical schools *in general* from schools of a *non-theoretical* kind, for example schools of painting or musical composition, one must mention their aim of advancing *some theory or other*. It does not follow that *individual* schools *within* philosophy must be defined by adherence to a *specific* theory. One might just as well reason that different schools of representational art must be distinguished by the sorts of things they depict, simply because pictorial art in general is defined as art that depicts things (i.e. has depicting things as one of its differentia).

Accordingly, even if all philosophical schools, movements or traditions had to aspire to theories, individual schools would not have to be united by acceptance of a theory; they could just as well be held together by adherence to a certain method for arriving at theories. Given the colourful diversity of positions and interests within the analytic movement, definitions that are methodological or stylistic promise a way of avoiding the narrowness of doctrinal and topical definitions. Furthermore, they capture an idea cherished by many contemporaries who have given up on analytic philosophy's early promises of providing lasting and definitive solutions or dissolutions of philosophical problems: essential to analytic philosophy is the *value of the process* rather than the *durability of the result*. Nevertheless, it will transpire that these formal definitions tend to be too wide, and that they suffer from other shortcomings as well.

A blindingly obvious suggestion is to take seriously the 'analytic' in 'analytic philosophy', and to define the movement as one that pursues philosophy as analysis. In section 1 I shall argue that this proposal is both too narrow and too wide, even though it is less out in either direction than some of the material definitions discussed in the previous chapter. Section 2 turns to the idea that analytic philosophy is guided by an interest in science and imbued with a scientific ethos, in contrast to the continental orientation towards art and the humanities. It turns out that this proposal does not fit paradigmatic representatives of the analytic movement throughout its progression. In section 3 I discuss and reject assorted specific features of method and style that have been used to characterize analytic philosophy, notably the idea that it proceeds in a piecemeal fashion. Section 4 turns to the view that analytic philosophy stands head and shoulder above its rivals by dint of its superior clarity. I find myself compelled to conclude that the achievement or even the pursuit of a clear style is no longer a hallmark of analytic philosophy. The fact that some non-analytic authors are perfectly capable of clear writing is less unfortunate, but equally damaging to the proposed definition. This leaves the suggestion that analytic philosophy aspires to a more fundamental type of clarity, one of thought rather than linguistic expression. That idea leads to a *prima facie* attractive rationalistic conception of analytic philosophy, according to which its defining feature is its ambition to resolve philosophical problems through the use of arguments (section 5). Surprisingly, however, this definition does not even include all analytic philosophers, since some of them attach little importance to argument. And if it is weakened to cover any philosopher who occasionally employs arguments of some kind or other, it makes analytic philosophy co-extensive with philosophy as such.

1   PUTTING ANALYSIS BACK INTO ANALYTIC PHILOSOPHY

Many contemporary explanations of what analytic philosophy is are curiously silent on the issue of analysis. Yet the idea of putting the idea of analysis back into the definition of analytic philosophy is hardly far-fetched. Predictably, it also has quite a few adherents. For instance, having criticized Dummett's linguistic definition for barring Russell from being an analytic philosopher, Monk emphatically insists that Russell must qualify because he believed in the overriding value and importance of analysis (1997: 49–50). Similarly, in his excellent survey of conceptions of analysis, Beaney writes: 'If anything characterizes "analytic" philosophy, then it is presumably the emphasis placed on analysis.' He recognizes that 'such a characterization says nothing that would distinguish analytic philosophy from much of what preceded it', simply because various types of analysis have played a central role since the dawn of the subject'. Nevertheless, Beaney concludes:

analytic philosophy should really be seen as a set of interlocking subtraditions held together by a shared repertoire of conceptions of analysis upon which individual philosophers draw in different ways. (Beaney 2003)

The idea is *prima facie* compelling: analytic philosophy is tied to analysis, and its undeniable diversity is owed to diverse though largely overlapping conceptions of that single unifying method. But there remains a daunting obstacle to defining analytic philosophy as that kind of philosophy which employs the method of analysis. The term analysis and its cognates pervade the whole history of our subject. To be sure, Hegel and his followers purport to overcome both analysis and synthesis by incorporating it in the dialectic method. But many other non-analytic philosophers and movements have promoted or pursued analysis of a kind which has strong affinities with procedures popular among analytic philosophers. Under this rubric one would for a minimum have to include the Socratic quest for definitions, Descartes' search for simple natures, the empiricists' psychological resolution of complex ideas and Kant's 'transcendental' analysis of our cognitive capacities.

To do service in a definition of analytic philosophy, therefore, the notion of analysis needs to be severely constrained. Unfortunately, even *within* the context of the analytic tradition, 'analysis' signifies not just diverse but often incompatible procedures. None of these forms of analysis is accepted by all analytic philosophers, and some of them can also be found outside of analytic philosophy. The only gloss of the notion of analysis which would capture all commonly recognized analytic philosophers is so general, it includes any sustained philosophical investigation of a specific subject matter.

It is both common and natural to understand the term 'analytic' *au pied de la lettre*, namely as referring to a decomposition of complex phenomena into simpler constituents (e.g. Monk 1997: 41–50; Hacker 1996: 3–4; 1997b: 56). It is a contentious issue whether this ever was Frege's aspiration. He arguably countenanced the possibility of alternative analyses of one and the same proposition (Baker and Hacker 1983: ch. 6; Kenny 1995: 15–16; Beaney 2003; cf. Dummett 1981: ch. 17). A simple proposition like

(1) Uranium is heavier than lead

can be analysed either as the value of the function *x is heavier than lead* for the argument Uranium or as the value of the function *uranium is heavier than x* for the argument lead. This sets Frege's position apart from classical paradigms of philosophical analysis such as Descartes and the British empiricists, but also from the logical analysis of Leibniz, Russell and the early Wittgenstein. In some respects it prefigures the non-reductive type of analysis which prevailed in mid-century conceptual analysis.

On the other hand, decompositional analysis was at the forefront of Moore's project. He tried to define complex concepts in terms of simpler ones, up to the point at which one has reached indefinable simple notions like goodness. The decompositional project also fuelled the endeavours of the logical atomists. Admittedly, in the first instance their *logical* analysis amounts to a *paraphrase* of *propositions*, a translation into an interpreted formal language, rather than a decomposition of *concepts*. But this paraphrase involves a breakdown of complexes into their simple components.

According to the logical atomists, many apparent components of ordinary propositions – such as ordinary proper names or definite descriptions – turn out to be incomplete symbols that can be paraphrased away in context. At the same time, however, analysis is expected to progress towards an ultimate level. The components of propositions fully analysed are logical or semantic atoms – signs which resist further analysis and which are immune to referential failure. And these signs stand either for metaphysical atoms, the basic and ultimate components of reality, as in the *Tractatus*, or for sense-data the existence of which cannot be doubted, as in Russell.

Sticking to the *Tractatus* version, we set out by paraphrasing a sentence like

(2) Excalibur stands in the corner

along the lines of Russell's theory of description: 'Excalibur' is replaced by a definite description – e.g. 'King Arthur's sword' – which in turn is paraphrased as an incomplete symbol through quantifiers and concept-words. Thus we get

(2') There is one and only one x which is a sword of King Arthur, and that x stands in the corner.

This is only the beginning, since both King Arthur and the corner are themselves complex, entities with parts. 'Every statement about a complex can be resolved into a statement about their constituents and into those propositions that describe the complex completely' (Wittgenstein 1922: 2.0201, 3.24; see Glock 1996: 203–8, 269–74). The complex is described completely by specifying its constituents and the way in which they are related. A complex consists e.g. of a component a standing in the relation R to another component b. A proposition which ascribes a property to it – '$\Phi[aRb]$' – comes out as 'Φa & Φb & aRb'. By this token, (2) is analysed into

(2*) The blade is in the corner & The hilt is in the corner & The blade is fixed in the hilt.

Even this is not the end of the matter. For both the blade and the hilt are themselves complex and need to be decomposed analytically. Ultimately we need to analyse (2) into logically independent elementary propositions which consist of simple signs immune to referential failure because their referents are indestructible metaphysical atoms.

Decomposition plays a role in reductive analysis more generally, even though the components need not necessarily be indefinable concepts as in Moore or logico-metaphysical atoms as in Russell and the *Tractatus*. The decompositional aspect is obvious in the case of metaphysical or new-level analysis, whether it be of the Cambridge or the Viennese variety. Here the ambition is that analysis will unmask the ultimate constituents of propositions, and thereby the primitive elements of the 'facts' that they represent. Even when such analysis remains agnostic on the question of whether analysis ever reaches a bedrock of unanalysable notions or entities, it remains committed to the idea that complex concepts or entities can be broken down into simpler and ontologically more basic ones.

New-level analysis runs into serious difficulties, and not just if it is tied to the atomistic mirage of necessarily existent entities. Attempts to analyse all empirical propositions into those about sense-data foundered: the occurrence of sense-data is neither necessary for the presence of a material object, since we may fail to perceive an object even under favourable conditions, nor sufficient, because of the possibility of illusion and hallucination. Even the apparently innocuous new-level analysis of

(3) Every economist is fallible

as

(3') Adam Smith is fallible & Paul Ricardo is fallible & Maynard Keynes is fallible, etc.

presents problems. As Black (1933) pointed out, (3) and (3') do not mean the same, unless 'means' here merely amounts to 'entails'. Furthermore, analysis cannot even display the entailed propositions without prior knowledge of the name of every economist. The correct analysis, according to Black, is instead:

(3*) $\forall x$ (x is an economist $\rightarrow$ x is fallible).

But this is a logical analysis of structure rather than a metaphysical uncovering of more basic facts or entities.

Such same-level analysis still purports to rephrase propositions into their 'correct' logical form, the one they really possess underneath their misleading grammatical surface. This idea remains a guiding theme in contemporary theories of meaning. Such theories detect a hidden logical structure in all sentences of natural languages, and they credit ordinary speakers with knowledge of a formal system. In Davidsonian truth-conditional semantics, for instance, that system tends to be the predicate calculus, the whole predicate calculus, and nothing but the predicate calculus.

In retreating from logical atomism, Wittgenstein repudiated both the decompositional and the formal aspect of his earlier vision. In 1929 he condemned Moore's 'hellish idea' that it takes analysis to find out what our humdrum propositions like (2) or (3) mean (1979: 129–30; see 1953: §§60–4). Even if Excalibur has ultimate constituents and we are capable of discovering them, this will contribute to our knowledge of its physical make-up, rather than to our understanding of the sense of (2). Wittgenstein insists that there are no 'surprises' or 'discoveries' in logic and semantics, since he rejects the idea that speakers have *tacit knowledge* of a complex formal calculus or arcane logical forms (1953: §§126–9). A 'correct logical point of view' (1922: 4.1213) is achieved not through a quasi-geological excavation, but through a quasi-geographical overview, which displays features of our linguistic practice that lie open to view. Philosophical analysis cannot reveal the hidden constituents of language, and in this respect analysis is *toto caelo* different from chemical analysis. Insofar as it is legitimate, it either amounts to the description of the rule-guided use of philosophically contested expressions, or to the substitution of one kind of notation by another, less misleading one (1979: 45–7; 1953: §§90–2).

When he wrote 'Systematically Misleading Expressions' (1932), Ryle assumed that every statement had an underlying logical form that was to be exhibited in its 'correct' formulation. Later he denied that there is a logical form to be discovered underneath the surface of ordinary language (Rorty 1967: 305). Yet he did not abandon the underlying motivation – to show what is wrong with misleading expressions. The aim of analysis is no longer to discover a hidden structure, but to avoid the philosophical problems generated by misleading features of grammatical form. In *The Concept of Mind* Ryle sought to overcome what he called the 'category-mistake' involved in talk of the mind as a kind of thing. His ambition was to 'rectify the logical geography of the knowledge which we already possess' (1949: 9). But this amounted to spelling out rules and conceptual connections ordinary speakers are capable of recognizing, rather than novel discoveries concerning either the world or arcane logical systems underlying linguistic competence.

In a similar vein Strawson (1952) argued at length that the predicate calculus – the weapon of choice for previous logical analysts – does not reveal the true structure of ordinary discourse. The gulf between the truth-functional connectives and their vernacular correlates is wider than commonly accepted. Similarly, by trying to paraphrase away singular referring expressions, Russell's theory of descriptions misconstrues their distinctive role, which is to pick out the things we talk about. The subtlety and variety of ordinary language is mangled by the Procrustean bed of formal logic, and the latter is not a sufficient instrument for revealing all the structural (logical) features of a natural language.[1]

Accordingly, Wittgensteinians and Oxford conceptual analysis reject the idea that propositions have ultimate components or even a definite structure. As a result, analysis in their hand means neither decomposition into ultimate or more basic components nor logical paraphrase. Instead, it means the explanation of concepts and the description of conceptual connections by way of implication, presupposition and exclusion. This activity still qualifies as 'connective analysis' in Strawson's sense (1992: ch. 2). But as Strawson himself points out, the term 'analysis' is misleading in so far as this procedure is no longer analogous to chemical analysis, and it might be more apposite to speak of 'elucidation' instead.

In its heyday in the 1950s and 1960s, many conceptual analysts emulated Moore's decompositional analysis in one important respect. Although they did not regard concepts as constituents of reality, they sought analytic definitions of them, definitions that specify individually necessary and jointly sufficient conditions for the application of the terms which express the concepts. This ambition has been waning. To take the most spectacular case, following Gettier's classic criticism of the tri-partite definition of 'knowledge' as 'justified true belief', the current tendency is to forego an analytic definition and to focus more on the role of the concept of knowledge in our practices (Hanfling 2000: ch. 6; Craig 1990). The specification of necessary and sufficient conditions is no longer regarded as the only or even primary aim of conceptual analysis, especially in the case of concepts such as 'knowledge', which are complex and fiercely contested.

Decompositional and logical analysis do not even capture the self-image of all ideal language philosophers. The idea of a breakdown into ultimate components and of a real logical form should be anathema to strict Quineans, on account of their faith in the indeterminacy of meaning and the inscrutability of reference. For Quine, there is no fact of the matter as to whether the terms of a natural language refer, for instance, to animals or undetached animal parts. Unlike Davidson, Quine denies that natural languages are *au fond* really structured by the predicate calculus. Indeed, in one respect the idea of real components and a real logical form sits uneasily with the whole project of logical constructionism. In that strand of

---

[1] Russell (1957) summarily dismissed this criticism on the grounds that he was not interested in natural languages. But Strawson's case did concern vernacular sentences like 'The King of France is bald', to which, after all, Russell himself had applied the theory of descriptions. Later Strawson (1971: chs. 2–5) further argued that *any* language must possess genuinely referring definite descriptions.

analytic philosophy, analysis is not the decomposition of a given complex into its components; rather, it is an act of *construction*. Thus for both Carnap and Quine analysis means 'logical explication'. The objective is not to provide a synonym of the *analysandum*, or even an expression with the same necessary and sufficient conditions of application. Nor is it to identify the true constituents and form which it possesses underneath the grammatical surface. It is rather to furnish an alternative expression or construction which serves the cognitive purposes of the original equally well, while avoiding its scientific or philosophical drawbacks (Quine 1960: 224, §§33, 53–4).

There may be a vague notion of analysis which still fits all of these cases: certain kinds of sentential paraphrase, formal or informal, still play a central role, and so do considerations about the applicability or non-applicability of concepts to certain cases. But not even these procedures cover all recent analytic philosophers. Neither conceptual elucidation nor sentential paraphrase play a prominent role in some contemporary practitioners of moral philosophy and moral psychology. Harry Frankfurt and Williams, for instance, count as analytic philosophers. Nonetheless, the only sense in which they *analyse* phenomena like motivation or truthfulness is so general, it also includes a large chunk of the activities pursued by non-analytic philosophers.[2] For in this catholic sense, to analyse X means nothing more specific than to provide a sustained examination of X (whether it be philosophical or scientific). Nietzsche's genealogy of morality passes this test on precisely the same grounds as that of Williams.

To this one might still respond that analytic philosophy is simply *analysis in the twentieth century* (with perhaps a few decades added on at the start). But non-analytic thinkers of the twentieth century are equally included. Husserl and his disciples specialized in 'phenomenological analysis' (1900: II 7). And even an arch-bogey of analytic philosophy like Heidegger pursued an 'ontological analysis' or 'analytic of Being', which is supposed to reveal the meaning of existence (1927: 14–15). Consequently, while weightier and more specific notions of analysis no longer cover the whole range of analytic philosophy, the less demanding and wider notions

---

[2] Thus Strawson operates with both a very specific and a very wide notion of analysis. On the one hand he repudiates atomistic and reductive analysis, and qualifies his own advocacy of connective analysis on the grounds that it 'might be better to use the word "elucidation" rather than "analysis", since the latter so strongly suggests the dismantling model' (1992: 19). On the other hand he maintains that there is a more comprehensive sense of analysis, which covers 'any systematic account of a problem-situation' (1995: 17).

are too indiscriminating. Analysis, therefore, cannot be used to define analytic philosophy.

2 THE SCIENTIFIC SPIRIT

Our second methodological definition is not as obvious as the first, but equally popular. It associates analytic philosophy with the scientific spirit. Thus Wang defines analytic philosophy as 'science centered', and contrasts it with the 'art centered' philosophy of Wittgenstein:

Unlike Russell, Carnap and Quine, Wittgenstein is art centered rather than science centered and seems to have a different underlying motive for his study of philosophy. (1986: 75; similarly Lurie 1997)

This proposal is more general than the naturalistic one discussed in chapter 5.3. It is compatible with the view that philosophy is neither part of nor continuous with the natural sciences, in the sense that it does not have the same task, namely the study of the natural world, but functions as a second-order discipline.

The idea is that any philosophical investigation, even a second-order logical or conceptual one, should proceed in a scientific spirit, guided by the same ethos and methodological principles. This is what Rorty has in mind when he contrasts the 'scientific' style of analytic philosophy with the 'literary' style of continental philosophy: "'scientific" now means something like "argumentative"', rather than the truly scientific discipline that Reichenbach had hoped for (1982: 220). Quinton conceives of analytic philosophy in similar terms, even though his evaluation of it, unlike Rorty's, is unequivocally enthusiastic: analytic philosophers 'think and write in the analytic spirit, respectful of science, both as a paradigm of reasonable belief and in conformity with its argumentative rigour, clarity, and its determination to be objective' (1995a: 30).

The proposal that analytic philosophy is scientific philosophy in this more relaxed sense is corroborated by many paradigmatic specimen. There is Russell's mission to introduce 'scientific method' into philosophy. Combating what he regarded as wrong-headed and woolly manifestations of irrationalism – Bradley's idealism, James' pragmatism and Bergson's evolutionism – Russell wrote:

A truly scientific philosophy will be more humble, more piecemeal, more arduous, offering less glitter of outward mirage to flatter fallacious hopes, but more indifferent to fate, and more capable of accepting the world without the tyrannous imposition of our human and temporary demands. (1925: 37)

By the same token, logical atomism represents

the same kind of advance as was introduced into physics by Galileo: the substitution of piecemeal, detailed, and verifiable results for large untested generalities
recommended only by a certain appeal to imagination. (1914: 14)

Next, there is the worship of science as the epitome of human knowledge
practised even by those logical positivists who distinguished philosophy
from science. Thus they often spoke of their philosophy as 'scientific
philosophy', in order to signify that it tried to emulate the precision and
cooperative nature of science:

over the years a growing uniformity appeared; this too was a result of the specifically scientific attitude: 'What can be said at all, can be said clearly' (Wittgenstein);
if there are differences of opinion, it is in the end possible to agree, and therefore agreement is demanded. It became increasingly clear that a position not
only free from metaphysics, but opposed to metaphysics was the common goal
of all. (Carnap, Hahn and Neurath 1929: 6; see also Reichenbach 1951)

Wittgenstein was neither amused nor flattered by being turned into a
'leading representative of the scientific world-view' (Carnap, Hahn and
Neurath 1929: 20). His famous 'The philosopher is not a citizen of a
community of ideas. That is what makes him a philosopher' (1967: §455)
was an excessive reaction to the equally excessive intellectual collectivism
propagated and often practised by the logical positivists in the name of
science.

Nevertheless, Wittgenstein's attitude to science was more complex than
Wang, among others, supposes (Glock 2001: 213–14). He had a background
in engineering and an abiding interest in certain kinds of scientific investigation, namely those that appealed to his craving for conceptual clarity.
Furthermore, one must distinguish Wittgenstein's personal ideology and
his philosophical methodology. The latter rejects not science but *scientism*,
the imperialist tendencies of scientific thinking which result from the idea
that science is the measure of all things. Wittgenstein insists that *philosophy*
cannot adopt the tasks and methods of science. There should be a *division
of labour* between science and philosophy's second-order reflection on our
conceptual apparatus, a division that is difficult to uphold given the
twentieth-century obsession with science.

Still, Wang is right to think that Wittgenstein's philosophy is not science
centred. Wittgenstein was personally hostile to the scientific spirit of the
twentieth century. He loathed the belief in progress and the 'idol worship'
of science, which he regarded as both a symptom and a cause of cultural
decline. He also declared:

I may find scientific questions interesting, but they rarely grip me. Only *conceptual* and *aesthetic* questions do that. At bottom, I am indifferent to the solution of scientific problems, but not the other sort. (1980: 79)

The fact that a science centred definition would exclude Wittgenstein might be regarded as irrelevant or even welcome. For there is an ongoing debate about whether Wittgenstein was a *bona fide* member of the analytic tradition. In one corner, Hacker has made out a powerful case for regarding him as the moving force behind analytic philosophy in the twentieth century. In the other corner, there has been a proliferation of non-analytic interpretations, most recently those sailing under the flag of a 'New Wittgenstein'. In my view it is incontestable that the *Tractatus* has earned a place in the pantheon of analytic classics. After all, it was the first work to think through the consequences of an atomist programme by combining Moore's conceptual and Russell's logical analysis. Russell had to confess that for all he knew 'analysis could go on forever' (1918: 202). Wittgenstein adopted a more stringent atomism, albeit at the price of refusing to specify its atoms. He transcendentally deduced that there *must be* objects that are metaphysically simple and semantically indefinable – in the sense of Moore's conceptual analysis – from the possibility of symbolic representation. The *Tractatus* also initiated the linguistic turn that dominated the middle phase of analytic philosophy. But there are some grounds for doubt with respect to the later work (see ch. 8.4).

In any event, the scientific conception also rules out other important figures and movements. Moore showed no inclinations to subordinate common sense to the extraordinary philosophical conclusions often drawn from scientific investigations. The same holds for Oxford conceptual analysis. While Austin toyed with the idea of an *Aufhebung* of philosophy in linguistics (1970: 181), this ideal is firmly rejected by Ryle and Strawson. The latter two not only distinguish philosophy from science in theory, they do not emulate the methods of science in practice either. In fact, Ryle proudly relates the following anecdote from school:

I remember another master saying: 'Ryle, you are very good on [philosophical] theories, but you are very bad on [scientific] facts.' My attempts to repair this latter weakness were short-lived and unsuccessful. (1970: 1)

According to the testimony of Geoffrey Warnock, Oxford ordinary language philosophers were hostile 'to technical terms and aspirations to "scientific" professionalism' (1998). It was precisely this attitude that provoked Quine to poke fun at their 'steadfast laymanship' (1960: 261). In doing so, Quine promoted the ideals of 'scientific philosophy' or 'philosophy in a scientific spirit' (e.g. 1970: 2; 1994: 47–57; 1987: 209) that he had imbibed from the logical positivists and with which he imbued contemporary naturalists. For all that, however, a definition of analytic philosophy that excludes not just Wittgenstein but also Moore and Oxford philosophy is a non-starter. Conceptual analysis in its various manifestations is far from dead, but has undergone a revival recently. Furthermore, the day-to-day practice of contemporary analytic philosophy is unthinkable without its legacy. Indeed, analytic discussion in practical philosophy owes significantly more to conceptual analysis than it does to logical constructionism. Even if the aforementioned figures had been a mere blip in the analytic tradition, they could not be excluded from that tradition on the grounds that their views have been superseded. For those grounds would equally disqualify Russell and the logical positivists. Whether or not they are the flavour of the month, none of these thinkers can be written out of the history of analytic philosophy.

To strike a final yet sadly familiar note, the scientific conception also *includes* too much. Whereas metaphilosophical naturalism is a recent position, the more general orientation towards science currently under consideration dominates Western philosophy. Mathematics and logic played a very important role in ancient and medieval philosophy, which in some respects foreshadows their role within analytic philosophy. Natural science and psychology were central to modern philosophy from Descartes onwards. Kant, for instance, had an elaborate philosophy of the natural sciences, and contributed to the explanation of the birth of the solar system. Some historians of analytic philosophy have suggested that Kantian philosophy was pursued in isolation from developments in the special sciences (Wedberg 1984: 1–2; Coffa 1991: 22). This is sheer prejudice. One group of Neo-Kantians (loosely so called) consisted of eminent scientists such as Helmholtz and Hertz. Moreover, even Neo-Kantian philosophers like Natorp (1910) and Cassirer (1921) tended to know more about the science of their day – both natural and social – than average analytic philosophers tend to know about present-day science. And the Southwest school of Neo-Kantianism included the social and historical sciences to produce comprehensive philosophies of science.

Even within contemporary continental philosophy there is the occasional preoccupation with certain scientific topics. Sadly, as we shall see in chapter 9.1, that preoccupation has been far from healthy. Even without that particular exhibit, however, the case against the scientific conception of analytic philosophy remains compelling. For better or worse, neither a preoccupation with science nor illumination by the scientific spirit defines analytic philosophy.

3   MAKING A PIECEMEAL OF IT

It is tempting to think that the shortcomings of methodological definitions can be rectified by modifying them into a *stylistic* definition. What separates analytic philosophy from other types of philosophizing is not so much a more or less specific technique or procedure, but rather a more general style of thinking and writing. Before turning to a strictly speaking stylistic conception of analytic philosophy, I shall consider some other features that have occasionally been mooted as setting it apart.

The first is clearly on the methodological side, namely the use of puzzle cases and thought experiments (Aschenberg 1982: 23). Conceptual analysts, in particular, have considered exotic cases, often fictional, in order to explore the precise range of application for certain terms. Most famous (or notorious) in this respect is the long-lasting debate about personal identity going back to Locke. We are invited to consider, for instance, cases in which the brain of N.N., or her memories, are transplanted into the body of M.M. The question is then raised whether N.N. now inhabits M.M.'s body, and this is supposed to establish whether her identity is determined by her brain, her memories or her body. Puzzle cases also play a role in Kripke's and Putnam's realist semantics. We are asked to consider whether, e.g., a substance which has all the phenomenal qualities of water but a fictional molecular composition XYZ still qualifies as water, or whether cats would continue to count as animals even if we discovered that they are automata controlled from Mars. During the heyday of the linguistic turn, puzzle cases were invoked to ascertain 'what we would say' under certain circumstances, in order to delineate the rules governing the use of philosophically contested terms. This setting has now been replaced by considerations of our tutored intuitions concerning puzzle cases and thought-experiments, though what precisely that difference amounts to is less than crystal clear (Hanfling 2000: chs. 4 and 12).

But in spite of its undeniable importance and value, the pondering of puzzle cases and thought-experiments does not mark the limit of analytic philosophy. For one thing, they also play a role in the British empiricists and in Kant, for instance. Furthermore, there are manifestations of analytic philosophy which do not consider them. The *Tractatus* is one instance, because it attempts to deduce what language must be like on the basis of certain general views about the nature of representation. Logical constructionism is another, because it devises new terms rather than exploring the precise extension or meaning of established ones.

A second feature, still more on the methodological side, is prominent in Russell: 'A scientific philosophy such as I wish to recommend will be piecemeal and tentative like other sciences.'

The essence of philosophy, thus conceived, is analysis not synthesis. To build up systems of the world, like Heine's German professor who knit together fragments of life and made an intelligible system out of them, is not, I believe, any more feasible than the discovery of the philosopher's stone. What is feasible is the understanding of general forms, and the division of traditional problems into a number of separate and less baffling questions. 'Divide and conquer' is the maxim of success here as elsewhere. (1925: 109)

Later he recommended logical positivists for their piecemeal methods, procedures that had proved their mettle in natural science. Traditional philosophy, by contrast, strove to 'produce a complete theory of the universe on all occasions' (1950: 381). In one respect, at least, this pat on the shoulder was deserved. Among the numerous bogeys targeted in the *Manifesto* of the Vienna Circle were not just traditional and school philosophy, but also *systematic* philosophy (*Systemphilosophie*) (Carnap, Hahn and Neurath 1929: 18).

Remnants of this attitude are found in Lewis, who confesses:

I should have liked to be a piecemeal, unsystematic philosopher, offering independent proposals on a variety of topics. It was not to be. I succumbed too often to the temptation of presupposing my views on one topic when writing on another. (1983: ix)

And very recently, Soames (2003: xiv–xv) has identified a 'piecemeal approach' as one of the distinctive features of analytic philosophy. Conversely, continental philosophers take pride in their systematic or 'synoptic' approach (Prado 2003a: 10–11; Schroeder 2005). Whereas analytic philosophers tend to lose the plot through their obsession with technical details, continental philosophers emulate the philosophical tradition at least in one respect: they seek an overall vision of the world and our place in it. These proponents of continental philosophy thereby revert Russell's evaluation of a piecemeal approach, while confirming his characterization of analytic philosophy.

The suggestion which emerges is that analytic philosophy tackles philosophical problems step-by-step, thereby resulting in edifices that are smaller in scale while at the same time being more dependable. The first thing to note is that piecemeal procedures and systematic ambition do not preclude each other. Austin recommended a piecemeal approach for precisely the same reasons that endeared such an approach to Russell – namely that it makes grandiose and potentially confusing problems manageable. Yet he had systematic ambitions. What is more, other conceptual analysts brought such systematic ambitions to fruition. Neither Strawson's *Individuals* nor Hampshire's *Thought and Action*, for instance, are lacking in systematic vision.

The formally oriented side of analytic philosophy has also produced eminent systems from Russell onwards (Putnam 1983: 170–83, 287–303). We have already heard about Lewis, systematic thinker *malgré lui*. Even more obviously, Quine is a system-builder in the vein of Descartes, Kant or Hegel. His reflections on various philosophical topics (philosophy, necessity, language, knowledge and the mind) are part of a systematic and comprehensive theory. The same goes for Davidson, in spite of the fact that he has developed his system through a series of overlapping and criss-crossing articles rather than in a single book. The most fascinating feature of their oeuvres is how they link problems and concepts from various fields – metaphilosophy, semantics, epistemology, philosophy of science, philosophy of mind – and weave them into a striking whole. It can also be an exasperating feature, especially for critics. Claims from one area which are *prima facie* implausible are supported by ideas from another, and thus form a single, powerful and coherent perspective.

Although Quine and Davidson tackle with relish the detailed technical problems beloved by their post-positivist colleagues, they move rapidly from small-scale to large-scale questions. Thus Quine has turned the apparently recherché question of whether there are objective standards of translation into the linchpin of a whole new conception of philosophy. In a similar style, Davidson argues that the 'charitable' presuppositions of radical interpretation rule out seemingly irrefutable positions like scepticism and relativism. What is more, their systematic edifices are not uniformly owed to piecemeal procedures. Consider Quine's discussion of sentence meaning and propositions. Instead of breaking the problem down into smaller and more manageable parts, he immediately becomes embroiled in complex issues concerning belief-formation and scientific method, with the striking result that there is no such thing as sentence meaning and that we believe sentences rather than what they express. One may well suspect that a more circumspect approach might have led to more reliable if less iconoclastic results (Glock 2003a: 36–7). In our context, however, the upshot is that analytic philosophy *per se* is neither more piecemeal nor less systematic than its rivals.

Russell's allusion to Heine does have a point, though. It was the aspiration of every self-respecting German philosophy professor in the nineteenth century to leave behind a system of philosophy in at least three volumes: logic, including epistemology; metaphysics and practical philosophy including aesthetics. This specific ambition is still alien to analytic philosophy. But there are quite a few famous analytic philosophers who can look back at a similar and systematic progression of their interests, notably Putnam and Dummett. And because the average size of the resulting volumes is smaller, and the average life expectancy of philosophers higher, we are even more likely to reap the benefits of the crowning volumes concerning ethics, politics and cultural criticism than was the case in the nineteenth century (e.g. in the case of Lotze and Rickert).

Speaking about long tomes, there is a lingering suspicion that continental philosophers regularly succumb to bouts of logorrhoea. Expressed in less loaded terms, the impression prevails that analytic texts tend to be shorter than traditional or continental ones (D'Agostini 1997: 70, 205–6). Now, it is perfectly correct that analytic philosophers find it easier to build a career on the basis of short articles than their continental counterparts: witness Grice, Davidson and Putnam (Cohen 1986: 139). But the alleged brevity of analytic treatises is illusory. In recent vintages, block-busters abound – just think of Dummett's *Frege: Philosophy of Language*, Nozick's *Philosophical Explanations* or Brandom's *Making it Explicit*. Once more, we are not dealing just with a recent phenomenon. Neither *Principles of Mathematics* nor *Principia Mathematica* is short, and the same goes, e.g., for Broad's *The Mind and its Place in Nature* and Nagel's *The Structure of Science*. And at the very dawn of the analytic movement, Bolzano's *Wissenschaftslehre* dwarfs anything ever to issue from the pen of Kant or Hegel. Frege's *Grundlagen der Arithmetik*, Russell's *Problems of Philosophy* and Wittgenstein's *Tractatus* are the exception rather than the rule.

We have now reached matters of style. Let me end this section by mentioning briefly one other feature of presentation. Few continental philosophers would join Ryle in complaining about 'foot-and-note disease'. In some analytic philosophers, fear of that affliction has provoked a comprehensive cull (Armstrong 1997: xi). Indeed, Dummett published his aforementioned tome about Frege initially not just without footnotes, but also without a single quotation or reference. Once more, however, there is no absolute and pervasive contrast here between analytic philosophers and their non-analytic colleagues. When they write on historical issues, for example, analytic philosophers employ footnotes just as liberally as traditionalist philosophers, and quite properly so. Even outside such areas, what one might call the *defensive footnote* has become a notable feature of analytic writings. While the less compelling objections to the author's position are dispatched with great aplomb in the main body of the text, the really tricky ones are dealt with in footnotes, or better yet in endnotes. This way the author can demonstrate that she is aware of the difficulty, while still depriving it of the oxygen of publicity.

4 'CLARITY' IS NOT ENOUGH!

The specific stylistic features mentioned at the end of the last section stand little chance of uniting all of analytic philosophy. It is for good reasons, therefore, that the most common stylistic definition latches on to a much more general matter of style – clarity. Conversely, the positivist charge that traditional-cum-speculative philosophy is unintelligible lives on in the less focused charge that continental philosophy is obscure, mystery-mongering, gnomic, oracular, or the work of charlatans. Thus Rosen summarizes the stereotypical contrast between analytic and continental philosophy as follows: 'precision, conceptual clarity and systematic rigour are the property of analytic philosophy, whilst the continentals indulge in speculative metaphysics or cultural hermeneutics, or, alternatively, depending on one's sympathies, in wool-gathering and bathos' (quoted Critchley: 1998: 7).

In 1945, H. H. Price gave an address to the Joint Session under the title 'Clarity is not Enough'. It was an attack on the rising tide of linguistic philosophy, albeit a very measured and clear one. Austin, who was one of the main targets, reacted in an equally clear and telling manner:

Clarity, too, I know, has been said to be not enough: but perhaps it will be time to go into that when we are within measurable distance of achieving clarity on some matter. (1970: 189)

Both sides in this exchange took for granted that there is an intimate connection between clarity on the one hand, linguistic philosophy and analytic philosophy more generally on the other. Price was one of the first to use the term 'analytic philosophy'. He introduces the movement as 'Analytic or clarificatory philosophy', and credits it with the credo that 'clarification is the fundamental aim of philosophy' (1945: 16–17).

Down the years, even some of its detractors have accepted that, for better or worse, analytic philosophy aspires to greater clarity than its rivals. Thus Moore tried in *Principia Ethica* to 'distinguish clearly' different kinds of question which previous moral philosophers 'have always confused' (1903: vii–viii). Wittgenstein was even more emphatic. He wrote of his passionate 'work of clarification' (1980: 19) and assigned to philosophy the task of achieving clarity.

The purpose of philosophy is the logical clarification of thoughts. Philosophy is not a doctrine but an activity. A philosophical work consists essentially of elucidations. The result of philosophy is not 'philosophical propositions', but the clarification of propositions. Philosophy should clarify and sharply demarcate our thoughts, which would otherwise be cloudy and blurred, as it were. (1922: 4.112)

The logical positivists pursued a similar goal, though for different reasons. They regarded themselves as heirs of the Enlightenment. Prominent among Enlightenment values, along with progress and scientific cooperation, is the virtue of clarity. 'Neatness and clarity are striven for, and dark distances and unfathomable depths rejected' (Carnap, Hahn and Neurath 1929: 15). Carnap placed this aspiration in a wider context:

We [those with a 'basic scientific attitude'] too have 'emotional needs' in philosophy. But they are fulfilled by clarity of concepts, precision of methods, responsible theses, achievement through co-operation in which each individual plays his part. We do not deceive ourselves about the fact that movements in metaphysical philosophy and religion which resist such an orientation, again exert quite a strong influence today. What then, in spite of that, gives us the confidence that our call for clarity, for science without metaphysics will succeed? It is the insight, or, to put it more carefully, the belief, that those opposing powers belong to the past. We feel there is an inner kinship between the attitude on which our philosophical work is founded and the intellectual attitude which presently manifests itself in entirely different walks of life; we feel this orientation in artistic movements; especially in architecture, and in movements which strive for meaningful forms of personal and collective life, of education, and of external organization in general. We feel all around us the same basic orientation, the same style of thinking and doing. It is an orientation which demands clarity everywhere, but which realizes that the fabric of life can never be quite comprehended. (Carnap 1928: xvii–xviii)

Nazism and Stalinism subsequently made a mockery of Carnap's political hopes. But they made it all the more tempting for British philosophers to turn the ideal of clarity into a stick with which to beat what they began to label 'Continental philosophy'. In 1957, R. M. Hare toured Germany with a lecture entitled 'A School for Philosophers'. In it he explored what he calls the 'two different ways' in which philosophy is currently studied, namely British and German (1960: 107).

According to Hare, in the Oxford tutorial system, a student of philosophy will be taught 'how to think more clearly and to the point'; taught, that is, 'to express his thought clearly to himself and to others; to make distinctions where there are distinctions to be made, and thus avoid unnecessary confusion – and not to use long words (or short ones) without being able to explain what they mean'. Furthermore, British philosophy at large is guided by the intellectual virtues taught at Oxford, viz., 'clarity, relevance and brevity'. Such virtues will then ensure that arguments between 'British philosophers' can circulate and develop through the defence and refutation of work with 'an unambiguously stated thesis' (1960: 108, 112).

German philosophy, by contrast, enjoys the 'delights of erecting, in solitary thought, imposing edifices – of writing huge volumes which only a handful of people will ever understand'. The typical author of these 'long or difficult books', these 'monstrous philosophical edifices', likes to 'collect a private coterie to listen to him'. Furthermore, he will not shy away from turning 'philosophy into *mystique*', or from producing 'verbiage' disguised as 'serious metaphysical inquiry'. 'German philosophy' thrives on and finds 'uplifting' work characterized by 'ambiguities and evasions and rhetoric,' i.e. just those characteristics which 'British philosophers' regard 'as the mark of a philosopher who has not learnt his craft' (1960: 110–15). (One hopes that the craft of the British diplomat differs somewhat from that of the British philosopher.)

Analytic philosophers continued to contrast analytic clarity and continental obscurantism into the 1980s and 1990s, when much of the strident self-confidence of post-war analytic philosophy had dissipated. Thus Ayer gives us a piece of his mind.

[the tradition of British empiricism] is a commonsensical tradition ... Sticking close to the facts, and close to observation, and not being carried away by German Romanticism, high falutin' talk, obscurity, metaphysics. It's a tradition, on the whole, of good prose. That is very important. If you write good prose, you can't succumb to the sort of nonsense we get from Germany and now also from France. (1991: 212)

Later he makes a concession, though not without blowing his own trumpet:

I think it's perfectly true that people who write very clearly *may* be superficial. One way of writing clearly is to avoid difficult questions. But I think it isn't at all true that someone who writes clearly *has* to be superficial. On the contrary, I think that a good philosophical writer is someone who can put difficult theories – as for instance my Constructionalism, which is extremely difficult – in a clear fashion. One of the great dangers in philosophy is woolliness, and woolliness, particularly among Germans, is always marked by very unclear writing. (1991: 224–5)

Finally, Warnock in 1998:

To a more than trivial extent, membership of the group in question was a matter of style. There was a conscious hostility to the lofty, rather loose rhetorical manner of, for example, its idealist predecessors; ... There was an even more emphatic distaste for the riddle-spinning, paradox-delighting 'deep' discourse of most contemporary continental philosophers, with whom, indeed, any kind of academic communication was neither sought nor, probably, practicable. (In this particular distaste there was, I think, an element of moral disapproval; it was felt that the weird, mind-boggling pronouncements of some continental sages were not only unprofitable but largely bogus – an intellectual fraud.) So far, the doggedly plain-man manner of G.E. Moore was a significant influence; nor, so far, does the 'ordinary language' style much diverge from that of logical positivism. (1998: 149)

The idea that analytic philosophy is inherently clearer than its rivals asserts itself even in those commentators who tend to be more reserved about its achievements. Thus Williams assures us that what marks out analytic philosophy is 'a certain way of going on which involves argument, distinctions, and, so far as it remembers to try to achieve it and succeeds, moderately plain speech'. Unfortunately, the speech of many contemporary analytic philosophers is as plain as a baroque church and as clear as mud. Indeed, many of them seem to regard this as an achievement, because it shows that their work does not suffer from the alleged superficiality of the logical positivists and ordinary language philosophy, both of which were marked by lucid prose. As an analytic philosopher, Williams has a comeback to this objection:

As an alternative to plain speech, [analytic philosophy] distinguishes sharply between obscurity and technicality. It always rejects the first, but the second it sometimes finds a necessity. This feature peculiarly enrages some of its enemies. Wanting philosophy to be at once profound and accessible, they resent technicality but are comforted by obscurity. (1985: vi)

Analytic philosophers for their part will no doubt find comfort in the idea that the indigestible nature of their writings is a necessity, and a sign of technical proficiency, by contrast to the wilful and whimsical obscurantism of continental authors. In fact, however, many so-called technicalities serve no purpose other than that of adopting a certain intellectual posture.

According to Charlton (1991: 5), 'peppering your papers with logical symbols . . . is considered uncouth' among analytic philosophers. Passmore's view of this landscape is less blinkered. He points out that 'logical symbols proliferate' and that they 'are often decorative abbreviations rather than elements in philosophical derivations' (1985: 6–7). For instance, McGinn's (1991) idea of 'cognitive closure' is simply that certain phenomena transcend the cognitive capacities of creatures like ourselves. But he explains it as follows: 'A type of mind M is cognitively closed with respect to a property P or a theory T if and only if the concept-forming procedures at M's disposal cannot extend to a grasp of P (or an understanding of T).' Dennett comments: 'Don't be misled by the apparent rigour of this definition; the author A never puts it to any use U in any formal derivation D' (1991: 10).

Clarity, including clarity achieved by formal devices, may have been a characteristic feature of analytic philosophy when it was dominated by writers such as Frege, Moore, Tarski, Ryle, Austin, Carnap, Reichenbach, Hempel, Quine or Strawson. But at present aspiring philosophical authors could gain more by studying continental writers like Schopenhauer, Marx or Nietzsche, than by emulating articles in leading analytic journals (Glock 1998: 91–3; 2004: 432–5; see also Cohen 1986: 42; Leiter 2004c: 11–12; Williamson 2006: 183–5).

Even in the olden days there were notable exceptions. There is a striking irony about Wittgenstein's work. He devoted his philosophy to the pursuit of clarity, but he pursued this end in a fashion which is at times extremely obscure. C. D. Broad referred to the marmoreal remarks of the *Tractatus* as 'syncopated pipings' (1925: vii). Wittgenstein himself acknowledged the justice of that remark, admitting that every sentence in the *Tractatus* should be read as the heading of a chapter, needing further exposition (Rhees 1984: 159). *Philosophical Investigations* is discursive by comparison. The writing is lucid and non-technical (except for individual remarks that are extremely condensed and hence opaque in the manner of the *Tractatus*). Nonetheless, the *Investigations* as a whole is a very difficult book, largely because the structure and the targets of the argument remain unclear. Neither work makes any concessions to the reader.

It will not even do to modify the thesis of the inherent clarity of analytic philosophy by exempting *both* Wittgenstein *and* a sizable part of recent practitioners. In many instances, middle Russell is almost as indigestible as early Wittgenstein. The Grey's Elegy argument of 'On Denoting' enjoys a well-deserved notoriety, and so do his attempts to shore up the ramified theories of types (see Hart 1990: 197). Russell's equally well-deserved and widespread reputation for lucidity rests mainly on works which he composed after he was forced to make a living from writing 'shilling-shockers' for a wider audience. Or consider Elizabeth Anscombe and Wilfrid Sellars. Seminal analytic philosophers – certainly! Lucid authors – surely not!

It should go without saying that writing clearly is not sufficient for being an analytic philosopher. Plato, Descartes, Hume and Lichtenberg, to name just a few, are supremely clear, yet they do not form part of the analytic tradition. What does bear saying is that several writers which are commonly classified as continental were not just eloquent but also clear.

Schopenhauer modelled his style on Hume, and declared literary style to be the 'physiognomy of the spirit', a faithful image of the movement of thought (1844: I 446; II 73). Schopenhauer's great strength lies in his ability to tell a gripping philosophical yarn, aided by his ability to construct a dynamic interplay between different themes. It is a gift which has frequently been compared to that of a great composer, but not one that is much in evidence among authors of the analytic tradition.

Marx and Engels, for their part, wrote well by-and-large, except in the early Hegelian manuscripts which were not published during their lifetime.[3] Nietzsche, finally, was one of the most lucid writers ever to put pen to paper. *Zur Genealogie der Moral* meets all the stylistic standards that analytic philosophers have been fond of preaching if not practising: it is brief, lucid, well crafted and straightforward, a pleasure to read. The obstacles to understanding Nietzsche are largely the creation of contemporary commentators, especially those of an analytic bent. If one approaches him on the assumption that he must *au fond* have been a closet proponent of reason and logical rigour, or of liberalism, peace and racial equality, then his texts must appear utterly opaque. If, however, one abandons such wishful misinterpretation, one can easily recognize him for someone who tried to debunk the ideals of objectivity, truth and morality. But then one can also pay due homage to him as a great philosophical wordsmith.

I would not go as far as saying that within continental philosophy Hegel, Heidegger, Lacan, Deleuze and Derrida are the exception rather than the rule. But they are less representative than analytic philosophers like to assume. And that contention could be further buttressed by looking at the early writings of Husserl and Sartre.

There are two morals. First, whatever distinguishes analytic philosophy from continental philosophy, it is neither the pursuit nor the attainment of clarity. Secondly, it is high time that analytic philosophers started to think seriously about the nature of clarity. Whether or not clarity is enough, it is certainly not enough to throw around the term 'clarity'. For that term obviously means very different things to different people, and it stands in urgent need of clarification. Surprisingly, there is hardly any discussion of this issue. In contemporary philosophy, clarity is discussed only in the context of Descartes' doctrine of clear and distinct ideas, if it is discussed at all. I know of only two articles which explicitly address the idea of clarity in analytic philosophy (Price 1945; Hart 1990), and even they are mainly devoted to wider metaphilosophical issues. This is a scandal, not 'the scandal of philosophy', to be sure, but *a* scandal of *analytic* philosophy nonetheless.

[3] No less a writer than Russell commented on the *Communist Manifesto* that it was 'unsurpassed in literary merit' (1896: 10).

5 THE VOICE OF REASON

This is not the place to get on with the substantial task of providing either a historical survey or a proper analysis of the concept of clarity (see Glock 2002). Instead, let us turn to an immediate response to my challenge. What marks out analytic philosophy, the response goes, is a clarity of *thought* rather than *expression*, one which involves conceptual distinctions and ultimately aims at transparency of arguments. This suggestion is captured by what I call the *rationalist* conception of analytic philosophy.[4] It holds that analytic philosophers are marked out by their rational approach to the subject, by their attempt to solve philosophical issues through argument.

The rationalist conception is contained in the passage from Williams just quoted. Elsewhere he recommends analytic philosophy for 'being answerable to argument' and its 'workmanlike truthfulness'. At the same time, contrary to metaphilosophical and epistemic naturalism, he insists that these virtues are not exclusive to science, and that they are 'much more important than any attempt to make philosophy look like a science' (1996a: 26–7). The rationalist conception is, among other things, an attempt to preserve a kernel of truth in the proposal that analytic philosophers are enamoured to science. The idea is that the essence of analytic philosophy is furnished by cognitive ideals that are exemplified by, though not necessarily confined to, science, namely rational inquiry and debate.

In this spirit, Jonathan Cohen has referred to analytic philosophy as *The Dialogue of Reason*.[5] In a less lyrical fashion, Dagfinn Føllesdal explains analytic philosophy as a general attitude towards philosophical problems and doctrines, namely one that tackles them in a rational way, through argument.

The answer to our question [What is analytic philosophy?] is, I believe, that analytic philosophy is very strongly concerned with argument and justification. An analytic philosopher who presents and assesses a philosophical position asks: what *reasons* are there for accepting or rejecting this position? (1997: 7)

In line with this definition, Føllesdal treats 'analytic' as a scaling adjective. He classifies thinkers from very disparate schools, including apparently continental ones like phenomenology or hermeneutics, as more or less analytic depending on the role rational argument plays in their work.

---

[4] I use the term 'rationalist' to include not just the continental rationalists with their emphasis on innate or *a priori* knowledge, but any position which stresses that our beliefs should be subject to critical scrutiny and supported by arguments, no matter whether these invoke reason or experience.
[5] Cohen (1986: Part I) combines a rationalist with a topical definition: he maintains both that analytic philosophers employ reason and that reason is the ultimate topic of their investigations.

The rationalist conception has the advantage of allowing for the fact that analytic philosophy is a very broad church indeed. Nevertheless, it suffers from two shortcomings. One, which I shall pursue in chapter 8.1, is that it amounts to a 'persuasive definition'. The immediate problem, which it shares with doctrinal and other methodological approaches, is that it is not in keeping with the commonly recognized extension of 'analytic philosophy'. In driving home this point, we need to turn the spirit of the rationalist conception against the letter, and draw a few distinctions.

The first is that between *theory* and *practice*, the second the one between *ambition* and *achievement*. If extolling the virtue and importance of reason in theory were the decisive test, then Hegel would qualify with flying colours, notwithstanding Einstein, who compared Hegel's writings to the 'drivel of a drunk'. At the same time, the later Wittgenstein and some of his followers would be excluded. For, as Monk points out, Wittgenstein 'had a great deal of sympathy' for the 'tradition of continental anti-rationalist thought' (1990: 250). Lest this might once more be greeted with glee, note that on this understanding the rationalist conception would also exclude Humeans, pragmatists and sceptics, both inside and outside of analytic philosophy as commonly recognized. All of them maintain that the scope of reason is severely restricted and that it is at best an overrated icing on the predominantly pre-rational cake of human existence.

Accordingly, we must distinguish between

- *irrationalism*, a neglect of empirical science, logic, conceptual clarity and rational argument in favour of religious, political or artistic styles of thinking;
- *anti-intellectualism*, the denial that reason and intellect have the exalted position accorded to them by philosophical tradition.

Unlike irrationalism, anti-intellectualism has been advocated by numerous Anglophone philosophers at least since Hume, and by numerous analytic philosophers of whatever tongue. A suitably revised version of the rationalist conception therefore runs as follows: analytic philosophy eschews irrationalist practice, without necessarily repudiating anti-intellectualist doctrine.

At this juncture the contrast between ambition and achievement comes into play. Do you need to *succeed* at backing your claims by arguments in order to qualify as an analytic philosopher by rationalist lights? Or is it sufficient to make *bona fide* efforts? In the former case, 'analytic philosopher' would be a category that can be used rarely, if ever, with any degree of confidence. In the latter case, the rationalist definition still faces counter-examples.

Though it may come as a surprise, the rationalist definition still *excludes* too much. It is notorious that the later Wittgenstein managed to convey the impression of being an irrationalist. Like Ramsey, Carnap was taken aback by Wittgenstein's authoritarian style of debate, which tolerated 'no critical comment' and treated insights as a kind of divine inspiration.

I sometimes had the impression that the deliberately rational and unemotional attitude of the scientist and likewise any idea which had the flavour of 'enlightenment' were repugnant to Wittgenstein. (1963: 25–9; see Monk 1990: 241–3, 260)

Even the early Wittgenstein, who cannot be written out of the canon of analytic philosophy, was not exactly keen to spell out the arguments behind his statements. Doing so would 'spoil their beauty', he maintained, to which Russell trenchantly replied that he should acquire a slave to take over this task (Monk 1996a: 264).

In his gem of an article 'How I see Philosophy?', Waismann, a one-time member of the Vienna Circle and Wittgenstein disciple, felt emboldened to write:

There are many things beyond proof: the existence of material objects, of other minds, indeed of the external world, the validity of induction, and so on. Gone are the days when philosophers were trying to prove all sorts of things: that the soul is immortal, that this is the best of all possible worlds and the rest, or to refute, by irrefutable argument and with relish, materialism, positivism and what not. Proof, refutation – these are dying words in philosophy, though G.E. Moore still 'proved' to a puzzled world that it exists. What can one say to this – save, perhaps, that he is a great prover before the Lord? (1956: 1)

Outing himself as an anti-intellectualist rather than an irrationalist, Waismann himself proceeds to argue at length that deductive arguments are of little use in philosophy. Even if such arguments can be established as valid, the debate will inevitably turn to the truth and plausibility of the premises. For philosophy is a fundamental discipline in which nothing can be taken for granted and no stone can remain unturned. Even *reductio ad absurdum* arguments are not rigorous or compelling in philosophy, Waismann contends, since there always remains elbow room for wriggling out of a dilemma (1956: 22–34). More recent analytic admirers of Wittgenstein, such as Baker and McDowell, have been equally immune to the ethos of the knock-down argument. Indeed, the importance of argument is played down even by some perfectly mainstream figures (e.g. Martin 2002: 133–6).

Proponents of the rationalist conception might respond that these counter-instances are owed to an excessively narrow conception of what constitutes an argument or rational debate (Føllesdal 1997: 10–12). Philosophers have used a confusing variety of types of reasoning. Traditional styles of argument include deductive, inductive and abductive (inference to the best explanation), demonstrative and elenctic, direct and indirect (*reductio ad absurdum*), logical and pragmatic, vicious regress arguments, and charges of self-refutation. Analytic philosophers are famous mainly for devising critical arguments, like the argument to meaningless or category-confusions and paradigm-case arguments. More recently they have also come up with constructive or defensive lines of reasoning, such as the appeal to tutored intuition in post-Kripkean metaphysics, the trade-off between ontological parsimony and explanatory power, or the 'my theory is the only game in town' argument popular in cognitive science.

I shall not pretend to provide as much as a snap-shot of this dauntingly expansive field (Passmore 1970; Cohen 1986: Part II). Instead I shall grant, and not just for the sake of argument, that anyone who can be deemed an analytic philosopher employs arguments of some kind. But this still leaves the problem that many of them have not accorded a central role to argument. Furthermore, a catholic understanding of argument only exacerbates the second difficulty facing the rationalist conception, namely that it *includes* too much. In this context Hacker remarks:

in a loose sense, one might say that all, or the bulk of, philosophy is analytic . . . If the term 'analytic philosophy' is to be useful as a classificatory term for the historian of philosophy, it must do more work than merely to distinguish mainstream Western philosophy from the reflections of philosophical sages and prophets, such as Pascal or Nietzsche, and from the obscurities of speculative metaphysicians, such as Hegel, Bradley or Heidegger. (1996: 3)

One might dismiss this type of objection and insist that there is nothing wrong with revisionary definitions that make the bulk of philosophy analytic. Perhaps one should abandon the assumption that analytic philosophy is a *distinct tradition* and simply regard it as the norm, a period within the mainstream of Western philosophy, with continental philosophy as a deviation.

However, while analytic philosophy is in many respects closer to that mainstream than continental philosophy, it is not just more of the same. By sharp contrast to traditionalist philosophy, the pioneers of analytic no less than those of continental philosophy brought about a revolutionary break with the past (see chs. 3.5, 4.1, 5.1). They might occasionally draw (highly selective) inspiration from the past, but they also sought to transcend it.

This holds not just for the positivist replacement of 'traditional' or 'school' by scientific philosophy. Wittgenstein regarded his 'new method' as a 'kink' in the 'development of human thought', on a par with the Galilean revolution in science. He even portrayed it as a 'new subject', one of the heirs of what was once called philosophy, rather than merely a stage in its evolution (1958: 27–8; 1993: 113–14). Russell entertained similar Galilean aspirations on behalf of scientific philosophy. Even more modest figures (Moore, conceptual analysts) proclaimed to overcome systemic weaknesses of past philosophizing. The same goes for the condemnations of 'armchair philosophy' by Quinean naturalists. What is more, the resulting movement differs in numerous – though hardly clear-cut – respects *not just* from continental philosophy, *but also* from the academic philosophy that preceded it, *and* from current traditionalist philosophy.

In the case of the rationalist definition, the problem is more pronounced still. If all that is required is a genuine attempt to construe arguments of some kind or other, then Pascal's wager obviously qualifies, as does Nietzsche's *Genealogy of Morals*, Hegel's attack on the categorical imperative, Bradley's animadversions against external relations, and Heidegger's reflections on mortality. Accordingly, the rationalist conception threatens to make not just the *bulk* of philosophy analytic, but *the whole* of it. This would turn 'analytic philosophy' not just into a very blunt taxonomic instrument, but deprive it of any distinct classificatory role. The reason for this unpalatable consequence is simple yet compelling. At least since Socrates, and arguably since the dawn of our subject, the attempt to tackle fundamental questions at least partly by way of reasoned argument, rather than, e.g., through an appeal to authority or revelation, has been regarded as one of the features that distinguishes philosophy as such from religion or political rhetoric. It cannot, therefore, be used to demarcate a particular kind of philosophizing.

CHAPTER 7

Ethics and politics

This chapter discusses the role of ethics and politics within the analytic tradition. The main purpose is to criticize certain views about what analytic philosophy amounts to. As in the case of history, however, conceptions of analytic philosophy relating to ethics and politics cut across some of the parameters along which I have distinguished conceptions of philosophy in the last two chapters. The idea that analytic philosophy is characterized by the exclusion of moral philosophy and political theory constitutes a topical conception, and will be dismissed in section 1. In addition, there are two doctrinal conceptions relating to ethics and politics. These areas have occasioned two conflicting prejudices. On the one hand, many continental philosophers and members of the political intelligentsia believe that analytic philosophy shirks ethical and political commitments and hence inclines to being apolitical and conservative. Conversely, many proponents of analytic philosophy regard it as a progressive or liberal political force. For most participants in this debate, epithets like 'apolitical' and 'conservative' tend to carry negative connotations and epithets like 'progressive' or 'liberal' positive ones. I am no exception, and I shall not disguise my disapproval of extreme views on both the right and the left. Nevertheless, my aim is *not* to defend a partisan political line, but to question the idea that analytic philosophy is intrinsically linked to any particular ethical or political outlook.

In section 2 I shall debunk the first prejudice. Eminent members of the analytic tradition have been politically committed, and on the left rather than the right. More importantly, while the doctrines of some early analytic philosophers may create difficulties for regarding such commitment as part and parcel of the philosophical enterprise, this does not hold for analytic philosophy as a whole, least of all for the current mainstream. Section 3 corrects the comforting but, alas, overly optimistic idea that analytic philosophy inculcates a saner and more responsible approach to moral and political issues than alternative philosophical movements. Important analytic philosophers have not been strangers to political

179

extremisms and misjudgement. Furthermore, there are plausible explanations why there is no automatic link between analytic philosophy and a wholesome moral-cum-political stance. At the same time I concede in section 4 that the Singer affair displays sharply contrasting attitudes towards specific moral and political dilemmas in analytic and non-analytic philosophy. The final section considers the question whether the analytic tradition might at least be characterized by an avoidance of ideology. Important analytic voices have indeed warned against tailoring philosophical theories to suit political prejudices. But that aberration is not entirely absent from analytic philosophy, and it is not pervasive among its rivals.

I DOES ANALYTIC PHILOSOPHY SHUN ETHICS AND POLITICAL THEORY?

In chapter 5.4 we considered the possibility that analytic philosophy might be defined through the topics which it focuses on or ignores. But I postponed discussion of one widespread view, namely that analytic philosophy sticks out by virtue (or by vice) of ignoring the areas of moral philosophy and political theory. Although it may strike connoisseurs of the current scene as absurd, this idea is not entirely without foundation.

At the time when the label 'analytic philosophy' gained currency, during the 1950s, most of the leading analytic philosophers shunned ethics in favour of logic, epistemology, philosophy of language and philosophy of mind. Figures like Ryle, Austin, Strawson, Carnap, Reichenbach, Hempel, Quine, and Goodman hardly shared any views. But at that stage, at least, none of them paid much attention to the non-theoretical side of the subject.

With respect to the precursors and early pioneers of analytic philosophy, the picture is more complicated. Both Bolzano (1834) and Brentano (1889) had elaborate ethical theories, the former advocating a form of hedonistic utilitarianism, the latter a theory of intrinsic value. But while both thinkers, and in particular Bolzano, had clear affinities to analytic philosophy, they did not influence developments within analytic philosophy until quite recently; even at present their moral philosophy is ignored within the analytic mainstream.

Russell is a weightier counter-example to the idea that analytic philosophy tends to ignore ethics. He wrote as freely about egoism, universal love, education, pacifism and guild socialism as about classes, definite descriptions, logical forms, universals and knowledge. Furthermore, the logical positivists had a rather larger interest in matters ethical and political than is commonly appreciated. Neurath wrote extensively on political, economic and social issues. Schlick and Ayer, for their part, took a strong interest in ethics. The question remains, however, whether these figures regarded their ethical writings and political interventions as unconnected to their strictly philosophical endeavours (see section 2).

But at least one trailblazer of analytic philosophy defies that qualm. Ethical considerations loom large in Moore's rebellion against idealism (Baldwin 1990: 8, 35–8). Furthermore, *Principia Ethica* proved pivotal to the further development of Anglophone moral philosophy. The charge of the naturalistic fallacy and the idea that moral properties are unanalysable non-natural properties that can be intuited remain central to this day. Finally, the book is also a founding document of analytic philosophy, notably through its emphasis on clarifying questions, its propagation of analysis, and its role in alerting later generations to the paradox of analysis. On the other hand, it has to be admitted that Moore's interest in ethics quickly faded after 1903. Post World War I, his meta-ethical and ethical ideas were taken up not by the analytic avant-garde, but rather by 'old-fashioned' traditionalist philosophers like Ross and Pritchard. Right into the fifties, there was a pervasive if largely tacit feeling within analytic philosophy that moral and political philosophy are less kosher than theoretical philosophy, or that they are in crisis.

Reasons such as these might have swayed Passmore (1966: 7) to provide a survey of analytic philosophy without discussing areas outside theoretical philosophy. In the sequel he remarked that at the time this choice was 'as much symptomatic as stipulative', while recognizing the subsequent proliferation of moral and political theory within analytic philosophy (1985: 1). As regards one area of practical philosophy, however, the idea of a blind spot soldiers on. Topics concerning human existence continue to be associated with continental philosophy. Thus Strawson claims that 'more or less systematic reflection on the human condition' belongs to 'a species of philosophy' that contrasts with analytic philosophy (1992: 2). This claim is underwritten by Cooper (1994: 3). It also chimes with Young's definition of continental philosophy as 'philosophy which, as its primary task, seeks to respond to the question of what can be said about the meaning of life in the light of the death of the God of Christianity' (2003: 4).

This characterization is tailored to the Nietzschean strand of continental philosophy. It fits neither phenomenology nor Marxism: the former revolves around issues in theoretical philosophy; and in so far as the latter conceives of itself as engaged in practical *philosophy* (as opposed to economics or sociology), it tends to focus on more mundane issues. More importantly, as far as this book is concerned, the claim that analytic philosophy tends to exclude practical philosophy of any kind is unsustainable. Wittgenstein, Russell and the logical positivists engaged in existential reflections. Perhaps these can be dismissed by maintaining that they pursued these 'off duty', or at least outside of their philosophical brief as they themselves understood it. After the war, any topical constraints on moral and political philosophy were swept aside by three interconnected developments – the rise of cognitivism in moral philosophy, the emergence of applied ethics, and the rehabilitation of grand political theory in the wake of Rawls. As a result of these developments, over the last fifty years practical philosophy in an analytical vein has come to rival if not exceed the theoretical branches in importance. This trend includes not just meta-ethics and normative ethics, but also political theory and jurisprudence. Even existentialist topics are very much involved. The meaning of life, for instance, is often held up as the archetypal profound-yet-arcane issue which hard-headed analytic philosophers have gladly left to woolly minded continentals. Yet as a recent survey article demonstrates, even this issue has come in for a lot of attention from analytic philosophers (Metz 2002), attention, moreover, that is more straightforward than that of continental thinkers like Heidegger and Sartre (e.g. Hanfling 1987; Cottingham 2003).

Indeed, many recently popular issues in moral and political theory have first and foremost been explored by analytic philosophers rather than their rivals. For instance, both environmental and bio-ethics evolved out of applied ethics pursued in an analytic vein. And an important topic like animal welfare has been pioneered by analytic philosophers like Singer (1975). Continental philosophers seriously lag behind in this respect, unless they simply display a complete moral blind spot (see Atterton and Calarco 2004).

2   IS ANALYTIC PHILOSOPHY MORALLY NEUTRAL AND CONSERVATIVE?

Accordingly, analytic philosophy cannot be understood as a movement that tends to exclude practical philosophy. This leaves open the possibility that it has characteristic views in this area, or that these views restrict the range of practical issues that can legitimately be pursued, at least by philosophers in their professional capacity.

Many early proponents of both logical constructionism and conceptual analysis confined moral philosophy to meta-ethics (see 2.9). As a result, analytic philosophy has frequently been portrayed as *neutral* with respect to ethical issues and hence as *apolitical*. Both features are in turn associated with being conservative, since they preserve the status quo. As a result, analytic philosophy is sometimes accused even of lending succour to exploitation and suppression. By contrast, continental philosophy is often regarded as inherently political and progressive, not just by practitioners but also by members of the educated public. Marxism and critical theory are officially keen to overcome the dichotomy between 'theory and practice' (as in Habermas 1963). This is to say that they regard their intellectual efforts as an integral part of a social and political struggle for emancipation. Something similar holds for continental philosophers that champion new social movements, especially feminism.

The prejudice that analytic philosophy is apolitical and by implication right wing goes back to early proponents of critical theory. Horkheimer, the founder of the Frankfurt School, went as far as associating logical positivism with fascism. He maintained that 'radical [i.e. logical] positivism' – no less than the 'Neo-romantic metaphysics' (*Lebensphilosophie* and Heidegger) it attacks – is connected 'to the existence of totalitarian states'. For it is equally rooted in the fear of social upheaval which makes the bourgeoisie pliable to fascistic tyranny (1937: 140). For Marcuse, analytic philosophy is part and parcel of a novel and particularly insidious form of repression. In spite of its 'rigidly neutral approach ... the intrinsically ideological character of linguistic analysis' is revealed in its prostration before ordinary use – a case of 'academic sado-masochism' – and in its zealous erection of barriers to thought and speech.[1] A vague yet suggestive association of analytic philosophy with the political right was further enshrined by the badly mislabelled 'positivism dispute' (*Positivismusstreit*) which raged in the 1960s between the Frankfurt School (Adorno, Habermas) and critical rationalists (Popper, Albert), who were actually keen to distance themselves from logical positivism. Though largely spurious and contrived, this conflict did pit the idea of 'critical theory', which investigates social reality *ab initio* with a view to changing it, against the orthodox view that the social sciences should remain neutral with respect to moral and political issues.[2]

Nevertheless, at least *prima facie* the idea that analytic philosophy is apolitical or conservative, let alone reactionary or authoritarian, is flabbergasting. Note first that leading analytic philosophers have been politically

---

[1] 1964: 171–3, 178, 192. Marcuse uses 'linguistic analysis', 'analytic philosophy' and '(neo-) positivist philosophy' interchangeably, even though he is dimly aware of the difference between logical construction and conceptual analysis (1964: 182–4, 187).

[2] Adorno *et al.* 1969. Dahms 1994 places this dispute in the wider context of the relations between critical theory, logical positivism, pragmatism and critical rationalism. Of particular interest is the fact that before Horkheimer's polemical attack on logical positivism of 1937, there was an astonishing degree of interaction and collaboration between the Frankfurt School and the Vienna Circle, in particular between Horkheimer and Neurath, precisely because of shared left-wing views.

184 Ethics and politics

active, and that they have tended to support progressive rather than conservative or reactionary causes.

No philosopher of any age has ever trumped Russell's political engagement on the side of the down-trodden and oppressed. His activities included theoretical discussion – notably his account of German social democracy and his critiques of both capitalism and Bolshevism. But he also put his nose to the grind in day-to-day political activities, from running for Parliament, through his valiant opposition to World War I, to his role in the Campaign for Nuclear Disarmament and the resistance to the Vietnam War (see Ryan 1988).

Horkheimer's invidious remarks notwithstanding, the Vienna Circle was the most political philosophical group of note in the twentieth century. It certainly surpassed the more notorious critical theorists of the Frankfurt School, who remained aloof from actual political struggles. On the so-called 'left wing' of the Vienna Circle we find an outspoken if unorthodox Marxist like Neurath, a socialist activist like Hahn and a more theoretically inclined humanist socialist like Carnap. By contrast, Schlick and Waismann constituted the apolitical or 'right wing'. Schlick not only resisted the attempt of harnessing logical positivism to specific political goals. He went as far as trying to ingratiate himself to the clerical fascists of Dollfuß, if only for the sake of preserving the *Verein Ernst Mach*. This was an embarrassing and unsuccessful gambit, strongly condemned by Neurath and Carnap (1963: 57–8). Yet even Schlick explicitly opposed Nazism as a liberal humanist, pacifist and cosmopolitan (1952).

Admittedly, although the basic political attitudes of the logical positivists may have survived their exodus to America, their activism did not (see Riesch 2004). Part of the explanation must be that Neurath, the leading political firebrand, died in 1945. Another part lies presumably in the post-war political situation in the USA. Democratic left-wingers faced a political scene polarized between Stalinism and McCarthyism. Their willingness to oppose the second, in any event far lesser, evil would have been dampened further by their status as immigrants with ample reason to be grateful for the sanctuary they had received.

There is no licence here for diagnosing a generic link between analytic philosophy and political abstinence. For a similar political constellation also had paralysing effects on the political commitment of the Frankfurt School. After World War II, Horkheimer and Adorno no longer qualified even as champagne socialists. To be sure, Marcuse turned into the guru of the student rebellion of the 1960s. But Russell also retained political fire in his belly. Indeed, his collaboration with Sartre in the 'International War

Crimes Tribunal' condemning the US war in Vietnam marks a political consensus across philosophical barriers (Russell 1967–9: 667–8).

Nevertheless, the accusation that analytic philosophy tends to be ethically neutral and apolitical has not yet been deflected entirely. Critical theorists are not alone in suspecting that the ethical reflections and political stances of analytic philosophers do not form an integral part of their philosophical endeavours. In pronouncing on matters moral and political, analytic philosophers appear to be moonlighting outside of their day-job.

There is some evidence to this effect. Russell frequently pronounced not just on normative ethics and policy-making, problems of what we nowadays call applied ethics, but also on specific political events and decisions. But he did so in a popular style, and for a general audience. Admittedly, he also wrote in a more academic vein about meta-ethical issues such as the definability of 'good' and the possibility of objective moral judgement. Yet he himself regarded even these discussions as *extrinsic* to philosophy as he conceived it. For that philosophy is essentially scientific, aspiring to *a priori* knowledge about the most general features of reality and of possible facts. By contrast, ethical notions and statements are essentially subjective and non-factual; they are disguised manifestations of our desires and emotions. This means that they are beyond the purview of science, and indeed of knowledge in general (1925, chs. 1 and 6; 1935). For related reasons, although Russell pined for a synthesis of his artistic and scientific, emotional and rational aspirations, he never achieved it (see Monk 1996a: 27, 245, 395–6).

The case of Chomsky is similar. For better or worse, he is the leading left-wing intellectual of our age, and it is hard to imagine a more vocal champion of sundry political causes. Furthermore, through his interaction with mainstream philosophy of language and of mind he is at least an associate of the analytic movement. At the same time, Chomsky denies that there is a direct connection between his technical work in linguistics and cognitive science on the one hand, and his moral and political convictions on the other (1979: Part 1). Dummett has been a prominent campaigner against racism and a champion of refugees for a long time. But in his recent *On Immigration and Refugees* he writes: 'At the invitation of Routledge and the series editors, I have tried in this book to bring together two things that interest me: philosophy and the politics of race, something I had never thought of doing before' (2001: ix).

By contrast, in the early days of logical positivism its left wing representatives actually drew a closer connection between their scientific philosophy and their moral and political convictions. They conceived of their scientific world-view as a vehicle not just of intellectual, but also of moral and social progress (see Geier 1992: 57–99; Stadler 1997: chs. 11–12; Cartwright *et al.* 1996). Neurath was in the vanguard as regards both the condemnation of metaphysics and the promotion of political activism, and he explicitly linked the two (see Uebel 1991: Part III). But others were not lagging far behind. For Hahn, 'otherworldly philosophy', i.e. metaphysics, is a frequently used means for 'fobbing off with another world the multitude of those who are rightly dissatisfied with *this* world' (1930: 21). Carnap eloquently connected the scientific world-view and progressive cultural and political aspirations in the *Logische Aufbau*. Later he declared more bluntly that the struggle against metaphysics was part of the struggle 'which we lead against superstition, theology ... traditional morality and the capitalist exploitation of the worker' (1934a: 258). Small wonder, then, that the Circle's *Manifesto*, which bears the stamp of Neurath, handed out a cigar even to those not directly engaged in politics:

To be sure, not every proponent of the scientific world-view will be a fighter. Some [presumably Carnap], glad of solitude, will lead a withdrawn existence on the icy slopes of logic; some [presumably Schlick] may even disdain mingling with the masses and regret the 'trivialized' form that these matters inevitably take on spreading. However, their achievements too will take a place among the historic developments. We witness the spirit of the scientific world-view penetrating in growing measure the forms of personal and public life, in education, upbringing, architecture, and the shaping of economic and social life according to rational principles. *The scientific world-view serves life, and life receives it.* (Carnap, Hahn and Neurath 1929: 19–20)

With the benefit of hindsight, such hopes appear extremely optimistic. But it is clear that the political commitment of leading positivists was not simply a matter of coincidence. One thorny issue remains, however. It is far from clear how these uplifting ethical thoughts and rousing political exhortations can be reconciled with the positivists' image of philosophy and their account of evaluative and normative judgements. On the whole, they confined the role of practical philosophy to the analysis of moral discourse; and their favoured non-cognitivist analysis seemed to belittle moral issues by severely restricting the scope of rational ethical debate. Admittedly, the logical positivists pointed out that many ethical and political conflicts arise from divergent views about matters of fact, which they regarded as amenable to a rational resolution. But they would have been the first to insist that every judgement about what is good or ought to be done has an ineliminable evaluative or normative component. Again, the logical positivists could consistently (if naïvely) proclaim that by overcoming metaphysics the scientific world-view would undermine the foundations of the evaluative/normative views they opposed. Still, it is hard to fathom how that purely factual world-view could sustain their *alternative* evaluations and norms, and hence how they could consistently propound their positive moral and political views in their capacities as philosophers. Roughly the same holds for Stevenson's emotivism and, to a lesser degree, for Hare's universal prescriptivism (although the latter moved from a strictly neutral perspective to one in which the analysis of moral discourse has substantive moral implications). Accordingly, at the time when analytic philosophy gelled into a reasonably distinct movement, many of its standard bearers did indeed maintain that legitimate practical philosophy reduces to the logical and conceptual analysis of moral discourse. They also denied that moral statements are capable of stating facts and of embodying knowledge. Finally, they confined philosophy either to an appendix to scientific knowledge (the naturalistic option epitomized by Neurath), or to the analysis of non-philosophical forms of discourse (the 'Kantian' option epitomized by Carnap and conceptual analysis).[3] Consequently, the combination of the meta-ethical and the meta-philosophical views of many classic analytic philosophers is inimical to the idea of treating normative ethics and political theory as an integral part of the philosophical enterprise.

Leading non-analytic moral theorists, notably Apel (1980) and Habermas (1979), have felt that these semantic strictures condemn analytic philosophy to being existentially and politically insignificant, a scholastic exercise incapable of addressing the profound problems of human life and of social organization. To them it is all part of a schizophrenic world-picture. While modern science allows us to understand reality in a completely rational way, the questions which matter most, namely questions concerning morality, religion, art and the meaning of life, are treated as *a*rational, incapable of a rational answer. Rationality is confined to means–ends reason – what the Frankfurt School called 'instrumental reason' – i.e. to the efficient marshalling of means in the service of ends which are arbitrary and incapable of justification (Horkheimer and Adorno 1947). In a similar vein more recent critics from both left (e.g. Rorty 1998) and right (e.g. Kekes 1980) continue to blame analytic philosophy for failing to

---

[3] A third alternative, pursued by Schlick (1930), is to assign to moral philosophy both the analytic task of elucidating moral discourse and the psychological task of explaining why human beings (often) comply with moral demands. But even this more catholic approach precludes moral philosophers – by contrast to moralists – from issuing moral evaluations or prescriptions.

live up to philosophy's ancient aspiration of providing moral guidance, of being 'politically relevant' in the social sphere and giving 'meaning to life' in the private sphere (see also Borradori 1994: 4; Prado 2003a: 11).

Many analytic philosophers plead guilty to this kind of charge. Some have done so wistfully. Thus Wittgenstein (1922: Preface; 1980: 9) acknowledged 'how little has been achieved' when the logico-semantic problems analytic philosophy addresses have been solved. And in his reply to critics Russell reveals the sorrow of someone who cannot reconcile his yearning for an objectively binding morality with his philosophical convictions (1944). Other analytic philosophers have accepted the ethical and existential irrelevance of analytic philosophy light-heartedly. Thus Strawson and Quine, two great antipodes within post-war analytic philosophy who agree on little else, happily join hands in condemning students who look for 'inspirational or edifying writing in philosophy', on the grounds that such students are not moved by intellectual curiosity (Strawson 1990: 312; Quine 1981: 193). And really, how could serious students of philosophy possibly desire inspiration and edification, if instead they can have Strawson's acute observations about the use of the definite article or Quine's deft permutations of logical symbols?

For all that, there is no intrinsic link between analytic philosophy on the one hand and the two claims that offend its politically motivated critics, namely that moral judgements are non-cognitive and that philosophy should remain ethically neutral. Neither Moore nor the contemporary mainstream accepts either of these views. Indeed, at present the idea of ethical neutrality is almost universally rejected. Many contemporary analytic philosophers specialize in normative ethics of a kind that their predecessors would have described as lay sermonizing. Some of them reject the fact/value distinction(s) on which non-cognitivist accounts of moral judgement were based. Others reject the idea that philosophy cannot pronounce on matters of value or norms. Finally, as Williams has stressed, they are not faced by the question which deterred their predecessors, namely of how philosophers could have a special authority on such practical issues (2006: ch. 14). For they no longer regard (moral) philosophy as a 'pure' discipline with goals and methods entirely distinct from those of other disciplines, whether these be the natural sciences or the humanities. This is not to deny that some analytic ethicists and political theorists lay claim to special attention for their normative views. Yet they do so not on account of presuming a privileged intuitive grasp of moral facts (as in Moore), but on account of an ability to argue about these issues in a clear and cogent manner, an ability acquired through their training in analytic philosophy.

Admittedly, analytic philosophers may not have succeeded in demonstrating and explaining the possibility of universally binding practical standards and of objective moral knowledge. But it has not been for lack of trying on the part of thinkers like Rawls or Nagel (who, incidentally, share a left-wing political agenda with many of the aforementioned noncognitivists). It is doubtful, moreover, that their continental colleagues have fared any better. Finally, while strong versions of moral objectivism and cognitivism have been pursued by Apel and Habermas, this cannot be said of either Adorno or Horkheimer, not to mention Nietzsche and Heidegger. Nor can it be said of French philosophers from Sartre to Foucault and Derrida.

3 IS ANALYTIC PHILOSOPHY PROGRESSIVE AND EMANCIPATORY?

Critchley proclaims that 'so much philosophy in the continental tradition can be said to respond to a sense of crisis in the modern world, and to attempt to produce a critical consciousness of the present with an emancipatory intent' (2001: 111). But there is a case for holding that the emancipatory boot is actually on the analytic foot.

From its inception, continental philosophy has been a negative response to the Enlightenment ideals of reason and emancipation, and especially to Kant. This response ranged from conservatives like Hegel to reactionaries like Jacobi and Schelling. Later on, the most original and influential continental thinkers – Nietzsche and Heidegger – initiated what Critchley himself calls 'reactionary modernism', a critique of modernity which violently repudiates the ideals of liberty and equality. Extremely right-wing political recipes have also issued freely from the pens of Carl Schmitt and Leo Strauss. Then there is the awkward question of whether the Leninism and Stalinism supported by eminent continentals like (the early) Bloch, Sartre and Merleau-Ponty qualify as emancipatory in even the most attenuated and perverted sense. Finally, there are figures like Foucault and Derrida, who have campaigned on behalf of progressive causes, but whose writings are inimical to the humanist ideals that have fuelled progressive political movements since the Enlightenment. Indeed, Critchley himself admits that from Bentham vs Coleridge to Carnap vs Heidegger it has been the 'continental' side that has tended to resist progressive change (2001: 45, 87–8).

The first positive prejudice about analytical philosophy pertains to this point. It is the idea that analytic philosophy contrasts favourably with continental philosophy, because it occupies a more humane and

emancipatory ethical-cum-political perspective. Perhaps few would consider this as the defining feature of analytic philosophy. But for some
proponents of analytic philosophy it is a characteristic feature associated
with (allegedly) defining features such as the advocacy of reason.

As we have seen, many of the logical positivists presented 'scientific
philosophy' as a *progressive* political force. Indeed for Neurath it was a
virtual panacea against right-wing political ideologies, which he associated
with metaphysics in general and post-Kantian German philosophy in
particular. At present, proponents of a rationalist conception of analytic
philosophy such as Føllesdal insist that it has beneficial effects not just for
philosophy or in the wider cognitive sphere, but also in the area of
'individual and social ethics'. For its characteristic emphasis on

argument and justification . . . will make life more difficult for political leaders and
fanatics who spread messages which do not stand up to critical scrutiny, but which
nevertheless often have the capacity to seduce the masses into intolerance and
violence. Rational argument and rational dialogue are of the utmost importance
for a well-functioning democracy. To educate people in these activities is perhaps
the most important task of analytic philosophy. (1997: 15–16)

Similarly, Cohen assesses the 'direction of [analytic philosophy's] socio-
political influence' as follows:

By its systematic exploration of reasons and reasoning, analytic philosophy
helps to consolidate the intellectual infrastructure that is needed for systems of
social organization within which disputes are reflected in argument and counter-
argument, rather than in the use of violence. By virtue of its preoccupation with
rationality it promotes awareness that the intellectual merit of a person's opinion
does not hinge on his membership of a particular party, priesthood, or hermetic
tradition.

Analytic philosophy, according to Cohen,

deserves respect as a cultural movement that makes for tolerance, universal
suffrage, ethical pluralism, non-violent resolution of disputes, and freedom of
intellectual enterprise, and is in turn promoted by them. Doctrinaire tyrannies
certainly have good reasons to ban it. (1986: 61–2)

Although I cannot defend them here, I emphatically share Føllesdal's and
Cohen's social and political ideals of a liberal democracy based on rational
argument, dialogue and non-violence. As regards the statement that analytic philosophy *promotes* such values, we need to distinguish two possible
claims: it could either mean that analytic philosophy has *propagated* these
values, or it could mean that it has actually *advanced* them in the public and
political sphere. Both Føllesdal and Cohen imply that analytic philosophy

will actually militate against fanaticism and tyranny, and thereby suggest that they subscribe to both claims. As we shall see, however, both of these claims stand in need of serious qualification.

This is not to deny that there is at least a *prima facie* connection between analytic philosophy and the propagation of certain liberal and progressive values. Neither employing nor extolling reason and argument is the distinguishing feature of analytic philosophy, or so I argued in chapter 6.5. In both respects it was incontrovertibly preceded by the Enlightenment. Nonetheless, the analytic movement has done more to scrutinize and uphold rationality than traditionalist and continental philosophy. Furthermore, following serious teething problems it has extended this pursuit of reason to the moral and political sphere. Otherwise highly diverse thinkers like Hart, Rawls, Thomas Nagel, Dworkin, Raz and Jerry Cohen have provided sophisticated justifications for the rule of law, liberal democracy, tolerance, altruism, and moderate versions of egalitarianism.

At the same time, analytic philosophy cannot lay claim to being the sole or even the most significant philosophical champion of such civic values. That accolade arguably belongs to theorists of the democratic left (radical liberals, social democrats, suffragettes, pacifists, anti-colonialists, etc.) on the one hand, pragmatism on the other. Habermas, to mention a recent example, has been as vocal a champion of liberal democracy as any analytic philosopher, and politically more effective to boot. And the pragmatist case for democracy has been taken up just as enthusiastically by a more 'continental' neo-pragmatist like Rorty (1998) as by a more analytically minded neo-pragmatist like Putnam (1992: ch. 9).

That analytic philosophy has no monopoly on supporting liberal and democratic values militates against characterizing it by reference to those values. But it should be a cause for celebration, even among its most partisan supporters. More sobering is the thought that there is no uniform connection between these values and analytic philosophy, even if we leave aside the question of actual impact. For there have been eminent analytic philosophers who have opposed liberalism, democracy and non-violence. In supporting this contention, I shall leave aside the personal behaviour of great analytic philosophers. There is no reason to accept that their failure to live up to ethical ideals (whether ours or their own) has been more pronounced than that of other mortals. But when it comes to assessing the question of whether there is an intrinsic link between analytic philosophy and (presumed) moral and political rectitude, it is imperative to consider the ethical and political views of its proponents, and their political activities.

In this respect aberrations to both the left and the right abound. Frege opposed democracy and liberalism. He was a virulent nationalist and anti-Semite. He abused his towering intelligence by contemplating plans for expelling the Jews from Germany and for suppressing the Social Democrats and Catholics. Indeed, he can fairly be regarded as a proto-Nazi on account of his sympathies for Hitler's and Ludendorff's defence of their failed putsch of 1923. That analytical skills and logical acumen offer no protection against political aberrations of even the most heinous kind is further demonstrated by Gentzen, a logical prodigy who was not just a proto-Nazi but a Nazi *tout court* (see Menzler-Trott 2001).

By comparison, Wittgenstein's ruminations on moral, cultural and political issues qualify as a blessing, albeit a mixed one. They feature culturally conservative qualms about twentieth-century scientism and the obsession with progress, which are contestable yet worthy of serious consideration. But they also feature objectionable ideas, notably doubts about the creative powers of Jews (see Monk 1990: 73, 247–8; ch. 17; Glock 2001). To be fair, many of these remarks were made in conversation, and, as in the case of Frege, none of them were intended for publication. Nevertheless they suggest that in matters cultural and political Wittgenstein was a loose canon. He detested Russell's pacifism and humanist socialism, while at the same time sympathizing with the hard left in the thirties and forties, and even considered emigrating to the Soviet Union. In so far as an underlying principle can be detected in his political views, it was a Tolstoyan ideal of a simple life of manual work, coupled with a mild predilection for authoritarian ideologies – bolshevism, catholicism – which place individual liberty and well-being below the pursuit of 'higher' goals.

To some readers it might occur that these lapses, though deplorable, are atypical. For they pertain to Germans and Austrians during a period in which these countries were dominated by political extremisms. As we shall see, the socio-historical context must indeed be taken into account. But this holds for non-analytic philosophers as well. In any event, political aberrations by analytic philosophers extend beyond central Europe.

Whatever his personal demeanour, in the equally fraught area of social ethics and politics, Russell generally acquitted himself well. As against countless intellectuals, Wittgenstein included, he was right to resist World War I and to loathe Soviet Russia from the 1920s onwards. Nonetheless, his political ruminations do not uniformly conform to the high standards of his writings in theoretical philosophy. Thus during World War I he propounded that Slavs are racially inferior to Germans. Furthermore, he is widely held to have advocated a pre-emptive nuclear strike on the Soviet Union between 1945 and 1948. Whether he ever did in so many words is a subject of considerable dispute. What is not in dispute is that he regarded such a 'preventive war' as preferable both to the Soviet Union acquiring nuclear weapons of its own and to appeasement. It is also clear that he favoured an aggressive strategy of containment, a policy of which he believed, quite sensibly, that it might well lead to such a pre-emptive strike. In the converse direction, but in an equally irresponsible mode, in the sixties Russell reached the conclusion that the USA rather than the Soviet Union was the embodiment of all evil. As a result he egged on the latter to intervene militarily on the side of North Vietnam, even though he must have realized that this would in all likelihood precipitate the outbreak of World War III.[4]

More recent analytic luminaries have not been immune to political extremes either. During the sixties, Putnam valiantly opposed the Vietnam War as a member of Students for a Democratic Society. But he was also, more problematically, a member of the Progressive Labor Party, a Maoist splinter group, and he radicalized some of his students such as Hartry Field and Richard Boyd in a similar direction. To his credit, Putnam retracted his support later on (see Ben-Menahem 2005). Chomsky, by contrast, has not undergone a similar change of mind. His political views, especially on US foreign policy and human rights, have been subject to endless controversies that have created more heat than light. Even if one disregards slanders and distortions propagated by his countless enemies, however, one must take issue with the haste with which he draws con-clusions on weighty matters such as freedom of expression and holocaust denial, and with his tendency to play down or trivialize the atrocities committed by opponents of the USA such as the Khmer Rouge or the Bosnian Serbs.[5]

In combination with the fact that distinguished non-analytic philoso-phers have been on the side of the angels, these examples suggest that analytic philosophers should think twice before adopting a holier-than-thou attitude. They also indicate that there is no intrinsic incompatibility between analytic philosophy and political extremisms of various kinds. Yet if analytic philosophy were inherently rational, and if rationality in the sphere of public morals and politics *per se* militated against extremism and

---

[4] See Griffin 2001: 410, 426–9; Monk 2000: 297–304, 468–9; http://www.economist.com/books/displayStory.cfm?Story_ID=699582 accessed 21 May 2006.
[5] See 'Criticisms of Noam Chomsky' in Wikipedia, The Free Encyclopedia. Retrieved 13 October 2006, from http://en.wikipedia.org/w/index.php?title=Criticism_of_Noam_Chomsky&oldid=80748085.

favoured liberal democracy, then we should expect such an incompatibility. There are three possible explanations of this divergence between analytic philosophy and liberal political views.

One explanation lies in the fact that one can be an analytic philosopher without extolling the virtues of rational argument. This anti-intellectualism plays a role, for instance, in Wittgenstein's apparent soft spot for authoritarian modes of thought. A second possible explanation is that the link between rationality and political rectitude is weaker than assumed by rationalists. It is at least arguable that there *can be* such a thing as *excessive* emphasis on argument and a particular kind of intelligence, at least in the moral and political sphere.[6] Ever since Plato, philosophers have shown an uncanny willingness to follow the argument wherever it leads. Even on reaching absurd or repugnant conclusions, they have rarely engaged in soul-searching or questioned their own premises. Instead, they have devised clever arguments for dismissing the judgements, values and practices of ordinary mortals as unreflective and obsolete. This propensity is not confined to analytic philosophers. But as we shall see in the next section, it is particularly pronounced in those branches of the analytic movement aligned with consequentialism. And it is arguably such exaggerated confidence in the powers of philosophical judgement and reasoning which explains some of Russell's political blunders.

Finally, even if analytic *philosophy* had a tendency to encourage wholesome moral and political views because of its special relationship to reason, its individual *practitioners* would not have to be morally or politically superior. There are *blind spots* of reason. The capacity to think critically and argue cogently in one area does not guarantee the capacity to do so in another. Our approach to moral and political issues is particularly susceptible to extraneous influences, reaching from prejudices imbibed by upbringing through wishful thinking occasioned by personal experiences to sheer coincidence. It is the historical context that determines the options for the exercise of an individual's moral and political judgement. In a different setting, Frege would still have been an embittered misanthrope

---

[6] At the same time I cannot underwrite Sluga's denial of any link between Nazism and irrationalism (1993: 99–100). The distinction between anti-intellectualism and irrationalism (ch. 6.5) helps to bring out my reservations. Some Nazi sympathizers like Frege and Rickert did not subscribe to anti-intellectualism. Nevertheless, Nazi ideology was both aggressively anti-intellectual and risibly irrational. Therefore a failure of reason was a necessary condition for supporting their cause. Furthermore, the most important philosophical Nazis – Rosenberg, Baeumler, Heidegger, Krieck – opposed reason in a (predominantly) unreasoned manner.

and Gentzen would still have been an opportunist. But they could not have manifested these vices through political allegiances quite so pernicious.

The paramount importance of context also goes to defuse a potential comeback for those who regard analytic philosophy as ethically and politically wholesome. If the big philosophical beasts are anything to go by, then culpable political lapses may be rarer within the analytic movement than in continental philosophy. Even if this claim survives a statistical survey, however, it must be put in perspective. Numerically speaking, most analytic philosophers have grown up in societies that were liberal and democratic, at least by the standards of their time. As a result, they have faced fewer political temptations and dilemmas than some other groups of intellectuals. Conversely, as Sluga (1993) has shown, it was the upheaval of World War I and the ensuing sense of crisis that fostered extreme right-wing sympathies among German philosophers of all persuasions, Frege included. If we contemporary analytic philosophers are relatively immune to extreme political aberrations, this is due not to our intrinsic moral or intellectual virtues, nor to our sound grounding in modal logic, formal semantics, externalist theories of content, contextualist epistemology or the hedonistic calculus. It is rather due to the fact that we, or at least most of us, have enjoyed the benefits of liberal democracies, and have had the additional privilege of going through systems of higher education that are generally geared to humane social and political values, quite independently of the analytic faction in a numerically small and socially insignificant discipline like philosophy. Finally, while contemporary analytic philosophers are more immune to certain radical left-wing views that have lost whatever appeal they had in the 1960s, later generations may well have reason to condemn our failure to be more radical in the pursuit of pressing environmental causes such as climate change.

4 THE SINGER AFFAIR

An analytic orientation is not necessary for inculcating liberal and democratic values in individual philosophers. Nor is it sufficient, either because its link with rationality is weaker than supposed by proponents of a rationalist definition, or because the unfettered pursuit of rationality can be a mixed blessing, or because of contingent historical circumstances. But might it not at least help to advance such values at a social level? Might it not actually support and reinforce a general atmosphere in which moral debates and political processes are based on peaceful coexistence, mutual tolerance and rational argument?

This idea can draw some support from the so-called Singer affair. In 1989 the Australian philosopher Peter Singer was to give lectures on applied ethics throughout the German-speaking parts of Europe. He was soon confronted by protesters from disabled pressure groups, the hard left, and the religious right. They alleged that by promoting active euthanasia Singer's *Practical Ethics* (1979) condoned 'mass extermination' of the same kind as the euthanasia programme of the Nazis, and that his ideas were 'fascist' and 'murderous'. The anti-Singer alliance opposed not just euthanasia, but any *debate* about euthanasia. They prevented Singer's lectures through whistles, noise-machines, and chants; in one case he was even physically assaulted. University seminars using *Practical Ethics* were obstructed, and petitions signed to remove his supporters from academic posts. Matters came to a boil with the Wittgenstein Symposium at Kirchberg. In 1991, this important platform of analytic philosophy was to have 'Applied Ethics' as its theme. Initially, the organizers refused to revoke invitations to Singer and his supporters. But the anti-Singer alliance threatened to stage an exhibition 'Kirchberg under the Nazis'. Faced with this prospect, the local innkeepers resolved not to serve participants of the conference, which had to be cancelled.

The idea of Austrian innkeepers joining the anti-fascist struggle in order to conceal the Nazi past of their village is striking, to say the least. The spectacle would have been as instructive as any philosophy conference, and more entertaining, even in the absence of beer and schnaps. There has been another ironic result, in which Singer himself found consolation. Because of the media coverage, the taboo about discussing euthanasia has been broken; indeed, since 1991 issues in applied ethics have increasingly been debated in the Germanophone world. The affair had yet another ironic result. Singer has been one of the champions of the Hegelian ideal of *substantielle Sittlichkeit*, the shared ethos of a cohesive community. This ethos does not respect the purely 'negative freedom' of individuals to have their own goals and opinions, but seeks to imbue them with specific moral values. For Hegel and his Marxist admirers, such an organic community is entitled to curtail civil liberties, including freedom of expression. Accordingly the protesters share with Singer the ideal of a community which is not based on the agreement to disagree about many moral issues, but imposes specific moral ideals, even at the expense of civil liberties. The difference is that for Singer's opponents the sanctity of human life is part of this substantial ethos, which means that the discussion of euthanasia can be restricted. In the land of Hegel and Marx, Singer got more *substantielle Sittlichkeit* than he may have bargained for when writing his *Past Masters* introductions (1983 and 1980) to these thinkers.

Liberal *Schadenfreude* aside, my last observation only seems to support the association between analytic philosophy and liberal values on the one hand, non-analytic philosophy and the restriction of liberty on the other. Many of Singer's left-wing opponents subscribed to Marxism, while some of his right-wing opponents drew on traditional Christian philosophy and on Hegel. More generally, the affair reinforces a stereotypical contrast. On the one hand, Anglophone analytic philosophers have reacted with incredulity to this outbreak of Teutonic intolerance. For them, unfettered argument is the very lifeblood of the academy, and the possibility of questioning even the most fundamental and cherished assumptions the hallmark of philosophy. On the other hand, German and Austrian academic institutions and some professional philosophers have not only tolerated the attacks on applied ethics, but even supported them. A German philosopher, it seems, is not expected to muster nine arguments for and ten against any given position, but to utter profound wisdoms, preferably wisdoms which are in line with a shared communal ethos.

Before appending QED to this argument, however, a few points need to be borne in mind. First, the utilitarian views on euthanasia for which Singer was attacked are indeed severe. He condones active *non-voluntary euthanasia*, the killing of innocent human beings that are incapable of understanding or making the choice between life and death – such as severely defective infants or grown-ups in a vegetative state. Moreover, he favours such a course of action not just in cases in which it is in the interest of the patient, but also in cases in which it is best for *the patient's environment* – the family or society. This includes both infants with Down's syndrome and haemophiliacs. Singer admits that the life of these patients 'can be expected to contain a positive balance of happiness over misery', and that adult haemophiliacs tend to 'find life definitely worth living'. Nevertheless he maintains that it is *permissible* to kill them on the request of their parents for up to a month after their birth. Indeed, he *favours* killing them. Their 'life prospects are significantly less happy than those of a normal child', and they are a constant burden to their parents. It is therefore best to 'replace' them by healthy children (1979: 131–5). This position is hardly a showcase for the idea that analytic philosophy erects intellectual safeguards against extremism.[7] It is more of a showcase for a particular failure of rationality, albeit one associated more with utilitarianism than

---

[7] Singer mellowed his stance in the second edition, but this is immaterial to whether the protests against his initial position were legitimate. For his reaction to the affair, see Singer 1992. For a defence of my take on the ethical and jurisprudential issues it raises see Glock 1994.

with analytic philosophy as such: the failure to reconsider one's premises in the light of unpalatable consequences, and the tendency to seek refuge instead in self-serving animadversions against 'orthodox' or 'conventional' morality and 'lay' intuitions.

Accordingly, the Singer affair casts a negative light not just on continental enemies of free speech, but also on some analytic philosophers working in applied ethics. They have approached sensitive moral problems in a gung-ho spirit that sets them apart unfavourably from the characteristically serious air of Germanophone moral philosophy. Most applied ethicists – Singer and his followers included – are what right-wing commentators are fond of calling 'politically correct'. That is to say, they favour linguistic expressions that are calculated to cause minimum offence to minority groups. As a result, they would have scruples about calling people in wheel-chairs 'handicapped' or 'disabled'. But this has not stopped some of them from telling the very same people that, for the sake of maximizing overall utility, the world would be a much better place without them.

The same cavalier approach is evident in a particular style of example and dilemma beloved by many analytic ethicists. On the one hand, it is to their credit that they consider specific moral problems and test their theories by reference to puzzle cases. On the other, many of these cases are not just extremely far-fetched, but also in exquisitely bad taste. The following is not much of a travesty, alas:

On your way to the airport for the sake of attending an Oxfam conference you pass a pond in which an (innocent) child and an (irreplaceable) genetically modified sheep are drowning. Should you save the child, in line with the dictates of 'conventional' morality, the sheep, for the benefit of scientific understanding, or ensure that you catch your flight to bestow a maximum of good on the Third World? And what difference, if any, would it make if the drowning child were splashing water on a sandwich you were about to devour?

There may be a place for casuistry; but that place is in the consideration of genuine moral dilemmas, dilemmas that could confront minimally decent and sane human agents. In this kind of casuistry, by contrast, moral problems seem to be treated mainly as an excuse for trying out one's pet theory or showing how clever one is.

A further observation concerns once more the context. To a considerable degree the disconcerting aspects of the Singer affair reflect not so much the logophobia of continental or traditionalist philosophers but political sensitivities created by the ghastly legacy of the Nazis. At the time of the Singer affair Switzerland was still dominated by non-analytic philosophy. Yet, in marked contrast to their German and Austrian equivalents, Swiss academic institutions staunchly defended Singer's right to speak, and applied ethics flourished there long before it gained a foothold in Germany and Austria. Conversely, after these sensitivities had been eroded in these parts, a prominent 'continental' philosophical journalist like Sloterdijk (1999) showed no scruples to suggest that Nietzsche's ideal of the *Übermensch* ought to be pursued by means of genetic selection and engineering.

There is a final objection to the rationalist case of Føllesdal and Cohen. Anyone who subscribes to the hope that analytic philosophy actually advances liberal and democratic values such as rational debate and the peaceful resolution of conflict needs to face up to an awkward fact. Before the USA, Great Britain and Australia were dominated by analytic philosophy (roughly till the end of World War II), they were clearly in the international vanguard of promoting such values. But now that they have become the powerhouses of analytic philosophy the situation is rather different. At present these countries are the most belligerent in the world. If we confine our comparison group to contemporary Western democracies, the result is even less flattering. On issues ranging from weapons of mass destruction and political correctness to evolutionary theory and climate change, the voices of reason, of science and of empirical fact play second fiddle at best to political propaganda, media glitz, economic expedience and religious fundamentalism. Furthermore, it would be ludicrous to suggest that in these countries the level of public debate is higher than in European countries in which continental philosophy has a significant presence. The British tabloid press and American TV and radio, for instance, enjoy a hard-earned reputation for being among the worst of their respective kinds in the Western world.

Of course it is complex social and political circumstances that are to blame for this melancholy development rather than analytic philosophy. Nevertheless, three observations are in place. First, although analytic philosophy *per se* is neither rational nor progressive in the political and moral sphere, there have been many rational and/or progressive voices within analytic ethics and political theory. The question arises why these voices have not had more of an impact. We shall return to this issue in chapter 9.2. Secondly, these observations do not refute Føllesdal's and Cohen's claims conclusively. That could only be done through extensive empirical investigations of the actual political impact of analytic philosophy on individual practitioners and their societies. But, thirdly, they support the fear that their hopes may be Utopian. There is no evidence that *everything else being equal* analytic philosophy has greater public benefits than other forms of philosophy. This counts against Cohen's claim that analytic philosophy actually promotes liberal values in the wider political and public sphere. Nor is there any evidence for his second claim, namely that analytic philosophy is in turn favoured by a general liberal climate. Its early roots reach back to the Habsburg Empire and to Prussia, which were authoritarian even by the exacting standards of the nineteenth century. And the same socio-political context that spawned logical positivism in Austria and Germany also gave rise to Nazism.

5 AN ANTIDOTE TO IDEOLOGY?

There remains a final potential advantage of analytic philosophy. Irrespective of the views of individual practitioners and of its actual ethical and political effects, at least analytic philosophy properly separates theoretical and practical issues. Even when the practical recommendations of analytic philosophers are controversial, it is tempting to hold, they are based on dry hard reasoning rather than on a dubious mixture of philosophical ideas, ideology and political allegiances. Conversely, non-analytic philosophy appears marred by a tendency to conflate cognitive and moral pursuits.

In this spirit, Soames maintains that analytic philosophy is committed to argument. He thinks that this is 'connected with a second underlying theme'. Analytic philosophy aims for

truth and knowledge, as opposed to moral or spiritual improvement ... In general, the goal in analytic philosophy is to discover what is true, not to provide a useful recipe for living one's life. (2003: xiv–xv)

The point here is not that analytic philosophy *ignores* moral questions, or that it remains *neutral* on them, but that in dealing with them it is motivated by the desire to provide *true* answers rather than *practical guidance*.

The case of ancient philosophers like Socrates demonstrates that one can seek moral or spiritual improvement, yet do so through the reasoned pursuit of truth and knowledge. More importantly, several analytic philosophers also aspire ultimately to moral and spiritual improvement. Wittgenstein springs to mind, at least in some moods. As do the politicized members of the Vienna Circle, and perhaps even Russell. Finally, numerous analytic philosophers presently work on applied ethics. Yet one hopes that at least some of them are motivated by a desire to provide moral and political guidance.

Conversely, many non-analytic philosophers have been driven by curiosity rather than a moral-cum-spiritual mission. What is more, these include thinkers that count as continental, at least in the wider sense. It is not for nothing that Marx and Engels attacked their Hegelian predecessors for merely 'interpreting the world'. For most phenomenologists moral and political guidance is a secondary concern at best, indeed, their method professes to be purely descriptive. Finally, even if Nietzsche, Heidegger and Sartre sought moral and spiritual improvement, their postmodernist successors seem to pursue the less serious objective of playing around with ideas, words and texts in ways that they deem elegant, irrespective of practical concerns.

Lack of practical *motivation* is neither a characteristic of analytic philosophers nor a boon. The real issue is whether moral and political aspirations dictate the *content* of philosophical arguments, methods and conclusions. There may be a sense in which even theoretical research ought to be relevant. But that simply means that it ought to pursue questions which make sense and which are interesting and important from a cognitive point of view. It does not mean that theoretical research must try to yield practical results, whether these be of a technical or of a moral-cum-political kind. As the history of science and of the academy shows, theoretical research is often most fruitful and beneficial when it is not subjected to the demand of yielding practical results. Furthermore, even though theoretical research ought to be theoretically relevant, relevant to furthering our knowledge and understanding, it is far from clear that it flourishes when it is explicitly driven by this desire, rather than by curiosity.

If philosophy advises on moral and political matters, that guidance should be based on philosophical reasoning, rather than the other way around. Even that philosophy *can* give such counsel at all is not a foregone conclusion, but subject to theoretical reflection. To adapt one's philosophical views in logic, epistemology and metaphysics to prior moral or political commitments is misguided in two respects. First, it confuses practical questions concerning what ought to be the case, or what is valuable, with theoretical questions in the widest sense, concerning what is actually the case, what might be the case or what can be shown to be the case. Secondly, even within the practical sphere it commits the sin of dogmatism, in so far as certain moral and political doctrines are treated as sacrosanct instead of being subject to critical reflection. Of course it is perfectly legitimate to engage in theoretical philosophy out of moral and political motives. But a philosophy the methods and results of which are predetermined by prior practical commitments is wishful thinking at best, and deceitful rhetoric at worst. Marxist incantations about the primacy of practice over theory notwithstanding, a refusal to bow to the clamour of being politically relevant and to tailor philosophical methods and views to preconceived moral and political ideals, is actually an advantage.

Eminent analytic philosophers have indeed combated this type of error. Austin wrote: 'I am not sure importance is important; truth is' (1970: 271). Russell, implacable enemy of 'ordinary language philosophy' though he was, would have agreed. He ended his 1957 BBC television interview with the advice to future generations always to distinguish strictly between what one would *like* to be true and what one can *show* to be true. In a similar vein Cohen is satisfied that analytic philosophy can afford resisting 'the claims of other philosophies to superior social relevance', not just because of its liberal and democratic credentials, but also because it 'can be counter-productive to design the programme of philosophical enquiry with an eye to the social benefits that this enquiry may achieve' (1986: 62). Even the later Putnam, who actively pursues a pragmatist apology of democracy, criticizes deconstructivism for lapsing into a kind of 'para-politics', a politicized philosophy which sees its objectives primarily in social and political terms (1992: 197). The same can be said about some manifestations of pragmatism; not, to be sure, of the more analytic pragmatism of Putnam and Haack, but of the brand represented by Rorty and West. And it might also be said of certain traditionalist philosophers whose religious convictions predetermine their arguments in other areas.

At the same time, a systematic running together of philosophy and politics is certainly not constitutive of either traditionalist philosophy or of phenomenology in the vein of Husserl. Nor is all analytic philosophy immune to this vice. Because of the shared Marxist background, Neurath no less than critical theory regarded theorizing about society as inseparable from theorizing on behalf of a harmonious social organization (see Cartwright and Cat 1998). Furthermore, we have seen that some opponents have tried to compromise analytic philosophy by associating it with right-wing political views. Alas, they have no monopoly on drawing flimsy connections between philosophical positions and political commitments. Neurath's association of metaphysics with conservative or reactionary political attitudes is wishful speculation, as the case of Kant, Bolzano, Brentano and Russell should have demonstrated to him (the same goes for his association of analytic or 'scientific' philosophy with Catholicism). In general, Neurath's extreme loathing of metaphysics comes across as politically rather than philosophically motivated. Other logical positivists, including politically interested figures like Carnap, softened their stance towards metaphysics when they recognized the problems in their anti-metaphysical arguments. Neurath, by contrast, remained adamantly opposed even when this led to a split with his former comrade Carnap (see Carnap 1963: 22–3). Nor are we dealing exclusively with sins of the past. There persists an unfortunate tendency in some quarters to taint assorted non-analytic thinkers with the brush of Nazism or Stalinism, enormous temporal and intellectual gaps notwithstanding.[8]

Consequently, while a certain separation of theoretical from practical and of philosophical from political issues is salutary, it is not a distinguishing feature of analytic philosophy. Still, there remains a lingering suspicion that contemporary analytic philosophy contrasts favourably with important strands of continental philosophy in this respect. This suspicion is linked to wider issues concerning the role of analytic philosophy within culture at large. There is one area in which analytic philosophers even of the theoretical brand have had an impact on general cultural and political debates, an impact that has on occasion reached the mainstream press. I am thinking of the science and culture wars that have been raging on American campuses for some time and which later spilled over into French academies. These hostilities, along with similarly grand issues concerning the merit and future of analytic philosophy, will occupy the last chapter. In the next chapter I shall finally get round to presenting and defending my own conception of analytic philosophy.

---

[8] In the course of defending Neurath's anti-metaphysical diatribes Köhler (1991: 138 and n) detects an immediate route from Kant's 'lamentable incomprehension of logic' to Hegel's 'apology for totalitarianism'. What is lamentable instead is Köhler's random association of Kant's philosophical logic with Hegel's political theory, and his comprehension of totalitarianism. He is either clueless as to the meaning of this term, which was coined in the 1920s for a distinctively modern type of dictatorship; or, more ominously still, he cannot tell the difference between the Prussian monarchy of the 1820s that Hegel did indeed defend and the murderous regimes of Mussolini, Hitler and Stalin.

CHAPTER 8

Contested concepts, family resemblances and tradition

Geo-linguistic, historiographical, formal, material and 'ethical' conceptions of analytic philosophy have all been found wanting. Have we reached
the end of the line? We certainly face an impasse. It may seem that we are
forced to conclude (with Preston 2004) that analytic philosophy does not
constitute a distinctive phenomenon. At the very least it looks as if we have
to agree with Leiter when he claims: '*I don't think anyone knows what
"analytic philosophy" is*' (2004b).

Fortunately, we do not have to throw in the towel quite yet. So far we
have considered different kinds of *analytic* definitions of analytic philosophy, definitions in terms of conditions which are individually necessary
and jointly sufficient for being part of analytic philosophy. But there are
legitimate concepts that do not allow of an analytic definition. Indeed, we
have encountered such concepts in our odyssey up to this point. Neither
the family resemblance concepts that feature in Wittgenstein's later attack
on his youthful quest for the essence of language (ch. 2.5) nor the genetic
concepts central to Williams' argument in favour of historicism (ch. 4.2)
are defined analytically. What is more, there is yet another possibility. It
arises straight out of the rationalistic conception discussed in chapter 6.5.
That conception in effect turns 'analytic philosophy' into an honorific title,
one that signifies what has come to be known as an essentially contested
concept. In section 1 I concede that there is such an honorific use, while
insisting that it is less entrenched than the descriptive use. I also consider
the merits of a revisionary definition of 'analytic philosophy' along rationalist lines. My conclusion is that such a revision would lead down the
garden path to a persuasive definition, one which is less propitious to
philosophical debate than a descriptive definition.

In section 2 I turn to the question of whether analytic philosophy is a
family resemblance concept. Though hugely influential, the idea of family
resemblance concepts has also been fiercely contested. Against the sceptics,
I shall argue that it is coherent, and that it has some purchase in the case of

analytic philosophy. But a definition in terms of family resemblances draws the lines of analytic philosophy irrespective of any historical timeframe, thereby once more exceeding its commonly recognized extension. Furthermore, like an essentially contested concept, a family resemblance concept requires some central paradigmatic cases around which other cases are clustered. These paradigmatic cases, I shall argue in section 3, are provided by a conception of analytic philosophy which treats it as a historical tradition, thereby revealing analytic philosophy to be a partly genetic concept. On the other hand, it is to some extent by reference to the features that figure in family resemblance conceptions of analytic philosophy that we can establish membership in the tradition. This facilitates identification of paradigmatic members of the tradition and allows one to exclude thinkers that have influenced members of that tradition, but whose general outlook is too remote for them to be added.

The answer to the title question, then, is that analytic philosophy is a tradition held together *both* by ties of mutual influence *and* by family resemblances. But who precisely is part of that tradition, who founded it, and when did it emerge as a distinct intellectual movement? The answers suggested by my approach are in keeping with the commonly acknowledged extension, as I show in the last section. Analytic philosophy gradually emerged when the Fregean revolution of formal logic combined with debates about the nature of propositions necessitated by Moore's and Russell's rebellion against idealism, and with the linguistic turn of the *Tractatus*.

1 AN ESSENTIALLY CONTESTED CONCEPT?

Most if not all proponents of a rationalistic conception proffer it with an *apologetic* intent, as part of a defence of analytic philosophy. The rationalist conception shapes the image of analytic philosophy projected by societies dedicated to promoting it. The European Society for Analytic Philosophy presents it as follows:

Analytic philosophy is characterized above all by the goal of clarity, the insistence on explicit argumentation in philosophy, and the demand that any view expressed be exposed to the rigours of critical evaluation and discussion by peers. (URL = http://www.dif.unige.it/esap/ accessed 04/10/05)

The combination of definition and defence is nicely expressed in the title of Føllesdal's essay: 'Analytic Philosophy: what is it and why should one engage in it?' Answering both questions, he draws the following 'final conclusion':

We should engage in analytic philosophy not just because it is *good* philosophy but also for reasons of individual and social ethics. (1997: 15)

A similarly uplifting spirit seems to have prevailed at the founding session of the *Gesellschaft für Analytische Philosophie* (GAP) at Berlin in 1990. Having listened to the proposed aims of the society, one pundit summed it all up by saying: 'Perhaps we shouldn't establish a society for analytic philosophy, but simply one for *good* philosophy!'[1]

Less tongue-in-cheek, a former president of GAP, Ansgar Beckermann, explicitly connects the rationalist conception of analytic philosophy to the idea that it equates to good philosophy. According to Beckermann, analytic philosophy originally set out to overcome philosophy by dissolving its problems through the logical analysis of language. But 'what characterizes analytic philosophy today' – after its original ambitions have been frustrated – is acceptance of two views: first, that philosophy seeks to answer substantive (rather than historical) questions in a way that is both systematic and governed by universally applicable standards of rationality; secondly, that this ambition can only be achieved if the concepts and arguments philosophers employ are made as clear and transparent as possible. 'And in my view these are indeed also the distinguishing features of good philosophy' (2004: 12).

More or less deliberately, proponents of the rationalistic conception use 'analytic philosophy' as an *honorific* title. Rightly so, given their assumptions. For it is surely advantageous and indeed indispensable to philosophy that it should be pursued in a rational fashion, through arguments informed by logic and conceptual distinctions. Even on the rationalist conception, analytic philosophy need not simply equate to good philosophy. For there are other philosophical virtues with which the unfettered pursuit of rational debate and philosophical criticism might come into conflict, for instance a concern with insights rather than argument, or for a non-aggressive academic environment. But for a rationalist, analytic philosophy is *pro tanto* good philosophy, since it satisfies an essential desideratum of sound philosophizing.

If the rationalist definition is correct, then analytic philosophy will be similar in certain respects to what Gallie has labelled 'essentially contested concept' (1956). Essentially contested concepts are notions like art, democracy, justice or repression. Among the features ascribed to them in the wake of Gallie, the following are pertinent to an understanding of analytic philosophy.

First, there is a pervasive practice of using these expressions in a *value-laden* manner, one that carries strong positive or negative connotations.

---

[1] Communication from Ansgar Beckermann, 31 August 2005.

Secondly, there is *disagreement* on both the extension and the intension of the concept, which is to say (for present purposes), on what the concept applies to, and by virtue of what properties.

Thirdly, disputants typically share a small core of *paradigmatic exemplars* and differ over which additional candidates are relevantly similar.

This final feature certainly applies to debates about the nature of analytic philosophy. And the first two features will apply, *if* the rationalist-cum-honorific conception is correct. In that case, debates surrounding analytic philosophy will never concern the question of whether it is a good thing, at least among those philosophers who aim to pursue the subject in a rational manner. Instead they will focus on what it takes to be an analytic philosopher, and on who actually makes the grade.

Some features of the philosophical landscape lend this suggestion a certain plausibility. The internal controversies over the roots and nature of analytic philosophy have gone hand in hand with clashes over the proper course of analytic philosophy. Many participants have tended to identify analytic philosophy with the kind of philosophizing they regard as fruitful. This goes at least some way towards explaining the popularity of definitions with unpalatable consequences of which their proponents are fully cognizant. Thus Dummett favours the linguistic turn, and bites the bullet of defining analytic philosophy in a way that excludes Evans and Peacocke. Hacker regards philosophy as a second-order conceptual investigation, and hence allows that Quine and his disciples may no longer be part of the analytic tradition. Some contemporary naturalists regard analytic philosophy as based on the conviction that philosophy is part of natural science, and seem willing to exclude Moore, Wittgenstein and Oxford conceptual analysis from the analytic club.

Even some outsiders attach a certain kudos to analytic philosophy. The most extreme case is a response given by the late Derrida to a paper by Adrian Moore:

> at the beginning of your paper, when you were defining conceptual philosophy, or analytic philosophy as conceptual philosophy, I thought: well, that's what I am doing, that's exactly what I am trying to do. So: I am an analytic philosopher – a conceptual philosopher. I say this very seriously. That's why there are no fronts . . . I am not simply on the 'continental' side. Despite a number of appearances, my 'style' has something essential to do with a motivation that one also finds in analytic philosophy, in conceptual philosophy. (2000: 83–4)

Surely some mistake, and not just if analytic philosophy is an inherently rational pursuit. Still, it is a mistake that supports the suggestion that 'analytic philosophy' is first and foremost a coveted label, just like democracy, though on grounds which are sometimes somewhat flimsy.

Nevertheless, unlike parenthood and apple pie, analytic philosophy is *not* something that everyone is keen to be associated with. More importantly, the refusniks include not just Nietzscheans and postmodernists, but also figures who extol rationality, at least in theory. In Germany, for instance, there are several thinkers who lay claim to the mantle of the Enlightenment tradition, *without* purporting to be analytic philosophers, for instance Apel, Habermas and Henrich (2003), notwithstanding the fact that some of their Anglo-American friends present them as analytic philosophers in order to make their acquaintances look more respectable. Furthermore, counter-instances include not just representatives of 'Old Europe', but also figures within Anglophone philosophy. Here are just a few examples taken from very diverse quarters.

The one with most clout is Popper, his intellectual proximity and debt to the Vienna Circle notwithstanding. In the Preface to the English edition of *Logik der Forschung*, he distanced himself from analytic philosophy (1959). He refers to it as 'logical' or 'linguistic analysis'. That is, he includes logical constructionism and conceptual analysis, and thereby *both* strands of analytic philosophy at the time. Popper explicitly subscribes to the ideals of 'rational discussion' and the 'critical' solution of problems around which the rationalist definition revolves. In fact, Popper declares that he values analytic philosophers not just as opponents, but also as allies, since they keep rational tradition in philosophy alive. At the same time, he conceives of analytic philosophy as a much more specific phenomenon, one which wages a 'no nonsense' campaign against metaphysics and tries to dissolve philosophical problems through logico-linguistic analysis in either the Viennese or the Oxonian mould. This is a Wittgensteinian idea which Popper abhors. In line with Russell, he insists that philosophy confronts 'genuine problems', and that it seeks knowledge about the world rather than thought or language.

My next witness is Simon Critchley (2001: ch. 7), an accomplished expositor of continental philosophy. Critchley shuns analytic philosophy, which he disparages as 'scientistic'. But he does so not in the name of a postmodernist autodafé of reason. For he also distances himself from the 'obscurantism' of religion and New Age thinking, which he portrays as the reverse side of the scientistic coin (a figure of thought also prominent in the Frankfurt School).

Finally, Fodor, who vehemently disavows being an analytic philosopher:

Who among the living counts as an analytic philosopher by these jaundiced criteria? Not me, for sure. But practically everybody in Australia; Peacocke . . . McDowell, Brandom, Travis (when he isn't being simply a nihilist), everybody in cognitive science without exception. And so forth. You needn't aim; just pull the trigger and you'll hit one. (in Leiter 2004b)

Admittedly, the criteria on which this disavowal is based are even narrower than those employed by Popper. Fodor makes being an analytic philosopher depend *not just* on the linguistic turn – also known as 'semantic ascent' – *but also* on subscribing to an even more specific doctrine – 'semantic pragmatism'. For Fodor this doctrine is the scourge of any serious attempt to understand the mind, since it explicates 'intensional content' as 'some sort of "know how"'. I presume that a paradigmatic type of 'intensional content' is *propositional content*, something like *that bureaucracy breeds corruption*. And I am clueless as to what it could possibly mean to treat such a propositional content as a know how. Furthermore, I do not know of an analytic philosopher who has ever advanced such an adventurous account. Admittedly, some of them have treated *believing* that bureaucracy breeds corruption as a disposition. And some have treated *concepts* like that of corruption as an ability. However, even those positions had few friends among analytic philosophers before the later Wittgenstein; and they are repudiated by a majority of contemporary philosophers of mind. Be that as it may, the crucial point in the present context is this: whether rightly or wrongly, Fodor and Popper are happy to renounce analytic philosophy as they conceive it.

Analytic philosophy is a *contested* concept among *some* philosophers and within *certain* debates, notably debates about the origins and nature of analytic philosophy among its practitioners. But it is *not* an essentially contested concept. The most fundamental feature of its intension is not that it refers to a commendable intellectual activity – whatever it may look like. While there is an honorific use, the descriptive use is more widely spread and more firmly entrenched. Understanding of the term 'analytic philosophy' is tied to the ability to specify certain figures, movements, texts and institutions, and perhaps some of their prominent features. It does not require the belief that analytic philosophy is at any rate a jolly good thing.

The rationalist definition is not purely stipulative. It purports to pay heed to paradigmatic instances. Furthermore, it captures – more or less – one existing way of using the label 'analytic philosophy'. One might argue, therefore, that this honorific use is superior to the descriptive one. By the same token, the rationalist conception might be defended as a revisionary definition or logical explication, one which avoids the shortcomings of the standard descriptive use.

Yet the only potential shortcoming of that use that we have encountered so far is that it is vague, in the sense of allowing for borderline cases. This would mean that an explication should take the form of a so-called 'precising definition'. For instance, we can make a vague term like 'wealthy' more precise by defining it, for instance as 'having assets 10,000 times the median figure'. By the same token, one might claim that a rationalist definition of analytic philosophy simply makes an otherwise vague term more precise.

It is a moot question whether vagueness is indeed undesirable in the area of philosophical-cum-historical taxonomy. But let us grant, for the sake of argument, that there is a premium on avoiding this vagueness. Even then the rationalist definition is not an option. For instead of tidying up the rough edges of the descriptive employment of 'analytic philosophy', it yields an *entirely different* extension, one that reaches way back to the sixth century BC and includes figures that are standardly classified in completely different terms (see also 6.5).

The boot is on the other foot. Rather than solving problems, the honorific use creates new ones. The danger of cross-classification can be avoided, to be sure, if 'analytic philosophy' is consistently employed as a taxonomic label of a different order to that of other labels, whether these be historical – e.g. scholasticism or German Idealism, or doctrinal, such as Platonism or naturalism. Føllesdal achieves this by allowing members of other philosophical groups to be more or less analytic, in proportion to the weight they attach to rational argument.

But the honorific use still has disadvantages as compared to its descriptive rival. The first is that it is either *too undiscriminating* or *too demanding*. Remember Fodor's disavowal of being an analytic philosopher by his (extremely narrow) doctrinal definition. When pressed on this score by Leiter he writes:

Oh, well, there's an uninteresting notion of 'analytic philosopher' which just means 'philosopher who tries to argue for his claims.' I am, or at least hope some day to be, an analytic philosopher in THAT sense. (in Leiter 2004b)

I may be a step ahead of Fodor here. I don't just *hope* to try to argue for my claims some day, I already *do* try to argue for them. My hope is that some day I shall succeed. Accordingly, I already satisfy the notion of 'analytic philosopher' that Fodor describes as uninteresting. He is right to do so. For my achievement is rather minimal. As mentioned at the end of the last chapter, most if not all philosophers have *tried* to argue in some way or other for their claims. But a classification which implies that all or most philosophers qualify as analytic does less work than one which draws a line between significant phenomena.

But if we turn from ambition to achievement, the honorific label once more causes trouble. If soundness or even validity is required, the label will be way too demanding. For its application would presuppose accreditation of an achievement which is notoriously and, it appears, incurably contested between philosophers. The alternative is to allow for a category of genuinely arguing rather than merely trying which does not presuppose that the argument is compelling. Even if this category could be reasonably well defined, however, it would still imply a substantial achievement. This consequence militates against an important desideratum of philosophical taxonomy. It should be possible to classify someone as an analytic philosopher without having to decide whether he or she is a good philosopher, or at least good enough to present something that looks like it might be a compelling argument. *Classification* should be easy and *evaluation* difficult, rather than the other way around.

This problem is intimately connected to a second worry. To put it bluntly: just as theists should not be allowed to define God into existence, analytic philosophers should not be allowed to define themselves into excellence! Of course proponents of the rationalists definition will disavow any such underhand scheme. Remaining faithful to their rationalist aspirations, they would have to grant that all bets are off. The question of who qualifies as an analytic philosopher would have to be decided afresh, without any preconceptions stemming from the descriptive use. Alas, this is easier said than done! Consider in particular the one arena in which the honorific use plays its greatest role, namely the notoriously acrimonious and ill-tempered exchanges with the despised 'continentals'. In this context it is particularly tempting to move from one's uncontentious membership of an intellectual tradition to pretensions of intellectual superiority. Mulligan relates the following anecdote: 'As Searle once said, on being introduced to a friend of mine who (modestly under-) described himself as a phenomenologist, "I am an analytic philosopher. I think for myself"'(2003: 267). It is not just Searle who assumes a supremacy of analytic philosophy here. Even Mulligan, who is sympathetic to phenomenology, intimates in parenthesis that being a phenomenologist is a lesser achievement than being an analytic philosopher.

When it is used or assumed in exchanges of the kind just mentioned, the rationalist conception clearly amounts to a 'persuasive definition', as Stevenson (1944: 206–26) calls it. Such definitions appeal to certain preconceptions of the party to whom they are given, in order to make a claim or position more persuasive. One example is to define politicians as 'self-serving manipulators' in a debate about whether all politicians are immoral. The definition clearly prejudges the issue, since to manipulate others for one's own purposes is (*pro tanto*) immoral. Similarly, defining analytic philosophers as 'philosophers who pursue their subject in a rational manner' prejudges the issues if one is debating the merits, or otherwise, of analytic philosophy and its rivals.

The only way of avoiding this 'persuasive' abuse of an honorific label is to keep it out of certain debates. Yet this is a momentous drawback in its own right. Definitions should prejudge as few substantive and interesting questions or debates as possible. And among these are indisputably certain questions about analytic philosophy as identified by the standard descriptive use: is analytic philosophy good philosophy? Has it made significant advances over its predecessors? Is it superior to its current rivals? Is it making progress or at least going in the right direction? Or is it in a state of stagnation and retrogression?

2 ANALYTIC PHILOSOPHY AS A FAMILY RESEMBLANCE CONCEPT

The rationalist conception is not a precising definition, and its disadvantages outweigh its advantages when it is considered as a revisionary definition. Nevertheless, one may well sympathize with the desire for such a definition. After all, the non-honorific use I defended just now has defied all attempts to come up with a definition that is proof against counterexamples. While 'analytic philosophy' has a generally recognized extension in this use, it is too wide and diverse to be captured by an analytic definition, one which specifies conditions that are individually necessary and jointly sufficient for a thinker or work to qualify as analytic.

Sluga has a strong point, therefore, when he suggests that it 'may well be hopeless to try to determine the essence of analytic philosophy'. But not all definitions need to be analytic. Sure enough, Sluga continues:

analytic philosophy is to be characterized in terms of overlapping circles of family resemblances and of causal relations of 'influence' that extend in all directions and certainly far beyond the boundaries we hope to draw. So our question should not be: what precise property do all analytic philosophers share? But: how can one draw the boundaries of analytic philosophy most naturally and most usefully and to what uses are we putting the term when we draw them in one way rather than another. (1998: 107)

There are several pregnant suggestions in this passage. In the next section I shall discuss the suggestion that analytic philosophy is a historical category. Right now I consider the proposal that we should take a leaf out of

Wittgenstein's *Philosphical Investigations*, and treat analytic philosophy as a *family-resemblance concept*. Roughly the same line is taken by Stroll (2000: 7) and Hylton:

I do not think that it is possible or useful to give a strict definition, with necessary and sufficient conditions, for being an analytic philosopher [footnote omitted]. Our understanding of the idea proceeds from certain paradigmatic figures and works and ways of conceiving philosophical problems. In all of this we have, as Wittgenstein said of games, overlapping strands, rather than one (or two or three) continuous threads. (1998: 54)

This approach promises to heed the lessons from our failures so far. While none of the features we have discussed (e.g. reservations about history or metaphysics, the linguistic turn, the use of analysis, a scientific ethos, aspirations to stylistic clarity and argumentative rigour) are common to all and only analytic philosophers, they nevertheless capture important strands within the analytic family, strands which overlap partially. And yet, the family resemblance conception faces serious hurdles at three levels. First, there are objections to the coherence of the very idea of family resemblance. Secondly, there are qualms about whether one could ever be in a position to determine whether a given notion is a family resemblance concept. Finally, there are specific worries whether the idea can be applied to analytic philosophy. I shall address these different types of challenges in turn, setting out from Wittgenstein's own famous example of the concept of a game (see Glock 1996: 120–4) and transposing the lessons to the concept of analytic philosophy.

When we '*look and see*' whether all games have something in common, Wittgenstein tells us, we notice the following: they are united not by a single common feature, but by a complex network of overlapping and criss-crossing similarities, just as the different members of a family resemble each other in different respects (build, features, eye colour, etc.). What holds the family together and gives it its unity is not a 'single thread' running through all cases, but an overlapping of different fibres, as in a rope (1953: §§66–7).

Wittgenstein is inaccurate in this passage. He suggests that when we look at the variety of games we will not see 'something that is common to *all*'. Yet it is obvious that games do have something in common. They are all activities, and Wittgenstein himself refers to them collectively as 'procedures'. The real crux is that this falls short of a definition, since there are many activities which are not games. The claim is that there is no set of conditions which all and *only* games satisfy, and hence no analytic definition of 'game' in terms of necessary and sufficient conditions. Properly understood, to conceive of a concept *F* as a family resemblance concept is not to rule out the idea that there are features common to all *F*s. This point is equally missed by those critics who complain that

loosening the conditions on a concept's application from 'defining' conditions to mere 'family resemblances' risks leaving that application far too unconstrained. Everything after all bears some resemblance to everything else (Goodman 1970 [in L. Foster and J. Swanson, *Experience and Theory*, Amherst]): returning to Wittgenstein's example, anything, x, resembles standard games in some way or other (if only in belonging to some arbitrary set that contains all games and that thing x!). The question is which resemblances are essential to the concept, and which merely accidental . . . (Rey 1998)

It is part and parcel of our concept of a game that they are activities of a particular kind. The real challenge is not to rule out contrived 'resemblances' *à la* Goodman. It is rather to draw the line between those activities which are and those which are not games. To this there is a threefold response. First, we must distinguish between *concept-formation* on the one hand, *concept-application* on the other. As regards the latter, grasp of a family resemblance concept is acquired through exposure not to a single instance, but to a whole cluster of examples of different kinds, preferably supplemented by a specification of similarities that hold them together. At some stage, to be sure, one must decide whether a candidate is sufficiently similar, in a relevant respect, to an acknowledged specimen to be included. But in this respect family resemblance concepts are no worse off than analytically defined terms such as 'drake'. Even in their case there is a point when we must decide whether a given object satisfies a term which is part of the *definiens*. As regards concept-formation, the inclusion of some activities and some similarities and the exclusion of others is simply a matter of convention, that is to say, it is up to the way we explain and employ the relevant term (Schroeder 2006: ch. 4.1). Furthermore, the fact that these conventions are subject to partial change nicely reflects the dynamic character of concepts like game or analytic philosophy.

Finally, in shaping the concept one way rather than the other, speakers are guided *both* by paradigmatic instances and by paradigmatic features that they share, what Wittgenstein himself called 'centres of variation'. For example, a game like chess is a central case, because it is not solitary, involves winning and losing, and the actions performed have no significance outside of the context of the game.[2]

---

[2] This appeal to paradigmatic or typical games need not create a vicious regress (*pace* Williamson 1994: 87). The concept of a *paradigmatic* game is open ended, to be sure. But there is no reason why it should itself be a family resemblance concept.

Returning to our target concept, Stroll is right to repudiate the claim that 'there is no feature that characterizes the activities of all those commonly known as analytic philosophers'. The reason why such a naïve family resemblance account fails, however, is not the one Stroll himself states, namely that the work of all analytic philosophers 'is directed toward articulating the meaning of certain concepts' (2000: 7–8). As we have seen in our discussion of the linguistic turn and naturalism (5.2–3), this task is shunned by enemies of conceptual analysis, who are keen to keep their eyes on the world rather than thought or language. It is rather the humdrum if incontrovertible fact that all analytic philosophers engage in *philosophical* activity: they tackle philosophical problems, analyse philosophically important notions, advance or dispute philosophical claims, discuss philosophical texts, etc. How do we draw the line between analytic and non-analytic philosophers? By reference to paradigmatic figures such as Russell, Carnap and Ryle on the one hand, paradigmatic features like logical analysis, sentential paraphrase, an interest in language and a suspicion of speculative metaphysics on the other. There is a finite list of candidates for the pantheon of analytic figures, and an even shorter list of candidates for relevant similarities. But this is no bar to analytic philosophy operating as a family resemblance concept, as long as peripheral cases can be added on the grounds of diverse similarities to distinct central figures, without having to share a feature that is possessed by all and only analytic philosophers.[3]

This model may invite another worry, however. According to Rundle, the proper conclusion to draw from the fact that we explain 'game' in a variety of different ways, is that it is not a univocal term, but has different, albeit related, meanings (1990: 48–63). Wittgenstein seems to have rejected this possibility. He insisted that e.g. in the case of 'understanding' we do not have a *family of meanings*, but family resemblances within a single concept (1953: §§531–2). Against him one might invoke his own idea that the meaning of a word is its use, and that diversity of use entails diversity of meaning. We apply 'game' to different pairs of instances on diverse grounds. Indeed, Wittgenstein himself intimates that a term is ambiguous if and only if in one and the same context it can make for both a true and a false statement

---

[3] As Wittgenstein recognized, the *branches* of a family resemblance concept may be united by necessary and sufficient conditions. Thus the various types of numbers – natural, rational, real, complex, p-adic, etc. – cannot be defined by a common property. But each such type is precisely defined (1953: §135; see also Russell 1919: 63–4). By this token, a family resemblance conception of analytic philosophy which has it that no single feature unites e.g. the rebellion against idealism, logical positivism, Wittgensteinians and current neo-Nietzscheans, is compatible with the idea that there may be necessary and sufficient conditions for belonging to one of these groupings.

(1958: 58). But on the account just given, saying for example that war games are games can be true or false depending on what strand of the family resemblance rope one considers (in our case, whether one treats being a rule-guided activity with winning or losing as sufficient, or whether one treats having a goal that is of little point outside of the game as necessary).

One could accept this and still insist that 'game' differs from a genuinely ambiguous term like 'light' or 'bank' which lack the overlapping similarities that allow one to speak of *the* concept of a game or number. One might insist that we must distinguish three different cases – univocality, family of meanings, ambiguity – since to reduce the second to the first stretches the notion of univocality beyond breaking-point. However, it is doubtful whether the criteria for what constitutes identity or difference in meaning or concepts are either as hard and fast or as context independent as the maxim 'same concept, same marks' suggests (see Wittgenstein 1953: §§67–71, 547–70).

In any event, the objection is not really apposite in our context. 'Analytic philosophy' may be ambiguous as between an honorific title and a descriptive label. But as long as we focus on metaphilosophy rather than semantics, it is not much of an issue whether the overlapping similarities between instances make for a family of meaning or a single family resemblance concept. Either way, the proper explanation of analytic philosophy proceeds differently from an analytic definition. The crux of Wittgenstein's idea of family resemblances is simply that there are perfectly legitimate concepts that are explained through such similarities rather than analytically. So far we have no compelling reason for gainsaying him.

The problems facing family resemblance accounts at the second level are more pertinent. Wittgenstein presents his characterization of the concept of a game as 'the result' of an examination (1953: §66). But he has only argued for it by counter-examples to some *prima facie* plausible definitions. He is therefore open to the charge that 'game' might after all be analytically defined, e.g. as a rule-guided activity with fixed objectives that are of little or no importance to the participants outside the context of the game.[4]

---

[4] Rundle 1990: ch. 3. The definition is arguably too wide, since it includes e.g. athletic events like running, and too narrow, since not all games need be rule governed (certainly this is not a necessary condition for something being a *Spiel*). Most proposed definitions have been far less plausible. With great fanfare Hurka chides 'anti-theorists' like Wittgenstein for 'simply being lazy' and defines 'game' as follows: 'in playing a game one pursues a goal that can be described independently of the game, such as directing a ball into a hole in the ground, while willingly accepting rules that forbid the most efficient means to that goal, such as placing the ball in the hole by hand' (2004: 251–2). Not all of the individual conditions are necessary, since children playing football in school do not need to submit to the rules willingly (I, for one, would have much preferred to tackle some of my opponents in a more robust manner). Nor are they jointly sufficient: someone who willingly follows the rules of the traffic

Cohen levels that same charge against family resemblance definitions of analytic philosophy. He holds that 'such an account would be much more difficult to establish than a unitary explanation', because the fact that the similarities we have so far come up with only constitute a weave of overlapping threads does not

> exclude the possibility that some tacitly unifying theme pervades the whole movement . . . In order to exclude such a possibility altogether a space of mutually exclusive, and jointly exhaustive, unitary explanations would have to be demonstrated, and then each of these unitary explanations in turn would have to be shown inadequate to its task. (1986: 5–6)

But qualms about the claim that games *do not* have any common characteristics leave intact the more modest claim that they *need not* have anything in common. This suffices to resist the essentialist position that there *must* be an analytic definition. Furthermore, even if one could specify conditions which necessarily all and only games satisfy, these would not automatically be constitutive of our concept of a game. Necessarily, all and only equilateral triangles are equiangular triangles, yet the two concepts differ. Similarly, our concept of a game is not defined by a yet unheard of set of conditions, since it can, and has been, explained by reference to examples and similarity riders rather than to such a common characteristic.

The case of analytic philosophy invites a family resemblance approach for the same reasons. As we have seen, there is no plausible analytic definition. Furthermore, while there is no algorithm for generating all the possible explanations, it is plausible to suggest that the concept of a philosophical movement can appeal only to the features which we have gone through, features relating to geo-linguistic identity, an attitude to the past, doctrines, topics, methods or style. To render Cohen's animadversions compelling, one would have to establish three things: first, that there is an additional parameter for distinguishing philosophical movements; secondly, that this parameter affords a unitary explanation; thirdly, that it (implicitly) guides our practice of classification. Once more, the fact that the concept in hand limits the range of parameters is no bar to its being a family resemblance concept.

This leaves objections at the third, and more specific level. Two such objections have been raised by Hacker. The first is that there is no point in following Wittgenstein's advice 'don't think, but look!', because 'analytic

code in trying to travel from *A* to *B* (a goal that can be described independently of the activity of driving in accordance with the traffic code) is not thereby playing a game, even if a more efficient route is available.

philosophy' lacks a well-established use (1997a: 14). As pointed out in 1.2, however, the term has an established use, even though it is a relatively technical one. Furthermore, a chart of resemblances within analytic philosophy can be given which closely resembles those available for family resemblance concepts like 'game'.

Analytic philosophy at a glance

	Frege	Russell	Vienna Circle	Quine	Oxford	TLP	PI
linguistic turn	(×)	×	✓	✓	✓	✓	✓
rejection of metaphysics	×	×	✓	×	(✓)	(✓)	✓
philosophy ≠ science	(×)	×	(✓)	×	✓	✓	✓
reductive analysis	(×)	✓	✓	(✓)	×	✓	×
formal logic	✓	✓	✓	✓	(×)	✓	×
science oriented	✓	✓	✓	✓	×	×	×
argument	✓	✓	(✓)	(✓)	✓	(×)	(✓)
clarity	✓	(✓)	✓	(✓)	✓	×	(×)

Parentheses indicate either that the verdict is contestable or that the feature is partly present or partly absent.

Hacker's second objection carries greater weight:

There is extensive controversy over the correct characterization of analytic philosophy. Some have tried to define it in terms of a set of necessary and sufficient conditions. The result has been the exclusion of most of the philosophers of the twentieth century who lauded the methods of 'analysis' (variously conceived) and who deemed themselves analytic philosophers. Others have tried to define it as a family resemblance concept. The result has been the unavoidable inclusion of some of the ancient Greeks. (2007: 125; see also 1996: 4–5)

As we have seen, analytic definitions can be both too narrow and too wide. In fact, the dialectic that emerges from our previous discussions is that all attempts to avoid the exclusion of analytic specimen seem to lead inexorably to the inclusion of non-analytic ones. It is clear nonetheless that a family resemblance conception exacerbates the inclusion of *philosophus non grata*, since it provides a multitude of features by which to qualify. It is also clear that there is no plausible way of avoiding the inclusion of Aristotle on account of his proximity to conceptual analysis or of Leibniz on account of his similarity to logical constructionism, and so on, and so forth.

The trouble is that my chart could be extended in the horizontal direction well beyond the limits of analytic philosophy, without any significant decrease in the fibres uniting the additions to the specimen on the list. Thus we can confidently add not just philosophers who wrongly disassociate themselves from analytic philosophy, such as Popper and Fodor, or definite ancestors like Bolzano. We are also forced to include Kant, the British empiricists, the continental rationalists, much scholastic philosophy, and a whole raft of ancient thinkers.

To this one can add one final problem. In defending the feasibility of family resemblance conceptions both in general and in our particular case, I had to invoke the existence of *paradigmatic cases*. This means that we need a list of uncontested core examples to start out from. But how is this list to be established? In the next section I shall suggest that it is done by reference to a historical tradition.

3 ANALYTIC PHILOSOPHY AS A HISTORICAL OR GENETIC CATEGORY

Although the extension of 'analytic philosophy' is causing such mischief for conscientious attempts to define the term, it is stated easily enough. Here is, for instance, Sluga:

Following common practice, I take analytic philosophy here as originating in the work of Frege, Russell, Moore, and Wittgenstein, as encompassing the logical empiricism of the Vienna Circle, English ordinary language philosophy of the post-war period, American mainstream philosophy of recent decades, as well as their worldwide affiliates and descendents. (1997: 17n)

Sluga is right to assume that there is a common practice (in 1.2 I defended that idea against objections and gave positive reasons in its support). Moreover, Sluga's list indeed conforms to that practice in its extension. But how is that extension determined?

The quote contains a suggestion on this score. It is a suggestion, more-over, that has been explicitly supported by other commentators, and it seems to be taken for granted by many both inside and outside of analytic philosophy. Thus Hacker favours using analytic philosophy 'dynamically', to signify 'a historical phenomenon . . . in a constant process of change and evolution'. Although it cannot be defined by reference to any non-trivial doctrines or principles, 'analytic philosophy' does not express a family resemblance concept,

for so to conceive it would diminish its usefulness in characterizing a *very particular historical movement of the twentieth century* . . . Nevertheless, there is a kinship with family resemblance concepts, inasmuch as each phase in the evolution of analytic philosophy shares methodological, doctrinal and thematic features with its antecedent and subsequent phases. Since the various phases overlapped temporarily . . . each fructified the other by stimulus and challenge. Hence the phenomenon of analytic philosophy must not be viewed as a simple linear development. It has a complex synchronic, as well as a diachronic, dimension. (1996: 4–5; my emphasis)

To signify this concern with a specific historical phenomenon, Hacker frequently refers to analytic philosophy as 'twentieth century analytic philosophy'.

I shall call such a conception *historical* or *genetic*. According to this approach, analytic philosophy is first and foremost a historical sequence of individuals and schools that influenced, and engaged in debate with, each other, without sharing any single doctrine, problem or method.

A first challenge for such an approach is to specify what *kind* of historical phenomenon analytic philosophy is. More specifically, what kind of philosophical group are we dealing with. Three possible categories are in the fray here: analytic philosophy is variously termed a school, a movement or a tradition. I reckon that few would follow Preston in assimilating all three (see the beginning of chapter 6). Nonetheless, I know of no discussion of the differences within metaphilosophy or philosophical historiography.

In my view, it is plausible to treat a *school* as a tightly knit group based on relatively intimate personal contact and a direct transfer of certain doctrines or methods. This is the sense in which we speak of schools in the history of art, such as the school of Raphael or of Rubens. Such schools consist of disciples that learnt their trade from the master and try to emulate his style. It is also the sense in which we speak of schools in philosophy: groups bound together by personal contacts and theoretical commitments alike. By contrast to most artistic schools, however, philosophical schools can continue long after the death of the original founder; they renew themselves along a sequence of disciples turned teachers. The most striking case of such philosophical schools are the ancient schools: Plato's Academy, Aristotle's Peripatetic School, the Megarian School, etc. There were also schools in medieval philosophy, such as the school of Chartres (though when Descartes chides the schoolmen his target was a wider phenomenon, namely Aristotelianism). And there were schools in this sense in twentieth century philosophy, such as the Vienna Circle or the Frankfurt School.

As stated at the beginning of chapter 5, analytic philosophy may comprise such schools, but it is itself a much looser phenomenon, a philosophical *movement*. In the words of Charlton, analytic philosophers 'constitute not so much a school as a straggling, undisciplined movement' (1991: 4). In this respect, analytic philosophy resembles not so much the Peripatetic School as Aristotelianism, not so much the Vienna Circle as logical positivism. Indeed, it is obviously more general than the latter, more akin to wider intellectual movements like seventeenth-century rationalism, or British empiricism.

There is yet another respect in which analytic philosophy transcends transient phenomena like logical positivism and Oxford conceptual analysis. Analytic philosophy amounts to a *tradition*. It is not just a blip on the radar screen, a fashion, fad or vogue, though of course it has thrown up numerous such blips. Rather, its various doctrinal, methodological and stylistic features have been transmitted and transformed over at least five generations. A plausible historical conception treats analytic philosophy as an evolving philosophical tradition, a body of problems, methods and beliefs that is socially transmitted from the past and evolves over time.

This leads us to the second challenge facing the historical conception. How does a historical or genetic definition cope with the extension of 'analytic philosophy'? Can one specify a web of mutual influence which encompasses all and only analytic philosophers?

To answer that question, we first need to lay down certain parameters concerning two questions: What counts as a philosophically relevant influence? Under what conditions are we justified in maintaining that one thinker *A* has influenced another *B*?

As regards the first question, influence is primarily a causal notion. But philosophical influence is not simply a case of efficient causation. *A* cannot philosophically influence *B* by administering a drug to her which makes her accept his pet theory *T*. Even if reasons are indeed causes (something Davidson affirms and analytic hermeneutics deny), they are causes of a special kind. It is only if *A*'s theory figures in the way in which *B* reasons, or, less stringently, in the way she thinks about the topic of *T*, that *A* will have influenced her. This point can be brought out by using Cohen's terminology: analytic philosophy is a 'dialogue', a 'critical interchange' between different thinkers and movements: the 'analytical dialogue' as Cohen calls it (1986: 3, 58).

Of course, this dialogue takes place within a real world of academic and cultural institutions (all too real, some would say). From this perspective, analytic philosophy and continental philosophy are constituted as different traditions at least partly because 'they neither read each other's journals nor attend each other's conferences'. By contrast, analytic philosophers 'go to conferences together, read and write for the same journals and examine each other's pupils' (Charlton 1991: 3–4). Analytic philosophy is not just an abstract or idealized dialogue, but an institutionalized and historically evolving one.

222 Contested concepts, family resemblances and tradition

Under what conditions are we licensed to ascertain this kind of influence? Clearly, mere parallels between the ideas of A and the ideas of B do not suffice. It is for roughly the same reason that Dummett's 'history of thoughts' rather than 'history of thinkers' (mentioned in 4.3) is a doxographical rather than genuinely historical exercise. By contrast, Baker and Hacker insist that a 'genuine causal connectedness' can be established only by showing that B has noted a particular view in A 'and consequently reached such and such conclusions' (1983: 7n). By these standards, one can diagnose a genuine influence only in cases in which B explicitly acknowledged it and we have reasons for accepting the statement as sincere and accurate. In my view, this is too demanding. Philosophers are no saints, and some of them deliberately conceal certain influences on their thinking. Other philosophers show little concern for lines of influence, and fail to state influences without being in bad faith.

In view of this situation, I propose the following compromise between the extremes of mere doxography and philosophical depth biography. We are entitled to state that A has influenced B positively if there are clear affinities and convergences between the ideas of B and those of A, and B was familiar with the latter through reading or conversation. Replace 'affinities and convergences' by 'disagreements and divergences', and you get a criterion for negative influence. It ought to be uncontroversial, furthermore, that when it comes to membership in a philosophical movement like analytic philosophy, positive influence counts for more than negative influence, inspiration for more than provocation.

Does analytic philosophy really constitute a reasonably distinct philosophical tradition? Obviously, to count as an analytic philosopher, it is not enough to have influenced individual analytic philosophers. Otherwise one would have to include Plato and Aristotle for starters. They not only score well on the family resemblance model. They also influenced most philosophers. What is more, they influenced some analytic philosophers substantially, notably conceptual analysts. But one would also have to include paradigmatic *non-analytic* thinkers, e.g. Hegel (on account of Brandom or McDowell), Schopenhauer (on account of Wittgenstein), Nietzsche (on account of Danto and Williams), and Marx (on account of Neurath and Jerry Cohen). Conversely, it is not enough to have been influenced by analytic philosophers. Otherwise one would have to include, for instance, not just Apel and Habermas (who draw on speech act theory and Wittgenstein), but also Lyotard (who invokes the latter).

Some of these cases are easily excluded if we insist on *mutual* influence, just as the idea of a dialogue demands. Though its sources reach back into a distant and non-circumscribed past, analytic philosophy may nonetheless be a 'well-bounded dialogue' (Cohen 1986: 5). Even this needs to be considered, however. For there are at least some cases of reciprocal influence. By my criteria, it is clear that Frege influenced Husserl's anti-psychologism, much less obvious that there was traffic in the opposite direction. Similarly, while Searle and Derrida exchanged views, they did not influence each other in a constructive fashion, let alone a positive one (see 9.3). However, there has been mutual positive influence between Putnam and Habermas, and between Davidson and Gadamer.

These are minor phenomena in the wider scheme of things. But we should expect such give-and-take to become more common over time, *if* there is a rapprochement between analytic philosophy and other traditions. In any event, these phenomena suggest that the historical or genetic account requires supplementation by a family resemblance perspective. Such a perspective is fruitful not just with respect to the diachronic continuities and discontinuities within the analytic tradition, but also when it comes to determining the *synchronic* identity of the movement. We want to distinguish between dialogues within the analytic tradition on the one hand, dialogues conducted between analytic and non-analytic philosophers on the other. Here the family resemblance model provides a handle, though of course it will not lead to clear-cut verdicts in an algorithmic fashion.

There is at least one other reason for involving family resemblances. It is important to preserve a kernel of truth in the rationalist conception as articulated by Føllesdal. Philosophers that do not form part of analytic philosophy understood as a twentieth-century tradition can be more or less analytic, and may be among the precursors of analytic philosophy. Such claims have been made, for example, on behalf of Aristotle, Aquinas, Descartes, Leibniz, the British Empiricists, Bolzano, Brentano, Husserl and the Kantian tradition.

For this reason, I want to argue in favour of *combining* a historical and a family resemblance approach. We learn most about analytic philosophy by regarding it as a tradition that is held together *both* by ties of influence *and* by a family of partially overlapping features. Methodological and stylistic ideas which are less general than clarity and argument play a particularly important role here. For example, most analytic philosophers rely on methods of sentential paraphrase and conceptual articulation, whether or not these methods are guided more by artificial logical calculi or more by the subtleties of ordinary use. They also tend to show an interest in logic and language (variously conceived). There is even one point of widespread consensus as regards the role of science. Naturalists *à la* Quine, Kantian or Wittgensteinian anti-naturalists and even proponents of essentialist metaphysics *à la* Kripke reject the ultra-rationalist Hegelian idea that philosophy can pronounce *a priori* on the nature of the world, independently of the special sciences.[5]

4 THE CONTOURS OF THE ANALYTIC TRADITION

I want to end this chapter by delineating the contours of the analytic tradition thus conceived; as precisely as possible, I feel obliged to add, but that may not be all that precise.

It is clear that one can subscribe to a historical conception of analytic philosophy and yet draw the limits of the historical tradition inaccurately, or in a one-sided manner. Consider Hylton's statements: 'in speaking of analytic philosophy here I have in mind that tradition which looks for inspiration to the works of Frege, Russell and Carnap' (1990: 14). The historical conception embodied in this passage is too narrow, since it excludes Moore, the later Wittgenstein, Oxford philosophy and contemporary Nietzscheans.

The endeavour to right these wrongs will steer us in the direction of the questions which have so far occupied centre stage in debates about analytic philosophy, but which I have postponed till now:

Who founded the analytic tradition?

and

Where precisely does the analytic/continental divide have its source?

Keeping in mind the difference between continental and traditional-cum-traditionalist philosophy, one should ask:

Where precisely did analytic philosophy split off from other branches of Western philosophy?

Scholars of the analytic tradition have not been coy in volunteering answers to these questions.

In one passage, Dummett presents Frege as the 'true father' of analytic philosophy (2007: 12). In another passage, he casts him in the role of grandfather, while also insisting that the linguistic turn, and with it analytic

---

[5] Some analytic metaphysicians such as Lowe would challenge this view. So it is not a necessary condition for being an analytic philosopher.

philosophy, were born in 1884 with the context principle of *Grundlagen* (1991: 111–12). In yet another passage, Dummett treats Bolzano as the 'great-grandfather of analytic philosophy', Frege as the grandfather, and implies that the honour of having fathered the movement and the linguistic turn goes to the early Wittgenstein. Even in that passage, Russell and Moore are demoted from direct ancestors to mere uncles or great-uncles (1993: 171), with a whiff of poor relations about them.

According Bolzano the role of a great-grandfather is unobjectionable and indeed mandatory if one employs the family resemblance scheme. In terms of argumentative rigour, exploration of formal means, semantic sophistication and analytic tools, he qualifies fully. But it is problematic from a genetic perspective. Bolzano exerted an influence on analytic philosophy only very late in the day, after the movement was already firmly entrenched. Unlike Brentano, he was not a major influence on Twardowski and the Polish School. He only came into his own from the 1950s, when his groundbreaking ideas were placed in an analytic context by scholars like Chisholm. Therefore I shall not include Bolzano among the founders of analytic movement, even though he was a highly impressive forerunner.

As regards Frege, Dummett is both too emphatic and too modest. As we have seen, Frege was not the first to espouse a contextualism. The context principle does not mark a decisive turn to language, and the latter post-dated the birth of analytic philosophy (5.2). Dummett is too modest, in my view, when he describes Frege as a grandfather. This modesty is taken to extremes by Hacker. He relegates Frege to the role of 'one of the many precursors of twentieth century analytic philosophy', on a par with Bentham (Hacker 1996: 28n). Once the difference between the rise of analytic philosophy and the linguistic turn is recognized, a different assessment suggests itself. Unlike Bentham and Bolzano, Frege directly influenced the other pioneers of analytic philosophy. Admittedly, before the 1950s Frege's work was noted by only three philosophers. But these three were Russell, Wittgenstein and Carnap, the crucial forces behind the rise of analytic philosophy!

All three acknowledged their debt handsomely. I have already mentioned statements by Wittgenstein and Russell to this effect. One might object that Frege's influence on Russell post-dates the latter's revolt from absolute idealism. Yet, without the influence of Frege's pioneering work in logical analysis – acknowledged, e.g., in the Prefaces of *Principia Mathematica* and *Our Knowledge of the External World* – Russell might never have offered something distinct, and ultimately more influential, than Moore's conceptual analysis based on Platonism. Indeed, he might not even have risen above the parapet of other realists such as Ward, Stout, Meinong, or Cook-Wilson. A comparison of Russell's work before and after *Principles of Mathematics* suggests that he owed to Frege not just the wherewithal to deal with quantification, but also the realization that there is a difference between use and mention, signs and the things they signify (see Stevens 2005).

Carnap mentions Frege's impact in *Logical Syntax* (1937: xvi) and he declares Frege's lectures to have been 'the most fruitful inspiration I received from university lectures' (1963: 4). And at present, for better or worse, the predicate calculus Frege invented is not just seen as *the* logical system, but also as the prime or even exclusive tool for the analysis of language and thought (see Ben-Yami 2004: 1–2). Returning to our criterion of mutual influence, Frege took no notice of Carnap, who silently attended his lectures. Even Wittgenstein's *Tractatus* was like water off a duck's back. But he had to take painful notice of Russell's paradox, which spelled ruin for his logicist system. So Frege is an integrated member of the analytic club, though one that was curiously snubbed between the 1920s and the 1950s.

On the other hand, it is ungenerous of Dummett to belittle the role of Moore and Russell in turning analytic philosophy into a prodigiously burgeoning, multi-polar and multi-faceted field. There is the rather academic dispute over whether it was Moore or Russell who led the revolt from idealism.[6] But there can be no dispute about the decisive role that this revolt played in the emergence of the analytic tradition. Analytic philosophy achieved lift-off only when the logicist programme and the Frege–Russell revolution of formal logic combined with attempts to solve problems concerning propositions, concepts and facts that Moore and Russell faced in their fight against idealism. And it took a linguistic turn when the *Tractatus* linked these problems to the nature of philosophy and of logical necessity, and tried to resolve the lot by reference to linguistic representation.

The later Wittgenstein, by contrast, is a contestable case. While some regard him as the crowning achievement of the analytic tradition, others fervently deny this (see Glock 2004). But when we look at the historical criterion, Wittgenstein's membership in the analytic tradition becomes

---

[6] E.g. Stroll 2000: 86, Baldwin 1990: 1–2, 39; Bell 1999 vs Magee 1986: 10. This priority dispute might be resolved amicably by acknowledging Russell as a pioneer of logical and Moore as a pioneer of conceptual analysis.

clear. He was mainly influenced by analytic philosophers (Frege, Russell, Moore), and he in turn mainly influenced analytic philosophers (Russell, Moore, logical positivism, conceptual analysis). This is not to deny that he was also influenced by (Schopenhauer, James, Spengler) and influenced (hermeneutics, postmodernism) non-analytic philosophers. But these historical connections can be distinguished from the others, because the authors concerned do not qualify on a family resemblance conception of analytic philosophy.

A very rough historical chart of analytic philosophy might look something like this:

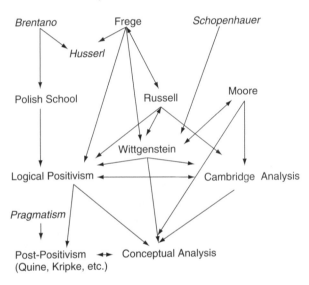

A family tree of analytic philosophy

I have included a *select* few non-analytic figures and movements (italicized), to indicate the fact that lines of influence run across the limits of analytic philosophy.

When we look at a family resemblance chart, Wittgenstein turns out to be almost as firmly entrenched in the analytic tradition as, for example, Quine. To be sure, Quine's membership has also been contested, namely by Hacker. But I have already argued that Quine's attack on the idea of a qualitative contrast between philosophy and science does not exclude him (ch. 5.3). Furthermore, the overlaps with paradigms like the logical positivists and his unrivalled influence on post-positivist philosophy make his inclusion imperative.

As regards the contours of the analytic tradition, I have little reason to diverge from the standard conception embodied in the quote from Sluga. If that quote has any lacunae, it is the failure to mention the Polish School of metaphysics and logic. But it is only by applying my conception of analytic philosophy to potentially problematic cases, and by resisting various exclusionary strategies, that we are in a position to appreciate why the lines should be drawn roughly where they are standardly drawn.

As regards the origin of the analytic/continental split, Dummett writes:

> Frege was the grandfather of analytical philosophy, Husserl the founder of the phenomenological school, two radically different philosophical movements. In 1903, say, how would they have appeared to any German student of philosophy who knew the work of both? Not, certainly, as two deeply opposed thinkers: rather as remarkably close in orientation, despite some divergence of interests. They may be compared with the Rhine and the Danube, which rise quite close to one another and for a time pursue roughly parallel courses, only to diverge in utterly different directions and flow into different seas. Why, then, did this happen? What small ingredient in the thought of each was eventually magnified into so great an effect? (1993: 26)

For an answer, Dummett turns to Husserl's response to Brentano's problem of intentional inexistence (certain mental acts lack real objects, without being directed towards mere representations). Husserl distinguished between the meaning and the object of a mental act, extending a Fregean distinction between meaning and reference to non-linguistic acts. A Fregean sense is *not intrinsically linguistic*, since Frege does not exclude the possibility of naked thoughts without linguistic clothing. Nevertheless, Dummett argues, it is essentially *capable* of being expressed in language. For as a 'mode of presenting the referent', the sense of a sentence (a thought) is not a trans-linguistic entity standing between an expression (a sentence) and its referent (a truth-value), as Frege's own Platonistic myth suggests, but rather 'a step' in determining the truth-value of a sentence (1993: ch. 11). This is the critical point which separates analytical philosophy and phenomenology: Husserl's extension of 'meaning' beyond language blocks the way to a linguistic turn, while Frege's notion of sense is incapable of such an extension, since it is restricted to the domain of the potentially linguistic.

While the analogy with the Rhine and the Danube is intriguing, I have my doubts about this diagnosis. Frege took less of a linguistic turn than Dummett believes. More importantly, two contrasting views on the relation between thought and language hardly make for a split between two grand strategic traditions, especially since both of them have featured lingualist and mentalist approaches to this issue (see 5.2). Mulligan's account strikes me as more plausible (1986: 93–4). While none of the many distinctions between realism and idealism coincides with the analytic/continental contrast, in Husserl's specific case the turn to a transcendental idealism was accompanied by a shift in style of reasoning as well as writing. And it was this later style that influenced the phenomenological tradition, and its existentialist off-shoots.

This does not yet amount to an analytic/continental divide. Even less does it amount to a branching off of analytic from traditional/traditionalist philosophy. Friedman's account in *A Parting of the Ways* (2000) is *prima facie* promising on this score, since it chimes with my tripartite classification. Friedman's protagonists – Cassirer, Heidegger and Carnap – represent in my scheme traditionalist, continental and analytic philosophy, respectively. Friedman argues that the meeting of these three at a 1929 conference in Davos was the crucial event in the analytic/continental divide and that Carnap, Heidegger and Cassirer are all reacting in diverse ways to problems presented by the Neo-Kantian tradition, the problem of reconciling the logical and the perceptual preconditions of experience.

Unfortunately, Friedman's explanation suffers from misplaced concreteness. It ignores the fact that long before Davos, Moore, Russell (see Monk 1996a: 235, 247–8, 313) and members of the Vienna Circle launched withering analytic attacks on British and German Idealism, Bergson and *Lebensphilosophie*. Indeed, in some respects these attacks go back to the contrast between Romanticism, empiricism and positivism and in the nineteenth century (see ch. 3.3). It is difficult to see how a different course of events at or after Davos could have papered over the widening cracks between the philosophical doctrines, methods, and intellectual demeanour epitomized by these three protagonists.

Furthermore, the idea that the analytic/continental divide springs out of a common root in Kant and Neo-Kantianism is the opposite extreme of the thesis of an Anglo-Austrian axis. While there is an important Kantian trend within analytic philosophy, large sways of the analytic tradition derive from a break with Kant and hark back to Leibniz. In fact, Friedman moves from a specific Kantian problem concerning sensibility and understanding to a different and much broader contrast between rationalism (Carnap), *Lebensphilosophie* (Heidegger) and a vaguely defined synthesis of the two (Cassirer). That contrast transcends niceties of Kantian epistemology, and it reaches back far beyond the late twenties.

I suspect that there is simply no single crucial philosophical event in the formation of these two movements. The Davos meeting no more fits this bill than the differences between Frege and Husserl over sense that Dummett singled out. And if personal contact is of paramount importance, one might regard Ryle's exchanges with Husserl as equally indicative. In any event, between these exchanges and the fateful Royaumont meeting, the analytic/continental split had become a *fait accompli*. What interceded was not a single philosophical watershed. There was, however, a political watershed: the rise of Nazism and the exile of the Central European pioneers of analytic philosophy. The analytic/continental divide results from a combination of a multitude of gradual philosophical developments with a single political catastrophe. In this respect, analytic philosophy as we now know it is partly a product of much larger cultural and geo-political forces.

CHAPTER 9

Present and future

In the last chapter I argued that analytic philosophy is a historical tradition held together by ties of influence on the one hand, family resemblances on the other. This final chapter leaves behind the question of how analytic philosophy should be defined. The issue is no longer whether certain features hold true of all and only analytic philosophers. Instead it asks whether certain features have a special relevance for *contemporary* analytic philosophy and for its place in a wider cultural context, and how such features are to be assessed.

Section 1 deals with the role of the analytic/continental contrast in the high-profile culture and science wars epitomized by the Sokal hoax. I urge that one must distinguish ideologically motivated abuses of science from relativist-cum-constructivist views about knowledge. Combating the former may be a genuinely analytic cause, but the debate about relativism, constructivism and the correspondence theory of truth features analytic voices on both sides. The culture and science wars cast a positive light on analytic philosophy, at least in comparison to postmodernism. In section 2 I turn to the question of whether analytic philosophy has vices as well as virtues, once more with an emphasis on its current self-image and practice. I shall discuss, in this order, the charges that analytic philosophy suffers from scholasticism, isolation from other disciplines and the public, internal factionalism, and an exclusionary demeanour towards various outsiders. I shall exculpate analytic philosophy in some respects, while underwriting other complaints from both within and without.

This leads on to the final section. If analytic philosophers should not simply ignore or remain aloof from other ways of philosophizing, is there any point in distinguishing them from their non-analytic colleagues? The existence of a tradition notwithstanding, perhaps that tradition is currently losing its distinct identity. This idea is strengthened by the fact that there have been notable attempts to synthesize the two. On the other hand, there are those on both sides of the divide who resist such bridge-building. Their stance is reinforced by continuing mutual neglect, and by the fact that the public debates between analytic and continental philosophy have exacerbated rather than ameliorated the alienation. Nor has the analytic/ continental divide been supplanted by other divisions, such as that between naturalism and its discontents. I conclude that it remains useful to distinguish analytic philosophy from continental and traditionalist philosophy, provided that these divisions are properly understood.

This leaves a final question: should philosophers try to overcome these divisions? I argue that synthesis is no more a goal in itself than preserving a distinct identity. Instead of trying to assimilate to other types of philosophy, analytic philosophy should simply try to do better by its own standards.

I IMPOSTERS, BUNGLERS AND RELATIVISTS

The term 'culture war' refers to ideological confrontations that have racked American public culture and politics since the 1960s (Hunter 1991). It pits a left-wing – secular and progressive – camp against a right-wing – religious and traditionalist one, on issues ranging from abortion and censorship through gun control and homosexuality to the separation of church and state. The front lines of this titanic battle for ideological hegemony run straight through American academia. Important factions within the progressive camp have alleged that not just traditional curricula but 'Western' science and academia as a whole are biased against minorities. In particular they are accused of being ethnocentric, favouring 'dead white males' and a Waspish or Eurocentric agenda.

One major engagement within these campus struggles is now known as the 'science wars', and concerns the nature, status and merit of scientific theories. The bone of contention is whether 'Western' science is capable of providing an objective account of reality, or whether it merely reflects 'local' concerns and prejudices which can be discarded on ideological and political grounds. A loosely speaking *realist* camp insists on the first stance. The opposing camp is generally referred to as *postmodern* or as *social constructivism*. It regards not just science but even the physical reality it purports to describe and explain as a mere construct of social forces, and denies that there is a universally valid standpoint from which Western science can be regarded as superior to other belief systems.

The science wars reached their climax through the well-known Sokal hoax. *Social Text* is a fashionable American journal in the field of cultural studies. In 1996 it published an article by the American physicist Alan Sokal with the intriguing title: 'Transgressing the Boundaries: Toward a Trans-formative Hermeneutics of Quantum Mechanics' (Sokal 1996). The article indeed transgressed boundaries in several respects. For, as Sokal soon revealed, it was a hoax. It purports to be a scholarly investigation of the philosophical and political implications of twentieth-century physics, yet is in fact a deliberate parody of postmodern thought. 'Transgressing the Boundaries' consists of a melange of scientific solecisms, howlers, *non-sequiturs* and sheer nonsense designed to pander to the ideological prejudices of the editors of *Social Text*. It starts off by chiding scientists for clinging to the

dogma imposed by the long post-Enlightenment hegemony over the Western intellectual outlook ... that there exists an external world whose properties are independent of any individual human being and indeed of humanity as a whole, that these properties are encoded in 'eternal' physical laws, and that human beings can obtain reliable, albeit imperfect and tentative, knowledge of these laws by hewing to the 'objective' procedures and epistemological strictures prescribed by the (so-called) scientific method (199).[1]

The article goes on to assert that this dogma has been thoroughly under-mined by modern physics, which shows physical reality to be 'at bottom a social and linguistic construct' (200). In fact, Sokal continues, recent developments not only substantiate postmodern denials of the objectivity of truth, but also furnish the beginnings of a 'postmodern and liberatory science' that can serve the ends of progressive politics. At this point, the piece becomes truly adventurous. Starting out from micro-physics it gen-erates political and cultural conclusions supported by nothing more than puns (mainly on the words 'linear' and 'discontinuous'), strained analogies and egregious falsehoods. Not content with his initial success, Sokal later teamed up with the Belgian physicist Jean Bricmont to produce a more sustained exercise of intellectual hygiene. Their *Intellectual Impostures* (1998) aims to catalogue and critically dissect some of the texts from which Sokal derived inspiration for his hoax, as well as other writings in the same genre.

Sokal's hoax immediately turned him into a *cause célèbre*. In the first instance, it shows that the ignorance about science among literary folks still persists, forty years after C. P. Snow castigated it (1959). But the Sokal hoax is more than *The Two Cultures* revisited. The editors of *Social Text* revealed not just scientific and mathematical illiteracy. They also demonstrated

---

[1] References are to Sokal and Bricmont 1998, which contains a reprint of Sokal's original article.

their willingness to publish sentences which anyone who understands the constituent terms must recognize as absurd, and, in consequence, their indifference towards the intelligibility and truth of the articles in their journal. Indeed, many commentators have felt that something even more sinister is afoot. To them, the hoax is indicative of a more general decline in scholarship, rigour and intellectual honesty within the humanities. Some right-wing cultural critics have claimed that even science is threatened by the postmodern malaise. This last claim has been vigorously denied by those familiar with the scientific scene, including Sokal. As regards the humanities, however, apocalyptic fears have racked even cool-headed philosophers.[2]

Finally, the Sokal hoax unmasks the sin of distorting theoretical issues for the sake of political and moral (or immoral) dogma (see 7.5). Postmodern ideas have been seized upon by sections of the academic left as a way of promoting the values of the new social movements (feminism, gay pride, multi-culturalism) and of the minorities for which they are taking up their cudgels. It is part of what Taylor (1994) supports as 'the politics of recognition': those minorities which have been victimized or marginalized by the Western mainstream are entitled to recognition of their cultures as equally valuable.

A non-dogmatic left-winger himself, Sokal resents the association of left-wing politics with postmodernism, not least because it provides right-wing critics with plenty of ammunition. Some analytic philosophers make similar attempts to insulate progressive causes from postmodern follies. Having noted the post-colonial motive behind constructivism, Boghossian (2006) rightly resists the move from the fact that it is immoral to subjugate other peoples in the name of spreading knowledge to the claim that there is no such thing as one culture possessing knowledge superior to that of another. Nagel wryly comments on Rorty's postmodern defence of left-wing politics: 'Apart from philosophy, Rorty has all the right views' (1998: 4). Left-wing resistance to postmodernism also alerts us to the fact that the front lines in the science wars do *not* run parallel to those of the culture war. On crucial issues like evolution and climate change it is the right-wing camp which dismisses the findings of science for reasons of ideology and political or economic expedience.

More to the present point, do the front lines of the science wars run parallel to the analytic/continental divide? The label 'postmodern'

---

[2] For a more elaborate discussion of the Sokal hoax see Glock 2000. Hacking 1999 provides a charitable account of social constructionism.

certainly associates one party with continental philosophy, and not without some licence. Like 'analytic philosophy' and 'continental philosophy', 'postmodernism' refers to a historical family of positions. Nevertheless, it standardly indicates a common negative tenet: a rejection of 'modern' (Enlightenment) values and convictions, among them the belief in the possibility of human progress, and the confidence that human reason is capable of revealing the secrets of nature and of establishing universally binding moral principles. The attack on the possibility of objective knowledge even in science is a central part of this stance. Most of the gibberish pilloried by Sokal was plucked or derived from the writings of leading postmodernists such as Lyotard, Lacan, Kristeva, Irigaray, Deleuze and Guattari. Moreover, the attack on the objectivity of science is clearly fuelled by a post-structuralist suspicion which ultimately derives from Nietzsche: the alleged authority of science, or of rational discourse more generally, is nothing but a rhetorical device in a power game. There is also a Nietzschean utopia in play, one which has affinities less with the gloomy outlook of Foucault and Derrida than with Rorty's happy-go-lucky brand of neo-pragmatism. It is the revolt against the idea that our beliefs must pay homage to a reality independent of us, and the defiant insistence that we human beings are in charge (see Rorty and Searle 1999: 30–1, 42–3, 47).

It is therefore tempting to suppose that the science wars pit a coalition of natural scientists and analytic philosophers against an unholy alliance of social scientists, humanities dons and continental philosophers. This would be inaccurate. We must distinguish between a war on *postmodernism* and a war on *relativism* or *constructivism*. The first war pits science and analytic philosophy against an important strand of non-analytic philosophy, albeit one which excludes traditionalist philosophy, pragmatism and even certain parts of continental philosophy. It is a strand which delights both in a cavalier and playful handling of intellectual questions and in an exceedingly obscure style. The second war pits absolutists and realists against relativists and anti-realists. The latter include important continental philosophers; but they also include eminent representatives of both analytic philosophy and natural science.

Unfortunately, some abolutists/realists have tried to make hay by equating relativism with postmodernism. Admittedly, Sokal and Bricmont state that *Intellectual Impostures* is directed at two distinct but related targets:

(A) the extraordinary misuse of scientific and mathematical concepts by famous French psychologists, philosophers and literary theorists such as Lacan, Kristeva, Irigaray, Deleuze and Baudrillard;

(B) relativistic tendencies in philosophy of science as exemplified by the work of Kuhn, Feyerabend and by the strong programme in the sociology of science (Bloor, Latour).

Sokal and Bricmont concede that there is a difference between (A), which amounts to an egregious 'abuse' of science, and (B), which they regard as based on more 'subtle' scientific errors and philosophical confusions. Nevertheless, many of their supporters have been quick to draw the conclusion that relativism is intellectually just as bankrupt and contemptible as the pseudo-scientific and would-be interdisciplinary work of some postmodernists.[3] Admittedly, there is a sociological link between the two, namely that they are popular in some of the same circles. But Sokal and Bricmont insist that there is also a 'weak logical link':

if one accepts relativism, there is less reason to be upset by the misrepresentation of scientific ideas, which anyway are just another discourse. (x, see also 15, 49, 194–5)

Yet, that a form of discourse fails to provide an objective, universally acceptable account of the world is *no reason whatsoever* for concluding that in representing this form of discourse one is free to distort it, or that claims about that form of discourse are arbitrary. By the same confusion of discourse and 'meta-discourse', we would have less reason to be upset by misrepresentations of religious fundamentalism than by misrepresentations of intuitionist logic, on the grounds that the former but not the latter is gobbledegook anyway. Perhaps what Sokal and Bricmont have in mind is this: if a form of discourse does not even *purport* to provide an objective account of reality, misrepresentations of it are less serious. This is hardly less suspect, however. To a significant extent, art does not even purport to provide an objective account of reality. But does that render grossly mistaken histories of the arts less repugnant than grossly mistaken histories of hydraulics? It is by no means obvious.

Boghossian detects another slippery slope from relativism to the sloppiness and bungling that characterizes so much of postmodern thought.

Simple-minded relativistic views about truth and evidence . . . license, and indeed typically insist upon, the substitution of political criteria for the historically more familiar assessment in terms of truth, evidence and argument. (1996: 14)

Boghossian pinpoints a recurrent motive in postmodernism: theories are assessed according to whether they fit certain political standards rather than

---

[3] Thus the *Scientific American* describes *Intellectual Impostures* as 'a dissection of what he [Sokal] calls "sloppy thinking" on the part of postmodernists, social constructivists, cognitive relativists and sundry other "-ists"', and simply speaks of the 'misuse of scientific ideas by nonscientists' (Mukerjee 1998: 17; see also Dawkins 1998).

reality or the facts, since the latter are a mere social construction. By this reasoning, feminist distortions of science are legitimate because they promote women's interests; First Nation creation myths are just as valid as scientific accounts, because they are the views of oppressed minorities, etc. Thus, there is allegedly no fact of the matter as to whether Native Americans originally arrived by crossing the Bering Strait, or whether they ascended from a subterranean world of spirits. Both accounts are valid, the first 'for' Western industrialized society, the second for certain American First Nations (see Boghossian 2006: 1–2).

Logically speaking, however, relativism is neither necessary nor sufficient for instrumentalizing truth and other cognitive values. One can hold that truth is relative to a group, and nevertheless separate it strictly from moral goodness, political correctness, or instrumental expedience. Conversely, pragmatists of both the postmodern and the naturalistic variety have advanced Darwinian accounts which reduce true beliefs to those it is expedient or good to hold. Such accounts are untenable, for reasons I hint at below. Yet they are perfectly compatible with insisting that there are *universal* standards of expedience or goodness, and hence that truth is *not* relative to individuals or groups.

Similarly, the asinine abuse of science is neither necessary nor sufficient for relativism. Hegel was the absolutist *par excellence*. Alas, as Sokal and Bricmont point out (1998: 150–5; following Russell 1956b: 21), Hegel's philosophy was partly based on slipshod mathematics. Conversely, while some sociologists of science might be accused of being impostors, this charge cannot be extended to all relativists. Kuhn and Feyerabend 'knew their stuff', however untenable some of their conclusions. In fact, the targets of Sokal and Bricmont also include anti-realist (instrumentalist) tendencies within science itself, notably Bohr's and Heisenberg's Copenhagen interpretation of quantum mechanics and certain 'popular' accounts of chaos theory (77, 242, ch. 7). This displays beyond doubt the difference between culpable errors and distortions of the postmodern variety on the one hand, and respectable scientific and philosophical views which happen to run counter to the staunchly realist conception of science favoured by Sokal, Bricmont and many of their supporters on the other.[4]

---

[4] Quantum mechanics poses several threats to such a conception: Heisenberg's uncertainty principle seems to limit the scope of objective measurement; light is described both in terms of waves and in terms of particles; and there is no compelling explanation of why the macroscopic world appears to follow classic rather than quantum mechanical laws (see Stairs 1998).

Boghossian is one of these supporters. He contrasts the tremendous influence of constructivism in the 'humanities and social sciences' with its 'weak' hold 'in philosophy itself, at least as it is practiced within the mainstream of analytic philosophy departments within the English-speaking world'. He sapiently points out, however, that in defence of constructivism 'one could cite a sizable proportion of that tradition's most prominent philosophers', among them Wittgenstein, Carnap, Kuhn, Goodman and Putnam (Boghossian 2006: 7). To this list one must add other instrumentalists, conventionalists or anti-realists such as Neurath, Quine, Feyerabend and Dummett, just for starters.[5]

As strategists of the science wars, contemporary analytic philosophers like Boghossian, Blackburn (2005), Nagel (1997) and Searle (e.g. 1995) have risen to public prominence (by academic standards) through attacking continental philosophers, among others. Nevertheless, the science wars do not reduce to analytic vs continental philosophy or even to analytic vs non-analytic philosophy. While resistance to postmodernism may be a *bona fide* analytic cause, the crusade against relativism and constructionism is not.

This answers the taxonomic question raised at the beginning of the section. It does not answer the philosophical one. A recurrent theme of my book has been that analytic philosophers are no strangers to error and confusion. Indeed, I regard such bungling as an occupational hazard of anyone struggling with philosophical problems. Perhaps then, the important substantive divide is not so much between analytic and continental philosophy as between level-headed absolutists/realists and muddleheaded relativists/constructivists. If so, the science wars would mark a point at which the category of analytic philosophy wanes in significance.

There are reasons for resisting this conclusion. Relativism draws its inspiration from the idea that there is significant diversity between different cultures, both diachronically and synchronically. But its claim goes beyond noting differences: there is not just diversity, we lack neutral canons for assessing the different options as better or worse. Relativism maintains that our beliefs, concepts or practices cannot be assessed from an

---

[5] One caveat is in place *both* for Boghossian's original list *and* for my addendum: not all of the constructivists listed are *social* constructivists. This holds notably for Carnap and Quine, who both subscribed to a methodological solipsism. Thus, for Quine physical objects are 'posits' no less than the Homeric gods (1953: 16–17, 44–5). But both are posited by an individual for the sake of explaining and predicting her private sensory experiences, rather than by a community. This caveat does not exculpate analytic constructivists, however. To regard reality as the product of lonely individual minds is even less plausible than portraying it as the product of collective processes of information gathering and processing.

impartial, universally acceptable vantage point, since they are valid (true, justified, good, etc.) or invalid (false, unwarranted, bad, etc.) only relative to a particular individual or group of individuals (societies or even species).

Admittedly, many relativistic claims are obligingly self-refuting, in that they present themselves as objectively true in a way that they explicitly renounce. Other relativists observe that even in science the choice of topics and methods is inevitably subject to – possibly local – biases and preconceptions; yet they fallaciously infer from this that the emerging theories cannot be objectively true, quite irrespective of the motives that made them look attractive, or that there is no point in seeking such truth.[6] But relativism *per se* is not committed to such errors. Thoughtful relativists avoid genetic fallacies. They also try to avoid claims of an absolute kind, and instead seek to proceed by reducing absolutist positions *ad absurdum*.

Furthermore, we should distinguish different kinds of relativism – alethic, ontological, conceptual and methodological. Most contemporary absolutists have in mind a promiscuous *alethic* relativism, a position which allows that incompatible views all have equal cognitive value, being either all true, or none true, or each of them true for its own proponents. To be sure, we occasionally speak of a belief as being 'true for' an individual or group. So we might say, for instance,

(1) That witches exist is true for society *A*, but that witches exist is false for society *B*.

But that amounts to no more than that it is *accepted* or believed by *A*, and it contrasts with being true *strictly speaking* or *simpliciter*. The alethic relativist, on the other hand, rejects this non-relational or 'absolutist' use of 'true'. For him *any* ascription of truth must be qualified by reference to a subject (individual or social) that accepts the belief at issue. Consequently, he is committed to the idea that the notion of truth which is in play in (1) is the *very same* as the one that features in the following two truisms about truth and falsehood:

(2) That witches exist is true $\Leftrightarrow$ witches exist

(3) That witches exist is false $\Leftrightarrow$ witches do not exist

As a result, the alethic relativist must accept the substitution of 'witches exist' and 'witches do not exist', respectively, for 'that witches exist is true' and 'that witches exist is false' in (1). This yields

(4) Witches exist for society *A*, but witches do not exist for society *B*.

---

[6] This genetic fallacy has been diagnosed by Boghossian (2006: 20, 113) and Searle (Rorty and Searle 1999: 63). But one significant realist camp is not entitled to this straightforward protest, namely those naturalists who also make the content and truth of beliefs dependent on their origins.

The relativist is not at liberty to gloss (4) in a harmless manner, namely as asserting that society *A* but not society *B believes* that witches exist. Instead, he is driven to conclude that members of *A* and members of *B* must inhabit different worlds, one populated by witches the other not. Alethic relativism thereby lapses into *ontological* relativism, the view that even what is *real* is relative, and that different individuals or groups literally *inhabit different worlds*. Such a radical position has occasionally been mooted by supporters of the Sapir-Whorf hypothesis in linguistics (Whorf 1956), of the incommensurability thesis in the philosophy of science (Kuhn 1962: 134), and by Goodman (1978). But it is surely absurd. Among other things, it makes it difficult to explain how members of *B*-type societies could have been so successful at exploiting, oppressing and killing members of *A*-type societies. Are we to suppose, for example, that the bullets which colonial troops fired at the unfortunate 'natives' managed to traverse an ontological gap between different worlds before hitting their targets?

At the same time there are other forms of relativism which are both more plausible and can more easily be pinned on the aforementioned *analytic* anti-realists. There are also versions of relativism that respect the distinction between belief, knowledge and fact, and avoid the pitfalls of alethic relativism. One of them is *conceptual relativism*. It admits that the truth-value of the statements we make is not up to us. At the same time it insists that our concepts, and hence the kind of statements we can make, is not simply dictated to us by reality or experience; in adopting or constructing such frameworks there are different options which cannot be assessed as more or less rational from a neutral bird's eye view. Our conceptual net does not determine whether we actually catch a fact, but it determines what kind of fact we can catch (see Wiggins 2001: ch. 5).

Searle is one absolutist who reckons with the difference between this conceptual relativism and alethic relativism (Rorty and Searle 1999: 37, 47). Unfortunately, he overplays his hand by holding that the only alternative to alethic relativism is the correspondence theory of truth, according to which a statement is true iff it corresponds to reality or to the facts. In fact, however, all it takes to avoid alethic relativism and other anti-realist conceptions of truth like the pragmatist-cum-Darwinist one is an insistence on alethic realism. As Künne likes to quip, alethic realism should not be confused with athletic realism, since it is not a very muscular affair (2003: 20). The doctrine for which I use the term is downright anaemic. It maintains no more than the conjunction of the following two principles:

(1) $\sim$ (It is true that $p \Rightarrow$ it is believed/stated by someone that p)

(11) ~ (It is believed/stated by someone that $p \Rightarrow$ it is true that p).[7]
In other words, the fact that a proposition is true neither entails nor is it entailed by the fact that the proposition is being stated or believed (etc.) to be true by someone, or that it would be useful to believe it, etc. Alethic realism allows one to reject alethic relativism. It also allows one to deny, against pragmatist-cum-Darwinist accounts, that the belief that God exists is true, even though empirical research demonstrates that holding that belief is advantageous in all the relevant respects (it promotes happiness, life expectancy, recovery from illness, biological fitness, etc.).

In spite of this salutary potential, alethic realism is respected not just by the correspondence theory, but also by so-called deflationary theories of truth which explain truth through the logical equivalence between 'It is true that p' and 'p', without invoking metaphysical notions like reality or fact. It is from this perspective, perfectly analytic and commendably realistic, that Strawson objected to Austin's attempt to make the correspondence theory more precise: 'The correspondence theory requires, not purification, but elimination' (1971: 190).

The purpose of this discussion has *not* been to vindicate relativism even of the conceptual kind. I am as opinionated as the next philosopher, and hence loathe to concede that either my views or my concepts are anything other than optimal. But among these views is that some popular objections to relativism are not as conclusive or as comprehensive as commonly assumed. In any event, while the contrast between absolutism and relativism may be one between truth and falsehood, it is not one between light and darkness, reason and insanity. Relativism differs from postmodern abuses of science in at least two respects:

• it is supported by serious arguments, whereas in postmodern discourse we rarely find comprehensible lines of reasoning (Mulligan 1998);
• not all relativistic claims or arguments suffer from obscurantism, charlatanism or even bungling (Glock 2007).

In consequence, the absolutism vs relativism distinction is not more significant than the analytic vs non-analytic distinction. Strategically, the difference between analytic and postmodernist thought remains more important.

In the course of the science wars, absolutists have not just gone astray by running together relativism and postmodernism, and by nailing their

---

[7] As regards scope, we need to exclude self-referential (and arguably ill-formed) statements like 'this statement is believed/stated by someone'. (11) needs to be further restricted to exclude statements like 'Some things are stated/believed by someone.'

anti-relativist flag to the mast of philosophical views that are too specific and contentious. They have also painted a doomsday scenario which verges on intellectual scaremongering. According to some of them, a rejection of realist positions destroys or at least threatens the values and standards on which the academy rests. In my view, analytic philosophers involved in this debate run the risk of being a bit too solemn and meretricious, perhaps in response to the excessive playfulness of their bogeys Derrida and Rorty. This holds even for those with a certified sense of humour like Searle.

To be sure, the values of the academy will not survive an 'anything goes' approach. Such an attitude has been affected by relativists like Feyerabend, and it may well be actually implemented in the practice of some post-modernists. Fortunately, one can avoid such frivolity even if one rejects alethic realism and succumbs to errors like alethic and ontological relativism. There have to be standards or norms that distinguish between doing things correctly or well, and doing them incorrectly or badly. But these standards need not be furnished by what analytic realists are fond of calling mind-independent objective reality. They can be furnished instead by standards of coherence, originality, clarity, validity, acumen and sheer panache. It would be slightly disconcerting if analytic philosophy lost sight of the possibility that one might get things wrong, indeed badly wrong, and yet display prodigious intelligence in the process, and advance human understanding and the life of the mind.

2 WHAT, IF ANYTHING, IS WRONG WITH ANALYTIC PHILOSOPHY?

We have already encountered several accusations that are frequently levelled against it: that it is ahistorical or anachronistic (ch. 4), that it is limited in its interests (5.4) or doctrinaire, either in rejecting metaphysics, or in being obsessed with language at the expense of reality, or in being scientistic by slavishly following natural science (5.3 and 6.2), that it lacks systematic vision (6.3), that it is ethically neutral and politically conservative (7.1). I have more or less rejected these allegations, either because the diagnosed features are not in fact genuine weaknesses, or because they affect only parts of the analytic tradition without being inherent to analytic philosophy itself. At the same time, I have dampened paeans of praise. Clarity and rationality are no more the prerogative of analytic philosophers than scholarship and education are the prerogative of continental and traditionalist philosophers. Nevertheless, these slogans mark tendencies in a more general academic and cultural sense. This is hardly surprising, given certain brute facts about university education in Anglophone and non-Anglophone countries. Having to write an essay every week is no more conducive to assiduous scholarship and *Bildung* than seeing your supervisor only once a year is conducive to clear and cogently argued doctoral theses.

In this section I discuss accusations which may be justified with respect to contemporary analytic philosophy, irrespective of whether they can be levelled against the whole tradition. In sifting these complaints I shall try to refrain from two types of wail:

- animadversions against *doctrinal* trends in contemporary analytic philosophy
- general Jeremiads about unsavoury features of current academic life.

The reason for this abstinence is not lack of opinions on my part. I have strong feelings in particular about Mad Assessment Disease, a syndrome which in our subject is epitomized by 'The Philosophical Gourmet Report', an unofficial yet highly influential ranking of Anglophone philosophy departments <http://www.philosophicalgourmet.com>. But a discussion of these issues would lead us into sociology and educational policy, without telling us much about analytic philosophy in particular. And a fair assessment of doctrinal trends would require lengthy considerations of intricate philosophical and metaphilosophical problems.

When it comes to the current state of analytic philosophy, there is a striking divide among prominent commentators. On the one hand we find optimists who detect a new dawn. Williamson has recently proclaimed that we have finally arrived at 'the end of the beginning' of philosophy; courtesy of the 'rigour and precision' afforded by technical tools like the predicate calculus and modal logic, our subject is now in a position to establish metaphysical truths about the nature of reality that will pass the test of time (2006). This confident pronouncement echoes not just Kant, who was convinced that he had at long last set metaphysics 'on the secure path of a science'. It also echoes similar statements of analytic philosophers down the ages: from Russell's hope to have hit upon the correct scientific method in philosophy, through Wittgenstein's announcement 'to have found, on all essential points, the solution of the [philosophical] problems' (1922: Pref.) and the positivists' self-assured promises of replacing speculative by scientific philosophy, to frequent *eurekas* by contemporary members of the artificial intelligentsia who believe that they have at last discovered the philosopher's stone by naturalizing meaning and mind.

A generation before Williamson, Dummett had issued a similar announcement: 'philosophy has just very recently struggled out of its early stages into maturity'; because of advances in logic and philosophy of language it can now prove its mettle among the other previously more successful 'sectors in the quest for truth' (1978: 456–7). Both express the hope that analytic philosophy may succeed in turning philosophy into a scientific subject (though not necessarily a natural science) that furnishes definitive solutions to philosophical problems through systematic and cumulative research. But past experience and the peculiar nature of philosophical problems suggest that great expectations of transforming philosophy into a science which makes steadfast linear progress may be utopian, no matter whether this feat is attempted through the application of formal logic and semantics (as in the case of Dummett and Williamson) or by emulating natural science (as in the case of the naturalistic mainstream).

Of course, one need not harbour such strong ambitions to hold that philosophy is *capable* of making progress of a different kind. By contrast to the natural and formal sciences, this progress need not be cumulative, it often concerns questions, explanations and distinctions rather than theories, and it is sadly liable to being reversed. Analytic philosophy has arguably made such progress during its long career. Most informed commentators will agree that we are in a position to understand central problems in both theoretical and practical philosophy better than we did 150 years ago. We know or could know what the presuppositions of the questions and the options for answering them are, even if we cannot accept any of the extant solutions. At issue between the optimists and the pessimists is rather the question of whether analytic philosophy has made progress in *recent* years.

A sombre assessment of analytic philosophy's current record is supported by an equally impressive line-up. Hacker not only pours cold water on the 'millenarian' aspirations of Dummett and Williamson; he also regards the history of mainstream analytic philosophy from the sixties onwards as one of decline, a move back to scientistic and metaphysical ventures that fall foul of arguments developed by Wittgenstein and conceptual analysis (2006a; 1996: ch. 8). Putnam shares Hacker's dislike for naturalism-cum-scientism. He also complains about 'the *exclusionary tone* that has become pervasive in analytic philosophy'. And he deplores an increasing dogmatic tendency. Even claims of 'clarity' and 'respect for reason' are to be treated with care, according to Putnam, since the alleged arguments take current orthodoxies for granted and virtually ignore important alternatives (2007: 5–6). Indeed, Dummett himself seems to have lost some of his earlier confidence. For some time he has deplored the analytic/continental rift. He has also joined the chorus of complaints about naturalistic reductionism, with the added twist that he laments the increasing estrangement of philosophy and natural science. One common denominator between Dummett, Hacker and Putnam is that philosophers should be both more knowledgeable of and less overawed by natural science.

Finally, Williams concurs with Searle that analytic philosophy has become 'in various ways more interesting than it was 40 years ago' (1996a: 26). He also commends it for its 'undoubted virtues', such as its insistence on 'the values of unambiguous statement and recognizable argument; its patience; its lack of contempt for the familiar; its willingness to meet with the formal and the natural sciences; its capacity for genuine and discussable progress – in all this, and despite its many and often catalogued limitations, it remains the only real philosophy there is' (2006: 168). At the same time, however, he joins the chorus of plaintive melodies about its scientistic tendencies. Like Stroll (2000: 246), he emphasizes that philosophy is a *humanistic* endeavour, one which cannot be reduced or assimilated to a natural science in its aims or methods. His main grievance is the neglect of history implied by scientism. He also regrets the urge to remain 'pure' from the influences of other disciplines, including the humanities. Both tendencies, according to Williams, have prevented analytic philosophers from pulling their weight, especially in ethics and political theory (see 4.2 and 7.2). Finally, Williams deplores 'stylistic scientism'. This includes the 'pretence' that philosophy of mind is 'the more theoretical and less experimentally encumbered end of neurophysiology'. It also includes 'the well known and highly typical style of many texts in analytic philosophy which seek precision by total mind control, through issuing continuous and rigid interpretative directions', thereby trying 'to remove in advance every conceivable misunderstanding or misinterpretation or objection, including those that would occur only to the malicious or the clinically literal minded' (2006: 183).

Williams' notion of stylistic scientism thus includes a doctrine along with a style of writing. I for my part shall leave doctrinal disputes aside. As regards Williams' strictly stylistic gripe, spare a thought for those less famous authors who try to publish in mainstream journals. Especially if they refuse to toe the majority line in their area of research, they have no choice but to forestall every misunderstanding and objection they can anticipate. For they face the exacting scrutiny and occasionally the wrath of referees who can be counted on to be maliciously minded when their sacred cows are at stake. This is a partial excuse of a certain style of writing in many analytic texts, and one factor in the overall decline of literary standards deplored in chapter 6.4. At the same time, it casts a negative light on the style of contemporary analytic philosophy understood in a wider sense. I am thinking of the way in which it is conducted not just on paper but more generally, both as an intellectual endeavour and as an institutionalized academic practice. There is a veritable analytic industry, and it is a common butt of complaints, not just among old hacks hankering for a golden age, but even among some young Turks. I shall dwell on four grievances, concerning scholasticism, disengagement from other disciplines and the public, factionalism and the exclusionary demeanour towards non-Anglophone and non-analytic philosophy.

First and foremost, there is the palpable scholasticism into which a lot of analytic philosophy has descended. This vice manifests itself in, among other things, the focus on a very narrow range of issues and authors in what are regarded as the leading journals, a general disinclination to explain why these issues and authors are worthy of attention, the tendency to treat many fundamental issues as settled once and for all, and a predilection for technicalities irrespective of their usefulness. Although contemporary analytic philosophy can boast of a flurry of diverse activity, much of it is epiphenomenal and derivative. This vice has been nicely lampooned in MIND!, the spoof issue of *Mind* affectionately compiled by Roger Teichmann (2000). One of the titles on the front reads: 'Black on White on Brown on "Grue"'. As in the case of the Sokal hoax, it proves increasingly difficult to distinguish any would-be spoofs of mainstream analytic philosophy from the real article. It is sheer coincidence rather than systemic sanity which has spared us 'Black on White on Brown on Green on "Grue"', not to mention 'Reply to Black on White, etc....' Titles also reveal another stylistic feature.[8] In spite of the narcoleptic pedantry of much contemporary analytic philosophy, or perhaps precisely because of the need to conceal that scar, there is also a palpable desire to project an image of being easy going, up to date and cool, especially through forced attempts at humour. This desire is lampooned by another title on the cover of MIND!: 'Meanings, Shmeanings: You Bet They Ain't, and Noplace Else Neither'. A common butt of both jokes is a tendency towards navel gazing:

[8] Most books bear titles which are 2- (X and Y) or 3-place (X, Y and Z) permutations of terms from a list which is easily surveyable. Major items include: Logic, Logical Form, Truth, Language, Meaning, Semantics, Grammar, Necessity, Modality, Understanding, Knowledge, Justification, Mind, Thought, Concepts, Perception, Reality, Science, Holism, Prediction, Explanation, Causation, Action, Reason, Normativity, Rules, Morality, Law, Justice, Welfare. By the iron laws of combinatorics, analytic philosophy might eventually come to a grinding halt simply for lack of novel titles. Fortunately, analytic philosophers are resourceful. Peacocke, for one, got wind of the danger and deliberately rung the changes with his *Being Known* (1999: vii).

often the humour of analytic writings boils down to more or less artful take-offs from previous titles or dicta, in this case, Putnam's famous 'Cut the pie any way you like, "meanings" just ain't in the head' (1975: 227).

As with titles, so with content. There is a proliferation of epicycles on epicycles on quasi- or would-be scientific 'research programmes'. This spectacle may project an image of professionalism, which in turn may help to keep a trickle of grants flowing. But it will not revive analytic philosophy as a radical and unassuming (if not entirely presuppositionless) activity of questioning, clarification and argument. Whereas the optimists detect a new dawn, I fear that we are past the heroic age of analytic philosophy, and that the allegedly myopic logical empiricists and conceptual analysts, to say nothing of Wittgenstein and Quine, made greater contributions than its currently extant practitioners. To borrow a distinction from the history of architecture, there is a real danger that analytic philosophy has exhausted its capacity for structural progress, and is capable of progressing only with respect to the embellishments.

Scholasticism and specialization discourage interest from outsiders. We saw that analytic philosophy has plenty to offer that is of public relevance, for instance on relativism and matters moral and political. Yet these offerings have been largely ignored, and there is a widespread impression that analytic philosophy remains isolated in the Ivory Tower, a *l'art pour l'art* discipline that does not interact with other disciplines or the public. Thus Borradori complains that 'from the thirties to the sixties, from the eve of the Second World War to the Vietnam War, American Philosophy ceased to be a socially engaged enterprise, becoming instead a highly specialized occupation' (1994: 4). Confronted with Searle's statement that 'the sheer intellectual self-confidence of analytic philosophy has had the consequence that most of this [post-modern] stuff just passes them by', Rorty retaliates: 'On the other hand, analytic philosophy is not taken very seriously anywhere except by analytic philosophers' (Rorty and Searle 1999: 58; also Prado 2003: 11–12).

Appearances suggest that analytic philosophy faces acute difficulties at least in the PR and marketing department. It hardly figures in the educated public's perception of philosophy (such as it is). It nowhere features in the best-selling *Sophie's World* (Gaarder 1996) which has recently shaped that perception. And there have been numerous complaints by populist writers that analytic philosophy in particular and academic philosophy in general fails to provide *The Consolations of Philosophy* (as in the title de Botton 2001 took over from Boethius) for which alone the subject deserves attention and respect. Journalists (Jenkins 2001; cf. Gottlieb 2001) and even politicians (Glotz 1996) have entered the fray. Mainly because of the scholastic, technical and hence hermetic nature of analytic philosophy, it appears, philosophy is not up to the task set by Hegel, namely of 'apprehending its time in thought'. What a waste, one is inclined to exclaim, given the demand for philosophical support and guidance which the success of these populist voices demonstrates.

Fortunately, this is not the whole story. As Searle points out in response to Rorty, analytic philosophy is taken seriously in some other disciplines, such as linguistics and cognitive science. There are also portents that its profile in the life- and neurosciences is on the increase. Still, its present interaction with physics is surprisingly small, as Dummett (2007) notes. Even more surprisingly, analytic philosophy has had relatively little effect on the humanities and social sciences. Young writes: 'whereas analytic philosophy has proved of little or no interest to the humanities other than itself, the impact of Continental philosophy has been enormous. But there is also a great deal of (mostly French) humbug in the Continental tradition'. Mulligan wryly comments: 'From these observations [Young] concludes, not that there is something very wrong with the humanities, but that there is a powerful need for philosophers "equipped with analytic methodology" to sort the gold from the humbug.'[9]

The failings of other humanities notwithstanding, however, analytic philosophers cannot afford to be complacent. There is an ancient tension between the esoteric and the exoteric vocation of philosophy. Philosophers of any persuasion will have a gap to bridge in communicating their ideas, e.g. to politicians (Swift 2001). But this is a task they should be eager to undertake, especially if they have got something to say. I am far from confident that the forbidding style that prevails in contemporary analytic philosophy is licensed by either subject matter or message. To the extent that it is, however, it behoves analytic philosophy to make its ideas accessible to all concerned, whether they be other philosophers, scientists, scholars, professionals, politicians, artists or laypeople. Few of them have faced up to this challenge.

Perhaps the reason is that gaps are widening within analytic philosophy. It is widely agreed that analytic philosophy in the process of turning from a revolutionary movement into the philosophical establishment has become more diverse and even eclectic (e.g. Stroll 2000: ch. 9). According to Searle this tendency has made it 'a more interesting discipline'. Even he concedes, however, that it has thereby also lost some if its 'vitality' (1996: 12, 23). For

---

[9] *Times Literary Supplement*, Letters to the Editor 10 and 24 July respectively, 1998.

his part, Baldwin commends contemporary analytic philosophers for having shed the constraints of logical empiricism, and rightly so. But he also intimates that the emphasis on conceptual analysis and the workings of language paralysed analytic philosophy and that it could undergo a 'revival' only after these methods were discarded or at least sidelined. For Baldwin, the heterogeneity of the contemporary scene, with its appeals to all sorts of considerations from all sorts of fields, is a sign of 'vigour' (2001: 267, 12).

This diagnosis captures the fact that analytic philosophy continues to be a thriving and expanding academic field. Yet it is not necessarily a sign of *rigour* if philosophers fail to draw distinctions, for example between empirical investigations, historical descriptions, conceptual clarifications and moral exhortations. Furthermore, the variety one encounters in contemporary analytic philosophy is of a one-sided and potentially harmful kind. In matters of *doctrine* it has become more uniform, yet in matters of *method* less uniform. For instance, that one should be a naturalist or physicalist in the philosophy of mind is taken for granted within the mainstream; the only remaining question, it appears, is whether one should argue to this predestined conclusion in an *a priori* or an *a posteriori* manner.

This state of affairs augurs ill for the kind of rational debate on which analytic philosophy prides itself. It means that analytic philosophers disagree not just (or, in some areas, mainly) on what the correct answers are. Rather, they diverge even on fundamental issues like the following: what questions are the right ones to ask? How should they be tackled? By what standards are answers to be judged? More ominously, they also disagree over how even such methodological disputes might be settled. Indeed, there are no longer universally accepted rules and standards, whether of specifically philosophical or more general academic and intellectual quality.

The effect has been an unhealthy factionalism and dogmatism. Many analytic philosophers have lost either the ability or the inclination to distinguish between a refusal to share their views and methods on the one hand, and lack of philosophical talent on the other. There is a widespread presumption that those who do not conform to prevailing standards and preconceptions, who dissent or demand explanations, for example, are simply unprofessional (except for the non-analytic – continental, feminist or non-Western colleagues in one's own department, who, miraculously, tend to be exempted from such damning judgements). This factionalism is not confined to the mainstreams of the various sub-disciplines, but is also rife within dissenting splinter groups. It is all too common to find one and the same figure described as execrable by one analytic philosopher and as a veritable genius by another, with no rationale for the disparity in sight other than conflicting party allegiances.

The effects of factionalism have been exacerbated by a more ancient vice, the aggressive and occasionally bellicose nature of debate within analytic philosophy. In conversation, this feature is frequently deplored even by orthodox practitioners, especially when they have just been on the receiving end of a 'frank and robust' criticism. In print, however, the complaint is raised most often by figures who are either hostile to the analytic tradition or situated at its periphery, such as analytic feminists, people seeking to build bridges to continental philosophy, or non-philosophers who are keen to draw on analytic philosophy yet taken aback by the domineering tone of its devotees (e.g. Garry 2004: sections 4–5; de Gaynesford 2006: 3; Reno 2006: 31).

The reverse side of hostility towards outsiders is what Leiter calls 'cronyism and in-breeding' towards insiders. For reasons I have been unable to fathom, Leiter suggests that this failing afflicts mainly those who try to reconcile science and common sense. He singles out Dworkin and Putnam for censure, the latter because he 'appears to cite only to [sic!] his former or current students and colleagues' (2004a: 20–1). Paid up naturalists and Nietzscheans who shun reconciliation and appeal to intuitions, by contrast, seem immune. Naturally, therefore, it is *not* cronyism when Leiter himself waxes lyrically about the influential authors of his collection *The Future for Philosophy*:

It has been both a pleasure and a privilege to work with the distinguished contributors to this volume: they exemplify what Nietzsche most admired in scholars, their 'reverence for every kind of mastery and competence, and [their] uncompromising opposition to everything that is semblance, half-genuine, dressed up, virtuosolike, demagogical, or histrionic in *litteris et artibus*' (*The Gay Science*, sec. 366). (Leiter 2004c: Acknowledgements)

Unsurprisingly, the theme of exclusion casts an even longer shadow over analytic philosophy's 'external relations'. One of the less savoury, if predictable, reactions to Sokal's and Bricmont's *sottisier* has been to attack their motives rather than their arguments. In this context, they have been accused of trying not just to divert research funds from the social to the natural sciences, but also of orchestrating an assault on French philosophy and culture. Julia Kristeva (1997: 122), one of their prime targets, accused them of spreading 'disinformation' as part of an anti-French political and economic campaign. 'What's the point of such a polemic, so far removed from present-day preoccupations?' she asked; and apparently the only answer she could think of was: 'It's an anti-French intellectual escapade'.

Sokal and Bricmont have been at pains to disavow francophobe motives: 'ideas have no nationality', and one should not feel obliged to follow the 'national line' on intellectual questions. They also point out that their second target, namely epistemic relativism, is 'much more widespread in the Anglo-Saxon world than in France' (1997: 17). Still, they regard epistemic relativism as less asinine than postmodern abuses of science. And those abuses they illustrate predominantly through French rather than Anglo-American authors, even though there would have been plenty to choose from. This selection hardly reflects anti-French motives on the part of Sokal and Bricmont, however (which, in any event, would be immaterial to the validity of their case). It is more likely to reflect the fact that the original copyright for this specific genre lies with French thinkers rather than their Anglo-American imitators. It is no coincidence, therefore, that their book has been widely perceived as directed against *French philosophy*, whereas Sokal's original hoax was clearly at the expense of *American cultural studies*.

Even to some with less axes to grind than Kristeva, there is a geo-cultural side to the contrast between analytic and continental philosophy. For reasons rehearsed in chapter 3, geographic and linguistic divisions serve us ill when it comes to *defining* analytic philosophy, even when one disregards the latter's continental roots. But such divisions nevertheless matter for the public profile and the self-image of current analytic philosophy.

Two opposing yet connected cultural trends on either side of the Channel are important in this context. Looking west, there is the increasing insularity of Anglo-American culture vis-à-vis continental Europe during the twentieth century. Before 1914 there was exchange and even rapprochement. Around 1900, Frege, Husserl and Russell were very close, as Dummett pointed out. But proximity and exchange was not confined to these revolutionaries, it included large sways of the respective mainstreams. German Neo-Kantians, British Absolute Idealists and American pragmatists, had common protagonists (notably Kant), antagonists (e.g. Hume) and interests (especially in the possibility of knowledge). By contrast, the current notion of *continental* as opposed to European philosophy suggests something foreign and set apart. This reflects a more general change of fortunes. During the course of the last century, political, military and economic developments have alienated the Anglophone world from the European continent, world war by bloody world war. In the academic sphere, the Germanophone world started out as a role model, then became a bogey, and is now treated with superior indifference.

Turning east, on the European continent, or at any rate in what is now called 'old Europe', we encounter fears of Anglo-American 'cultural imperialism' among parts of the elites. Perhaps the most significant target of this reaction is the ascendancy of English to a universal *lingua franca* and the creation of mixed languages like *Franglais* and *Denglisch*, which craft English terms and constructions onto an entirely different and largely inhospitable substrate language. Predictably, these large-scale phenomena cast a shadow on the much smaller stage on which the clash between analytic philosophy and its rivals is played out. The importation of analytic philosophy into France and its re-importation into Germany often come across as an attack on 'indigenous' intellectual traditions, whether they be French structuralism and post-structuralism or German Idealism.

German philosophers like Henrich have never tired of defending the perennial importance of *die klassische deutsche Philosophie* and its superiority over new-fangled imports, whether Anglo-American or French. By contrast, contemporary German analysts have blamed the 'international insignificance' of Germanophone philosophy on its abiding insularity and provincialism (<http://www.information-philosophie.de/philosophie/deutschephilo1.html>). Although the ensuing exchanges have been less acrimonious than those over *Intellectual Impostures*, they have thrown up some of the same topoi. The analytic proponents of philosophical globalization (Beckermann and Spohn) complain that no Germanophone thinker except Habermas counts among the great innovators of recent decades. They maintain that Germanophone philosophers can reach an internationally respectable calibre only by dropping their reverend attitude towards the classics and by accepting English as the academic *lingua franca* even for philosophy. Their opponents accuse them of suffering from an intellectual inferiority complex, indeed, of a 'politically correct, colonized mentality'. They retort that it is Anglophone philosophy that is provincial, since it ignores anything written in languages other than English. They concede the international dominance of Anglophone philosophy, but attribute it to the economic might of the Anglo-Saxon academic industry rather than its inherent superiority.

In this debate, there is truth on all sides, yet the result is still unedifying. In spite of numerous burials at midnight, there is no doubt that predominantly Anglophone analytic philosophy is triumphing on the global academic market, at the expense of other trends within Western philosophy. At the same time, it is perfectly legitimate to wonder whether such success derives from the quality of the product or from the quality of the marketing and from the conditions of trade.

On the basis of my reasonably well-developed acquaintance with the various sides of these linguistic and philosophical divides, I entirely accept that the analytic emperor does have clothes. And although many of its original sources were Germanophone, the bulk of its contributions to philosophical understanding have come from Anglophones.

This is no excuse, however, for the notable failure of many analytic philosophers to pay due attention to figures and ideas that hail from beyond their philosophical, their linguistic or their national horizons. Note certain national divisions even *within* Anglophone analytic philosophy. The received (if misleading) distinction between American ideal language philosophy and British ordinary language philosophy has been supplanted by a difference between a predominantly naturalistic American scene and a more sceptical attitude in Britain. This goes back to the resistance of early British analyticians to the naturalism of the pragmatists. With the naturalistic fallacy in mind, Broad quipped: 'all good fallacies go to America when they die, and rise again as the latest discoveries of the local professors' (1930: 55). Dummett is right to insist, therefore, that the original emergence of analytic philosophy owed most to continental sources, and virtually nothing to American influence (2007: 11, 16). And ontological naturalists though they may be, Australian philosophers like Jackson have joined British colleagues in defending conceptual analysis against its Quinean and Kripkean detractors. A more distinct note of transatlantic disharmony enters into the conflicts between new and old Wittgensteinians (read 'New' and 'Old world'), and into the current controversy between Soames (2006) and Hacker (2006b) over whether it was the Americans or the British who provided the insights of analytic philosophy. A special relationship, perhaps, but not uniformly one of reciprocal adoration.

All of which is small beer compared to the indifference and condescension with which many Anglophones greet non-Anglophone philosophy. This holds not just of those contemporaries who indulge in hackneyed jibes at the 'continentals'. It also afflicts some (first-time) visitors to the continent who note, with genuine surprise, that some of the natives are neither Hegelians, nor Heideggerians, nor postmodernists, and may even be capable of intelligent questions and objections.

The exclusionary demeanour of the Anglophone mainstream is indisputably an intellectual disadvantage when the grounds of exclusion are linguistic or geographic rather than philosophical. Two mutually reinforcing factors are in play – the declining interest in foreign languages among the Anglophone educational elites and the increasing switch to English as the global academic language. Given these factors it is unsurprising that Anglophone philosophers take little notice of analytic texts in languages other than English. But it is a pity that there are so few translations of worthy texts, and an even greater pity that even work that has been translated tends to be ignored.

There is a bitter irony here, and one which marks a chink in the armour of analytic proponents of philosophical globalization. In so far as non-Anglophones are noted by the Anglo-American mainstream, they tend to be *non-analytic* philosophers. Beckermann's list of figures with a top-notch international reputation features only two from outside of the Anglophone world, namely Habermas and Derrida. And in hard-core analytic departments in the Anglophone world, even second-rate continentals are better known than accomplished analytic philosophers like Beckermann, Bouveresse, Garcia-Carpintero, Künne, Marconi, Recanati or Tugendhat, to name but a few. This explains the grudging respect for Derrida I have encountered among some Germanophone analytic philosophers. Whatever their assessment of his philosophical merits (and disgression forbids divulging details), they tend to pay homage to the fact that he managed to make the arrogant Anglo-Saxons listen up. *Chapeau!*, as we used to say in old Europe. Because of cultural stereotyping, a continental European philosopher is much more likely to be taken seriously if she produces something that strikes Anglo-American academics and intellectuals as 'indiginous', mostly on the side of continental philosophy. The easiest route to a modicum of fame is not analytic reasoning, however astute, or even scholarship, however erudite, but something weird and wonderful with a 'local flavour'.

Even with respect to non-analytic philosophy, the exclusionary tone is a weakness of the contemporary mainstream. Rorty reports that 'a distinguished analytic philosopher ... urged that "intellectual hygiene" requires one not to read the books of Derrida and Foucault' (1982: 224). Putnam professes that he came to realize 'that analytic philosophy was no longer characterized by a set of issues or new and exciting approaches to these issues, but by the advice that teachers gave to students as to what those students must *not* read'. And he adds, rightly, that such indifference is especially deplorable when it concerns non-analytic yet perfectly rationalist thinkers such as Habermas (Putnam 2007: 2–3). As I urged in chapter 6.4, if analytic philosophy still retains a general advantage over its rivals in terms of clarity, the clarity at issue must be of a substantive (conceptual, argumentative) rather than merely stylistic (literary) kind. This does not mean that we should all devour as many continental works as possible. *Ars longa, vita brevis!* It does mean, however, that condemnation, not to mention contempt, cannot be based on a perfunctory browsing of continental texts, but must be based on a reasonably sustained examination of their conceptual and logical merits. It is therefore the prerogative of people like Mulligan, Philipse, Searle and Tugendhat, who have put in the hard work.

3 WHITHER ANALYTIC PHILOSOPHY?

Given that analytic philosophers should not wilfully erect barriers against alternative traditions, is there still a point in distinguishing them from their colleagues? Is 'analytic philosophy' still a useful category? Or have the label and the analytic/continental distinction outlived their usefulness?

When it comes to the question of whether analytic philosophy should still be distinguished from other styles we once again encounter opposing camps. In one corner we find the commentators mentioned at the beginning of the introduction. They include a pioneer of analytic philosophy like von Wright, who worries that it is dying on its feet because it has lost its distinctive identity.

Against this are aligned those on both sides who regard such bridge-building between analytic and continental philosophy as pointless or perhaps even invidious. In this corner we find many continental philosophers, notably Rorty, who feel that the analytic/continental divide has become a possibly permanent but equally harmless fixture of Western philosophy (1982: ch. 12; similarly Rockmore 2004: 474). We also find, perhaps surprisingly, Williams. He maintains that analytic philosophy has overcome some of its 'earlier limitations' as regards political philosophy, yet he denies that 'reform has changed or will change it out of all recognition'. What is more, while analytic philosophy does not have 'definite bounds', even on a generous view of its scope it does not coincide with philosophy period (2006: 167).

Unlike von Wright, most of those who question the continuing viability of a separate category of analytic philosophy and of the analytic/continental divide feel that this development is a positive one, philosophically speaking. Many of them invoke, and some of them have contributed to, attempts to build bridges between the two. Sometimes, for instance in the case of many papers assembled in Prado 2003, these bridges look more like (hastily constructed) siege towers for an assault on analytic philosophy. There is no gainsaying the fact, however, that there are some thinkers who have genuinely tried to synthesize the two, or at least to mediate between them, such as Føllesdal, Tugendhat, Dreyfus, Charles Taylor, Cavell and Mulhall.

Does this show that the barriers are finally coming down? I think not. While these various syntheses are distinguished and interesting, it is fair to say that they have not set the agenda on either the analytic or the continental side. They have not produced any seismic shift towards the proverbial middle ground. It is not even clear what this middle ground could amount to. One possibility is post-analytic philosophy, i.e. continental philosophy presented by Anglophone commentators who refer to analytic thinkers like Wittgenstein, Quine and Davidson (e.g. Taylor, Cavell and Mulhall). Another possibility is 'post-continental' philosophy, the philosophy of apostates from thinkers like Hegel, Husserl or Heidegger, who incorporate continental themes or ideas into a purely analytic mode of philosophizing (e.g. Føllesdal and Tugendhat). For better or worse, neither option looks like carrying the day. Even if, in combination, they were to narrow some doctrinal differences, they seem unsuitable for overcoming the abiding methodological, stylistic and institutional differences.

Such a feat might be achieved by communication between more emblematic representatives of both sides. But consider the famous direct debates between analytic and continental philosophers. Many of them have already featured in this book. A complete list would have to include the following:

- Ryle's review of Heidegger's *Sein und Zeit*;
- Carnap's attack on Heidegger's 'The Nothing noths';
- the 1958 Royaumont encounter between British and French philosophers;
- Bar-Hillel's attack on Habermas' appropriation of speech act theory;
- the spat between Searle and Derrida over Austin's speech act theory and the alleged ubiquity of writing;
- the protests against Derrida's honorary degree in Cambridge;
- the aftermath of the Sokal hoax.

Two points are noteworthy. Considering the high profile of the analytic/continental distinction, these confrontations have been few and far between. Furthermore, I see little ground for hope that even now these clashes could be resolved in a more amicable way, or that we are at any rate closer to conducting them in a more controlled and fruitful manner. For instance, in spite of their much vaunted 'analytic training', recent Anglophone defenders of Heidegger remain unwilling to acknowledge some important points: Carnap's paper does not simply rely on verificationism, it considers various ways of making sense of Heidegger's dictum, and it rejects them for noteworthy reasons. They also seem to think that a sentence occurring in a philosophical treatise cannot be condemned as meaningless simply because one can assign a meaning to this *combination of words* (indeed any meaning one pleases), even if on that understanding the sentence can in no way shoulder the argumentative weight it needs to in its original context.

Or take the most extended rally between analytic and continental philosophers. One might argue over whether Searle's (1977) response to Derrida's (1972) critique of Austin is harsh yet fair (as I feel), or unnecessarily abrasive. But there is no arguing over the fact that Derrida's reaction (1988) amounts to a complete refusal to engage with the issues at a rational level. Instead, it consists of obscure evasions, wails and linguistic puns. Derrida suggests that Searle's acknowledgement of help with his response indicates lack of intellectual responsibility and integrity. And he stoops to attributing the response to a fictitious 'SARL' (*Société à Responsabilité Limitée*), a Limited Inc. or Society with Diminished Responsibility.

In short, exchanges between the two camps have made matters worse rather than better. If past experience is anything to go by, serious engagement between analytic and continental philosophy will not lead to conciliation, but to more pronounced estrangement. Perhaps it is the terms of engagement that are to blame. Dummett has recently recommended that the analytic/continental divide should be overcome by founding a journal in which an analytic philosopher writes an article followed by a 'continental' response, or vice versa. I am far from confident that this procedure would overcome the failure of communication Dummett rightly deplores. More probably, the outcome would be as described by Marconi in a discussion following Dummett's paper. Responding to a continental article, the analytic commentator would engage in a flurry of 'What do you mean by this?', 'What is the justification for that?', and 'How are we to understand the next thing?' The continental respondent to an analytic piece, by contrast, would ignore the general gist, pick out some tiny detail, and engage in comments about etymological or historical aspects surrounding that detail.

If the analytic/continental contrast has become obsolete, it is not because we have moved on to a new and thriving synthesis. But perhaps it has simply been superseded by other divides. Thus it has been suggested that the analytic philosophy/continental philosophy distinction is no longer relevant, and that the real fault-line within current philosophy runs between naturalists and non-naturalists. It is striking, furthermore, that this suggestion has found favour across the divide.

Commenting on Kantian Oxford philosophers in the wake of Strawson an analytic naturalist like Papineau writes:

... a new and potentially more fruitful division is emerging within English-speaking philosophy. In place of the old analytic–Continental split we now have the opposition between the naturalists and the neo-Kantians. The naturalists look to science to provide the starting point for philosophy. The neo-Kantians start with consciousness instead. But at least the two sides can understand what the other is up to. (2003: 12)

Similarly, a post-analytic non-naturalist like Glendinning writes:

Perhaps the dominant kind of analytic philosophy today, at least in America, although it's growing here too, is philosophical naturalism. This is the tradition opposed to the one I see myself located in, the post-Kantian tradition which doesn't see that kind of continuity between philosophy and science. For me, and I think for many others, this is where the most fundamental issues and disputes lie today. And this is why concern with the demarcation of analytic philosophy from continental philosophy is becoming less and less significant and is being abandoned by more and more people within the profession. (2002: 214–15)

What emerges has points of contact with the idea attacked in chapter 5, namely that unless analytic philosophy were defined by certain doctrines, it would not count as a proper philosophical movement. The proposal is this: because analytic philosophy can no longer be defined by reference to any doctrines, the analytic/continental divide should be replaced by a doctrinal distinction that marks the real fault-line.

While appreciating the reasons behind this proposal, I do not regard them as overwhelming. One of my qualms emerges by looking at the end of Papineau's quote. He places weight on the fact that the opposing sides in a philosophical dispute nonetheless understand each other. As regards naturalists and non-naturalists within analytic philosophy he worries: 'Whether they will stay in touch remains to be seen. Philosophical engagement depends on a shared context of basic assumptions, or at least a willingness to debate points of underlying conflict. If John Campbell's *Reference and Consciousness* is anything to go by, prospects for continuing dialogue are not rosy.' Why? Because 'the basic ideals that structure Campbell's overall argument will seem alien to naturalistic readers, and he displays a worrying disinclination to explain them to this wider audience'. Leaving aside this particular case, I can empathize with this *type* of frustration, since much contemporary analytic philosophy is not as clear as it could and should be, and fails in its duty of accounting for its assumptions. Parting company with Papineau, however, I feel that unclarity also afflicts naturalists, though perhaps to a lesser degree, and that the tendency to take *their* assumptions simply for granted actually afflicts them to a greater degree.

More importantly, Papineau is right to value the importance of mutual communication. Yet surely such communication is considerably easier between naturalists and non-naturalists arguing in an analytic vein than between analytic philosophers of any *couleur* and most of their continental colleagues. If Papineau has genuine difficulties understanding Campbell, he should be at a complete loss reading continental thinkers like Lacan, Deleuze or Guattari.

Philosophy is not about sharing doctrines, but about having a rational and civilized debate even about one's own most cherished assumptions. Such a debate remains easier among analytic philosophers than between analytic and continental philosophers.

This takes me to a final question, one in prescriptive rather than descriptive metaphilosophy. Should we deliberately try to overcome the remaining barriers dividing analytic philosophy from continental and traditionalist philosophy, and from pragmatism, in so far as it constitutes a movement at the same level of generality?

One message of this book is that mainstream Anglophone analytic philosophy should abandon some of its superior airs. But the reason is not the one often given, namely that continental philosophy is *better* than generally assumed. I am not in a position to pronounce on this claim with authority, though my evidence does not support it. It is rather that contemporary analytic philosophy is *worse* than most practitioners like to believe; at any rate, it is not as good as it should and could be.

Admittedly, there are now very competent expositors of continental philosophy, mostly Anglophone philosophers with some analytic background. But the genuinely continental and original voices in that field, in so far as any remain, strike me to be as obscure as ever. It also seems to me that their intellectual impact is on the wane. If analytic philosophy is in crisis, continental philosophy is in serious trouble. To modify Willy Brandt's old joke about capitalism and socialism: Analytic philosophy is staring into the abyss. And what does it see? Continental philosophy!

Like Baldwin (2006) I think that one should not expend energy on 'fortifying and patrolling' the border between analytic and continental philosophy, yet remain true to the virtues of 'open-minded clarity and rigour'. One should remain open to interesting ideas from any quarter, while insisting that they be presented in a manner that makes them amenable to fruitful debate.

That much ought to be uncontroversial. But we can draw a stronger and potentially more contentious conclusion. There is no overriding *intellectual* imperative for analytic philosophy to alter course solely to achieve rapprochement with other philosophical currents, assimilation to other intellectual styles, or recognition in other academic disciplines. While there may be a premium on reconstituting philosophy as a unified sphere of discourse, this must not go at the expense of rigour, clarity, scholarship and intellectual honesty. Accordingly, neither division nor synthesis should be sought for its own sake, but simply philosophical quality. What the analytic scene needs is not a deliberate switch to continental, traditionalist or pragmatist modes of thought, but analytic philosophy in a different vein: engaging and engaged instead of scholastic and isolationist, collegial, undogmatic and open minded instead of factionalist and exclusionary.

Analytic philosophy can be proud of its achievements without succumbing to self-serving preconceptions about itself and the continental 'other'. Freed of its excesses and weaknesses, it remains capable of advancing not just the resolution of traditional philosophical problems, but also human self-understanding. Finally, it can facilitate the pursuit of non-philosophical debates in a clearer and more cogent fashion. Analytic philosophy could do worse than taking seriously its vocation as critical thinking writ large: a means of improving debate in other areas, but one which, from case to case, engages with the details of these debates, rather than legislating from above on the basis of preconceived generalities. Asked at a party, what he actually did, an analytic philosopher replied: 'You clarify a few concepts. You make a few distinctions. It's a living' (Swift 2001: 42). To qualify for a pay hike, one must put these activities in the service of resolving conceptual difficulties in all walks of life, and of constructing and assessing arguments on pertinent issues. And if, contrary to my expectations, it is ontologists rather than physicists that can pronounce on the ultimate make-up of reality, I'd be the last to begrudge them a fat top-up bonus.

One remedy for the ills of current analytic philosophy may simply lie in recovering some of the virtues of earlier stages. A cherished self-image of analytic philosophy notwithstanding, the inspirational figures from its past have not bequeathed us a series of indisputable demonstrations or knockdown arguments. But they have shown us how one can question deepseated assumptions and resolve tempting confusions in a way that is striking, innovative and illuminating; they have also shown us how one can broach fundamental and complex problems in a manner that is clear, profound and honest. At its best, analytic philosophy conforms to Russell's ideal of 'cold steel in the hand of passion' (Monk 1996a: 262). At a time when religious ideologies and economic dogmas are ruling the planet with scant regard to either logic or science, analytic philosophy might even have beneficial effects in a wider sphere, provided that it is wielded to slay a few intellectual monsters.

Bibliography

Adorno, T. W. *et al.* (eds.) 1969 *Der Positivismusstreit in der deutschen Soziologie* (Neuwied and Berlin: Luchterhand); Engl. trans. *The Positivist Dispute in German Sociology* (London: Heinemann, 1970).

Agostini, F. D. 1997 *Analitici e Continentali* (Milan: Raffaello Cortina).

Alcoff, L. and E. Potter (eds.) 1993 *Feminist Epistemologies* (London: Routledge).

Anderson, R. L. 2005 'Neo-Kantianism and the Roots of Anti-Psychologism', *British Journal for the History of Philosophy* 13, 287–324.

Annas, J. 2004 'Ancient Philosophy for the Twenty-First Century', in B. Leiter (ed.), *The Future for Philosophy* (Oxford University Press), 25–43.

Anscombe, G. E. M. 1958 'Modern Moral Philosophy', *Philosophy* 33, 1–19.

Apel, K. O. 1980 *Towards the Transformation of Philosophy* (London: Routledge & Kegan Paul).

Armstrong, D. [1980] 'The Causal Theory of the Mind', in W. Lycan (ed.), *Mind and Cognition* (Oxford: Blackwell, 1990), 37–47.

1983 *What is a Law of Nature?* (Cambridge University Press).

1997 *A World of States of Affairs* (Cambridge University Press).

Aschenberg, R. 1982 *Sprachanalyse und Transzendentalphilosophie* (Stuttgart: Klett-Cotta).

Atterton, P. and M. Calarco (eds.) 2004 *Animal Philosophy* (London: Continuum).

Austin, J. L. 1970 *Philosophical Papers* (Oxford University Press).

Ayer, A. J. [1936] *Language, Truth and Logic* (Harmondsworth: Penguin, 1971).

1947 *Thinking and Meaning* (London: Lewis).

(ed.) 1959 *Logical Positivism* (New York: Free Press).

1991 'An Interview with A. J. Ayer', in A. P. Griffiths (ed.), *A. J. Ayer: Memorial Essays* (Cambridge University Press), 209–26.

Ayer, A. J. *et al.* 1956 *The Revolution in Philosophy* (London: Macmillan).

Ayers, M. 1978 'Analytical Philosophy and the History of Philosophy', in Rée, Ayers and Westoby 1978, 42–66.

Babich, B. E. 2003 'On the Analytic/ Continental Divide in Philosophy', in Prado 2003b, 63–104.

Baggini, J. and J. Strangroom (eds.) 2002 *New British Philosophy: the Interviews* (London: Routledge).

Baker, G. P. 1988 *Wittgenstein, Frege and the Vienna Circle* (Oxford: Blackwell).

Baker, G. P and P. M. S. Hacker 1983 *Frege: Logical Excavations* (Oxford: Blackwell).
  1984 *Language, Sense and Nonsense* (Oxford: Blackwell).
Baldwin, T. 1990 *G. E. Moore* (London: Routledge).
  2001 *Contemporary Philosophy: Philosophy in English since 1945* (Oxford University Press).
  2006 'Editorial', *Mind* 115.
Beaney, M. 2003 'Analysis', *The Stanford Encyclopedia of Philosophy* (Summer 2003 Edition), E. N. Zalta (ed.), URL = <http://plato.stanford.edu/archives/sum2003/entries/analysis/>.
  2007 *The Analytic Turn: Analysis in Early Analytic Philosophy and Phenomenology* (London: Routledge).
Beck, L. (ed.) 1962 *La Philosophie Analytique. Cahiers de Royaumont* IV (Paris: Editions de Minuit).
Beck, L. W. 1967 'German Philosophy', in Edwards 1967, 291–309.
Beckermann, A. 2001 *Analytische Einführung in die Philosophie des Geistes* (Berlin: Walter de Gruyter).
  2004 'Einleitung', in P. Prechtl (ed.), *Grundbegriffe der Analytischen Philosophie* (Stuttgart: Metzler), 1–12.
Bell, D. 1999 'The Revolution of Moore and Russell: a very British Coup?' in O'Hear 1999, 193–208.
Bell, D. and N. Cooper (eds.) 1990 *The Analytic Tradition* (Oxford: Blackwell).
Beneke, F. E. [1831] 'Kant und die philosophische Aufgabe unserer Zeit', in J. Kopper and R. Malter (eds.), *Immanuel Kant zu Ehren* (Frankfurt: Suhrkamp, 1974).
Ben-Menahem, Y. 2005 'Introduction', in Y. Ben-Menahem (ed.), *Hilary Putnam* (Cambridge University Press), 1–16.
Ben-Yami, H. 2004 *Logic and Natural Language* (Aldershot: Ashgate).
Bennett, J. 1966 *Kant's Analytic* (Cambridge University Press).
Bentham, J. [1817] *Chrestomathia* (Oxford University Press, 1983).
Bergmann, G. 1945 'I – A Positivistic Metaphysics of Consciousness', *Mind* 44, 193–226.
Berlin, I. [1950] 'Logical Translation', in *Concepts and Categories* (Oxford University Press), 56–80.
Bieri, P. 2005 'Was bleibt von der Analytischen Philosophie, wenn die Dogmen gefallen sind?', CD-Rom (Potsdam: Einstein Forum).
Biletzki, A. and A. Matar (eds.) 1998 *The Story of Analytic Philosophy* (London: Routledge).
Blanshard, B. 1962 *Reason and Analysis* (La Salle: Open Court).
Black, M. 1933 'Philosophical Analysis', *Proceedings of the Aristotelian Society* 33, 237–58.
Blackburn, S. 2005 *Truth: a Guide for the Perplexed* (London: Allen Lane).
Blumberg, A. and H. Feigl 1931 'Logical Positivism: a New Movement in European Philosophy', *Journal of Philosophy* 28, 281–96.
Boghossian, P. 1996 'What the Sokal Hoax Ought to Teach us', *Times Literary Supplement* 13, 14–15.

2006 *Fear of Knowledge: against Relativism and Constructivism* (Oxford University Press).

Bolzano, Bernard [1810] *Beiträge zu einer begründeteren Darstellung der Mathematik* (*Contributions to a More Well-founded Presentation of Mathematics*) (Darmstadt: Wissenschaftliche Buchgesellschaft, 1974).

(1834) *Lehrbuch der Religionswissenschaft* (*Textbook of the Science of Religion*), (Sulzbach: Seidel, 4 vols).

[1837] *Wissenschaftslehre* (Sulzbach: Seidel, 4 vols); selections, trans. and ed. R. George, in *Theory of Science* (Oxford: Blackwell, 1972).

[1851] *Paradoxien des Unendlichen* (Leipzig: Reclam; repr. Hamburg: Meiner, 1975); trans. and with intro. by D. A. Steele, *Paradoxes of the Infinite* (London and New Haven, Conn.: Routledge, 1950).

Bonjour, L. 1998 *In Defense of Pure Reason* (Cambridge University Press).

Boole, G. [1854] *An Investigation of the Laws of Thought* (New York: Dover, 1958).

Borradori, G. 1994 *The American Philosopher* (Chicago University Press).

de Botton, A. 2001 *The Consolations of Philosophy* (London: Penguin).

Bouveresse, J. 1983 'Why I am so Very Unfrench', in A. Montefiori (ed.), *Philosophy in France Today* (Cambridge University Press).

2000 'Reading Rorty: Pragmatism and its Consequences', in R. Brandom (ed.), *Rorty and His Critics* (Oxford: Blackwell), 129–46.

Brandom, R. 2002 *Tales of the Mighty Dead* (Cambridge, Mass.: Harvard University Press).

2006 'Between Saying and Doing: Towards an Analytic Pragmatism', The 2005–2006 John Locke Lectures, <www.pitt.edu/~brandom/locke/index.html>.

Brentano, F. [1874] *Psychologie vom Empirischen Standpunkte* (Hamburg: Meiner, 1973).

[1889] *Vom Ursprung sittlicher Erkenntnis* (Leipzig: Duncker & Humblot); 4th edn, ed. O. Kraus, (Hamburg: Meiner, 1955); trans. R. M. Chisholm and E. H. Schneewind, *The Origin of our Knowledge of Right and Wrong* (London: Routledge, 1969).

Broad, C. D. 1925 *Mind and its Place in Nature* (London: Routledge & Kegan Paul).

1930 *Five Types of Ethical Theory* (London: Routledge & Kegan Paul).

Brogan, W. and J. Risser (eds.) 2000 *American Continental Philosophy* (Bloomington: Indiana University Press).

Bubner, R. 1996 'Gedanken uber die Zukunft der Philosophie', *Deutsch Zeitschrift fur Philosophie*, 743–57.

Bunnin, N. and E. P. Tsui-James (eds.) 1996 *The Blackwell Companion to Philosophy* (Oxford: Blackwell).

Burge, T. 1979 'Individualism and the Mental', *Midwest Studies in Philosophy* 4, 73–121.

2003 'Logic and Analyticity', in Glock *et al.* (eds.), *Fifty Years of Quine's 'Two Dogmas'*, *Grazier Philosophische Studien* 66, 199–249.

Butler, R. J. (ed.) 1962 *Analytical Philosophy* (Oxford: Blackwell).

Carl, W. 1994 *Frege's Theory of Sense and Reference* (Cambridge University Press).

Carnap, R. [1928] *Der Logische Aufbau der Welt* (*The Logical Structure of the World & Pseudoproblems in Philosophy*), trans. R. A. George (Berkeley: University of California Press, 1969).

[1932] 'The Elimination of Metaphysics through Logical Analysis of Language', in Ayer 1959, 60–81.

1934a 'Theoretischen Fragen und praktische Entscheidungen', *Natur und Geist* 2, 257–60.

1934b 'On the Character of Philosophical Problems', *Philosophy of Science* 1, 5–19.

1936a 'Die Methode der logischen Analyse', in *Actes du huitième Congrès International de Philosophie, à Prague 2–7 Septembre 1934* (Prague: Orbis), 142–5.

1936b 'Von der Erkenntnistheorie zur Wissenschaftslogik', *Actes du Congrès International du Philosophie Scientifique* (Paris: Hermann & Cie), 36–41.

1937 *The Logical Syntax of Language* (London: Routledge & Kegan Paul).

1956 *Meaning and Necessity* (University of Chicago Press).

1963 'Intellectual Autobiography', in P. Schilpp (ed.), *The Philosophy of Rudolf Carnap*, Library of Living Philosophers, vol. XI (La Salle, Ill.: Open Court), 1–84.

1964 'Interview mit Rudolf Carnap (1964)', in W. Hochkeppel (ed.), *Mein Weg in die Philosophie* (Stuttgart: Reclam), 133–47.

Carnap, R., H. Hahn and O. Neurath 1929 'Wissenschaftliche Weltauffassung: Der Wiener Kreis', in O. Neurath, *Gesammelte Philosophische und Methodologische Schriften*, vol. I (Vienna: Hölder-Pilcher-Tempsky 1981), 299–336.

Cartwright, N., J. Cat, K. Fleck, and T. Uebel 1996 *Otto Neurath: Between Science and Politics* (Cambridge University Press).

Cartwright, N. and J. Cat 1998 'Otto Neurath', in Craig 1998, 813–16.

Cassirer, E. 1921 *Zur Einsteinschen Relativitätstheorie* (Berlin: Bruno Cassirer).

Chalmers, D. 1996 *The Conscious Mind* (Oxford University Press).

Charlton, W. 1991 *The Analytic Ambition* (Oxford: Blackwell).

Chomsky, N. 1965 *Aspects of a Theory of Syntax* (Cambridge, Mass.: MIT Press).

1979 *Language and Responsibility* (Brighton: Harvester).

Churchland, P. M. 1981 'Eliminative Materialism and the Propositional Attitudes', *Journal of Philosophy* 78, 67–90.

Coffa, A. 1991 *The Semantic Tradition* (Cambridge University Press).

Cohen, J. L. 1986 *The Dialogue of Reason* (Oxford University Press).

Collingwood, R. G. 1939 *An Autobiography* (Oxford University Press).

1940 *An Essay on Metaphysics* (Oxford: Clarendon Press).

Cooper, D. E. 1994 'Analytical and Continental Philosophy', *Proceedings of the Aristotelian Society* 94, 1–18.

Corradini, A., S. Galvan and E. J. Lowe (eds.) 2006 *Analytic Philosophy without Naturalism* (London: Routledge).

Cottingham, J. 2003 *The Meaning of Life* (London: Routledge).

Craig, E. 1990 *Knowledge and the State of Nature* (Oxford: Clarendon Press).

(ed.) 1998 *The Routledge Encyclopedia of Philosophy* (London: Routledge).

Critchley, S. 1998 'Introduction: What is Continental Philosophy', in Critchley and Schroeder 1998, 1–17.

2001 *Continental Philosophy: a Very Short Introduction* (Oxford University Press).

Critchley S. and W. R. Schroeder (eds.) 1998 *A Companion to Continental Philosophy* (Blackwell: Oxford).

Czolbe, H. 1855 *Neue Darstellung des Sensualismus* (Leipzig: Teubner).

Dahms, H. J. 1994 *Positivismusstreit* (Frankfurt: Suhrkamp).

Dancy, J. 2004 *Ethics without Principles* (Oxford University Press).

Dancy, R. M 1983 'Alien Concepts', *Synthese* 56, 283–300.

Danneberg, L., A. Kamlah and L. Schäfer (eds.) 1994 *Hans Reichenbach und die Berliner Gruppe* (Brunswick: Vieweg).

Danto, A. 1967 'Naturalism', in Edwards 1967, 448–50.

Davidson, D. 1980 *Essays on Actions and Events* (Oxford University Press).

1984a *Expressing Evaluations*, The Lindley Lecture (monograph), (University of Kansas Press).

1984b *Inquiries into Truth and Interpretation* (Oxford University Press).

1994 'Donald Davidson', in S. Guttenplan (ed.), *A Companion to the Philosophy of Mind* (Oxford: Blackwell), 231–6.

1999 'Intellectual Autobiography', in L. E. Hahn (ed.), *The Philosophy of Donald Davidson*, Library of Living Philosophers, vol. XXVII (Chicago: Open Court, 1999), 3–79.

Davies, S. 1998 'Art, Definition of', in Craig 1998, 464–8.

Dawkins, R. 1998 'Postmodernism Disrobed', *Nature* 394, 141–3.

Dennett, D. 1991 'The Brain and its Boundaries', *Times Literary Supplement* 10 May 1991.

Derrida, J. [1967] *Of Grammatology* (Baltimore: Johns Hopkins University Press, 1976).

[1972] 'Signature, Event, Context', *Glyph* 1 (1977), 172–97.

1988 *Limited Inc* (Evanston, Ill.: Northwestern University Press).

2000 'Response to Moore', in *Ratio* XIII, 381–3.

Devitt, M. 1996 *Coming to Our Senses: a Naturalistic Programme for Semantic Localism* (Cambridge University Press).

Dipert, R. 1998 'Logic in the 19th Century', in Craig 1998, 722–9.

Dummett, M. A. E. 1973 *Frege: Philosophy of Language* (London: Duckworth, 2nd edn 1981).

1978 *Truth and other Enigmas* (London: Duckworth).

1981 *The Interpretation of Frege's Philosophy* (London: Duckworth).

1991 *Frege: Philosophy of Mathematics* (London: Duckworth).

1992 'The Metaphysics of Verificationism', in L. E. Hahn (ed.), *The Philosophy of A. J. Ayer* (LaSalle, Ill.: Open Court), 129–48.

1993 *The Origins of Analytical Philosophy* (London: Duckworth).

2001 *On Immigration and Refugees* (London: Routledge).

2007 'The Place of Philosophy in European Culture' (forthcoming).

Edwards, P. (ed.) 1967 *The Encyclopedia of Philosophy* (New York: Macmillan).

Engel, P. 1997 *La Dispute: une Introduction à la Philosophie Analytique* (Paris: Minuit).

Ewing, A. C. 1937 'Meaninglessness', *Mind* 46, 347–64.

Feigl, H. 1981 *Inquiries and Provocations: Selected Writings 1929–1974* (Dordrecht: Reidel).

Feigl, H. and W. Sellars 1949 *Readings in Philosophical Analysis* (New York: Appleton-Century-Crofts, Inc.).

Ferry, J. L. and A. Renaut 1985 *La Pensée 68. Essai sur l'anti-humanisme contemporain* (Paris: Gallimard).

Feyerabend, P. 1975 *Against Method* (London: Verso).

Floridi, L. (ed.) 2004 *The Blackwell Guide to the Philosophy of Computing and Information* (Oxford: Blackwell).

Fodor, J. 1974 'Special Sciences', *Synthese* 28, 77–115.

1975 *The Language of Thought* (New York: Crowell).

1987 *Psychosemantics* (Cambridge, Mass.: MIT Press).

2003 *Hume Variations* (Oxford University Press).

Føllesdal, D. 1997 'Analytic Philosophy: What is It and Why Should One Engage in It?', in Glock 1997c, 193–208.

Foster, J. 1982 *The Case for Idealism* (London: Routledge & Kegan Paul).

Fotion, N. 2000 *John Searle* (Teddington: Acumen).

Foucault, M. 1973 *The Order of Things* (New York: Random House).

Frank, P. 1935 'Die Prager Vorkonferenz 1934', *Erkenntnis* 5, 3–5.

Frede, M. 1987 *Essays in Ancient Philosophy* (Oxford: Clarendon Press).

Frege, G. [1879] *Conceptual Notation and Related Articles*, trans. and ed. T. W. Bynum (Oxford: Clarendon Press, 1972).

[1884] *The Foundations of Arithmetic*, trans. J. L. Austin (Oxford: Blackwell, 1953).

[1892] 'On Sense and Meaning', in B. McGuinness (ed.), *Collected Papers* (Oxford: Blackwell), 1984), 157–77.

[1893 and 1903] *Grundgesetze der Arithmetik*, vols. I and II (Hildesheim: Olms 1966).

1979 *Posthumous Writings* (Oxford: Blackwell).

1980 *Philosophical and Mathematical Correspondence* (Oxford: Blackwell).

1984 *Collected Papers* (Oxford: Blackwell).

1996 'Diary: Written by Professor Dr. Gottlob Frege in the Time from 10 March to 9 April 1924', *Inquiry*, vol. 39, 303–42.

Friedman, M. 1997 'Philosophical Naturalism', *Proceedings and Addresses of the American Philosophical Association* 71, 5–21.

1998 'Logical Positivism', in Craig 1998, 789–95.

2000 *A Parting of the Ways: Carnap, Cassirer, and Heidegger* (Chicago: Open Court).

Gaarder, J. 1996 *Sophie's World*, trans. P. Moller (London: Orion, 2004).

Gadamer, H. G. 1960 *Wahrheit und Methode* (Tübingen: Mohr).

[1967] *Philosophical Hermeneutics* (Berkeley: University of California Press, 1976).

Gallie, W. B. [1956] 'Essentially Contested Concepts', in his *Philosophy and the Historical Understanding* (London: Chatto & Windus, 1964).

Gardner, S. 1993 *Irrationality and the Philosophy of Pschoanalysis* (Oxford University Press).

Garry, A. 'Analytic Feminism', *The Stanford Encyclopedia of Philosophy* (Summer 2004 Edition), E. N. Zalta (ed.), URL = <http://plato.stanford.edu/archives/sum2004/entries/femapproach-analytic/>.

Gaynesford, M. de 2006 *Hilary Putnam* (Chesham: Acumen).

Geach, P. 1972 *Logic Matters* (Oxford: Basil Blackwell).

1977 *The Virtues* (Cambridge University Press).

Geier, M. 1992 *Der Wiener Kreis* (Reinbek: Rowohlt).

Gellner, E. 1959 *Words and Things* (London: Gollancz).

Gillies, D. 1999 'German Philosophy of Mathematics from Gauss to Hilbert', in O'Hear 1999, 167–92.

Glendinning, S. 1998a 'What is Continental Philosophy', in Glendinning 1998b, 3–20.

(ed.) 1998b *The Edinburgh Encyclopedia of Continental Philosophy* (Edinburgh University Press).

2002 'The Analytic and the Continental', in Baggini and Stangroom 2002, 201–18.

2006 *The Idea of Continental Philosophy* (Edinburgh: Edinburgh University Press).

Glock, H.-J. 1994 'The Euthanasia Debate in Germany: what's the Fuss?', *Journal of Applied Philosophy* 11, 213–24.

1996 *A Wittgenstein Dictionary* (Oxford: Blackwell).

1997a 'Kant and Wittgenstein: Philosophy, Necessity and Representation', *International Journal of Philosophical Studies* 5, 285–305.

1997b 'Philosophy, Thought and Language', in J. Preston (ed.), *Thought and Language: Proceedings of the Royal Institute of Philosophy Conference* (Cambridge University Press), 151–69.

(ed.) 1997c *The Rise of Analytic Philosophy* (Oxford: Blackwell).

1998 'Insignificant Others: the Mutual Prejudices of Anglophone and Germanophone Philosophers', in C. Brown and T. Seidel (eds.), *Cultural Negotiations* (Tübingen: Francke Verlag), 83–98.

1999a 'Schopenhauer and Wittgenstein: Representation as Language and Will', in C. Janaway (ed.), *The Cambridge Companion to Schopenhauer* (Cambridge University Press), 422–58.

1999b 'Vorsprung durch Logik: The German Analytic Tradition', in O'Hear 1999, 137–66.

2000 'Imposters, Bunglers and Relativists', in S. Peters, M. Biddiss and I. Roe (eds.), *The Humanities at the Millennium* (Tübingen: Francke Verlag), 267–87.

2001 'Wittgenstein and Reason', in J. Klagge (ed.), *Wittgenstein: Biography and Philosophy* (Cambridge University Press), 195–220.

2002 '"Clarity" is not Enough', in K. Puhl (ed.), *Wittgenstein and the Future of Philosophy: Proceedings of the 24th International Wittgenstein Symposium* (Vienna: Hölder-Pichler-Tempsky), 81–98.

2003a *Quine and Davidson on Language, Thought and Reality* (Cambridge University Press).

2003b 'Strawson and Analytic Kantianism', in H. J. Glock (ed.), *Strawson and Kant* (Oxford: Clarendon Press, 2003), 15–42.

2004 'Was Wittgenstein an Analytic Philosopher?', *Metaphilosophy* 35, 419–44.

2007 'Relativism, Commensurability and Translatability', in *Ratio* vol. XX (2007), 377–402.

Glotz, P. 1996 *Im Kern verrottet? Fünf vor zwölf an Deutschlands Universitäten* (Stuttgart: DVA).

Gottlieb, A. 2001 'Why We Need Philosophers', *The Spectator* 13 January 2001, 20–1.

Gödel, K. [1931] 'On Formally Undecidable Propositions of *Principia Mathematica* and Related Systems I', in S. G. Shanker (ed.), *Gödel's Theorem in Focus* (London: Routledge, 1990), 17–47.

Goodman, N. 1978 *Ways of Worldmaking* (Indianapolis: Hackett).

Grayling, A. (ed.) 1998 *Philosophy 2: Further Through the Subject* (Oxford University Press).

Green, K. 2001 'Analysing Analysis', Critical Study of Hans-Johann Glock *The Rise of Analytic Philosophy*, *Philosophia* 28, 511–29.

Grice, H. P. 1989 *Studies in the Way of Words* (Cambridge, Mass.: Harvard University Press).

Grice, H. P. and P. F. Strawson 1956 'In Defense of a Dogma', *Philosophical Review* 65, 141–58.

Griffin, N. 1996 'Denoting Concepts in *The Principles of Mathematics*', in Monk and Palmer 1996, 23–57.

2001 *The Selected Letters of Bertrand Russell* (London: Routledge).

Haaparanta, L. and I. Niiniluouto 2003 *Analytic Philosophy in Finland* (Amsterdam: Rodopi).

Habermas, J. [1963] *Theory and Practice* (Boston: Beacon 1973).

1979 *Communication and the Evolution of Society* (London: Heineman).

Hacker, P. M. S. 1996 *Wittgenstein's Place in Twentieth Century Analytic Philosophy* (Oxford: Blackwell).

1997 'The Rise of Twentieth Century Analytic Philosophy', in Glock 1997c, 51–76.

1998 'Analytic Philosophy: What, Whence and Whither', in Biletzki and Matar 1998, 3–34.

2001 *Wittgenstein: Connections and Controversies* (Oxford University Press).

2006 'Soames' History of Analytic Philosophy', *Philosophical Quarterly* 56, 121–31.

2007 'Analytic Philosophy: beyond the Linguistic Turn and Back Again', in Beaney 2007, 125–41.

Hacking, I. 1984 'Five Parables', in Rorty, Schneewind and Skinner 1984, 103–24.

1999 *The Social Construction of What?* (Cambridge, Mass.: Harvard University Press).

Hahn, H. 1930 'Überflüssige Wesenheiten', in *Empirismus, Logik, Mathematik* (Frankfurt: Suhrkamp), 21–37.

1980 *Philosophical Papers* (Dordrecht: Reidel).

Haller, R. 1988 *Questions on Wittgenstein* (London: Routledge).

1991 'On the Historiography of Austrian Philosophy', in Uebel 1991, 41–50.

1993 *Neopositivismus* (Darmstadt: Wissenschaftliche Buchgesellschaft).

Hamilton, W. 1859–60 *Lectures on Metaphysics and Logic*, vol. III (Edinburgh and London: Blackwood).

Hammer, E. 2003 'The Legacy of German Idealism', *British Journal for the History of Philosophy* 13, 521–35.

Hanfling, O. 1987 *The Quest for Meaning* (Oxford: Blackwell).

2000 *Philosophy and Ordinary Language* (London: Routledge).

Hanna, R. 2001 *Kant and the Analytic Tradition* (Oxford University Press).

Hardcastle, G. L. and A. Richardson (eds.) 2003 *Logical Empiricism in America*, Minnesota Studies in the Philosophy of Science XVIII (University of Minnesota Press).

Hare, P. 1988 *Doing Philosophy Historically* (Buffalo: Prometheus).

Hare, R. M. 1952 *The Language of Morals* (Oxford University Press).

1960 'A School for Philosophers', *Ratio*, vol. 2, 107–20.

Harman, G. 1977 *The Nature of Morality* (Oxford University Press).

Hart, H. L. A. 1962 *The Concept of Law* (Oxford University Press).

Hart, W. D. 1990, 'Clarity', in Bell and Cooper 1990, 197–222.

Hegel, W. F. [1812–16] *Wissenschaft der Logik* (Hamburg: Meiner, 1932).

[1821] *Grundlinien der Philosophie des Rechts* (Hamburg: Meiner, 1955).

Heidegger, M. 1927 *Sein und Zeit* (Halle: Niemeyer).

Hempel, C. G. [1950] 'The Empiricist Criterion of Meaning', in Ayer 1959, 108–29.

Henrich, D. 2003 *Between Kant and Hegel* (Cambridge, Mass.: Harvard University Press).

Hintikka, J. 1998 'Who is About to Kill Analytic Philosophy?', in Biletzki and Matar 1998, 253–69.

Honderich, T. (ed.) 2005 *The Oxford Companion to Philosophy* (Oxford University Press).

Hookway, C. 1998 'Charles Sanders Peirce', in Craig 1998, 269–84.

Horkheimer, M. [1937] 'The Latest Attack on Metaphysics', trans. in *Critical Theory. Selected Essays* (New York: Seabury, 1972), 132–87.

Horkheimer, M. and T. W. Adorno 1947 *Dialektik der Aufklärung* (Amsterdam: Querido); trans. *Dialectic of Enlightenment* (London: Verso, 1979).

Hornsby, J. 1997 *Simple Mindedness* (Cambridge, Mass.: Harvard University Press).

Hospers, J. 1973 *An Introduction to Philosophical Analysis* (London: Routledge & Kegan Paul).

Hügli, A. and P. Lübcke 1991 *Philosophielexikon* (Reinbek: Rowohlt).

Hunter, J. D. 1991 *Culture Wars: the Struggle to Define America* (New York: Basic Books).

Hurka, T. 2004 'Normative Ethics: Back to the Future', in Leiter 2004c, 246–64.

Husserl, E. 1900 *Logical Investigations* (London: Routledge & Kegan Paul).

Hylton, P. 1990 *Russell, Idealism and the Emergence of Analytic Philosophy* (Oxford: Clarendon Press).

1998 'Analysis in Analytic Philosophy', in Biletzki and Matar 1998, 37–55.

Hyman, J. 2006 *The Objective Eye* (University of Chicago Press).

Jackson, F. 1986 'What Mary Didn't Know' *Journal of Philosophy* 83, 291–5.

1998 *From Metaphysics to Ethics: A Defence of Conceptual Analysis* (Oxford: Clarendon Press).

2003 'Among the Naturalists', *Times Literary Supplement* 12 September 2003, 32.

Jacquette, D. 2002 *Ontology* (Chesham: Acumen).

James, W. [1907] *Pragmatism*, B. Kuklick (ed.) (Indianapolis and Cambridge: Hackett, 1981).

Jenkins, S. 2001 'Have We all Lost the Nerve to Think?', *The Times* 3 January 2001.

Jubien, M. 1997 *Contemporary Metaphysics* (Oxford: Blackwell).

Kant, I. [1783] *Prolegomena to any Future Metaphysics*, trans. P. G. Lucas (Manchester University Press, 1953).

[1790] *On a Discovery according to which any New Critique of Pure Reason has been made Superfluous by an Earlier One*, trans. H. Allison (Baltimore: Johns Hopkins University Press, 1973).

[1787] *The Critique of Pure Reason*, trans. P. Guyer and A. Woods (Cambridge University Press, 1998).

1992 'The Jäsche Logic', in *Lectures on Logic*, trans. J. M. Young (Cambridge University Press), 517–640.

Kanterian, E. 2005 *Analytische Philosophie* (Frankfurt: Campus).

Katz, J. J. 1990 *The Metaphysics of Meaning* (Cambridge, Mass.: MIT Press).

Keil, G. forthcoming 2008 'Naturalism', in D. Moran (ed.), *A Companion to Twentieth Century Philosophy* (London: Routledge).

Kekes, J. 1980 *The Nature of Philosophy* (Oxford: Blackwell).

Kenny, A. J. P. 1995 *Frege* (Harmondsworth: Penguin).

2005 'The Philosopher's History and the History of Philosophy', in Sorell and Rogers 2005, 15–24.

Kim, Jaegwon 2003 'The American Origins of Philosophical Naturalism', *Journal of Philosophical Research*, 83–98.

2004 'The Mind-Body Problem at Century's Turn', in Leiter 2004c, 129–52.

Klaus, G. and M. Buhr (eds.) 1976 *Philosophisches Wörterbuch* (Leipzig: VEB Bibliographisches Institut).

Kneale, W. and M. Kneale 1984 *The Development of Logic* (Oxford: Clarendon Press).

Köhler, E. 1991 'Metaphysics in the Vienna Circle', in T. Uebel (ed.), *Rediscovering the Forgotten Vienna Circle* (Dordrecht: Kluwer), 131–42.

Körner, S. 1979 *Fundamental Questions of Philosophy* (Brighton: Harvester).

Kripke, S. A. 1980 *Naming and Necessity* (Oxford: Blackwell).

1982 *Wittgenstein on Rules and Private Language* (Oxford: Blackwell).

Kristeva, J. 1997 'Une desinformation', *Le Nouvel Observateur*, 25 September 1997, 122.

Krüger, L. 1984 'Why do we Study the History of Philosophy?', in Rorty, Schneewind and Skinner 1984, 77–102.

Kuhn, Th. [1962] *The Structure of Scientific Revolutions* (University of Chicago Press, 1970).

Kuklick, B. 1984 'Seven thinkers and how they grew', in Rorty, Schneewind and Skinner 1984, 125–39.

Künne, W. 1990, 'Prinzipien wohlwollender Interpretation', in Forum für Philosophie (ed.), *Intentionalität und Verstehen* (Frankfurt: Suhrkamp), 212–34.
2003 *Conceptions of Truth* (Oxford: Clarendon Press).

Kusch, M. 1995 *Psychologism: a Case Study in the Sociology of Philosophical Knowledge* (London: Routledge).

Langford, C. H. 1942 'The Notion of Analysis in Moore's Philosophy', in P. A. Schilpp (ed.), *The Philosophy of G. E. Moore* (La Salle, Ill.: Open Court) 321–42.

Laurence, S. and C. Macdonald (eds.) 1998 *Contemporary Readings in the Foundations of Metaphysics* (Oxford: Blackwell).

Leiter, B. 2001 *Objectivity in Law and Morality* (Cambridge University Press).
2004a 'Introduction: The Future for Philosophy', in Leiter 2004c, 1–23.
2004b 'What is "Analytic" Philosophy? Thoughts from Fodor', *The Leiter Reports: Editorials, News, Updates 21 October 2004*, URL = <http://webapp.utexas.edu/blogs/archives/bleiter/002261.htm>.
(ed.) 2004c *The Future for Philosophy* (Oxford University Press).

Lewis, H. D. (ed.) 1963 *Clarity is not Enough* (London: Allen & Unwin).

Lewis, D. 1983 *Philosophical Papers*, vol. 1 (Oxford University Press).

Liebmann, O. [1876] *Zur Analysis der Wirklichkeit* (Strasburg: Truebner, 1880).

Lotze, R. H. 1874 *Logik* (Leipzig: Meiner).

Lowe, E. J. 1998 *The Possibility of Metaphysics* (Oxford: Clarendon Press).
2000 *An Introduction to the Philosophy of Mind* (Cambridge University Press).

Lurie, Y. 1997 'Wittgenstein as the Forlorn Caretaker of Language', in Biletzki and Matar 1998, 209–25.

MacIntyre, A. 1981 *After Virtue* (Notre Dame: University of Notre Dame Press).
1984 'The Relation of Philosophy to its Past', in Rorty, Schneewind and Skinner 1984, 31–40.

Mackie, J. 1977 *Ethics: Inventing Right and Wrong* (Harmondsworth: Penguin).

Maddy, P. 1998 'How to be a Naturalist about Mathematics', in H. G. Dales and G. Oliveri (eds.), *Truth in Mathematics* (Oxford: Clarendon Press), 161–80.

Magee, B. 1983 *The Philosophy of Schopenhauer* (Oxford: Clarendon Press).
(ed.) 1986a *Modern British Philosophy* (Oxford University Press).
1986b 'Preface', in Magee 1986a, vii–xi.

Manser, A. 1983 *Bradley's Logic* (Oxford: Blackwell).

Marcuse, H. [1964] *One-Dimensional Man* (London: Routledge & Kegan Paul 1986).

Margolis, J. 2003 *The Unravelling of Scientism* (Cornell University Press).

Martin, M. 2002 'The Concerns of Analytic Philosophy', in Baggini and Stangroom 2002, 129–46.

Marx, K. [1867] *Das Kapital. Band I. Marx/Engels Werke Vol. 23* (Berlin: Dietz Verlag, 1973).

Marx, K. and F. Engels [1932] *Die Deutsche Ideologie. Marx/Engels Werke Vol. 3* (Berlin: Dietz Verlag, 1981), 13–530.

May, T. 2002 'On the Very Idea of Continental (or for that matter Anglo-American) Philosophy', *Metaphilosophy* 33, 401–25.

McDowell, J. 1996 *Mind and World* (Cambridge, Mass.: Harvard University Press).

    1998 *Mind, Value, and Reality* (Cambridge, Mass.: Harvard University Press).

McGinn, C. 1991 *The Problem of Consciousness* (Oxford: Blackwell).

Menzler-Trott, E. 2001 *Gentzens Problem: mathematische Logik im nationalsozialistischen Deutschland* (Basle: Birkhäuser).

Metz, T. 2002 'Recent Work on the Meaning of Life', *Ethics* 112, 781–814.

Mill, James [1829] *Analysis of the Phenomena of the Human Mind* (Hildesheim: Olms, 1982).

Mill, J. S. 1840 'Essay on Coleridge', in Mill and Bentham 1987, 177–226.

    [1865] *An Examination of Sir William Hamilton's Philosophy* (New York: University of Toronto Press, 1973).

    [1873] *Autobiography* (Harmondsworth: Penguin 1989).

Mill, J. S. and J. Bentham 1987 *Utilitarianism and other Essays*, A. Ryan (ed.) (London: Penguin Books).

Monk, R. 1990 *Wittgenstein: the Duty of Genius* (London: Cape).

    1996a *Bertrand Russell: the Spirit of Solitude* (London: Cape).

    1996b 'Bertrand Russell's Brainchild,' *Radical Philosophy* 78, 2–5.

    1997 'Was Russell an Analytic Philosopher?', in Glock 1997, 35–50.

    2000 *Bertrand Russell: the Ghost of Madness* (London: Cape).

Monk, R. and A. Palmer (eds.) 1996 *Bertrand Russell and the Origins of Analytic Philosophy* (Bristol: Thoemmes).

Montefiori, A. and B. Williams 1966 *British Analytical Philosophy* (London: Routledge & Kegan Paul).

Moore, G. E. 1898 'Freedom', *Mind* 7, 179–203.

    [1899] 'The Nature of Judgement', in Moore 1993, 1–19.

    1903 *Principia Ethica* (Cambridge University Press).

    1942 'A Reply to my Critics', in Schilpp 1942, 660–7.

    1953 *Some Main Problems of Philosophy* (London: Allen & Unwin).

    1993 *Selected Writings*, T. Baldwin (ed.) (London: Routledge).

Moreland, J. P. 1998 'Should a Naturalist be a Supervenient Physicalist?', *Metaphilosophy* 29, 35–57.

Muirhead, J. H. 1924 'Past and Present in Contemporary Philosophy', in J. H. Muirhead (ed.), *Contemporary British Philosophy* (London: Allen and Unwin), 309–24.

Müller, M. and A. Halder (eds.) 1979 *Kleines Philosophisches Wörterbuch* (Freiburg: Herder).

Mukerjee, M. 1998 'Undressing the Emperor', *Scientific American* March 1998, 17–18.

Mulhall, S. 2002 'Post-Analytic Philosophy', in Baggini and Stangroom 2002, 237–52.

Mulligan, K. 1986 'Exactness, Description and Variation – How Austrian Analytic Philosophy was Done', in H. C. Nyiri (ed.), *Von Bolzano zu Wittgenstein – Zur Tradition der österreichischen Philosophie* (Vienna: Holder-Pichler), 86–97.

1990 'Genauigkeit und Geschwätz – Glossen zu einem paradigmatischen Gegensatz in der Philosophy', in H. Bachmeier (ed.), *Wien – Paradigmen der Moderne* (Amsterdam: Benjamins), 209–36.

1991 'Introduction: On the History of Continental Philosophy', in Mulligan 1991 (guest ed.), *Topoi* 2: 115–20.

1998 'The Symptoms of Gödel-mania', *Times Literary Supplement* 1 May 1998, 13–14.

2003 'Searle, Derrida, and the Ends of Phenomenology', in B. Smith (ed.), *John Searle* (Cambridge University Press), 261–86.

Mundle, C. W. K. 1970 *A Critique of Linguistic Philosophy* (Oxford: Clarendon Press).

Naess, A. 1989 *Ecology, Community and Lifestyle*, (Cambridge University Press).

Nagel, E. 1936 'Impressions and Appraisals of Analytic Philosophy in Europe', *Journal of Philosophy* 33, 5–24, 29–53.

1954 *Sovereign Reason* (Glencoe: Free Press).

Nagel, T. 1974 'What is it Like to be a Bat', *The Philosophical Review* 83, 435–50.

1997 *The Last Word* (Oxford University Press).

1998 'Go with the Flow', *Times Literary Supplement* 28 August 1998, 3–4.

Natorp, P. 1910 *Die Logischen Grundlagen der Exakten Wissenschaften* (Leipzig: Teubner).

Nedo, M. and M. Ranchetti 1983 *Ludwig Wittgenstein: sein Leben in Bildern und Texten* (Frankfurt-on-Main: Suhrkamp).

Neurath, O. 1931 'Soziologie im Physikalismus', in Neurath 1981 [1936], 533–62.

[1936] 'Die Entwicklung des Wiener Kreises und die Zukunft des Logischen Empirismus', in *Gesammelte Philosophische und Methodologische Schriften*, vol. II (Vienna: Hölder-Pichler-Tempsky, 1981), 673–702.

1983 *Philosophical Papers 1913–1946*, R. S. Cohen and M. Neurath (eds.) (Dordrecht: Reidel).

Nietzsche, F. [1882] *The Gay Science* (New York: Vintage, 1974).

[1886] *Beyond Good and Evil* (London: Penguin, 1990).

[1906] *The Will to Power* (New York: Vintage, 1967).

Nyeri, C. (ed.) 1986 *From Bolzano to Wittgenstein. The Tradition of Austrian Philosophy* (Vienna: Hölder-Pilcher-Tempsky).

O'Hear, A. 1998 'Tradition and traditionalism', in Craig 1998, 455–7.

(ed.) 1999 *German Philosophy since Kant* (Cambridge University Press).

Olson, R. E. and A. M. Paul (eds.) 1972 *Contemporary Philosophy in Scandinavia* (Baltimore: Johns Hopkins Press).

Pap, A. 1949 *Elements of Analytic Philosophy* (New York: Hafner).

Papineau, D. 1993 *Philosophical Naturalism* (Oxford: Blackwell).

2003 'Is this a Dagger?', *Times Literary Supplement* 14 February 2003, 12.

Passmore, J. 1961 *Philosophical Reasoning* (London: Duckworth).

1966 *100 Years of Philosophy* (London: Duckworth, 1st edn 1957).

1967 'Philosophy: Historiography of', in Edwards 1967, 226–30.

1970 *Philosophical Reasoning* (London: Duckworth).

1985 *Recent Philosophers* (London: Duckworth).

Peacocke, C. 1999 *Being Known* (Oxford University Press).

Peirce, C. S. 1934 *Collected Papers of Charles Sanders Peirce*, vol. V (Cambridge, Mass.: Harvard University Press).

Piercey, R. 2003 'Doing Philosophy Historically', *Review of Metaphysics* 56, 779–800.

Plantinga, A. 1995 'Essence and Essentialism', in Kim and Sosa (eds.), *Blackwell Companion to Metaphysics* (London: Blackwell), 138–40.

Popper, K. R. 1934 *Die Logik der Forschung* (Tübingen: Mohr).

1959 'Preface to the First English Edition', *The Logic of Scientific Discovery* (London: Hutchinson), 15–23.

Prado, C. 2003a 'Introduction', in Prado 2003b, 9–16.

(ed.) 2003b *A House Divided: Comparing Analytic and Continental Philosophy* (Amherst, N.Y.: Humanity Books).

Preston, A. 2004 'Prolegomena to any Future History of Analytic Philosophy', *Metaphilosophy* 35, 445–65.

2007 *Analytic Philosophy: the History of an Illusion* (London: Continuum).

Price, H. H. 1945 'Clarity is not Enough', in Lewis 1963, 15–41.

Putnam, H. 1975 *Mind, Language and Reality: Philosophical Papers Volume 2* (Cambridge University Press).

1981 *Reason, Truth and History* (Cambridge University Press).

1983 *Realism and Reason* (Cambridge University Press).

1992 *Renewing Philosophy* (Cambridge, Mass.: Harvard University Press).

1997 'A Half Century of Philosophy, Viewed from Within', *Daedalus*, 175–208.

1999 *The Threefold Cord: Mind, Body and World* (New York: Columbia University Press).

2007 'Is Analytic Philosophy a Good Thing? Why I am Ambivalent', unpublished.

Quine, W. V. 1951 'Two Dogmas of Empiricism', in Quine 1953, 20–46.

[1953] *From a Logical Point of View* (Cambridge, Mass.: Harvard University Press, 1980).

1960 *Word and Object* (Cambridge, Mass.: MIT Press).

[1966] *Ways of Paradox and Other Essays* (Cambridge, Mass.: Harvard University Press, 1976).

1969 *Ontological Relativity and Other Essays* (New York: Columbia University Press).

1970 'Philosophical Progress in Language Theory', *Metaphilosophy* 1, 1–19.
1974 *The Roots of Reference* (La Salle: Open Court).
1981 *Theories and Things* (Cambridge, Mass.: Harvard University Press).
1986 'Autobiography of W. V. Quine', in Schupp and Hahn 1986, 3–46.
1987 *Quiddities: An Intermittently Philosophical Dictionary* (London: Penguin).
1992 *The Pursuit of Truth* (Cambridge, Mass.: Harvard University Press).
1994 'W. V. Quine: Perspectives on Logic, Science and Philosophy: Interview with B. Edminster and M. O'Shea', *Harvard Review of Philosophy* 4, 47–57.
1995 *From Stimulus to Science* (Cambridge, Mass.: Harvard University Press).
2000 'Quine's Responses', in A. Orenskein and P. Kotatko (eds.), *Knowledge, Language and Logic* (Dordrecht: Kluwer), 407–30.
Quinton, A. 1995a 'Analytic Philosophy', in Honderich 1995, 28–30.
  1995b 'Continental Philosophy', in Honderich 1995, 161–3.
Railton, P. 1998 'Analytic Ethics', in Craig 1998, 220–3.
Rajchman, J. and C. West (eds.) 1985 *Post-Analytic Philosophy* (New York: Columbia University Press).
Ramsey, P. F. 1931 *The Foundations of Mathematics and other Logical Essays* (London: Routledge & Kegan Paul).
Rawls, J. 1972 *A Theory of Justice* (Oxford: Clarendon Press).
Reck, E. (ed.) 2002 *From Frege to Wittgenstein* (Oxford University Press).
Rée, J. 1978 'Philosophy and the History of Philosophy', in Rée, Ayers and Westoby 1978, 1–38.
  1993 'English Philosophy in the Fifties', *Radical Philosophy* 65, 3–21.
Rée, J., M. Ayers and A. Westoby 1978 *Philosophy and Its Past* (Hassocks: Harvester).
Reno, R. R. 2006 'Theology's Continental Captivity', *First Things* [April]: 26–33.
Reichenbach, H. 1951 *The Rise of Scientific Philosophy* (Berkeley: University of California Press).
Rescher, N. 1993 'American Philosophy Today', *Review of Metaphysics* 46, 717–45.
Rey, G. 1998 'Concepts', in Craig 1998, 505–17.
Rhees, R. (ed.) 1984 *Recollections of Wittgenstein* (Oxford University Press).
Rickert, H. [1892] *Der Gegenstand der Erkenntnis* (Tübingen: Mohr, 1904).
Riesch, G. 2004 *How the Cold War Transformed Philosophy of Science* (Cambridge University Press).
Rockmore, T. 2004 'On the Structure of Twentieth Century Philosophy', *Metaphilosophy* 35, 466–78.
Rorty, R. (ed.) 1967 *The Linguistic Turn* (University of Chicago Press).
  1979 *Philosophy and the Mirror of Nature* (Princeton University Press).
  1982 *Consequences of Pragmatism* (Minneapolis: University of Minnesota Press).
  1986 'Pragmatism, Davidson and Truth', in E. LePore (ed.), *Truth and Interpretation: Perspectives on the Philosophy of Donald Davidson* (Oxford: Blackwell), 333–55.
  1991 *Objectivity, Relativism and Truth: Philosophical Papers Vol. I* (Cambridge University Press).

1998 *Truth and Progress* (Cambridge University Press).

Rorty, R. and J. Searle 1999 'Rorty v. Searle, At Last: a Debate', *Logos* 2.3, 20–67.

Rorty, R., J. B. Schneewind and Q. Skinner (eds.) 1984 *Philosophy in History* (Cambridge University Press).

Rosch, E. and B. B. Lloyd 1978 *Cognition and Categorization* (Hillsdale: Erlbaum).

Rosen, M. 1998 'Continental Philosophy from Hegel', in Grayling 1998, 663–704.

Ruben, D. H. 1998 'The Philosophy of the Social Sciences', in Grayling 1998, 420–69.

Rundle, B. 1990 *Wittgenstein and Contemporary Philosophy of Language* (Oxford: Blackwell).

Russell, B. 1896 *German Social Democracy* (London: Longmans).

[1900] *The Philosophy of Leibniz*, with a new introduction by J. G. Slater (London: Routledge, 1992).

[1903] *The Principles of Mathematics*, with a new introduction by J. G. Slater (London: Routledge, 1992).

[1905] 'On Denoting', in Russell 1956a, 41–56.

[1910] 'Knowledge by Acquaintance and Knowledge by Description', in Russell 1925, 152–67.

[1912] *The Problems of Philosophy* (Oxford University Press, 1967).

[1914] *Our Knowledge of the External World*, with a new introduction by J. G. Slater (London: Routledge, 1993).

[1914] 'On Scientific Method in Philosophy', in Russell 1925, 75–93.

[1918] 'The Philosophy of Logical Atomism', in Russell 1956a, 175–281.

1919 *Introduction to Mathematical Philosophy* (London: George Allen and Unwin).

1925 *Mysticism and Logic* (London: Longmans, Green & Co.).

[1924] 'Logical Atomism', in Russell 1956a, 321–43.

1935 *Religion and Science* (London: Butterworth).

1940 *An Inquiry into Meaning and Truth* (London: George Allen and Unwin).

1944 'Replies to Criticisms', in P. A. Schilpp (ed.) *The Philosophy of Bertrand Russell* (Evanston: Open Court) 679–741.

[1950] 'Logical Positivism', in Russell 1956a, 367–82.

1956a *Logic and Knowledge: Essays 1901–1950*, R. C. Marsh (ed.) (London: George Allen and Unwin).

1956b *Portraits from Memory and other Essays* (London: George Allen and Unwin).

[1957] 'Mr Strawson on Referring', in Russell [1959], 175–80.

[1959] *My Philosophical Development* (London: George Allen and Unwin, 1985).

[1967–9] *Autobiography*, 3 vols., (publ. in one vol., George Allen and Unwin Paperbacks, 1978).

Russell, B. and A. N. Whitehead 1910–13 *Principia Mathematica* (Cambridge University Press).

Ryan, A. 1988 *Bertrand Russell: a Political Life* (London: Allen Lane).

Ryle, G. 1928 'Heidegger's *Sein und Zeit*', in Ryle 1971a, 197–214.

[1932] 'Systematically Misleading Expressions', in Ryle 1971b, 39–62.

[1937] 'Taking Sides in Philosophy', in Ryle 1971b, 153–69.

[1949] *The Concept of Mind* (London: Penguin, 1980).

1953 'Ordinary Language', in Ryle 1971b, 301–18.

1962 'Phenomenology vs. *The Concept of Mind*', in Ryle 1971a, 179–96.

1970 'Autobiographical', in O. P. Wood and G. Pitcher (eds.), *Ryle* (London: Macmillan), 1–15.

1971a *Collected Papers*, vol. I (London: Hutchinson).

1971b *Collected Essays*, vol. II (London: Hutchinson).

Schacht, R. 1975 *Hegel and After: Studies in Continental Philosophy between Kant and Sartre* (University of Pittsburgh Press).

Schilpp, P. A. (ed.) 1942 *The Philosophy of G. E. Moore* (Evanston Ill.: North-Western University Press).

Schilpp, P. A. and L. E. Hahn (eds.) 1986 *The Philosophy of W. V. Quine* (Evanston, Ill.: Open Court).

Schlick, M. [1918] *Allgemeine Erkenntnistheorie General Theory of Knowledge*, trans. A. E. Blumberg, intro. by A. E. Blumberg and H. Feigl (Vienna: Springer-Verlag, 1974).

1926 'Erleben, Erkennen, Metaphysik', in Schlick 1979, 99–111.

[1930] *Problems of Ethics*, trans. D. Rynin (New York: Dover).

1930/1 'The Turning Point of Philosophy', in Ayer 1959, 55–9.

1952 *Natur und Kultur* (Vienna: Humboldt).

1979 *Philosophical Papers*, ed. H. L. Mulder and B. F. B. Van de Velde-Schlick, trans. P. Heath (Dordrecht: Reidel).

Schnädelbach, H. 1983 *Philosophy in Germany 1831–1933* (Cambridge University Press).

Schopenhauer, A. [1844] *The World as Will and Representation*, trans. E. F. J. Payne (New York: Dover, 1966).

[1851] *Parerga and Parilepomena*, trans. E. F. J. Payne (Oxford University Press, 1974).

Schorske, C. E. 'The New Rigorism in the Human Sciences', *Daedalus* 126, 289–310.

Schroeder, S. 2006 *Wittgenstein: The Way out of the Fly-Bottle* (Cambridge: Polity).

Schroeder, W. R. 2005 *Continental Philosophy: A Critical Approach* (Oxford: Blackwell).

Searle, J. 1969 *Speech Acts* (Cambridge University Press).

1977 'Reiterating the Differences: a Reply to Derrida', *Glyph* 1, 198–208.

1980 'Minds, Brains and Programmes', *Behavioural and Brain* 3, 450–6.

1992 *The Rediscovery of the Mind* (Cambridge, Mass.: MIT Press).

1995 *The Construction of Social Reality* (New York: Free Press).

1996 'Contemporary Philosophy in the United States', in Bunnin and Tsui-James 1996, 1–24.

2004 'Toward a Unified Theory of Reality: Interview with John Searle', in *The Harvard Review of Philosophy* 12, 93–135.

Sellars, R. W. 1922 *Evolutionary Naturalism* (Chicago: Open Court).

Sellars, W. F. 1963 *Science, Perception and Reality* (London: Routledge & Kegan Paul).

1979 *Naturalism and Ontology* (Reseda: Ridgeview).

Shapin, St. 2001 'How to be Anti-Scientific', in J. A. Labinger and H. Collins (eds.), *The One Culture?* (Chicago University Press), 99–115.

Sigwart, C. 1873 *Logik*, vol. I (Tübingen: Mohr).

Simons, P. 1986 'The Anglo-Austrian Analytic Axis', in Nyeri 1986, 98–107.

1999 'Bolzano, Brentano and Meinong: three Austrian Realists', in O'Hear 1999, 109–36.

Singer, M. G. (ed.) 1985 *American Philosophy*, RIP Lecture Series 19 (Cambridge University Press).

Singer, P. 1975 *Animal Liberation* (New York: Random House).

1979 *Practical Ethics* (Cambridge University Press).

1980 *Marx* (Oxford University Press).

1983 *Hegel* (Oxford University Press).

1992 'A German Attack on Applied Ethics', *Journal of Applied Philosophy* 9, 85–91.

Skinner, Q. 1969 'Meaning and Understanding in the History of Ideas', *History and Theory* 8: 3–53.

Skorupski, J. 1993 *English Speaking Philosophy 1750–1945* (Oxford University Press).

Sloterdijk, P. 1999 *Regeln für den Menschenpark* (Frankfurt: Suhrkamp).

Sluga, H. 1980 *Frege* (London: Routledge).

1993 *Heidegger's Crisis* (Cambridge, Mass.: Harvard University Press).

1997 'Frege on Meaning', in Glock 1997c, 17–34.

1998 'What Has History to Do with Me? Wittgenstein and Analytic Philosophy', *Inquiry* 41, 99–121.

Smith, B. 1994 *Austrian Philosophy* (La Salle: Open Court).

2000 'Philosophie, Polity und wissenschaftliche Weltauffassung: zur Frage der Philosophie in Österreich und Deutschland', *Grazer Philosophische Studien* 58/59, 1–22.

Snow, C. P. [1959] *The Two Cultures: and a Second Look* (Cambridge University Press, 1964).

Soames, S. 2003 *Philosophical Analysis in the Twentieth Century*, vol. I (Princeton University Press).

2006 'Hacker's Complaint', *Philosophical Quarterly*, 56: 426–35.

Soble, A. 1998 'Sexuality, Philosophy of', in Craig 1998, 717–30.

Sokal, A. 1996 'Transgressing the Boundaries: Towards a Transformative Hermeneutics of Quantum Mechanics', reprinted in Sokal and Bricmont 1998, 199–240.

Sokal, A. and J. Bricmont 1998 *Intellectual Impostures* (London: Profile).

1997 'What is all the Fuss About?', *Times Literary Supplement* 17 October 1997, 17.

Solomon, R. C. 1988 *Continental Philosophy since 1750: the Rise and Fall of the Self* (Oxford University Press).

Sorell, T. and G. A. J. Rogers (eds.) 2005 *Analytic Philosophy and History of Philosophy* (Oxford University Press).

Stadler, F. 1997 *Studien zum Wiener Kreis* (Frankfurt-on-Main: Suhrkamp).

Stairs, A. 1998 'Quantum Mechanics, Interpretation of', in Craig 1998, 890–5.

Stebbing, L. S. 1932 'The Method of Analysis in Metaphysics', *Proceedings of the Aristotelian Society* 33, 65–94.

Stevens, G. 2005 *The Russellian Origins of Analytic Philosophy* (London: Routledge).

Stevenson, C. L. 1944 *Ethics and Language* (New Haven: Yale University Press).

Strawson, G. (ed.) 2005 *The Self* (Oxford: Blackwell).

Strawson, P. F. 1952 *Introduction to Logical Theory* (London: Methuen).

    1959 *Individuals* (London: Methuen).

    1963 'Carnap's Views on Constructed Systems vs. Natural Languages in Analytic Philosophy', in P. Schilpp (ed.) *The Philosophy of Rudolf Carnap*, Library of Living Philosophers, vol. XI (La Salle, Ill.: Open Court), 503–18.

    1971 *Logico-Linguistic Papers* (London: Methuen).

    1985 *Skepticism and Naturalism: some Varieties* (London: Methuen).

    1990 'Two Conceptions of Philosophy', in R. Barrett and R. Gibson (eds.), *Perspectives on Quine* (Oxford: Blackwell), 310–18.

    1992 *Analysis and Metaphysics* (Oxford University Press).

    1995 'My Philosophy', in P. K. Sen and R. R. Verma (eds.), *The Philosophy of P. F. Strawson* (New Delhi: Indian Council of Philosophical Research), 1–18.

    1997 *Entity and Identity* (Oxford University Press).

    1998 'Intellectual Autobiography', in L. E. Hahn (ed.), *The Philosophy of P. F. Strawson* (Peru, Ill.: Open Court), 1–21.

Stroll, A. 2000 *Twentieth-Century Analytic Philosophy* (New York: Columbia University Press).

Stroud, B. 1968 'Transcendental Arguments', reprinted in R. C. S. Walker (ed.), *Kant on Pure Reason* (Oxford University Press, 1982), 117–31.

Swinburne, R. 1986 *The Evolution of the Soul* (Oxford University Press).

Swift, A. 2001 'Politics v. Philosophy', *Prospect* August/September 2001, 40–4.

Tait, W. 1997 *Early Analytic Philosophy: Frege, Russell, Wittgenstein* (LaSalle, Ill.: Open Court).

Tarski, A. (1935) 'Der Wahrheitsbegriff in den formalisierten Sprachen', *Studia Philosophica* I, 261–405; ['The Concept of Truth in Formalized Languages'] (English translation in Tarski 1983).

    1936 'O pojciu wynikania logicz-nego', *Przegląd Filozoficzny* 39, 58–68; ['On the Concept of Logical Consequence'] (English translation in Tarski 1983).

    1983 *Logic, Semantics, Metamathematics* (Indianapolis: Hackett).

Taylor, C. 1984 'Philosophy and its History', in Rorty, Schneewind and Skinner 1984, 17–30.

    1994 *Multiculturalism and 'The Politics of Recognition'* (Princeton University Press).

Teichmann, R. (ed.) 2000 'Mind! 2000', *Mind* vol. 109 Supplement (Oxford University Press).

Thiselton, A. C. 1998 'Hermeneutics, Biblical', in Craig 1998, 389–95.
Trendelenburg, A. [1840] *Logische Untersuchungen*, vol. I (Leipzig: Hirzel, 1870).
Tugendhat, E. [1976] *Traditional and Analytical Philosophy*, trans. P. Garner (Cambridge University Press, 1982).
Uebel, Th. (ed.) 1991 *Rediscovering the Forgotten Vienna Circle* (Dordrecht: Kluwer).
  1999 'Otto Neurath, the Vienna Circle and the Austrian Tradition', in O'Hear 1999, 249–70.
Urmson, J. O. 1956 *Philosophical Analysis: its Development between the Wars* (Oxford University Press).
Waismann, F. 1956 'How I see Philosophy', in R. Harre (ed.), *How I see Philosophy*, (New York: St. Martin's Press, 1968), 1–38.
  1976 *Logik, Sprache, Philosophie; mit einer Vorrede von Moritz Schlick*; G. P.Baker and B.McGuinness (eds.), with the assistance of J. Schulte (Stuttgart: Reclam).
Wang, H. 1986 *Beyond Analytic Philosophy* (Cambridge, Mass.: MIT Press).
Warnock, G. 1998 'Ordinary Language Philosophy, School of', in Craig 1998, 147–53.
Wedberg, A. 1984 *A History of Philosophy*, vol. III (Oxford: Clarendon Press).
West, C. 1989 *The American Evasion of Philosophy: a Genealogy of Pragmatism* (Madison: University of Wisconsin Press).
Whorf, S. 1956 *Language, Thought and Reality* (Cambridge, Mass.: MIT Press).
Whitehead, A. N. 1929 *The Aims of Education* (New York: Mentor Books).
Wiggins, D. 1991 *Needs, Values, Truth* (Oxford: Blackwell).
  2001 *Sameness and Substance Renewed* (Cambridge University Press).
Willard, D. 1989 'The Case against Quine's Case for Psychologism', in M. A. Notturna (ed.), *Perspectives on Psychologism* (Leiden: Brill), 286–95.
Williams, B. 1985 *Ethics and the Limits of Philosophy* (London: Fontana).
  1996a 'Contemporary Philosophy – a Second Look', in Bunnin and Tsui-James 1996, 25–37.
  1996b 'On Hating and Despising Philosophy', *London Review of Books* 18 April 1996, 17–18.
  2002a *Truth and Truthfulness* (Princeton University Press).
  2002b 'Why Philosophy needs History', *London Review of Books* 17 October 2002, 7–9.
  2006 *Philosophy as a Humanistic Discipline* (Princeton University Press).
Williamson, T. 1994 *Vagueness* (London: Routledge).
  2004 'Past the Linguistic Turn?', in Leiter 2004c, 106–28.
  2006 'Must Do Better', in P. Greenough and M. P. Lynch (eds.), *Truth and Realism* (Oxford University Press), 177–87.
Wilshire, B. 2002 *Fashionable Nihilism: A Critique of Analytic Philosophy* (State University of New York Press).
Wilson, M. D. 1991 *Ideas And Mechanism* (Princeton University Press).
Windelband, W. 1892 *Geschichte der Philosophie* (Freiburg: J.C. Mohr).
  [1884] *Präludien* (Tübingen: Mohr, 1921).

Wisdom, J. 1934 'Is Analysis a Useful Method in Philosophy?', in Wisdom 1953, 16–35.

1953 *Philosophy and Psycho-Analysis* (Oxford: Blackwell).

Wittgenstein, L. [1922] *Tractatus Logico-Philosophicus* (London: Routledge & Kegan Paul, 1961).

(1958) *Blue and Brown Books* (Oxford: Blackwell).

[1953] *Philosophical Investigations*, trans. G. E. M. Anscombe (Oxford: Blackwell, 1967).

1967 *Zettel* (Oxford: Blackwell).

1979 *Wittgenstein and the Vienna Circle* [1929–32], shorthand notes recorded by F. Waismann, B. F. McGuinness (Oxford: Blackwell).

1980 *Culture and Value*, trans. P. Winch (Oxford: Blackwell).

1993 *Philosophical Occasions 1912–1951*, ed. J. Klagge and A. Nordman (Indianapolis: Hackett).

Wolterstorff, N. 1970 *On Universals: an Essay in Ontology* (Chicago University Press).

Wright, C. 1983 *Frege's Conception of Numbers as Objects* (Aberdeen University Press).

Wright, G. H. von 1971 *Explanation and Understanding* (Ithaca, N.Y.: Cornell University Press).

1993 *The Tree of Knowledge* (Leiden: Brill).

Young, J. 1998 'Analytic Philosophy', *Times Literary Supplement* 10 July: 17.

2003 *The Death of God and the Meaning of Life* (London: Routledge).

Index

absolute presuppositions 97; *see also* framework
academic/cultural institutions 10, 24, 59, 62, 221,
  243, 245–6, 252
acquaintance 35
action (intentional), *see* behaviour
Adorno, Theodor 184; *see also* critical theory;
  positivism debate
aesthetics 91, 146–7; *see also* art
aggressiveness 206, 250
American Philosophical Association (APA): 83
anachronism 17, 90, 93, 103, 105, 114
analysis 13, 18, 21–3, 27, 32, 128–34, 152, 153–60
  alternative 154
  connective vs. reductive (Strawson) 158, 159
  decompositional/progressive 18, 21, 22, 32,
    154–7, 158; *see also* reduction/reductionism
  as defining feature of analytic philosophy
  ontological 22, 159
  phenomenological 159
  psychological 22
  reductionist, *see* reduction/reductionism
  regressive 21–2
  same level vs. new level 39–40, 144, 156
  wide notion of 159
  see also conceptual analysis, logical analysis,
    logical construction, paraphrase paradox
    of analysis
analytic/synthetic distinction 14, 23, 37, 141, 145,
  148, 211
  in continental philosophy 149–50
  Quine's attack on 11, 45, 59
  rehabilitation of 141–2
analytic vs. synthetic method 22
analytic philosophy 44, 89, 204, 205
  at a glance 218, 227
  apologies for 3, 204, 205
  borderline vs. paradigmatic cases of 15, 214,
    218–19
  contemporary mainstream 121, 130, 176, 188,
    231, 246, 259
  contours of 204, 205, 224

crisis, demise or triumph of 1–2,
  243–7, 252
and culture 203
current state of 2, 20, 61, 231–61
definition of 58, 158, 231
disagreements within 115–17
a distinct movement 44, 70, 115, 151–77, 190,
  204, 222, 231, 258; *see also* crisis of
diversity of 1, 115–17, 148, 152, 153, 248–9
exclusionary tone 244
exodus from continental Europe 68–9, 86, 230
forerunners of 225
founder of 2, 20, 70, 122, 224–6
from contemporary continental Europe 254
future of 6, 20, 255–61
historical development of 1, 16
historical roots of 2, 20, 132, 253
histories of 2, 89
importance of methods rather than results 152
nature of *see* what is analytic philosophy?
post-Fregean 122, 224
precursors of 223
public relevance of 187–8, 190–1, 203, 238,
  247, 261
rapprochement with other traditions 223, 259
revolutionary movement 85, 87, 177–8, 248
virtues and vices of 20, 212, 231, 242–55, 259, 261
see also 'analytic philosophy'; conceptions of
  analytic philosophy; what is analytic
  philosophy
'analytic philosophy' 175, 183, 204, 205,
  209, 218
established use/extension of 13–16, 151, 210, 212,
  218, 219, 221
an essentially contested concept 207–9
honorific title or descriptive label 3, 19, 204,
  205, 206–9, 210, 211–12
loose sense of 177, 210
origins of the term 44, 168
scaling adjective 174, 210
a useful category? 231, 238, 241, 255–9